Child Survivors
of Genocide

Child Survivors of Genocide

Trauma, Resilience, and Identity in Guatemala

Shirley A. Heying

Foreword by Andre J. Holten

LEXINGTON BOOKS
Lanham • Boulder • New York • London

Published by Lexington Books
An imprint of The Rowman & Littlefield Publishing Group, Inc.
4501 Forbes Boulevard, Suite 200, Lanham, Maryland 20706
www.rowman.com

86-90 Paul Street, London EC2A 4NE

British Library Cataloguing in Publication Information Available

Library of Congress Cataloging-in-Publication Data

Library of Congress Cataloging-in-Publication DataNames: Heying, Shirley A., author. | Holten, Andre J., writer of foreword.
  Title: Child survivors of genocide : trauma, resilience, and identity in Guatemala / Shirley A. Heying ; foreword by Andre J. Holten.
  Description: Lanham : Lexington Books, [2022] | Includes bibliographical references and index. | Summary: "This book examines the experiences of orphaned child survivors of Guatemala's 36-year internal armed conflict and genocide who were raised in an in-country permanent residential home. Now adults, they have faced long-term consequences but also have become resilient, well-adapted adults with a strong sense of identity and belonging"-- Provided by publisher.
  Identifiers: LCCN 2022016600 (print) | LCCN 2022016601 (ebook) | ISBN 9781793602299 (cloth) | ISBN 9781793602312 (paperback) | ISBN 9781793602305 (ebook)
  Subjects: LCSH: Genocide--Guatemala--History. | Children and genocide--Guatemala. | Genocide survivors--Guatemala--Psychology. | Psychic trauma--Guatemala. | Resilience (Personality trait)--Guatemala. | Identity (Psychology)--Guatemala. | Belonging (Social psychology)--Guatemala.
  Classification: LCC F1466.7 .H49 2022 (print) | LCC F1466.7 (ebook) | DDC 364.15/083097281--dc23/eng/20220504
  LC record available at https://lccn.loc.gov/2022016600
  LC ebook record available at https://lccn.loc.gov/2022016601

Contents

Foreword

I was born two and half years before the Netherlands was invaded by the German Reich (Nazi Germany). During this occupation, which lasted five years, the country became an involuntary part of the German effort to occupy and rule all of Europe, the so-called Third Reich. Native Dutch labor and resources were confiscated and sent to the German home country to support the war effort. Adolf Hitler, the German Chancellor, had established the racial policy of Nazi Germany—a racist doctrine—that defined the superiority of the Aryan race. This meant that non-Aryan people, including Jews, needed to be exterminated. Consequently, the German occupying forces, assisted by Dutch police and German sympathizers, carried out frequent raids to find Jews, arrest them, and send them to camps in the Netherlands. From there, they were sent to extermination camps in Poland.

My parents faced horrendous conditions, arrests of Jews by the German occupiers, and frequent raids. When those raids took place, my parents had to decide on short notice how to handle the circumstances. Those situations were always very stressful. For example, my mother once decided to dress up as a nurse caring for my grandmother, while my father hid underneath the coal in the backyard shed. On another occasion, they were able to quickly walk a couple of blocks to stay with friends for the duration of the raid. As a small child, I would frequently spend days with nearby relatives or friends if a raid was expected. Needless to say, during those trying times there was little time for normal family socializing. Undoubtedly, this has had a lasting effect. I think the impact of missing out on receiving tender loving care for many years while growing up is beyond the scope of this foreword. Suffice it to say, I have made a lot of decisions about my life without the benefit of consultations with family members.

At some point, my parents decided to find a hiding place for the three of us. Good friends had initially agreed to take them in, but that ended up not working. My parents then decided to place me—I was five at the time—with a Christian family, the Meijers. Undoubtedly, it was an incredibly difficult decision for them. They must have believed that this way, I would have a better chance of surviving the war. As fellow Holocaust survivor Dr. Yaffa Eliach (1991) noted, "Families that stayed together, died together."

I always wonder what instructions, if any, my parents gave me. I certainly don't remember any. I was given a "hiding name." Again, I don't remember how I responded to that. I want to emphasize that my age at the time of our separation was an important factor in the memories that I have of events.

My life after separation from my parents was, as I remember it now, a period during which I did not develop any "enduring attachments." During my stay at the first four or five different places where I lived, I felt like a visitor. After that, I wound up "permanently" living with the Meijers in the town of Haarlem. However, while I was "officially" living with the Meijer family, I did spend time, once again, at several other places.

My parents were arrested approximately six months after they had placed me with the Meijers. I have no knowledge of the circumstances regarding their arrest. However, I did learn that after spending about one month in a camp in the Netherlands, they were placed on a transport to Auschwitz in Poland. There, my mother was killed immediately upon arrival, having been sent directly to the gas chamber. Meanwhile, my father was put to work at a nearby camp where he lasted for three months until exhaustion put him in a hospital. After two months, he still had not recovered and was sent to the gas chamber as well.

The Meijers (husband and wife) had three children. They had one son, Jan, and two daughters, Riek and Nel, all in their early twenties at the time. In addition, there were three men living in their house: Pete (a close friend of one daughter), Jacob (Jewish and friend of the other daughter), and Cor (close friend of Jan, the son). I don't think Cor was there every day. The men, all in their twenties at the time, were hiding from the Germans because they didn't want to be taken to German labor camps, especially as one of them was wanted for being Jewish.

The people living in the Meijers' home provided a pleasant surrounding for me. However, they probably did not provide me with the tender loving care (or TLC) that I would normally receive in a traditional family.

All of them must have had financial concerns since normal employment was not possible for everyone at that time. There also were shortages of food and energy for heating and lighting, as well as pressures from being occupied by hostile military forces. On several occasions, I was "moved" to other locations when it was deemed that I might be safer away from the Meijer residence. So, I spent a fair amount of time at a farm about forty miles from Haarlem where Nel was a teacher.

After liberation, the Meijers made an effort to let the community know that I was living with them so that if any of my relatives were looking for me, they would know where to find me. When no one came to claim me, the Meijers decided to keep me.

About two years after the end of the war, the Meijers officially became my guardians. During the war, the public school had denied me attendance since it was assumed that I was a hidden Jewish boy with no birth certificate with my hidden name. To get me into a school when I was six and seven years old, the Meijers enrolled me in a Protestant bible school that their children had attended about fifteen years earlier. This effort, at least, made it appear that I was a "normal" child. About a year and a half after the war was over and I had regained use of my real name again, I was finally able to enroll in the public school.

It was not until fifty-four years after the end of the war that I finally made contact with a blood relative. Through the use of the Internet and with assistance of people in the Netherlands and Israel, I finally was able to locate two great aunts and a number of distant cousins. It was a connection, not a reconnection, since I had not known about them before. When I went to actually visit a number of cousins in New York, it was emotional for me. The cousins, too, were very pleased to make contact with a cousin they didn't know they had. Ever since then, I've started to grasp all that happened to me and my family. I had hoped for a reunion; obviously at a later age, I knew that would not happen. I still get emotional when I hear or see people getting reunited.

Looking back at the period of the first five years after the war, I became more aware of ways the war had affected me. It was very important in developing my feelings about the events that had taken place. For one, I kept hoping that someone from my family would show up to claim me. The reason for this was definitely not that I was not treated well, but subconsciously, I was missing something. I remember at one time sort of forcing myself onto Mrs. Meijer's lap for some affection. I don't remember exactly when this was, but my guess is that it was three or four years after the end of the war. During those years, I was busy with schoolwork, had become a member of a very nice soccer club, and had a number of friends.

Another effect of the war was the fact that I was a Jew and yet, that had very little meaning for me. I did not go to Jewish religious services, so the concept of belonging to the Jewish community never entered my mind. The Meijers—I'll call them my foster parents—always claimed that my parents had left the instruction that I should not be brought up in the Jewish religion. The Meijers strongly abided by that direction for as long as I lived with them.

The fact that I was Jewish had not made a big impression on me. I remember receiving Hanukah presents every year from a Jewish organization around the same time that "everyone" celebrated Saint Nicolas's birthday. I thought that was nice. Yet the event that has stayed with me the most was during a biology class when I was seventeen and the topic being discussed was physical characteristics. One student asked the teacher what she would say my characteristics were. The teacher answered that I appeared to be Jewish. That made a big impression on me because I had never been told that I was a Jew.

After the war, I remained with my foster (hiding) family until I finished high school. As a young man nineteen years of age, I was able to then immigrate to the United States rather easily because in 1956, the US government had modified an immigration quota. The quota had been set up originally for survivors after the flood of 1953 in southwestern Holland that killed over 2,000 Dutch people. That particular immigration quota, however, was not used as much as expected, so the US opened it up to World War II survivors. Therefore, I was able to qualify and immigrate rather readily.

Once in New York City, I attended City College of New York, receiving a Bachelor of Science degree in physics. Throughout my school years, I also played a lot of soccer. While in high school in Holland, I was fortunate to receive excellent coaching. While in college, I continued to use my advanced soccer skills and played on a team with a lot of foreign-born players. Our team was selected for the first National Collegiate Athletic Association (NCAA) tournament for men's soccer, and I was fortunate to be selected to be an All-American athlete—even before I was officially an American.

After graduation I was eligible to become a US citizen and once sworn in, I signed up to become a US Air Force officer. During five years on active duty, I worked in a physics laboratory studying the effects of micrometeorite impacts on space structures. After that, I was a Minuteman missile launch control officer for one year. I then left the service and became an Air Force Civil Servant addressing, among other things, Combat Aircraft Survivability and Vulnerability with special emphasis on the A-10 combat aircraft design. Later, I took a position with a professional services company in Albuquerque supporting the Air Force Operational Test and Evaluation Center (AFOTEC). For a period, I also functioned as adjunct professor at the Air Force Safety Center, lecturing on aircraft structural integrity. Since retirement, I have been active as a substitute teacher in the Rio Rancho Public School system in New Mexico.

Initially, I did not talk about my childhood experience much because the people who had been to the camps in Poland and survived that experience received, very appropriately, most of the attention during the first four or five decades after the war. However, I clearly remember the first time I talked to a group of students about my experiences. It was when my son was in an Anne Frank play that was performed by his high school theater group. I gave a talk to the cast. I was forty-three at the time, meaning that thirty-six years had passed before I first spoke about my own experiences during the Holocaust.

The next major occasion that I spoke about my own experience as a war orphan occurred ten years later, in 1991, when I attended the first Symposium for Hidden Children of the Holocaust that took place in New York City. The fact that approximately 1,500 survivors attended was really eye-opening to me. I had no idea that so many people had survived the war in ways similar to what I had experienced. It was especially notable that only a portion of all the hidden children still alive were able or willing to attend the event. Other hidden children did not attend for various reasons such as the cost of the trip, unawareness of the event, or unwillingness to relive that period.

Since then, I have talked rather frequently about my experience. I participated a number of times with the Anne Frank Exhibit when it was in town—this happened three times over a fifteen-year period. In the last couple of years, I have been asked frequently by middle and high school teachers to talk about my experience during the Holocaust with their students.

I feel very fortunate that I was able to get a very good education. I got a solid foundation, through high school in the Netherlands and then a fabulous college education in the US. I feel that the education that I received helped me be a significant contributor to the organizations for which I worked during my lifetime.

I appreciate that Dr. Heying recognizes the impact that World War II wartime has had on children and the similarity of these effects on other children all over the world who have survived war, armed conflict, and genocide. Initially during conflict, the fact that there are orphaned children can pose a burden on a community. For example, facilities may need to be established to take care of children who have lost their families. This near-term effect—the issue of children who have lost their parents and are now in need of care—can be an imposition on the community. However, later on, the experiences of war orphans can play an important and positive role in a community that has undergone the ravages of war. In the course of these kids meeting their needs for meaningful social contact, they will undoubtedly study the history of their community during the hostilities. During their adolescence, when they have needs for finding a path to follow in adulthood, those needs can propel them to address the traditions and strengths that the people in the community exhibited before and during the hostilities. As they grow older, war orphans can actively revive the traditions and culture of their community. I, myself, have been quite active with presenting to students, as well as adults, my experiences during the war as a hidden child. Based on the feedback I receive from my talks, I can tell that students and adults feel fortunate to live in an environment that is free of the effects of war and the restrictions that war poses on people. I believe that *Child Survivors of Genocide* by Dr. Heying also can make a very important contribution for people who study and are concerned about the impact that war can have on the welfare of children, especially orphans, who grow up under similar wartime conditions.

Andre J. Holten
Albuquerque, NM

Preface

I put this book project on the back burner for several years after completing my research. I kept hoping that there would be a sustainable political opening in Guatemala that would permit child survivors who participated in my research project to write about their own experiences. I dreamt of their being able to tell their stories in their own ways outside the constraints of academic writing and zeitgeists of academic disciplines. There appeared to be some hope for a political opening on the horizon in 2013 when former Guatemalan president and general Efraín Ríos Montt was found guilty of genocide[1] and crimes against humanity. However, his conviction was thrown out by the Guatemalan Constitutional Court just ten days later, dashing the hope that Ríos Montt finally would be brought to justice and diminishing the chances that other perpetrators in the country would face a similar fate.

In September 2019, hope for a political opening further eroded as Guatemalan President Jimmy Morales shut down the International Commission against Impunity in Guatemala (known as CICIG). CICIG was established in 2007 to independently investigate high-profile crimes and to crack down on criminal networks and corruption in Guatemala's governmental institutions (Beltrán 2016; Bowen 2019). The dismantling of CICIG signaled further governmental oppression and, thus, the dminishing of any potential future political opening. Such potential closure, along with increased violence and unrest in the country, made it precarious, once again, for child survivors to publicly speak the truth about their experiences with the internal armed conflict and genocide.

With little hope for the political opening that child survivors in my research project would need to be able to share their stories publicly, I felt that I was faced with two choices. I could shelf this book project permanently in the hope that someday this group of child survivors would be able to share their own stories in print so that a record of their struggles, suffering, and resilience would be preserved. Or I could move forward with this book, with the full permission and endorsement of these child survivors. I have chosen the second option even though it has made me incredibly nervous because I question and will always question whether I am truly worthy of sharing their stories. As a white, middle-class, US American, I recognize that I have many privileges that participants in my research project will never have. This was never more apparent than the day that I left Guatemala after serving two years as a volunteer at the residential home where these child survivors grew up. It was 1996, just one month short of the signing of the peace accords. I felt the full gravity, guilt, and shame of stepping on that plane and leaving the country while child survivors, their surviving family members, and my friends were left behind to deal with the ongoing repercussions of the violence even after the peace accords were signed. Unfortunately, the two-year deferment of my university student loans had ended, and I had no choice but to return to the United States (US) to begin paying off my debt. I vowed that day, however, that I would return to Guatemala and help preserve child survivors' stories.

With their stories foremost in my mind, I entered graduate school six years later. My specific goal was to understand the factors that led to Guatemala's internal armed conflict and genocide, and to discuss the consequences of both on the lives of child survivors with whom I had lived and worked as a volunteer. As a first-generation college student from rural Minnesota, entering graduate school was no easy task and had not even been in the realm of possibility for me when I was growing up, or even when I graduated from college. I had no mentor and no idea what graduate school would entail. I did not even have an undergraduate degree in anthropology, which would become my field of study. However, I had been returning to Guatemala every year after my volunteer stint to visit and had seen first-hand how child survivors were working multiple jobs and going to college, which was not in the realm of possibility for them when they were children. Seeing them work hard and entering the unfamiliar arena of academia inspired me to take a giant leap of faith and start the graduate program in anthropology at the University of New Mexico in Albuquerque. After all, what excuse would I have not to at least try? Child survivors would try, and they would give it their all.

Midway through my graduate program, I returned to Guatemala for preliminary research and then full fieldwork two years later. I was amazed at what I witnessed and heard from child survivors, which I present in this book. They exhibit such impressive resilience in the face of both the horrendous atrocities they endured as children and the many unfair struggles with which they have grappled in adulthood. I am continually impressed by their perseverance and strength. Yet I also feel undeserving of collecting their stories, opinions, and perspectives in a manner to share with the world because of my positionality. Nonetheless, child survivors continue to show me such great support, and some, often in exasperation, have gently reprimanded me over the past several years, saying, "Shirley, you keep asking us the same question many times. Just write the book! The world needs to know what happened to us, and we don't have the time or the political safety in which to write one. Just write it already!"

Such support for this research project was also made apparent by friends in the town where I conducted most of my research. In the middle of my fieldwork, I was suddenly and most unexpectedly faced with a cruel, devastating divorce. My life was shattered into a million pieces and my goal to finish my research project, as well as my doctoral program, was in peril. I fell deeply into depression and could not muster the strength or energy to get out of bed for days. At the same time, I felt incredibly guilty for feeling devastated and depressed because, after all, this was not genocide. How could I complain while being in a community of people who had faced some of the worst behavior of humanity? My Guatemalan friends did not see it that way. They saw a friend suffering and in need of help. I vividly remembering one of my friends pounding on my door every morning after I had spent days in bed and forcing me to get out of bed, shower, and accompany her at work at the residential home. She fiercely vowed that she would not let me stay in bed another day. Another dear friend brought out the coffee and sweet breads in his Internet cafe and sat with me every time I had to use one of his computers to find a lawyer in the US, communicate with the lawyer, freeze financial assets, and deal with other unpleasant divorce matters. One of the most poignant moments, however, came when one of the respected elders in the town made a statement that continues to resonate with me to this day and likely will until my last breath.

I was having another particularly difficult day and went over to Doña Matilda's house for some sage advice and support. I entered her home and immediately started bawling my eyes out. In between sobs when gasping for air, I explained that I was ashamed that I was crying about my divorce because she was a genocide survivor. I assured her that I had no right to cry, but I was just so destroyed. Doña Matilda turned to me (she had been ironing clothes as I sobbed and told her my troubles), put her hands gently on my shoulders, looked me directly in the eyes, and sternly said, "Shirley, trauma is trauma." Then she hugged me while I sobbed some more and assured me that one day this pain would diminish, although a portion of it would likely accompany me for life. Doña Matilda's statement was profound for me and reignited my desire to continue with my research project since trauma is a central element of it. Not only was Doña Matilda a source of general inspiration and encouragement, but on that day, she decided to take an active role in spurring me every day to continue with my research project. Doña Matilda was not going to let my research or me go down in defeat. Without the persistent support of Doña Matilda and my friends (some of whom are among the child survivors who grew up at the residential home), I am not sure that this research project would ever have been completed.

The support of Doña Matilda and my friends demonstrates that while I am the author of this book and take full responsibility for its contents, the research is not mine alone. It is a composite of the gracious help and support of friends and child survivors, themselves, all of whom helped bring it to fruition. As such, I feel compelled to publish it while continuing to question my worthiness in doing so. I have worked diligently to remain objective and to maintain the authenticity of participants' words and experiences. However, I acknowledge that my experiences as a child abuse survivor may influence how I perceive and understand child survivors' own experiences and perspectives. At the same time, I understand childhood trauma physically and emotionally in a way that only a child survivor of any kind of trauma can, giving me insights that may not be apparent to other researchers. For example, I know first-hand that childhood trauma never completely goes away but remains ever present on the edges of one's being, ready to flare up again when triggered and often unexpectedly. I also have a deep sense of what it means to be resilient in the everyday. Resilience and trauma are often experienced at the same time rather than alternating or being experienced as two opposing ends of a single spectrum, which I discuss in relation to child survivors in this book. I can only hope that my experiences have helped open new ways of thinking about child survivor experiences overall without skewing them. With that in mind, I present this book as but one more step toward learning more about child survivor experiences, not only in Guatemala but also around the world. There is still so much more to learn, and it is imperative that longitudinal research continue with this segment of survivors to help fill the gaps in research and praxis. I hope that this book inspires others to continue this important work and encourages child survivors to share their own stories whenever and however they can, just like Mr. Andre J. Holten, who wrote the foreword for this book. Based on my research with Guatemalan child survivors and my relationships with survivors of other genocides, like Mr. Holten, I believe that child survivors truly are the light that can illuminate our path away from genocide and cruelty, which we need now more than ever.

NOTE

1. Genocide is defined under the United Nations' 1948 Convention on the Prevention and Punishment of the Crime of Genocide as "acts committed with intent to destroy, in whole or in part, a national, ethnic, racial or religious group" that include any of the following: (a) killing members of the group; (b) causing serious bodily or mental harm to members of the group; (c) deliberately inflicting on the group

conditions of life calculated to bring about its physical destruction in whole or in part; (d) imposing measures intended to prevent births within the group; and (e) forcibly transferring children of the group to another group" (UN 2022).

Acknowledgments

There are so many individuals and entities that have helped bring this book to fruition, and I am profoundly grateful for their support. I must first thank the individuals who participated in my research project, including both child survivors and their peers from Santa Teresa. They were generously patient and supportive of the entire process, including from initial fieldwork to my more recent follow-up research in 2019. I am grateful to their families as well. Family members often cooked food and supplied participants and me with goodies while we chatted in the interviews. In addition, I appreciate the insights and support of the alumni of the residential home who were not participants but still continued important conversations with me along the way. The community of Santa Teresa and my dear Guatemalan friends also were supportive throughout the entire process, especially my chosen sisters Chela and Tonita whose sisterhood is steadfast and unconditional. I also am incredibly grateful for the Catholic sisters who supported me when I initially was a volunteer at the residential home and have continued to support me and my research over the years. I have learned so much from my experiences living, working, and researching in Guatemala because of the good and kind peoples I have come to know and love there. What I have learned most from them, however, is true generosity and human connection that extends far beyond borders and backgrounds.

I sincerely thank my dissertation committee for their support of and guidance with my fieldwork and dissertation writing process that would eventually lead to this book. Thank you, Drs. Les Field, Ronda Brulotte, Beverly Singer, and Jane Ellen Smith of the University of New Mexico and Dr. Judith Gibbons of Saint Louis University. I appreciate that you did not give up on this first-generation college student or my large dissertation you had to review. I am especially grateful for Dr. Jane Ellen Smith and her generous mentorship in my graduate studies, in research, and in helping me learn how to navigate academia more generally. You will always be a role model for me. Similarly, I am incredibly grateful to Dr. Judith Gibbons for her ongoing enthusiastic support of my work and for her willingness to review one of the chapters of this book. ¡*Mil gracias*, Judy!

My gratitude also goes to several funding sources that helped make my research possible. The Latin American & Iberian Institute at the University of New Mexico provided a PhD Fellowship for my dissertation fieldwork. The Alfonso Ortiz Center for Intercultural Studies provided an Ortiz Public Policy Fellowship that helped support me during dissertation writing. In addition, various sources, such as the Student Research Allocations Committee, Graduate Research Project and Travel, and Department of Anthropology at the University of New Mexico, provided small grants and funds that directly supported my dissertation research and presentations of my research at academic conferences. As a faculty member, I received funding support from the Faulty Professional Development Committee and Faculty Research Support Committee of the Gallup branch of the University of New Mexico for follow-up research in 2016. More recently, I received generous funding from a Faculty Field Research Grant from the Latin American & Iberian Institute and a grant from the Research Allocations Committee, both of the University of New Mexico in Albuquerque. That funding made all the difference in permitting me to return to Guatemala to conduct important final follow-up research in preparation of this book. This book would not have been possible without that vital support.

Kasey Beduhn, former acquisitions editor at Lexington Books, was incredibly patient and kind throughout this manuscript preparation. I appreciate her guidance and generosity in helping me carefully prepare this book. I am also grateful to Alexandra Rallo, associate acquisitions editor at Lexington Books, for her effervescent support and encouragement. Many thanks also to their assistants who wielded questions and provided support at critical moments in the process. The professionalism and humanity of the staff at Lexington Books is unparalleled and is worthy of much praise and recognition.

Over my teaching career, I have come to know some especially brilliant, inspiring, strong, generous, and kind students. I am incredibly fortunate that some of them are now my friends and chosen family. I have felt truly blessed to observe their career and life trajectories, watching with joy as they have accomplished so many great things already. I am so proud of all of you that I really do think my heart might burst! I am especially grateful to B. Arneson, Hannah Brechtel, Christina Sarraf, and Nicole Larsen for graciously and patiently editing chapters of this manuscript. Your input was crucial, encouraging, and selfless. Thank you to soon-to-be Dr. Maria Mendez, as well as Sydney Hutson, Adrian Avila, Cobin Willie, Chelsey Willis, and Glenda Murphy for being constant sources of inspiration and encouragement as well. The world is such a better place because you are all in it and doing such impressive things. I am so proud of all of you!

Many additional friends and family also have been with me on this journey, supporting me and my writing process. Anna Dause and Dr. Carolene Whitman have offered such great joy and friendship along the way, making me laugh when I really needed it. Cheryl Branum, my sister-friend, and Gloria Mora offered immediate friendship and enduring support when I up and left New Mexico in the middle of the COVID-19 epidemic to take a job on the East Coast. Thank you for taking me under your wings and keeping me afloat as I navigated a new place and job amid quarantine. The Placitas gals (Susie Willis, Lisa Bixby, Jen Robins, Joy Colucci, Trina Poplett, Ali Willis, Susan Barcena, Pia Fugedy, and Sona Dawkins) have been pillars of strength and courage, challenging me in such positive ways to become stronger physically and emotionally in my endeavors. A very special thank you to Joy and Tony Colucci for offering me a pivotal writing space that provided just the right cozy, inspiring environment to spur my writing when I needed it most. My brilliant friend and fellow anthropologist, Dr. Iyaxel Cojti Ren, offered pivotal advice and countless insights for this manuscript. I appreciate her perspectives, and I can only hope that I can return the favor a thousandfold.

Mr. Ervin Tsosie has been a constant source of wisdom served with a large side of humor. His insights and perspectives always keep me grounded and humble, and his prayers make me feel loved and supported. Simone Nunez, my Europe travel buddy and co-survivor of that one time, continues to inspire me with her courage and brilliance. The world is your oyster! My amazing sister-friend, Ximena Araya Fischel, has been encouraging me in both my research and life for years. I am not sure you will ever truly know how much I appreciate you. I also appreciate the encouragement and support of her father, Dr. Manuel Araya Incera, whom I greatly admire. Hugh, Sandi, and Javier Woodruff also have offered such wonderful encouragement and support for years now. I especially appreciate all the great strolls through the neighborhood with Hugh and Javi, who provided much needed exercise and distraction that actually made my writing better. I am grateful to Christi Seelen, my sister-cousin, for her ongoing friendship and to her father (my uncle-dad), Ernie Seelen, who never quite understood what I was doing or why but supported me anyway. Rest in peace, Ernie. My life will never be the same without you.

I am further grateful for the love, encouragement, and support of my friend and hero, Regina Turner. I clearly remembering calling Regina's organization, New Mexico Human Rights Projects, for the first time when I was looking for a Holocaust survivor to speak to students in my Children in Genocide course at the University of New Mexico. One minute into that conversation and I already knew that I was talking with someone incredible and inspirational. Thank you, Regina, for all the years of support and for involving me in the good work of your organization. Much of what I have learned about the long-term effects of genocide, I have learned from you and your important work.

It is through Regina Turner that I met Andre (Andy) Holten, who wrote the foreword of this book. Andy spoke to students in my past courses, providing a powerful glimpse into the truth about the Holocaust and genocides more generally. He not only moved and inspired students but also gave me the courage and passion to see this book through to publication. And then he wrote the foreword on top of it all. I do not know if I can ever show you enough how grateful I am for all that you have done for my students and for me. I thank you profusely, Andy!

Adria Hartman has been an immense support throughout the editing process. She not only has been the best source of much needed fun and diversion but helped buffer the strain of moving across the country and reestablishing myself in a totally new environment during a pandemic. I am so fortunate to be your friend, and I only hope that you realize just how brilliant and strong you are. Adria for President! I am grateful to Teddy Hartman for so many delicious home-cooked meals and fun outings to restaurants and wineries, a great way to celebrate small accomplishments with my manuscript along the way. I also appreciate the patience and humor of their daughter, Cameron, who puts up with my frequent visits and food mooching. Your future is so bright, and I know you are going to strive to do some amazing things in life.

During the entire process of writing and throughout countless rounds of editing, I often kept my big brother, Rick Heying, in the forefront of my mind. I would constantly ask myself what he would need to know to make sense of what I am trying to get across. In many ways, the tone of this book was written for him. I can only hope that he will like how it turned out. My gratitude to my sister-in-law, Julie Heying, and my two brilliant, strong, and courageous nieces, Rachel and Emily Heying, for their support and encouragement as well. Your accomplishments and convictions continue to impress me.

My forever friend, Jane Rocha de Gandara, is another powerful source of inspiration for me. Thank you for the years of support and encouragement, picking me up when I fell and helping me reconnect to my passion to educate others about genocide and especially about what happened in Guatemala. I am so thrilled and grateful that you were able to accompany me to Guatemala on one of my return trips so that I could share the beauty and the humanity of the special peoples and places I have come to know and love there. Traveling with you throughout Central America and Mexico over the years has been one of the greatest joys of my life. I so admire your curious inquiries and keen insights, always asking important questions about any given topic. You have made me a better thinker and a better person. I cannot wait for our next adventure!

My sister-friend, colleague, and collaborator on all things academic and not, Dr. Tracy Lassiter, graciously edited early versions of my manuscript and then edited the entire final manuscript from top to bottom. That was a huge ask, and I am profoundly appreciative of her help. Her relentless encouragement and reminder that impostor syndrome gets us nowhere also has been vital throughout my writing process. I honestly would not have made it to publication without her continued support. I also was fortunate to have the unwavering support and encouragement of her partner, Richard Calabuig, who reminded us both of our accomplishments, especially in the light of being two first-generation college students who had to figure it all out on our own. Thank you, Richard, for your steadfast encouragement and wisdom.

I owe a massive debt of gratitude to Dr. David Witherington who has been there through dissertation writing up through this book publication. He has read and edited countless versions of my dissertation and books chapters. He has offered important cross-disciplinary insights and guidance, helping me overcome bouts of writer's block or uncertainty. David also helped create a conducive writing environment and never doubted that I could finish this book. He consistently reminded me of the worth of my research and the importance of having these stories told. His strength, love, and encouragement are unmatched and deeply appreciated. I am also grateful for the unconditional love of our pets Chiva, Cow, Luna, and Pinyon, who distracted me with their desires for walks and belly rubs. I never minded taking a break to have a chance to love on them and vice versa. Rest in peace and unconditional love, Chiva and Cow.

Lastly, I am forever indebted to and grateful for the support of my chosen family and forever friends, Dr. Lisa Froehling and Tony Rakow. We have been friends for over three decades now, and I profoundly appreciate their steadfast, unconditional love and friendship. They have been with me through it all from college to volunteering in Guatemala, then later through horrific divorce to graduation from a doctoral program and job searches, and finally through the challenges of getting this book published. Nobody knows the extent of my struggles, doubts, achievements, and resilience better than Lisa and Tony. Thank you for your unwavering support, especially knowing the sacrifices you have made to remain my chosen family and forever friends. I appreciate your support in bringing this chapter of my life to a fruitful close, and I look forward to where our adventures together will bring us next.

Introduction

What genocide in Guatemala? This is the question I have been asked countless times over the past twenty-some years, and I am often not surprised by it. Few people whom I have encountered outside of Guatemala since my mid-1990s volunteer stint there know about its history. I must admit that I, too, was previously unaware of what was happening there in the late 1970s and 1980s, even though I can vividly recall the armed conflicts in Nicaragua and El Salvador getting coverage on the nightly TV news. Sadly, my ignorance about the internal armed conflict and genocide in Guatemala at the time was not uncommon. Laurie Levinger (2009) found the same to be true and also questioned why she had not been more aware of the Guatemalan armed conflict and genocide when it was happening. She attributes this general lack of knowledge, especially among those in US society, to the disproportionate level of media coverage at the time.

To illustrate her point, Levinger conducted an article search for the period of 1976 through 1996 with three major US newspapers: *The New York Times, Washington Post*, and *Boston Globe*. Interestingly, her search yielded far fewer articles on the armed conflict and genocide in Guatemala than on those in Nicaragua and El Salvador. For example, the *Washington Post* published 361 articles on the conflict in El Salvador and 242 articles on the Nicaraguan conflict but only seventy articles during the same twenty-year period on the Guatemalan armed conflict and genocide. The *Boston Globe* published just twenty-six articles on Guatemala during that same time frame (Levinger 2009, 17). The US government, which was highly involved in the Guatemalan armed conflict and genocide, certainly downplayed what was happening at the time and released very little information to the public, evidenced in the disproportionately low media coverage (Grandin 2004; Perera 1993; Sanford 2003). Limited media attention was not a reflection of journalist choices but rather of military strategy and the cozy relationship between the US government and Guatemalan military leaders, such as dictator Efraín Ríos Montt, who sought to cover up such atrocities (CEH 1999; Grandin

2011). Levinger (2009) further reveals that general lack of public information and subsequent media coverage must certainly have played a central role in limiting US citizens' awareness of the Guatemalan armed conflict and genocide. Hidden in plain view from the public eye, most US Americans[1] were and still are unaware of the violence and brutality that took place in Guatemala for over three decades. They are even less familiar with how their own government supported it.

Since the first day I set foot on Guatemalan soil in 1994, I have sought to learn as much as I can about the armed conflict and genocide in the hope of bringing greater attention to the struggles, challenges, and long-term consequences that so many Guatemalans have been unjustly forced to endure. In particular, I have been determined to shed light on the life experiences of primarily Maya Indigenous[2] orphaned child survivors who are now adults. These child survivors have had to deal with difficult and often traumatic long-term consequences because one or both of their parents, who were unarmed, noncombatant civilians who had nothing to do with either side of the conflict, were murdered in, or died as a result of, Guatemala's thirty-six-year armed conflict and genocide. An estimated 150,000 to 200,000 children were orphaned during that period (CITGUA 1989, 18; WOLA 1989, 1). However, the numbers are likely much higher since there had never been a centralized effort to register orphaned child survivors. Recognizing that scores of children had been orphaned and having witnessed firsthand the struggles of some of them myself, I feared that they would face lifelong hardships and distress nearly impossible to overcome, their struggles remaining hidden in plain view from the public eye much like the armed conflict and genocide had been for decades.

Two principal truth reports, *Guatemala: Memoria del Silencio* (*Informe de la Comisión para el Esclarecimiento Histórico* [CEH] 1999) and *Guatemala: Nunca Más* (*Informe del Proyecto Interdiocesano de Recuperación de la Memoria Histórica* [REMHI] 1998), include some orphaned child survivor accounts and testimonies. However, research focused specifically and solely on their experiences remains limited, which is surprising given the large number of children orphaned. My research explicitly helps fill the gap of data regarding orphaned child survivors' experiences by focusing on a specific group of individuals who are now adults and were orphaned in childhood during the most brutal years of the genocide (1978 to 1983), which many locals and those in my research project commonly refer to as *la violencia* (the violence). The individuals in my research project had the additional challenge of having been legally enrolled and raised for the majority of their childhoods in a permanent residential home for orphaned children in the central highlands region of the country. My goals with *Child Survivors of Genocide* include elucidating the long-term consequences of the Guatemalan armed conflict and genocide on the lives of this particular group of grown orphaned child survivors, whom I simply refer to as "child survivors" throughout this book. I also aim to foment greater awareness of what child survivors, as a distinct group of survivors, have endured. Lastly, I seek to illuminate how they have responded to those consequences over their current life span now that they are adults in their thirties and early forties.

I acknowledge that the findings of my research project are not exhaustive and, therefore, are not representative of all grown Guatemalan orphaned child survivors of the armed conflict and genocide, including those who grew up in permanent residential care in other locations. Yet the research presented in this book is critical both for advancing our knowledge of child survivors' experiences and for validating those experiences. It is also important for recognizing that child survivors do, in fact, constitute a distinct group of survivors and deserve attention separate from that of adult survivors. In the past, child survivors have often been overlooked in research because various scholars and practitioners often assumed that children were either too young to remember what happened, lacked the cognitive skills necessary to understand the gravity of what was occurring, or had experiences indistinct from those of adults (Heberer 2011; Robinson, Rapaport-Bar-Sever, and Rapaport 1994). Orphaned child survivors in my research project, however, demonstrate that, even if they were too young to remember the actual murder or kidnapping of their parents, they are fully aware of the distress, hardships, and consequences they endured in childhood and in adulthood because of their orphan status, something with which adult survivors have not had to contend. Therefore, in this book I present research that contributes to conflict, genocide, anthropological, and other literature by focusing on orphaned child survivors who are now adults but grew up in a non-governmental residential home in Santa Teresa,[3] Guatemala, with the hope that it will spur further research with child survivors—both in childhood and adulthood—in Guatemala and around the globe. Unfortunately, the existence of wars, armed conflicts, and genocides shows no signs of ceasing (Anderson and Anderson 2013; Jones 2016). My research contributes to both research and practice by providing pivotal findings and information critical to assisting development programs and policymakers concerned with meeting the needs of orphaned children around the world and empowering them to develop into resilient, well-adapted adults.

CARING FOR GUATEMALAN ORPHANED CHILDREN

Child survivors who participated in my research were raised in a family-style permanent residential home for orphaned children. The residential home is referred to as an "*hogar*" (or home) rather than an orphanage because the term "*orfanato*" (orphanage) carries with it much stigma in Guatemala, just like in many other countries. Furthermore, the design of the residential home deliberately moves away from the structure of a single building institutional orphanage by consisting, instead, of small family-style homes that are modeled on family homes in the region. The residential home was founded in 1985 by an order of Catholic religious sisters[4] in the town of Santa Teresa, located within a department[5] in the central highlands of the country. This region was especially devastated during the height of *la violencia* because the military used it as part of a major route for infiltrating the highlands during its counterinsurgency campaign to eliminate Marxist-inspired Leftist guerrillas. Consequently, villages and mostly Maya Indigenous peoples[6] along this route were often falsely accused of supporting guerrillas and became targets of military-led murders, disappearances, torture, and displacement (CEH 1999; REMHI 1998). Recognizing the devastation and despair that had occurred in this area of the highlands, the Catholic sisters decided to establish a program specifically aimed at caring for the growing number of orphaned children they were seeing firsthand in the region.

The Catholic sisters, who are religious women from Guatemala and the US, explained to me that they were initially forced to flee the country during *la violencia*. Having received death threats and under constant fear of ongoing political violence, they, along with a group of young women training to become Catholic sisters in Guatemala, left for Chiapas, Mexico, in late 1980. However, recognizing the growing needs of Guatemalan peoples, they returned in 1982 to serve in solidarity with individuals and families who had remained in the country despite the tumultuous state-sponsored violence that was fully underway. Prevented from returning to their former mission sites because of impending death threats and further interrogation by the military, they looked for other areas of need and established new mission sites where they could best serve peoples and communities most devastated by the armed conflict and genocide. Within a relatively short period of time of returning to the country, they initiated new mission projects in marginal areas of Guatemala City and in the department of Alta Verapaz.

Through their initial work in the newly-established mission sites, the Catholic sisters became increasingly aware of thousands of orphaned children and widows living in despair within the country, especially in the highlands region. Taking a risk, the sisters decided to work toward meeting the needs of orphaned children and their surviving family members by establishing a permanent residential home for orphaned children with diverse ethnic and family backgrounds and who came from some of the hardest hit areas of the region. After nine months of initial investigative and preparatory work, they were invited by Bishop Eduardo Fuentes Duarte of the Sololá Diocese to establish the residential home in the town of Santa Teresa, a midway point in the diocese and located in the middle of the central route the military used to infiltrate the highlands. The sisters were familiar with the region as they had provided pastoral services to parishioners in the area prior to fleeing the country. Impressed with their previous work, the bishop invited the sisters to live in the rectory of the Catholic Church located in Santa Teresa and to reinitiate their pastoral work while they also began laying the groundwork for opening their proposed family-style permanent residential home for orphaned children. In return, the bishop and the diocese agreed to give them a ninety-nine-year lease free of charge for adjoining church property where construction of the residential home would begin. By February of 1985, the first of eight homes that would constitute the residential home complex was completed, and the sisters began receiving orphaned children. Children's enrollment was legally processed to legitimately and safely transfer custody from surviving family members to the residential home only with the full voluntary consent of surviving family members. Such legal transfer of custody helped protect the children from strangers who would often show up claiming that the child was to be given over for intercountry adoption (none of these claims was ever legitimate). Surviving family members could request that custody be returned to them at any time, as long as they could provide proof that the children would be able to continue their education and would be well cared for by the family. Several more homes were constructed in a few years following completion of the first home, and the residential home was in full swing, nurturing and educating up to 125 orphaned children of all ages and backgrounds on a daily basis.

Structure of the Permanent Residential Home

At its height of its operation, the permanent residential home came to include a total of eight small, family-style homes. Each home was equipped with four bedrooms, a dining room, a kitchen with a common *pollo* (or brick hearth) and a *bodega* (storeroom) for each home's supplies and foodstuffs. An average of ten to fifteen children lived in each home where they were cared for by Maya Indigenous and *ladina* Guatemalan women who were referred to as *tías* (aunts), many of whom had been widowed during the armed conflict and genocide. The Catholic sisters allowed widowed women to bring their own children to live in the residential home as well, providing much needed support for them and their families. The *tías* lived with and provided daily care for children enrolled in the residential home and also tried to help maintain children's primary Mayan language skills. The sisters intentionally hired women from diverse areas throughout Guatemala who spoke Mayan languages such as Kaqchikel, K'iche', Q'eqchi', Mam, and Tz'utujil.[7] With an average caregiver-to-child ratio of one-to-three for younger children and one-to-five for adolescents, the residential home offered ethnically and linguistically diverse orphaned children the guidance, care, and nurturing necessary for fostering a genuine family-style environment often atypical in an institutional-type residential care setting.

The residential home also offered children access to formal education, provided through the local public schools. This permitted orphaned children to further develop social skills with children outside of the residential home and to integrate into the local community. When orphaned children arrived at the residential home, they were immediately enrolled in the local schools where they were placed in grades according to their prior educational experience and academic abilities. Many initially came from distant and more isolated villages and often lacked any formal education whatsoever prior to arriving at the residential home. Many also had little or no Spanish language skills. With such limited exposure to formal education and minimal Spanish language skills, many of the initial group of children enrolled in the residential home were placed in one of the initial primary grades, regardless of age. Once placed at the appropriate educational grade level, orphaned children attended school daily to meet the Guatemalan educational standards for completing *primaria* (elementary education) and *básico* (secondary education). To supplement their formal education and help them catch up to their age mates, the Catholic sisters, staff, and volunteers offered daily tutoring at the residential home in subjects such as Spanish language, mathematics, reading, and sciences. This tutoring was vital in helping orphaned children make considerable gains in their academic skills and in preparing them for secondary education.

The formal education of orphaned children enrolled in the residential home also was supplemented with vocational training. When orphaned children reached the age of twelve, they were required to choose one of four vocational tracks: shoemaking, carpentry, sewing, or agriculture. Once each child selected a vocational track, they were required to attend the designated vocational workshop daily (Monday through Friday), using an alternating schedule with their formal education classes (most formal education classes took place either in the morning for elementary school or in the afternoon for junior high school). Children attended the shoemaking, carpentry, and sewing workshops directly at the residential home as the workshops are located within the complex itself. Agricultural students worked on several nearby plots of land purchased by the Catholic sisters over the years to help provide agricultural training, while at the same time raising crops to help sustain the residential home. When it was time for planting and harvesting, all children, Catholic sisters, *tías*, staff, and volunteers were involved in agricultural activities and participated in related events such as the traditional blessing of the seeds. All vocational workshops were taught by local trade specialists who brought with them a variety of practical work experiences and skills. The instructors also spoke Mayan languages, helping maintain and encourage children's natal language skills. These instructors worked to develop healthy relationships with their students and to serve as positive role models at a time when orphaned children were in most need of adult mentorship and guidance. Combining vocational training with formal education, the residential home was intentionally designed to foster the development of orphaned children's academic, technical, and social skills with the aim of helping them gain improved access to more sustainable employment and life opportunities once they became adults and were on their own.

Orphaned Children Enrolled in the Permanent Residential Home

The permanent residential home was initially established to support orphaned children who had lost one or both of their parents in military attacks, massacres, kidnappings, and murders during the armed conflict and especially during the period of *la violencia*. In many instances, children who enrolled in the residential home had lost their fathers in military-led massacres, extrajudicial killings, or kidnappings and could no longer be economically supported by their surviving widowed mothers. For many widowed mothers, economically maintaining their families after their husbands had been kidnapped and disappeared[8] was nearly impossible because they had little or no marketable job skills or formal education to attain wage-earning employment. Many widows also lost most of their belongings and land because of the death of their husbands who had the only legal title or inheritance rights to their property. When a husband died in such cases, his family often regained control of his land. Thus, their husbands' deaths left these women with no resources to eke out even the most basic sustainable living for their children, an experience quite common for many families especially in the central highlands (CITGUA 1989). Many widows voluntarily brought their children to the residential home as a final hope for keeping their children safe and meeting their basic needs. However, as the residential home moved past the 1980s and weathered the initial aftershock of *la violencia*, children continued arriving due to other circumstances.

Most children who arrived at the residential home after the 1980s were abandoned, abused, or neglected by family members. In some cases, extended family members brought children to the residential home fearing for their safety as their parents suffered from serious mental illnesses or substance addiction, often resulting from *la violencia*, and had physically threatened their children. In other cases, widowed parents may have died due to illness or ongoing violence, leaving their children completely orphaned and with no other family members either willing or financially able to care for them.

Additional children came as a result of their single or widowed parents' inability to financially support them because of extreme poverty. With no other means of financial support, these parents looked to the Catholic sisters and the residential home as a viable way of providing for their children, now and in the future, while allowing them to sustain some form of relationship with their children whom they were invited to visit a frequently as possible.

Marked by the signing of the peace accords, Guatemala's armed conflict and genocide officially ended in 1996. Despite this, the need for a nurturing residential home for orphaned, abandoned, and other disadvantaged children continued. When the Catholic sisters began their work at the residential home, their original aim was to close the residential home after the initial group of orphaned children reached the age of eighteen and became adults. However, continuing social and economic strain on families in Guatemala created an ongoing need for the residential home well into the 2000s. Today, the number of children arriving at the residential home has dwindled significantly due to increased child protection regulations and a push for in-country adoptions. In fact, the Catholic sisters announced in November 2021 that the home would no longer operate as a residential home for children but, instead, would serve as a center for young women who elect to advance their studies at the university level. Ultimately, over its thirty-six-year history, the residential home has served over two hundred children, aged newborn to seventeed, from a variety of backgrounds and experiences. However, it is the group of orphaned child survivors among the first to live in the residential home who became participants in my research project.

EXPLORING ORPHANED CHILD
SURVIVORS' LIFE EXPERIENCES

Three central research questions formed the foundation of my project with this group of survivors. First, what long-term consequences of the internal armed conflict and genocide have affected and continue to affect grown orphaned child survivors today in adulthood? Second, how have grown orphaned child survivors responded in their life experiences to the challenges of these long-term consequences? Third, how have the long-term consequences and grown orphaned child survivors' responses to them influenced child survivors' own senses of ethnic identity and belonging in the Guatemalan nation-state today? With these three central questions, I embarked on over a year of formal field-work, establishing my home base in Santa Teresa in a rental property separate from the residential home to reduce any influence that the Catholic sisters or residential home potentially could have on participants or my research findings. I also conducted follow-up research one, two, six, and eleven years[9] after my initial fieldwork was completed.

Utilizing a combination of qualitative and quantitative research methods, I worked closely with twenty child survivors (twelve women, eight men)[10] randomly-selected from the residential home database of eighty-two alumni. Twenty child survivor participants constituted one-quarter of the total alumni at the time of my fieldwork. Child survivor participants were selected among alumni with birth dates between 1973 and 1983, the time period immediately preceding and including the period of *la violencia.* Their age range at the time of initial enrollment in the residential home was six to thirteen years of age, and their mean length of stay was 8.9 years (SD = 2.85). Eight of the twenty child survivor participants are considered full orphans (both parents deceased or disappeared at the time of enrollment), and twelve are considered partial orphans (one parent deceased or disappeared at the time of enroll-ment). For ten of the child survivor participants, one or both of their parents were murdered or disappeared during *la violencia,* and six lost one or both parents due to illness or suicide that participants, themselves, associate with the armed conflict and genocide. Four were abandoned for either economic reasons or to save their lives as their parents likely were targeted for kidnap-ping and murder, which was reported by surviving family members at the time of enrollment. Ten child survivor participants recalled witnessing the kidnapping or death of one or both of their parents, while ten report having been too young to remember such events or their abandonment. Child survi-vor participants' mean age at time of initial participation in my fieldwork was 28.7 years of age (SD = 2.23). Fifteen self-identified ethnically as Kaqchikel, K'iche', Uspanteka, or Indigenous generally, three self-identified using the term *"mestizo"* (they defined the term as meaning of mixed Maya Indigenous and *ladino* ethnicity), and two identified as *ladino* (Heying et al. 2016).

In addition to twenty child survivor participants, I incorporated compara-tive analyses by also working with twenty peers who were raised in their fam-ily homes in Santa Teresa and also had birth dates that fell between 1973 and 1983. The group of twenty peer participants were randomly-selected from a list of over seventy peers compiled through consultation with residential home staff, local elders, and former local schoolteachers. Peers on the list attended the local public schools in the same time period as child survivors from the residential home and had established friendships with many of them in childhood and adolescence. Only one peer participant lost a father who was disappeared near the end of the genocide, but she remained living with her surviving family members in their home. None of the peer participants reported any major disruption or participation in any form of alternative care during childhood. Peer participants' mean age at time of initial participa-tion in my research project was 31.8 years of age (SD = 3.14). Eleven peer participants self-identified ethnically as Kaqchikel and nine self-identified using the term "*ladino*" (Heying et al. 2016).

I conducted formal interviews with each of the forty participants at a location of their choosing (typically their own home, or my rental property) so that they felt safe during the interview. I conducted interviews in Spanish as all participants are fluent Spanish speakers and many no longer speak fluent Mayan languages. Conducting the interviews in Spanish also allowed me to interview them directly without a translator since I am not fluent in a Mayan language. Each interview included a close-ended demographic survey and a semi-structured ethnographic interview consisting of sixty questions that covered four primary topic areas that had emerged as common themes for orphaned child survivors during preliminary research: politics, economics, ethnic identity, and trauma. At the end of the ethnographic portion of the interview, I administered three psychological assessment instruments to assess psychological distress, trauma, and post-traumatic growth. Each of these instruments is discussed in greater detail in chapter four. I present my qualitative research findings, along with a brief overview of my quantitative work, in this book and have replaced the names of participants, as well as the names of towns, with pseudonyms to protect participants and their families. In addition, I purposely am not including any images or maps as a further means of protecting participants and their families.

Theoretical Tools for Exploring Child Survivors' Experiences

Three primary areas of research literature undergird my work with child survivors and provided an appropriate foundation for understanding their experiences with and responses to the long-term consequences of Guatemala's internal armed conflict and genocide: trauma; resilience and post-traumatic growth; and ethnic identity and belonging. Trauma research literature helps make sense of child survivors' experiences with distress related not only to having lost parents and other family members in the armed conflict and genocide but also to having confronted ongoing repercussions and resulting sequential traumatization due to their orphan status. Resilience and post-traumatic growth literature offer vital insights regarding child survivors' positive responses to the trauma they have faced and underscores the importance of recognizing that individuals can be both traumatized and resilient at the same time. Ethnic identity and belonging literature specific to Guatemala highlights the country's distinctive history with ethnic identity construction and politics that have led to over five centuries of overt structural racism used to justify the armed conflict and genocide in the twentieth century. Drawing from the expertise of scholars who have worked in Guatemala for decades, I utilize key concepts to unpack how child survivors conceptualize their own sense of ethnic identity and belonging despite having lost certain aspects they associate particularly with Maya Indigenous identities (e.g., language, traditions, and cultural practices, etc.). While child survivors' experiences are complicated and nuanced and each experience is as unique as each individual, the areas of research literature that I engage help highlight some of the commonalities across their experiences, which can better inform and shape future research and praxis. With this in mind, I present the following overview of each of the three areas of literature that undergird my research.

Trauma

Taken from the Greek word for "wound," trauma has likely been experienced by human beings in various ways since the dawn of humankind (Jones and Cureton 2014; van der Kolk 2014). Trauma involves exposure to often overwhelming terror. It is caused by an event or an ongoing series of events (e.g., child abuse or domestic violence) that can lead to troubling memories, arousal, and avoidance (van der Kolk, Weisaeth, and van der Hart 1996). Saigh and Bremner (1999) argue that aspects of distress associated with trauma have long been chronicled in human history. For example, they note that reports from the 1666 Great Fire of London portrayed survivors suffering with trauma-like symptoms. They also point out a case in which a physician treating American Civil War casualties reported soldiers experiencing trauma-like symptoms, including increased arousal, irritability, and elevated heart rates (ibid.). Trauma-related symptomatology has been observed for centuries, if not millennia. However, it was only after World War I that trauma-related distress gained particular attention as reflected in concepts such as shell shock, war neurosis, war hysteria, transient situational disturbance, anxiety neurosis, and rape trauma syndrome (APA 1980; Bracken 2001; Schlenger, Fairbank, Jordan, and Caddell 1999).

Psychiatrist and world-renowned trauma expert Bessel van der Kolk (2014) underscores the importance of recognizing that trauma is more than simply experiencing a distressing event or series of events that have occurred in an individual's lifetime. Rather, trauma is an imprint left by a distressing experience or experiences, affecting the mind, brain, and body with ongoing consequences for how an individual will continue to survive (ibid., 21). Traumatic experiences affect our minds and emotions; they impact our capacity for joy and intimacy, our biology, and our immune systems (ibid., 1). Even when a traumatic event or series of events is long gone, it can be triggered and reactivated at the slightest hint of danger and can cause a distressing reaction that leaves an individual feeling out of control. Therefore, trauma can have long-term consequences for individuals and can breed further trauma if not effectively addressed and treated (ibid., 2).

For children—given their limited cognitive and linguistic development—trauma may be experienced differently than adults, resulting in distinct responses and long-term consequences (Jones and Cureton 2014). Symptoms associated with trauma for children may include temper tantrums, restless sleep, or decreased participation in play, for example. Symptoms may also manifest through behavior or play reenactment that can be related to the traumatic event or series of events (ibid., 264). Children who suffer trauma brought on by war, armed conflict, genocide, and disaster experience even greater distress and risks to their well-being. They are also at risk for maladaptive functioning and development, a risk that increases when children experience additional adversities before and after war, armed conflict, genocide, or disaster related events (Masten, Narayan, Silverman, and Osofsky 2015, 734). Other factors such as age and gender similarly influence how children respond to trauma. For example, older children typically face greater exposure because of their awareness and age-related activities; however, younger children are highly dependent on caregivers and are thus more sensitive than older children to disruption in caregiving, such as the death of a parent (ibid., 718). With gender, older girls report more internal distress, while older boys display greater disruptive or aggressive behavior (ibid., 734).

Individuals who face trauma in childhood, especially in relation to war, armed conflict, genocide, and disaster, have an increased likelihood of facing psychological repercussions for years to come—including well into adulthood—if they are not provided with a favorable recovery context in childhood. Given a favorable context, they can fare reasonably well and recover from their trauma experiences. However, advanced research involving longitudinal analyses of childhood trauma is needed to more fully understand the lifelong repercussions that child survivors confront (ibid.). Additional analyses on the cumulative effects of trauma and long-term consequences of war, armed conflict, genocide, and disaster can allow for a broader and better-informed understanding of how child survivors cope with childhood trauma and what impact it has on their well-being in adulthood (ibid., 735). This is precisely where my work contributes to cross-disciplinary trauma literature. My research with grown Guatemalan child survivors who have experienced sequential traumatization in childhood and early adulthood as a result of having been orphaned in childhood during the armed conflict and genocide offers important insights that advance this critical area of study.

While trauma provides a salient construct for understanding an individual's experiences with distress related to a terrifying event or series of events, scholars and practitioners simultaneously caution against its broad, undiscerning application (Bracken 2001; López and Guarnaccia 2000). They argue that trauma and the utilization of associated psychological assessment instruments, such as those assessing post-traumatic stress disorder that were developed primarily in "Western" societies, may not accurately or genuinely map onto the varied human responses to psychological distress experienced by diverse groups of peoples and societies around the world (Desjarlais and Kleinman 1994; Fassin and Rechtman 2009). For example, Derek Summerfield (2000) argues that Western psychological frameworks have been assumed to have universal validity and relevance, with post-traumatic stress disorder (PTSD) taking an almost hegemonic position in medical and psychological research and praxis. He insists that human experiences with a traumatic event or series of events may differ radically across cultures and from Western-led theory and practice based on a biopsychomedical paradigm (ibid., 421). Considering a more socially constructionist and culturally relativist approach to distress and health may be more appropriate and effective in other cultural contexts. Recognizing that individuals may conceptualize and interpret their experiences with distressing events in varied ways across cultures is imperative and has informed my own research with child survivors in Guatemala. Having extensively reviewed trauma literature prior to research, I made a concerted effort *not* to use the term "trauma" in any of my preliminary interviews conducted a few years prior to fieldwork. However, nearly all participants used the term "trauma" to describe the distress associated with their childhood experiences. Therefore, I intentionally included the term "trauma" in my fieldwork and found that it remains a salient concept for participants (see chapter four for further discussion). The use of the term "trauma" also was effective for helping to elucidate child survivors' experiences with resilience and post-traumatic growth.

Resilience and Post-traumatic Growth

Research on the construct of resilience began in the 1970s and gained much momentum in the 1990s and 2000s as a way of assessing and understanding an individual's positive adjustment following significant risk or adversity such as a traumatic event or series of events (Luthar, Crossman, and Small 2015). Internationally renowned developmental and clinical psychologist Dante Cicchetti defines resilience as one's capacity to successfully adapt and competently function following chronic adversity or exposure to prolonged or severe trauma (2010, 524; see also Masten, Best, and Garmezy 1990). Resilience typically consists of two distinct dimensions: adversity and positive adaptation. Adversity involves a high risk condition that increases the likelihood for maladjustment in its wake, such as losing one or both parents in armed conflict and genocide. Positive adaptation indicates adjustment that is better than expected given the high risk condition experienced, which I found in my research with grown child survivors. Positive adaptation, especially among children, may include success in meeting tasks associated with typical developmental stages or demonstrations of social competence evidenced in positive behavior. It can also include lack of serious psychopathology for those who have experienced major trauma, demonstrating that criteria denoting positive adaptation can vary based on the context and gravity of a traumatic event or series of events (Luthar, Crossman, and Small 2015, 248).

To understand how resilience develops, researchers explore and evaluate both vulnerability and protective factors that can impact, or modify, the effects of traumatic events. Vulnerability factors, such as extreme poverty or orphan status, can exacerbate the negative effects of traumatic events. Protective factors can positively modify the negative effects of traumatic events and may involve nurturing relationships, positive peer networks, positive coping skills, and consistent daily routines. Because resilience involves both vulnerability and protective factors, it is important to note that it should not be considered a personal trait. Instead, it is a process or phenomenon involving both external factors (e.g., nurturing caregivers, secure housing, positive routines) and internal traits (e.g., positive coping skills, self-confidence) (ibid.).

Some scholars argue that resilience is too vague a concept to prove useful in praxis (see Manyena 2006). Others contend that basic tools of resilience studies fall short of rigor regarding validity (see Atkinson, Martin, and Rankin 2009), or that resilience is a primarily "Western" concept that ignores local idioms of communal care and support (see Nguyen-Gillham, Rita Giacaman, Naser, and Boyce 2008). However, I found it critical in my research with grown Guatemalan child survivors for analyzing and understanding their particular experiences with post-traumatic growth.

Psychologists Richard Tedeschi and Lawrence Calhoun first introduced the clinical term "post-traumatic growth" (or PTG) in 1995 (Calhoun, Cann, and Tedeschi 2010). They use the term to encapsulate the experiences of individuals who engaged in positive change following major life crises or traumatic events. They point out that the notion of positive growth following an adverse experience, such as a traumatic event or series of events, has long been invoked in ancient religion, myth, and literature (Tedeschi and Calhoun 1995). For example, ancient Greek and Athenian tragedies reveal a common theme of individuals overcoming adversity in the face of tragedy, one that has appealed to readers for over two millennia (ibid., 3–5). Thus, the idea of PTG is not new, even though the systematic quantitative research and assessment of it is.

Assessment scales designed to specifically measure PTG were first developed in Western, English-speaking countries but have been translated, validated, and used with diverse peoples in many countries around the world (Calhoun, Cann, and Tedeschi 2010). PTG assessment considers sociocultural influences such as primary reference groups (formal or informal social groups to which individuals belong), social and cultural norms and rules, and societal narratives. The assessment, called the Post-traumatic Growth Inventory and detailed in chapter four, is based on Tedeschi and Calhoun's (1995) model of the process of PTG. The PTG process starts with an individual's pre-trauma experience and then proceeds through their experiences with trauma toward the endpoint of positive change. Tedeschi and Calhoun argue that it is the disruption of a person's assumptive beliefs instead of the traumatic event itself that initiates processes that can lead to PTG (ibid., 62). In many cases of traumatic events, individuals may experience loss that cannot be undone, or they may find that returning to their pre-traumatic life experience is not possible, countering their assumptive beliefs. Consequently, those who move toward PTG positively adjust to their new circumstances and challenged assumptions about the world rather than holding steadfastly to their original assumptive beliefs and becoming permanently mired in feelings of loss, devastation, and hopelessness. Tedeschi and Calhoun's model also acknowledges that various cultural influences can play a significant role in shaping an individual's assumptive beliefs, influencing the ways in which an individual perceives events (Calhoun, Cann, and Tedeschi 2010). What I find most useful about the PTG model is that it recognizes that people can experience both trauma-related distress and growth concurrently (ibid., 6), which is clearly the case with child survivors featured in this book. Furthermore, PTG is viewed as a particular form of resilience that may shape an individual's resilience to future stressors (Lepore and Revenson 2006). Together, resilience and PTG can lead to salutogenic outcomes (promoting health and well-being) that are imperative for survivors and evident among participants in my research project.

Ethnic Identity and Belonging in Guatemala

The third and final area of research literature that I draw upon for my work with Guatemalan child survivors focuses on ethnic identity and belonging specific to Guatemala. Since the moment Spanish conquistadors came to what is known as Guatemala today, ethnic identity and belonging have been highly contentious issues. These issues ultimately gave rise to genocide in the twentieth century and continue to affect quotidian experiences of Guatemalans today (Carey 2001; Smith 1990a–d). For over five centuries, a small group of oligarchic elites who control the state, starting with the conquistadores and continuing with their descendants and others who claim direct Spanish lineage, has imposed the identity category of "Indian"[11] on the majority heterogeneous Indigenous populations found within Guatemala's borders (Calvert 1985; Handy 1984; Smith 1990c). Ignoring diverse local perceptions and expressions of ethnic identity, the ruling elite sanctioned and imposed its overgeneralized and often lethal "Indian" category on all Indigenous peoples.

This subordinate category would come to be positioned in direct contrast to the identity category of *"ladino"* that is specific to Guatemalan history.

Individuals identified as "Indian" were considered by the ruling elite as underdeveloped, backward, and traditionalist natives of the region who would only hinder progress toward the development of a unitary, modern nation-state (Fischer 2004b; Grey Postero and Zamosc 2004; Smith 1990b; Stavenhagen 1998). Persons categorized as *ladinos*, on the other hand, were initially considered to be baptized and Hispanicized (or assimilated) Indigenous peoples who spoke Spanish. By the eighteenth century, however, the category of *ladino* soon came to encompass all individuals of "mixed race" (Indigenous and Spanish), and by the turn of the nineteenth century, it was expanded to demarcate any individual considered "non-Indian," including individuals who were *mestizos* (offspring of mixed Spanish and Indigenous parents), Creoles (American-born offspring of Spanish parents), and Spaniards. Thus, the dichotomous identity framework established by the ruling elite came to define *ladinos* by the early 1800s as "non-Indian" Spanish-speaking peoples in *opposition* to the racist notion of ignorant, backward "Indians" who were deemed intellectually and morally inferior to their *ladino* counterparts (Brown, Fischer, and Raxché 1998; Grandin 2000; Hale 1999). By developing a dichotomous *ladino* versus "Indian" hierarchical identity-making framework, the ruling elite created and maintained an arbitrary division of "us" (*ladinos*) versus "them" ("Indians") based on a system of social classification that was built on ideologies of culture, class, and language. The resulting dichotomous identity construct came to be one of the fundamental classifiers of personhood in the Guatemalan nation-state (Grandin 2000; Fischer and Brown 1996; Nelson 1999; Smith 1990a).

Despite this state-imposed dichotomous identity framework, Indigenous and *ladino* citizens alike have formed, understood, and expressed ethnic identity and belonging in creative and resistant ways that extend far beyond the *"ladino* versus 'Indian'" construct. Contemporary scholars respect the need for ongoing analyses of the state's often violent efforts to impose its external dichotomous identity construct on Indigenous populations. Such analysis helps construct a more accurate picture of the context in which ethnic identity is perceived, formed, expressed, and reworked at the local level today. Yet scholars also have simultaneously broadened the scope of inquiry regarding ethnic identity by including a focus on individuals' complex, dynamic, and often strategic perceptions and expressions of ethnic identity as situated within an increasingly multifaceted context of local, national, and global relations (e.g., Hale 2006; Montejo 1999; Warren 1998). I find this broadened scope helpful and hopeful with my own research with grown Guatemalan child survivors.

While many scholars have conducted valuable and insightful research on ethnic identity in Guatemala and elsewhere, there are three central figures whose work I find most informative and pertinent to my research: Kay Warren, Victor Montejo, and Charles Hale. Kay Warren (1998) recognizes the complexity and dynamic nature of ethnic identity in contemporary Guatemala, especially for Maya Indigenous peoples. Based on her analysis of the Pan-Maya movement and its projects for "self-determination" and the promotion of "Maya Culture," Warren discusses an alternative construction-ist formulation of ethnic identity that suggests that it is an ongoing process in which individuals and communities continually rework identities (ibid., 71–72). The dichotomous "*ladino* versus 'Indian'" identity construct imposed by the Guatemalan state as a mutually exclusive set of ethnic identity choices for its citizens ignores the dynamic, fluid processual nature of identity forma-tion. Warren notes that constructionists acknowledge that ethnic identities are "constructed, contested, negotiated, imposed, imputed, resisted, and rede-fined in action" and as a result, ethnic identity formation is a process that is "never-ending because identity never quite coalesces" (ibid., 73). She notes that the dichotomous identity framework is challenged by the diversity found among contemporary Maya identities. Such diversity is further fomented by "pan-Maya ethnic nationalism, the diaspora of political and economic refu-gees, and the waves of successful evangelizers across ethnic divides" (ibid.).

Recognizing that Maya identities in Guatemala can be construed as a fluid, diverse, and never-ending process, Warren examines the Pan-Maya move-ment's efforts to cultivate a unified "Maya culture" across heterogeneous Maya populations. In her view, "Maya culture" as proposed by leaders of the movement is defined as "the meaningful selective mix of practices and knowledge, drawn on and resynthesized at this historical juncture by groups who see indigenous identity as highly salient to self-representation and as a vehicle for political change" (ibid., 12). Warren suggests that those in the Pan-Maya movement are hoping that a "unity within diversity" approach "will bring Mayas powerfully into the mainstream" and lead to readdressing serious development issues in Guatemala (ibid.,13). She argues that activ-ists, "articulating a nationalist essentialism," have created the Pan-Maya social movement to realize the resurgence of Maya culture via areas such as language revitalization and education, as well as through concerted efforts toward the assertion of self-determination and human rights (ibid., 13, 39, 77). Through her analysis of the Pan-Maya movement, Warren demonstrates that Indigenous peoples continue to take an active role—albeit now as a much more formalized social movement—in not only transforming their own lives, identities, and cultures but in also *affecting* the state through the creation of new positioning such as "novel class-ethnic blends" (ibid., 201).

Jakaltek Maya anthropologist Victor Montejo (2005, 2004, 1999) provides further insight into the complexity and diversity of ethnic identity among contemporary Maya peoples today. He draws from his own personal experiences and ethnographic research with Maya refugees from the Kuchumatan highlands, his homeland area, who were forced to flee to Chiapas, Mexico during *la violencia*. Through both his firsthand experiences and anthropological research, Montejo demonstrates that instead of losing their sense of Maya identity while in exile, refugees have worked in interesting ways to both reaffirm and transform their sense of ethnic identity. Through creative practices such as renaming themselves with historically established Jakaltek names, reviving or creating new ceremonial practices, and asserting new positions within and beyond the refugee community, refugees report feeling strongly connected with their past while simultaneously interacting in creative ways with the changing realities of their current situations (2004, 252–253; 1999, 188–189).

Montejo contends that interrelations of continuity and discontinuity in Maya identities, as evidenced among Maya refugees in Chiapas, have long informed Indigenous experiences in Guatemala. To understand Maya identities, he first emphasizes that Maya peoples prefer to be called by the names of their linguistic communities (1999, 187). Therefore, Maya peoples identify principally with their linguistic communities (e.g., Kaqchikel, K'iche', Tz'utujil, etc.) and then with the aggregate of being a Guatemalan Maya. Montejo confirms that it is not common to hear a Maya person self-identify as an "*Indio*" (Indian), since the term is considered pejorative by most and highly politicized by some.[12] He asserts that to be Maya in Guatemala is not limited to any single place or time or to the state-imposed category of "Indian," and it is not forever rooted in the past (2004, 243; 1999, 243). Instead, Maya identities are and have long been a dynamic process of resistance, adaptability, and creativity that is not inextricably bound to the state-imposed dichotomous "*ladino* versus 'Indian'" identity-making framework (2004).

Montejo also argues that despite their subjugated position, Mayas have made important long-standing contributions to the Guatemalan nation-state. For example, they have contributed both ideologically and economically by playing a major role in the construction of the country's infrastructure (1999, 18). Yet the oligarchy has persistently denigrated Indigenous citizens to the state-imposed ethno-class category of "*indios*" ("Indians") and, as such, has overtly rejected Indigenous peoples as active participants in the social, economic, and political life of the country. Ironically, the oligarchy has nonetheless co-opted elements of Maya *traje* (traditional clothing), historical figures (e.g., ancient K'iche' warrior Tecún Umán), and other imagery to promote tourism both nationally and internationally.[13] Montejo argues that despite the state's particular appropriation of Maya imagery, especially in the tourism industry, and the denial of participation in national social, economic, and political life, Maya peoples' actual involvement in affecting the state is undeniable. However, their contributions have been overshadowed by the pejorative and subjugated category of "Indian" that has been used by the state to discriminate against and terrorize Maya citizens for centuries. Montejo suggests, "It is not for being 'Mayas' that the dominant classes have persecuted and killed us since Columbus but for being placed in the denigrating category of '*indios*'" (1999, 189).

Based on his own life experience and work with Maya refuges, Montejo also contends that the sense of solidarity found among various Maya linguistic communities is imperative for eliminating the denigrating, state-imposed category of "Indian." In its place, he proposes establishing a multicultural, pluriethnic Guatemala in which Maya peoples, whom he defines as native peoples of the *Mayab'* (or Maya region of the world), are recognized for their long-standing contributions to Guatemala despite the duress, subjugation, and exploitation they have endured since the time of the Spanish conquest (2005, 6; 1999, 18, 187). He further suggests that both Mayas and non-Mayas work together to build a multicultural, pluriethnic Guatemala to prevent the reconfigured structure from simply promoting new ways of marginalizing and essentializing Maya citizens in today's world. Montejo maintains that what has been lacking in Guatemala is "the genuine interest in walking shoulder to shoulder, Mayas and *ladinos*, toward true progress for this country, with the efforts and contributions of all of us applied to generating a new nationalist vision of unity and solidarity among the Guatemala people" (2005, 15).

The work of Charles Hale (2006) offers a third and final perspective that advances understandings of the complex, dynamic, and often strategic perceptions and expressions of ethnic identity present in contemporary Guatemala and in my own research. Unlike most scholars who have been studying identity in Guatemala primarily through the focal lens of Maya experiences, Hale conducted research with *ladino* inhabitants of the department of Chimaltenango in the central highlands (ibid., 15). Engaging in the ethnography of social interaction and political practice, he examines how *ladinos* negotiate, contest, and maneuver within spaces of structured inequality (ibid., 17). He emphasizes that, with new Indigenous political assertion and gains in Indigenous empowerment, *ladinos* are generally afraid of their centuries-long dominance slipping away. Yet they also desire greater equality for all Guatemalan citizens (ibid., 11).

Hale observes that Guatemalans who self-identify as *ladinos* also are a heterogeneous group of individuals who constitute "a wide range of economic and social positions," ranging from manual laborers to elite landowners and politicians (ibid., 3). Despite this heterogeneity, however, *ladinos* generally have absorbed the ideology that they are racially superior in relation to "Indians." As *ladinos*, they perceive themselves as "closer to the ideal of progress, decency, and all things modern," while they continue to consider "Indians" as regrettably backward (ibid., 4). *Ladino* perceptions of racial superiority are reflected in the notion that they consider themselves *más que un indio* (more than an "Indian") (ibid., 11). Simply stated, they feel they are certainly and necessarily better than a "mere Indian." Hale notes that the use of the term "race" in this context is not meant to equate with race-as-biology, although at times the biological perception of race can work back into *ladinos'* cultural discourse. Instead, "race" is a social construction, undergirding social hierarchies and identities and influencing meanings that "*ladinos* assign to the world around them" (ibid., 30).

Even though the racial hierarchy persists in Guatemala, with Indigenous peoples meant to continue to occupy the bottom, always below *ladinos,* Hale asserts that *ladino* political sensibilities have changed. Hale argues that "most ladinos in Chimaltenango now accept the idea that indigenous Guatemalans merit better treatment than they received in the past" (ibid., 11).. Therefore, *ladinos* are taking a self-critical stance toward the overt racism of the past, purporting that racism should be eliminated and that the principle of equality should prevail. Curiously, *ladinos'* cautious advocacy for multicultural equality stands in direct tension with their privileged hierarchical positioning. Hale argues that while *ladinos* generally advocate multicultural equality, they simultaneously fear that Maya ascendancy will necessarily result in losing their racial dominance and privilege in relation to "Indians." The desire for a multicultural and equal society on one hand and continued racial privilege on the other fosters what Hale terms "racial ambivalence" among *ladinos* today (ibid., 11). "Racial ambivalence" reflects the contradiction between the way people think about race and the actual position they occupy in terms of a racialized social hierarchy (ibid., 19).

Hale purports that racial ambivalence has contributed to the remaking of the racial hierarchy in Guatemala, albeit in a "gentler, less offensive, and more sustainable guise" that forms part of a broader process of political restructuring exemplified in neoliberal multiculturalism (ibid., 31). Neoliberal economic reforms, characterized by aggressive open markets, free capital flows, and structural adjustment of local economies according to global economic principles, swept across Latin America in the 1980s. Neoliberal reforms ushered in a new era of neoliberal politics that vigorously sought to promote not only aggressive market-oriented economics but also state-sanctioned multiculturalism for the benefit of the market (ibid., 34). Hale contends that rises in both neoliberal economic policies and political practices as the predominant mode of governance coincided with a shift away from nationalist ideologies focused on assimilation and toward a new multicultural ethic that has become woven into Guatemala's social fabric (ibid., 34, 36).

While the idea of multiculturalism through the endorsement of cultural rights and intercultural equality has taken hold in Guatemala, Hale asserts that it has done so in such a way as to selectively recognize Indigenous rights "without placing *ladino* racial dominance in jeopardy" (ibid., 36). He affirms that neoliberal multiculturalism has the potential for fostering equality and cultural recognition but typically only supports the latter while promoting intercultural exchange anyway (ibid., 38). Therefore, it is in the context of neoliberal multiculturalism that *ladinos* embrace the new ethic of cultural equality—mainly because quotidian relations with upwardly mobile Indigenous neighbors and co-workers increasingly require it—while continuing to limit Indigenous ascendancy because of the direct threat that it imposes (ibid., 36).

Hale's work reveals that *ladino* racial ambivalence, neoliberal multiculturalism, and resulting change in class structure, which has opened middle-class spaces now shared with increasing numbers of upwardly mobile Indigenous peoples, constitute a complex set of contexts demanding an expanded framework for examining and understanding ethnic identity (both Indigenous and *ladino*) in contemporary Guatemala. His research illustrates how vital it is to continue to analyze intercultural relations because those relations, although traditionally mapped across *ladino*-dominated social, economic, and political domains, are now clearly changing. His research also illustrates that the ways in which *ladinos* perceive and express their identities are as creative and dynamic as they are for Indigenous peoples (ibid., 3).

Understanding *ladino* identities is an increasingly important focus for anthropological and other research as Guatemala's citizens continue to move forward in an ever-changing, globally-connected world, which is a world that grants them access to unprecedented social, economic, and political resources with the potential for up-ending previous centuries-long racial hierarchies and ethno-class systems. Contemporary scholarship on ethnic identity and belonging in Guatemala, such as that of Warren, Montejo, and Hale, offers an invaluable framework for analyzing and understanding the ways in which ethnic identity is perceived and expressed by the child survivors who participated in my research project. As I demonstrate in the chapters that follow, similar to Maya peoples featured in the research of Warren and Montejo, child survivors are well aware of the state's efforts to brutally impose its dichotomous identity-making framework on them and their families during the armed conflict and genocide. After all, it was under the auspices of the state and its assimilationist efforts that child survivors' unarmed, noncombatant parents and relatives were murdered, forever changing the course of their lives. At the same time, child survivors discuss how creativity and transformation have been key aspects in the ways they now perceive and express ethnic identity and view their belonging in the nation-state. For orphaned child survivors, utilizing new openings in the social hierarchy has been especially influential in helping them develop their strong sense of belonging in Guatemala today.

SETTING COURSE FOR UNDERSTANDING CHILD SURVIVORS' EXPERIENCES

Child Survivors of Genocide offers an important view of the life experiences of grown Guatemalan child survivors who are now approaching middle adulthood. Having lived as a volunteer for two years with this group of survivors when they were adolescents, visiting them frequently afterwards, and having then initiated formal research with them some twelve years after my initial volunteer service, I offer a unique lens on their life trajectories, discussing both their struggles and their successes along the way. Through their own perspectives and insights encapsulated in this book, these survivors demonstrate that they, indeed, have faced long-term consequences of the armed conflict and genocide, consequences that they still deal with today and likely will for the rest of their lives. Those consequences include severed family and community ties, sequential traumatization exacerbated by their orphan status, and lost aspects they associate with ethnic identity, which continue to present challenges and obstacles even in middle adulthood. At the same time, they assert and demonstrate that they have responded to those consequences in resilient, creative, and transformative ways, reporting higher levels of post-traumatic growth than their peers and engaging in novel practices surrounding ethnic identity and belonging. Rather than succumbing to the state's efforts to destroy them, they have persevered and have done so with a strong, indestructible sense of ethnic identity and belonging in contemporary Guatemala. To explore their experiences and articulate these themes, *Child Survivors of Genocide* consists of seven principal chapters.

Chapter one offers an overview of the political origins and resulting political landscape that is important for understanding why the thirty-six-year internal armed conflict and genocide occurred in Guatemala in the twentieth century. It starts with a general review of the conquest and subsequent colonial era and includes the policies and systems stemming from those eras, which still factor heavily into contemporary social relations. In particular, I discuss the consequences of various mechanisms that resulted from those eras such as oligarchy, social hierarchy, and unequal land distribution. I also draw attention to independence from Spain and some of the resulting national systems, policies, and foreign influence that had taken hold by the turn of the twentieth century and further destabilized interethnic relations in the country. These systems, policies, and influence continued to erode the social fabric of the country until the 1940s when Guatemala experienced, for the first time in its post-contact[14] history, a period of democratic reform and relative calm called "*la primavera*" (or "the spring"). I also explore how this ten-year period of calm and new social reforms was undermined by the US government and its Central Intelligence Agency (CIA), which in 1954 staged and directed a Guatemalan military coup that overthrew the government. A full-fledged internal armed conflict broke out just six years later, lasting 36 years. During the armed conflict, full-scale genocide was carried out, claiming the lives of over 200,000 people, and leaving over 45,000 or more mainly Maya Indigenous women widowed and 150,000–200,000 children orphaned (CEH 2004, xviii; CITGUA 1989, 18; Green 1999, 4; Gugelberger 1999, 50; WOLA 1989, 1). I conclude chapter one with a brief summary of the signing of the 1996 peace accords and the search for justice and reconciliation in the wake of the armed conflict and genocide—a search that is being challenged by new waves of growing impunity, organized crime, transnational gangs, gender-based violence, and economic crisis. While much has already been written about Guatemalan history and is widely available in other sources, I present this historical overview because it cannot be separated from child survivors' experiences since the reason they are survivors in the first place has everything to do with Guatemala's complex and often violent history.

In chapter two, I further elucidate the context in which child survivors were orphaned by first revealing how the Guatemalan military deliberately targeted children in the armed conflict and genocide under the state-backed mandate of "destroying the seed," with the "seed" meaning Maya Indigenous children (REMHI 1999, 29). The military considered all Maya Indigenous children to be "bad seeds" who, if left alive and intact, would allow Maya Indigenous communities to rebuild, continue their Indigenous lifeways, and gain key sociopolitical control in the future (ibid., 31). Following a discussion of the practice of "destroying the seed," I examine how the Guatemalan military used the US Phoenix program in Vietnam as a US sanctioned and supported blueprint for explicitly justifying the murder, disappearance, and victimization of mostly Maya Indigenous children. These children were not simply collateral damage (or unintentional unarmed, noncombatant victims caught in the crossfire) but were intentional targets in the Guatemalan counterinsurgency campaign. I also discuss the internal and external tactics used by the Guatemala military to terrorize Maya Indigenous populations and follow with the specific childhood experiences of three orphaned child survivors who participated in my research project. Their experiences illuminate the ferocity with which the military targeted primarily Maya Indigenous children and their families. Deliberately targeting children has not been uncommon in history and was clearly a strategy executed in other cases of genocide in the 19th and

20th centuries as well, which I briefly review in this chapter. Consequently, the deliberate targeting of children in war, armed conflict, and genocide needs to be a primary topic of discussion on both global and local levels. I conclude chapter two with a brief discussion of human rights treaties and conventions pertaining to the rights of children, including during war, armed conflict, and genocide, and I reveal how these policies have largely failed and still fail child survivors around the world in the twenty-first century.

Chapter three centers on how orphaned child survivors in my research project perceive, understand, and explain their childhood experiences with trauma and loss. My findings demonstrate that their experiences are not only specific to armed conflict-and genocide-related events but also include challenging and marked life transitions made especially difficult because of their orphan status. Following an overview of the general psychological suffering reported by inhabitants of the highlands in the wake of *la violencia*, I present child survivors' own experiences with trauma and loss resulting from losing their parents and other relatives during the armed conflict and genocide. Delving deeper into the sequential traumatization they faced, I next discuss the trauma and difficulties they encountered as they transitioned from living with surviving family members to living in the residential home in Santa Teresa. Child survivors, once again, experienced trauma and difficulties when later transitioning from life in the residential home to adulthood alone and without an economic, familial, or emotional safety net. Unfortunately, contemporary research tends to focus solely on the specific traumatic events of war, armed conflict, and genocide when working with child survivors without fully recognizing that those events often set into motion a whole other series of traumatic events and loss throughout childhood and beyond. I conclude chapter three with a discussion of limitations of contemporary research and why it is imperative to recognize the entire experience of childhood trauma and loss for orphaned child survivors. The long-term consequences of sequential traumatization during and following armed conflict and genocide are just as real and distressing for child survivors as the immediate aftereffects and, therefore, are also deserving of validation and attention in both research and praxis.

In chapter four, I further explore and assess the sequential traumatization that orphaned child survivors in my research project have endured by examining the long-term sense of trauma they continue to experience today as adults. I achieve this by first discussing why utilizing the concept of trauma as a framework for examining psychological distress is valid and appropriate with this group of survivors. I then present an overview of qualitative findings from my research project, comparing the experiences of orphaned child survivors who grew up in the residential home with those of their peers who grew up mainly with their families in Santa Teresa. A comparative approach helps illuminate how the particular experiences of orphaned child survivors differed from those of other children who also were born and raised in the highlands during the armed conflict and genocide. I also present an overview of my quantitative findings culled from three psychological assessment instruments, two that gauge general psychological distress and trauma and one that measures post-traumatic growth. These quantitative findings provide additional insights into and corroborate child survivors' complex experiences with trauma and resilience and demonstrate the value of using a mixed-method approach when examining trauma and resilience among child survivors. I end chapter four with a discussion of factors that may have contributed to child survivors' resilience, and I call for a more comprehensive, holistic examination of both trauma and resilience among child survivors throughout the world. Such an examination necessitates rethinking how we approach and understand trauma and healing in the wake of armed conflict and genocide, especially for orphaned children who survive such atrocities.

Chapter five presents child survivors' experiences with and perceptions of ethnic identity and belonging within the context of the aftermath of the armed conflict and genocide. Their experiences reveal that, despite severed familial and natal community ties, child survivors have formed a strong sense of ethnic identity and belonging, one that has persisted into middle adulthood. Engaging in a dynamic conceptualization of ethnic identity, child survivors remain strongly rooted in their Maya cultural heritage while also transforming what it means for them to be Maya Indigenous Guatemalans today. To explore these themes further, I discuss how the Guatemalan state, via its military and counterinsurgency campaign, carried out ethnocide (the intentional destruction of ethnic identity and belonging) as part of its strategy to eliminate and assimilate the majority Indigenous populations. At the same time, Maya Indigenous peoples of Guatemala did not surrender to the military's brutal assimilationist agenda. I highlight some of the ways in which Maya Indigenous peoples, in general, resisted and rejected the national assimilationist project even during the most extreme genocidal period of *la violencia*. I next turn to the specific experiences of orphaned child survivors in my research project, revealing that they report having lost some aspects they associate with Maya Indigenous identities because of the severed ties with families and natal communities they experienced. However, they do not perceive those losses as adversely affecting their sense of ethnic identity because they perceive ethnic identity as being internally rooted within themselves where it cannot be eroded or destroyed. To understand where child survivors' strong sense of ethnic identity derives, I next discuss efforts made in the residential home to foster continuity in Maya Indigenous identity formation, as well as the efforts of child survivors themselves in forging a strong sense of ethnic identity in childhood despite the losses they have endured.

The scope of the success of the residential home's and child survivors' efforts is encapsulated in one child survivors' poignant proclamation, "I was born Indigenous. I will die Indigenous." I conclude chapter five by elaborating on how child survivors view their sense of ethnic identity and belonging today and how they have helped their own children forge a strong sense of ethnic identity and belonging in Guatemala's post-conflict context.

In chapter six, I explore the achievements and struggles that child survivors have had as adults with the aim of more fully depicting the entirety of their life experiences thus far and honoring their resilience, struggles, and accomplishments in adulthood. I begin the chapter by providing updates on several child survivors featured throughout this book, centering on their experiences in early and middle adulthood. The updates further illuminate several key themes that emerged in my research interviews and from my long-standing conversations with grown child survivors for over nearly three decades. These themes shed further light on child survivor experiences and sources of support that have helped them develop and build resilience throughout their lifetimes. The chapter concludes with reflections and advice that child survivors shared with me regarding ways in which they think nongovernmental organizations, governments, and individuals can more effectively address the distinct needs, circumstances, and contexts of other child survivors of war, armed conflict, and genocide in the world today.

In chapter seven, the final principal content chapter, I further consider child survivors' experiences and their own advice regarding how to effectively support other child survivors of war, armed conflict, and genocide with a specific lens on the often problematic adoption trade that has overshadowed in-country alternative care options such as the permanent residential home in Santa Teresa. In particular, I examine the intercountry adoption trade in Guatemala that had been ongoing for more than forty years and the various issues surrounding the illegitimacy of many of those adoptions, including outright child kidnapping and trafficking. I next highlight regulations and safeguards that the Guatemalan government was eventually pressured to put into place to regulate adoptions, as well as the negative publicity and blow-back that came from intercountry adoptive families mainly in the US. Many of these families campaigned to continue intercountry adoptions even though there clearly was significant, substantiated evidence that many illegitimate adoptions had taken place. The chapter continues with a presentation of the perspectives and experiences of several grown Guatemalan adoptees living in the US who, unlike child survivors in my research project, commonly struggle with loss of ethnic identity and belonging. Through their stories, they reveal the emotional and psychological distress of having been uprooted, often abruptly, from their biological families and country, only to be transplanted in mostly White, middle- and upper-class families and communities in the US and other European countries. The perspectives and experiences of Guatemalan intercountry adoptees provide a catalyst for placing greater emphasis on in-country alternative care and, in some cases, for reconsidering permanent residential care. I then turn to an evidence-based discussion of the efficacy of providing culturally astute residential care for orphaned and other child survivors when in-country loving, nurturing family-based care is not available. I also address the international community's current resolute aversion to endorsing any form of residential care (often termed "institutional care") and provide counter-evidence that supports residential care for some contexts, especially amid the chaos of human-made or natural disasters. I conclude chapter seven with examples of new trends of "child-grabbing" that are currently being used to assuage the global hunger for adoptable children. I highlight the imbalance of power between children, families, and women in low- and middle-income countries and individuals, couples, and families in wealthier countries, revealing how it has stripped many vulnerable peoples in low- and middle-income countries of their rights and of their own children. Residential care, while never capable of fully replacing a loving, nurturing family, can help protect families' and children's rights. Outright dismissal of healthy, nurturing residential care as a viable form of alternative care and calls for its full and automatic eradication worldwide, without considering the specific cultural, economic, social, and political contexts in which children are living, undercuts our ability to support children and their surviving family members. Instead of giving away their futures, we must help safeguard those futures, and residential care can be one way to do that.

I draw *Child Survivors of Genocide* to a close by discussing the primary conclusions drawn from my research. Mainly, I affirm that child survivors have, indeed, faced long-term consequences of the internal armed conflict and genocide, but rather than succumbing to those consequences, they have become resilient, well-adapted adults with a strong internalized sense of ethnic identity. They also engage in creative and transformative practices regarding ethnic identity and belonging that have contributed to their abilities to adapt to their life circumstances in positive, constructive ways, and have expanded what it means to be Maya Indigenous Guatemalans today. Many factors likely contributed to child survivors' abilities to develop into resilient, well-adapted adults with a strong sense of ethnic identity and belonging. However, I believe two sources of influence are central, mainly the residential home programming and child survivors' own ambition and drive, which I discuss in further detail. Based on these research findings, I call for the continued expansion of research with grown orphaned child survivors in Guatemala, who remain a largely overlooked segment of survivors of the armed conflict and genocide. Additionally, I contend that further research on the internalized sense of ethnic identity perceived and expressed by child survivors is warranted. This is especially timely given that large numbers of Maya Indigenous peoples have moved to urban centers or foreign countries, which challenges familial and natal community ties often associated with Maya Indigenous identities. I also challenge scholars and others to continue dismantling erroneous assumptions that participating in creative practices, such as accessing higher education, erodes Indigenous identities. Child survivors in my research project are a testament not only to how creative practices can help reinforce ethnic identity and pride but also can be a conduit for transforming institutions, such as higher education, into more pluricultural entities. Lastly, I reassert that in-country residential care should be reconsidered as a viable option in some contexts, even if temporarily, when other forms of loving, nurturing care are unavailable. Child survivors in my research project clearly demonstrate that residential care can provide the positive, nurturing environment that helps children develop into resilient, well-adapted adults with a strong sense of ethnic identity and pride. Given the implications of my research, I end this book by outlining several areas of fruitful future research and tell a story of hope that synthesizes much of what I have learned from child survivors and some of their surviving family members over the years and offers optimism for the future.

A NOTE ON ETHNIC IDENTITY TERMS

Words matter. This is especially true when writing about ethnic identity and identity categories that are fluid, dynamic, and often political. In the case of my research and this book, words associated with ethnic identity are particularly important. As previously noted, many Maya peoples in Guatemala often prefer to be called by the names of their specific Maya linguistic communities. These communities are spread across the *Mayab'* the area occupied by past and present Mayan-speaking peoples (Montejo 2005, xiv; 1999, 187). Identifying by Maya linguistic communities was common for participants in my research project as well. They most often self-identified as Kaqchikel, K'iche', or Q'eqchi', for example. While identifying by Maya linguistic communities is both important and common, Montejo highlights the importance of also using the term "Maya" generally as a unifying central identity of the Indigenous peoples of the *Mayab'* (1999, 187). He explains, "To call ourselves 'Mayas' is a political act, since Mayas have been called *indios, naturales,* or *primitivos* by politicians, anthropologists, missionaries, and other non-Mayas" (Montejo 1999, 188). Montejo further asserts that the term "Maya" has long been used by Indigenous peoples of the *Mayab'* to name themselves over time and was even recorded on Columbus's fourth voyage, from 1503 to 1504, and in other postconquest documents (1999, 188). Therefore, Montejo notes that as inheritors of the great Maya culture, contemporary Mayas are proud of calling themselves Maya and using the term is a way to awaken the Maya nation, which is imperative for their future (ibid., 188). Montejo rightfully points out, "Until now the power of naming has been in the hands of outsiders, and of course, the one who names is the one who takes control" (ibid., 188–189).

Montejo's arguments are powerful and vital to consider and incorporate when working with Maya peoples and communities. They also present me with a particular dilemma in my own research. Participants in my research project rarely, if at all, use the term "Maya" to identify themselves or other Maya peoples of the *Mayab*.' This is also the case in the small highland community where the residential home is located. All throughout the interviews with participants, they either identified themselves and others by their particular Maya linguistic communities, or by the general term *"Indígena"* (Indigenous). Consequently, I am faced with the dilemma of using the term "Maya" in the way that Montejo suggests, or using the terminology of my participants, as well as of their peers and residents of Santa Teresa, to stay true to their experiences and perceptions. Furthermore, there are two additional Indigenous groups in Guatemala who do not descend historically from Maya peoples of the *Mayab*.' Those two groups identify as Xinca (an Indigenous group) and Garífuna (a mixture of African, Arawak, and Carib Indigenous peoples). Thus, the term "Indigenous" can also include non-Maya peoples and, therefore, cannot be automatically assumed to only include Maya peoples when speaking about "Indigenous peoples" in Guatemala.

Given the complexities of using the terms "Maya" and "Indigenous," I directly asked participants which terms they suggest I use in this book. They suggested using the specific names of Maya linguistic communities when referring to individuals who use those terms and using the term "Indigenous" when including all Maya peoples generally. Based on their advice, I do incorporate ethnic identity terms specific to Maya linguistic communities when used by my participants or other scholars, for example. When referring to Maya peoples of the *Mayab*,' I have elected to use the combination terms of "Maya Indigenous" as a way of honoring Montejo's arguments for using the term "Maya" and, at the same time, respecting the term "Indigenous" more commonly used by my participants, their peers, and residents of Santa Teresa. I use the single term "Indigenous" when referring to all Indigenous peoples of Guatemala, including Xinca and Garífuna peoples. I use the term "Maya" alone when referring to a scholar's work in which they have elected to use that term. I recognize that the use of these terms is imperfect and has consequences that I cannot even begin to anticipate. However, I use them out of respect and with the hope that they allow me to stay true to participants in my research project and their experiences while honoring the work of Maya scholars and activists, as well as the lived experiences of Maya peoples past and present.

NOTES

1. I use the term "US American" out of respect for all those who live in the Americas. As one of my participants pointed out, all of us who live in the Americas are Americans. She is correct, and I respectfully acknowledge that fact by distinguishing peoples from the United States of America as "US Americans" rather than simply "Americans."

2. I am intentionally capitalizing the term "Indigenous" in an effort to recognize centuries worth of mistreatment and inequality for Indigenous peoples. By capitalizing the term, I acknowledge their struggles and the tremendous resilience, persistence, and strength they have developed and maintained in the face of overt, brutal racism and persecution. Capitalizing the term is my way of honoring their experiences in print.

3. I use the fictitious name of Santa Teresa throughout this book as a means of protecting participants in my research project. Political conditions have become increasingly contentious in Guatemala recently. Given that participants in my research project were witnesses to events that occurred during the internal armed conflict and genocide, they could be at risk for being targeted by the government or by those who perpetrated heinous acts against their families and communities. It should be noted that this permanent residential home is not associated in any way with the state-run residential home in San José Pinula that experienced a fire in 2017. That fire killed 41 girls, and various allegations of staff-perpetrated abuse of children at the facility have arisen (Reynolds 2017).

4. As with the name of the town, I am not identifying the specific Catholic order of the sisters as it will reveal the location of the permanent residential home and potentially jeopardize the safety of participants in my research project.

5. *Departamentos* (or departments) in Guatemala are similar to states in the US.

6. I purposely use the term "peoples" rather than simply "people" to acknowledge that any group of individuals belonging to a specific community, such as an ethnic community, consists of distinct individuals with their own unique experiences as well as shared experiences with other members. Thus, I use "peoples" to acknowledge and honor the heterogeneity among individuals in a community and to try to avoid objectifying human beings.

7. The Guatemalan Ministry of Culture, working with Maya linguists, adopted a standardized orthography for all Mayan languages in 1989, which is now in general use among both academics and Maya individuals. In this book, I utilize the standardized spelling of Mayan words, such as Kaqchikel, K'iche', and Q'eqchi' in all instances except when direct quotes from other scholars are presented in which they have used the alternate spellings of Cakchiquel, Quiché, or K'eqchi. For more information on the standardized orthography for Mayan languages, see López Raquec (1989).

8. The concept of "disappeared" (desaparecido) became both a verb and participle (e.g., "to be disappeared," "he was disappeared," etc.) in Guatemala nearly a decade before the notion was used in Chile and Argentina. It is a term specific to Latin America and denotes the state-sponsored kidnapping of an individual whose fate is unknown and whose bodily remains may never have been found. The Guatemalan military "disappeared" thousands of individuals as a way of eliminating potential subversive threats and instilling fear in survivors who could just as easily have been the next to be disappeared. By 1983, over 35,000 persons had been disappeared in Guatemala (Calvert 1985, 113), raising the total number of disappeared during the 36-year armed internal conflict to over 40,000 individuals (CEH 1999a, 73). La violencia, however, was undeniably the period constituting the largest number of desaparecidos. In this period alone, approximately 100 to 200 people were disappeared per month (Fischer and Hendrickson 2003, 66).

9. All research that I conducted, including preliminary research, fieldwork, and follow-up research, was reviewed and approved by the University of New Mexico Institutional Review Board.

10. Twelve women child survivors were ultimately randomly-selected rather than an equal ten women and ten men because the majority of alumni are women, and several men initially selected chose not to participate because they work in urban centers and/or in positions that made it more difficult to take time away to participate in my research project. In the quantitative analyses of my research project, preliminary analyses of variance (ANOVAs) revealed no main effect of sex for any of the quantitative measures I employed. Therefore, I feel confident that the slightly larger number of women participants in the child survivor group than in the peer group does not skew any of the findings from my research project.

11. I enclose the term "Indian" within quotation marks since it is an oversimplified and overgeneralized identity category that is based on Christopher Columbus's erroneous assumption that he had arrived in the Indies or the land of Cathay and has been forced upon heterogeneous Indigenous populations in what are now called the "Americas."

12. Montejo refers to the term "*Indio*" (or "Indian") as being used by some Maya intellectuals as a political whip to politically reaffirm "Indian" identity (1999, 187).

13. Carol Hendrickson (1995) offers an expanded discussion of the appropriation of Maya Indigenous imagery and especially the depiction of *traje* used to promote tourism in Guatemala.

14. Post-contact in this context denotes the period from the time of first contact with Spanish conquistadors forward.

Chapter One

Origins and Orientations

For centuries, Indigenous peoples in what is now the nation-state of Guatemala have been systematically murdered, tortured, enslaved, indentured, violated, exploited, and discriminated against by a small group of self-identifying non-Indigenous oligarchic elites (Carey 2001; Jonas 2000; Warren 1998). In the late 1970s, the subjugation and annihilation of Maya Indigenous peoples, in particular, reached heightened levels of brutality when the ruling elite, via the military and paramilitary groups, orchestrated full-scale genocide. The genocide resulted in the murder and disappearance of hundreds of thousands of unarmed, noncombatant Indigenous and *ladino* civilians who committed no crime against the state. To understand what happened in Guatemala and its relation to the country's contemporary political landscape, it is vital to examine the political and economic processes, structures, and systems that have been developed over the past five centuries by a non-Indigenous, elitist, and often inhumane oligarchy (Carey 2001; Schlesinger and Kinzer 2005). Therefore, information provided in this chapter offers a general historical[1] overview of state-imposed policies and practices fueled by the oligarchic elite's centuries-long drive to keep Indigenous peoples at the bottom of a self-serving dichotomous social hierarchy.

CONQUEST AND COLONIAL ERA POLICIES AND SYSTEMS IN THE GUATEMALAN HIGHLANDS

Prior to Spanish conquest in the early 1500s in what is now known as the Guatemalan highlands, Mesoamerican polities already had a long tradition of alliance-building that helped strengthen their political organizations and military forces (Asselbergs 2004). At times, competition for territory and resources between these powerful polities was contentious and added to growing political fragmentation and division among them (Asselbergs 2004; Lovell 2015; Restall and Asselbergs 2007). Sharply divided and even

warring factions, such as between Maya Kaqchikel and K'iche' populations, gave Spanish conquistadors and Mesoamerican polities with whom
they built alliances, such as Tlaxcalteca and other communities in what is
now Central Mexico, a fertile opportunity to use such divisions to conquer
various Indigenous territories and communities (Lovell 2015; Restall and
Asselbergs 2007). Spanish conquistadors and their allies also built further
alliances with some Indigenous polities in their efforts to conquer the region.
For example, in 1524 Spanish conquistador Pedro de Alvarado developed a
strategic political alliance with the Kaqchikel kingdom, enlisting the services
of its warriors and using its ongoing rivalry with the K'iche' polity to take
advantage of divisions and eventually overtake the central highlands region.
Much of the Spaniards' success was due to their alliances with Indigenous
allies who provided food, soldiers, and key knowledge of the region and
served as guides, translators, and key negotiators (Asselbergs 2004; Carmack
2012; Sharer 2005). However, alliances with Indigenous polities eventually
began to unravel. By May of 1530, for example, the Kaqchikel kingdom also
found itself swept under colonial rule and policies by Spanish conquistadors
who blatantly reneged on prior agreements and promises of riches and power
(Asselbergs 2004; Carey 2001; Sharer 2005).

From the 1524 conquest of the region onward, Alvarado and fellow
Spaniards sought to expand their wealth and territories. To satisfy these
desires, the Spanish Crown established colonial policies and systems that
exacted greater control over subjugated populations by exploiting their labor
for the benefit of the Crown and its conquistadors (Asselbergs 2004). These
new policies and systems initiated a deepening, centuries-long rift between
diverse Indigenous majority populations—whom the conquistadors came to
collectively refer to as "Indians"—and the elite minority of Spanish landowners and their descendants (Lovell 2015; Luján Muñoz 2018).

The Spanish Crown established the *encomienda* system in the 1500s to take
advantage of the sizable "free" Indigenous labor force. In the *encomienda*
system, the Spanish monarchy's right to tribute was transferred directly to the
Spanish conquistadors as a reward for their service and loyalty to the Crown.
The system also led to the development of a rural-centric economy through
the collection of tribute in the new colony (Thompson 2001). Through the
encomienda system, the Spanish conquistadors received *encomienda* grants,
giving them legal title to the labor and tribute exacted from particular plots
of land located within the conquered territory (Asselbergs 2004; Fischer and
Hendrickson 2003). These grants forced thousands of Indigenous peoples
into grueling labor for tribute, which gave rise to poor working conditions
and abusive treatment of laborers. Legal provisions in the *encomienda* system
called for a limitation on "Indian" labor, requiring Indigenous inhabitants to
work for the Spanish colonists only until tribute was paid (Asselbergs 2004;

Carlsen 2011). Contrary to Crown policies, however, many Spanish *encomenderos* (the individuals who held and shared *encomiendas*) forced Indigenous inhabitants to work in horrendous and life-threatening conditions well beyond the limitations of tribute (Asselbergs 2004; Lovell 2000; Thompson 2001). Recognizing the inherent flaws and abuses of the *encomienda* system, the Spanish Crown established the New Laws of 1542[2] to replace the *encomienda* system with the equally exploitative *repartimiento* system (Carlsen 2011; Montejo 1999).

The *repartimiento* system was designed by the Crown to "free" Indigenous laborers from the "enslavement" they had experienced in the *encomienda* system by relocating them and paying them nominal wages to work on specified plantations owned by Spanish colonists and making them direct vassals of the Crown (Asselbergs 2004; Carlsen 2011). In the new system, colonial officials arbitrarily assigned Indigenous laborers to petitioning landowners who offered the laborers meager pay for their strenuous and grueling work. Besides miniscule pay, the laborers were also required to travel long distances to the site of their forced labor (Lutz and Lovell 1990). Any time spent traveling to and from these sites was neither paid for nor considered time toward their required period of service. The *repartimiento* system proved detrimental to Indigenous populations who were forced, once again, into slave-like conditions in a system supposedly designed to "free" them. They were also displaced from their villages with over one-quarter of the inhabitants of any village displaced at any given time. The system proved quite advantageous for Spanish colonists, however, because they accumulated vast wealth and benefited exponentially from the system until it was abolished in 1812 (Carlsen 2011; Grandin 2000; Lovell 2015).

The *reducción* (reduction), or *congregacion* (forced resettlement), system was yet another divisive colonial enterprise developed to control and dominate Indigenous populations for the benefit of Spanish colonists (Castillo Méndez 2008). Lovell notes,

> As promulgated by Spanish law, *congregacion* was a means whereby Mayas found dwelling in scattered rural groups would be brought together, converted to Christianity, and moulded into harmonious, resourceful communities that reflected imperial notions of orderly, civilized life. To the Church, especially members of the Dominican and Franciscan orders, fell the difficult job of getting Indian families down from the mountains and resettled in towns built around a Catholic place of worship (2000, 117).

The *reducción* system was enforced by the Catholic Church, especially by Dominican, Franciscan, and Mercedarian orders (Lovell 2015; Lutz and Lovell 1990; Thompson 2001). The system permitted the Catholic Church to receive assistance from civil authorities to "reduce" the multitude of scattered Indigenous settlements by creating larger, concentrated villages where denizens could be more easily converted to Christianity and controlled (Lovell 2000; Perera 1993). After the Spanish conquest, many Indigenous peoples had retreated to more isolated areas to escape the *encomienda* and *repartimiento* systems. This scattering of Indigenous peoples made it difficult for the Catholic Church to convert those it perceived as "savage Indians" to Christianity. Thus, the *reducción* system, fueled by the drive to convert, was designed to round up thousands of scattered Indigenous peoples and settled them into roughly 700 concentrated, closely monitored towns (Martínez Peláez 2009, 185).

The *reducción* system and its policies essentially "freed up" Indigenous peoples' land for confiscation by Spanish elite. It also fed additional workers into the *repartimiento* system to satisfy growing demands for tribute, which were being frustrated by large numbers of Indigenous laborers who had fatally succumbed to disease and desolation (Castillo Méndez 2008). While colonial officials and the Catholic Church greatly benefited from the supply of labor and new tracts of land that the *reducción* system helped secure, most Indigenous peoples lost their homes, lands, lifeways, and abilities to sustain their traditional forms of subsistence agriculture (Fischer and Hendrickson 2003; Sharer 2005).

The agrarian policies developed in Guatemala, as well as in other Latin American regions, during the colonial era gave rise to the *latifundio-minifundio* model of land tenure. The model involves large rural estates (*latifundios*) owned by a small group of elites that are surrounded by tiny subsistence-oriented plots (*minifundios*) parceled out to Indigenous peoples who tended the *latifundios*. This pattern of grossly uneven land distribution fostered and perpetuated the elites' growing monopolistic control of land and the drastic decline in living conditions for Indigenous peoples (Martínez Peláez 2009). Vile antagonisms resulted and deep divides emerged and festered between Indigenous peoples and elite Spanish colonists and their descendants for centuries (Carlsen 2011; Lovell 2000; Sharer 2005).

Independence from Spain in 1821

Mounting tension between Indigenous and *ladino* (defined at the time as inhabitants of mixed Spanish and Indigenous descent) populations, as well as deepening economic depression and political shifts within the territory that would become Guatemala, fed the movement for independence from Spain in 1821. The independence movement was initiated by two key developments that also played a part in the growing dichotomous rift between Indigenous and *ladino* inhabitants (Carlsen 2011).

The first development was the diminishing influence and control of the Spanish Crown due to a long period of economic depression in the new colony. Unable to fund larger efforts to maintain the *reducciones* in the new territory, elite landowners could no longer afford to pay Indigenous workers even the meager wages they typically offered them. Consequently, many Indigenous peoples returned to their rural natal lands and settled outside of the colonial administrative units known as *municipios*, or municipalities (Montejo 1999). Purposely defying forced settlement, some Indigenous peoples partially escaped the control of government officials and began to reshape internal political and social relationships, reestablishing their own prior community hierarchies and initiating community funds to support their own Indigenous villages (Woodward 2008).

The second development was the lack of sufficient numbers of priests in remote villages to enforce Catholicism and loyalty to the Spanish Crown. In place of strict Catholic dogma, Indigenous villagers began to reincorporate preconquest religious practices in daily village life. The revitalization of Indigenous religious practices, coupled with reinstated Indigenous leadership, allowed Indigenous populations to reorganize and reinvigorate their communities (Carlsen 2011). With a renewed sense of community and solidarity, Indigenous peoples worked vigorously to defend their rights and customs against the rule of the Crown, leading to numerous revolts throughout the late 18th and early 19th centuries. Despite long-standing consequences of the conquest, extreme poverty, and disease, Indigenous peoples steadfastly defended their positions. The Indigenous movement to regain control of their economic, social, and political situations became an important precursor to Independence from Spain, which was declared on September 15, 1821 (Grandin 2000; Lovell 2015).

INDEPENDENCE FROM MEXICO AND THE CENTRAL AMERICAN ALLIANCE

For the first two years following the Declaration of Independence from Spain, the territory that is now Guatemala remained under provisional rule of the Mexican Empire proclaimed by Agustín de Iturbide, who had been selected to take control of the emerging Mexican empire and who had led the Independence movement (Kinsbruner 2000). Iturbide's empire soon collapsed, however, and left the Central American provinces to develop their own collective forms of government. In 1823, leaders of what is now Guatemala and four remaining Central American nation-states (Honduras, El Salvador, Nicaragua, and Costa Rica) joined together to declare independence from the Mexican Empire and to proclaim the establishment of an independent United Provinces of Central America (Spinden 1999; Weaver 1999). Not long after this alliance was formed, however, warring factions and tensions between liberal and conservative elites began to threaten its cohesion. By 1839, a revolt against the alliance, under the leadership of José Rafael Carrera, ultimately persuaded politicians to renounce Guatemala's membership in the United Provinces of Central America and to declare Guatemala an independent nation (Carlsen 2011; Castillo Méndez 2008). Although independent from the Central American provinces, it was not until March 1847 that President Carrera declared the Republic of Guatemala as a formal, independent nation-state. The next fifty-three years, however, were marked by long-term presidencies that fortified the powerful position of elite landowners over Indigenous populations, deepening the growing chasm between the wealthy oligarchic elite and majority Indigenous populations that would ultimately foment genocide in the twentieth century (Casaús Arzú 2008; Grandin 2011; Thompson 2001).

TURN-OF-THE-CENTURY NATIONAL SYSTEMS, POLICIES, AND FOREIGN INFLUENCE

The turn of the twentieth century in Guatemala brought more contention and expanded elite control of resources, labor, and wealth, further displacing and disenfranchising the country's majority Indigenous populations. In the early 1900s, foreign powers also became major players in controlling Guatemala's political economy and in further destabilizing interethnic relations in the country. Following President Estrada Cabrera's overthrow in 1920, foreign entrepreneurs, especially those from the US, quickly gained ground in building powerful economic monopolies, with the United Fruit Company of the US becoming one of the most powerful and influential among them (Booth, Wade, and Walker 2010; Carey 2001).

The United Fruit Company's core crop in Guatemala consisted of banana cultivation in the humid eastern lowlands. This crop proved quite successful for the company. After purchasing its first land holding in 1901, the company exponentially increased its capital. Taking advantage of the sluggish economy, United Fruit bought massive tracts of land and quickly exploited the large mass of "cheap" Indigenous labor within Guatemala in its fruit production (Booth, Wade, and Walker 2010; Schlesinger and Kinzer 2005). It also came to control vast distribution networks, railways, Caribbean shipping, and the most fundamental source of power: the actual mechanisms of Central American governments (Kahn 2006; Schlesinger and Kinzer 2005). By the 1930s, the United Fruit Company owned forty percent of the country's economy with its fruit production and began to seriously challenge the predominance of coffee as Guatemala's major export crop (Handy 1984, 80). Through these monopolistic efforts, banana cultivation became an extremely serious business in Guatemala, and its players secured a major position in influencing and directing the state governing apparatus itself (Carey 2001; Schlesinger and Kinzer 2005).

During the 1930s, the United Fruit Company was dubbed *El Pulpo* (the octopus) for having many "tentacles" of influence wrapped around various business and political ventures and elites within the country (Booth, Wade, and Walker 2010; McPherson 2006). The company benefited significantly from generous and favorable terms in contracts provided by the Guatemalan government such as access to vast tracts of land along the Río Motagua, displacing scores of Indigenous populations in the process. It also enjoyed exemption from taxes for twenty-five years (Jonas 1991; Schlesinger and Kinzer 2005). Owing to the government's many accommodations and concessions to the company, Guatemala and its citizens received little in return. Concessions made to the United Fruit Company would become even more exaggerated and detrimental to Guatemala's majority Indigenous populations when General Jorge Ubico Castañeda took office as president from 1931 to 1944 and helped to support the company's west coast expansion (Luján Muñoz 2018; Saavedra 2001; Sabino 2007).

THE REGIME OF GENERAL JORGE UBICO CASTAÑEDA

Ubico's rule was characterized as military-like in that he was said to preside over a strict "model jail" (Calvert 1985, 70). Ubico had what Jim Handy refers to as "a brutal obsession with stability and a penchant for administrative detail" (1984, 90). Concerned by weak economic conditions of the nation-state, Ubico pushed hard for expansion of the coffee market, established new taxes to alleviate financial shortfalls, and supported duty-free trade of coffee and bananas with the US (Booth, Wade, and Walker 2010; Saavedra 2001; Sabino 2013, 2007). He also called for primary schools to be established in all towns so that all children (both Indigenous and *ladino* children alike) could be enrolled, ensuring a more educated future labor force. At the same time, Ubico suppressed unions and centralized power in the national government (Booth, Wade, and Walker 2010; Carey 2001). He also abandoned trade agreements with European countries to secure US trade and its capital dominance within Guatemala. This greatly benefited US interests by drastically increasing production and exportation. Handy notes that 90 percent of Guatemalan produce was being sold to the US by 1940 (1984, 94). While offering some small token incentives to inhabitants, Ubico's harsh rule and rigid efforts to stabilize the country's economy ultimately resulted in even greater concessions to the United Fruit Company, which had long-lasting negative consequences (Booth, Wade, and Walker 2010; Sabino 2007; Schlesinger and Kinzer 2005).

Ubico insisted on ensuring a sufficient supply of Indigenous laborers who were continuously paid low wages. He accomplished this by establishing strict vagrancy laws requiring all male citizens to carry a work card to show the number of days each had worked in the past year (Little 2008; Perera 1993). If an individual did not have an adequate number of workdays listed, he was forced to work on the plantations and to provide two weeks of hard labor on the national road system (Carey 2001; McCreery 1994; Montejo 1999). Ubico rigidly enforced these and all other laws by mobilizing and directing the national police, which he established in 1931. Through strict enforcement, tyranny, and violence, Ubico gained firm control of Guatemala's resources, economy, populace, and political system (Carey 2001; Grandin 2011).

As with previous presidents, Ubico further advanced Guatemala's close ties with US interests (Luján Muñoz 2018; Saavedra 2001). A paranoid ruler, Ubico trusted no one in his own government and, instead, developed tight relations with US business leaders and government officials who advised him on issues and influenced the future direction of the Guatemala nation-state (Luján Muñoz 2018; Sabino 2007). Ubico did mostly what the US government in Washington, DC., had asked of him. An example of his compliance with demands by US interests was his confiscation of German property in 1941. US producers continued to feel threatened by German coffee producers who had long controlled the bulk of coffee production in Guatemala. The US involvement in World War II further escalated tensions between US interests and German planters in Guatemala (Guillén 2007; Sabino 2013). Faced with reelection, Ubico agreed with US demands to confiscate all German-owned property in Guatemala and to force German settlers out of the country and into internment camps in North Carolina and Texas. This move won Ubico additional US approval, securing his reelection and garnering him a "gift" of Q200,000 (or Guatemalan quetzales, the national currency), a small fortune at the time, for his "contribution" to assisting the US government (Guillén 2007; Sabino 2007).

Although Ubico satisfied US interests, his leadership came under scrutiny by Guatemala's mass population (Saavedra 2001; Sabino 2013, 2007). While citizens recognized that Ubico did indeed provide some order in the country, he also took away their liberty. Guatemalans grew tired of their loss of freedom and of Ubico's exclusive support of the United Fruit Company and other US interests (Jonas 1991; Sabino 2007). They recognized that the US monopoly of capital controlled the Guatemalan economy at the expense of smaller European interests, Guatemalan elites who were not directly tied to the United Fruit Company, and the country's masses. Guatemalan producers and individuals outside of the United Fruit Company were angered and frustrated by Ubico's exclusive US-friendly administration. Student politicians, middle-class professionals, members of congress, and young reformist military officers soon began to withdraw their support and to publicly oppose Ubico's rule (Saavedra 2001; Sabino 2007). Even Ubico's "foolproof" relationship with the US was challenged when a new ambassador, Boaz Long, recognized the growing tensions within Guatemala and deemed Ubico's rule unstable (Sabino2013; Schlesinger and Kinzer 2005). Following massive student demonstrations, growing opposition to his rule, and a general strike in 1944, Ubico resigned in July of that same year and fled the country (Guillén 2007; Saavedra 2001; Schlesinger and Kinzer 2005).

LA PRIMAVERA (1944–1954)

The ten years following Ubico's resignation constituted a relatively calm period in Guatemala. Referred to as *La Primavera* (the spring), this period of democratic reforms and relative calm was sustained by two prominent Guatemalan presidents. The first was President Juan José Arévalo, who brought a new philosophy to the presidency (Luján Muñoz 2018, Tischler Visquerra 1998). Sympathy for the working man, democratic ideals, and socialism shaped his administration and were embodied in the new constitution of 1945 (CEH 1999; Schlesinger and Kinzer 2005). In the new constitution, all males (literate or illiterate) and females (literate only) over the age of eighteen were given the right to vote (Guillén 2007; Jonas 1991). The new constitution also prevented presidential reelection, required the military to play an apolitical role in the government, and gave autonomy to the public University of San Carlos. In addition to these ground-breaking reforms, Arévalo moved to improve access to healthcare in rural areas, establish potable water projects, and install sewers in the cities (Carey 2001; Guillén 2007; Schlesinger and Kinzer 2005). Arévalo's reforms were effective in raising the standard of living for all Guatemalans, which fostered a fall in mortality rates by 2.5 percent each year over the ten years of *la primavera* (Handy 1984, 107).

Arévalo also made other important strides to improve conditions within Guatemala for all its citizens, including Indigenous and *ladino* peoples alike. He established the Guatemalan Social Security Institute (or *Instituto Guatemalteco de Seguridad Social,* or IGSS) in 1946 to provide injury compensation, maternity benefits, and healthcare for all. He increased educational spending, expanded schools throughout the country, and initiated literacy campaigns to help educate the masses. He also pushed for the implementation of the Labor Code, which recognized the right to strike and collective bargaining, established minimum wages, restricted child labor, and legislated work hours (Guillén 2007; Luján Muñoz 2018; Schlesinger and Kinzer 2005). To further improve workers' conditions, Arévalo abolished the vagrancy laws established by Ubico, finally ending forced labor in Guatemala, and implemented a project for allocating uncultivated land located in sparsely populated areas to poor farmers from the highlands (Montejo 1999). These reforms played a vital role in establishing a new framework for radical social, economic, and political reforms in Guatemala. This framework allowed Arévalo to endure a contentious and challenging presidency, as his drastic reforms benefited the masses but angered the landowning oligarchic elite. Following his presidency, Arévalo's reforms were advanced by his successor, Colonel Jacobo Árbenz, who in 1951 became the second Guatemalan president during *La Primavera* (Guillén 2007; Luján Muñoz 2018; Sabino 2013).

Árbenz, an intelligent and strong-willed leader, deliberately centered his presidency on economic reforms. He was determined to achieve Guatemala's economic autonomy by focusing on economic modernization and agricultural diversification (Carey 2001; CEH 1999; Grandin 2011; Poitevin 2001). To achieve this goal, Árbenz fostered vigorous efforts to increase the production of crops such as sugarcane and cotton. He moved to expand access to agricultural credit and promoted the Bank of Guatemala's increased role in financing Indigenous development. Árbenz increased the number of rural schools and had them focus more on agricultural education to further strengthen and advance the country's agricultural base. Through increased production, lending, and education, Árbenz pushed for greater national autonomy on the world stage. At the same time, he worked to develop a nation-state that allowed all citizens, regardless of ethnicity, to experience an unprecedented level of freedom and democracy that had been absent in the history of the Guatemalan nation-state up to this point (Guillén 2007; Saavedra 2001).

Of all Árbenz's presidential acts, the most notable was the Agrarian Reform Law of 1952 (Grandin 2000; Perera 1993). Árbenz created the law to advance the agrarian system within Guatemala by promoting increased crop production. The Reform Law called for measures to empower a small group of farmers as a capitalist class and to lead the way to an independent, fully capitalist economy rather than one that was feudal and dependent on foreign interests (García Ferreira 2013). To achieve this aim, Árbenz focused on finding more efficient means of using uncultivated land. He believed inefficient landlords should be deprived of their excess fallow land. Instead, that land should be given to landless Indigenous farmers who Árbenz asserted would be able to cultivate it more efficiently and intensively. As a result, Árbenz passed Decree 900 that called for inactive land to be handed over to the government for resettlement purposes. Through Decree 900, the state agreed to pay for the land in the form of amortized bonds so large landowners would recoup some of the value of their retracted land. This bold move would come to have a tremendous impact on economic and social relations within Guatemala in the twentieth century (Carey 2001; Gálvez Borrell 2008; Guillén 2007).

By 1954, over 917,659 acres of uncultivated land were expropriated and distributed to 87,589 individuals who received an average of 10.5 acres each. In addition, 61 of 107 national *fincas* (large plantations) were divided among 7,822 small farmers and another 46 became cooperatives (Handy 1984, 128). All told, Árbenz's agrarian reform efforts permitted 100,000 landless peoples to receive valuable farmland within eighteen months of the enactment of Decree 900 (Booth, Wade, and Walker 2010; García Ferreira 2013, 62). The efforts of those who received land proved successful by directly contributing to increasing the production of corn by 11.8 percent between the years of 1950 and 1953 alone (Handy 1984, 129). Árbenz's plan for agricultural growth was working, and the country was well on its way to obtaining unprecedented levels of economic growth. However, his expropriation of land did not sit well with elite landowners or with US interests such as the United Fruit Company, which had lost major fallow land holdings in the country as a direct result of the reforms. Not surprisingly, Árbenz's efforts to pry Guatemala from the confines of coffee and banana export, the United Fruit Company and other US interests, and excess elite landownership, as well as from former dictators and the military, soon came under direct fire from the US government (Schlesinger and Kinzer 2005; Tischler Visquerra 1998).

The US government viewed Árbenz's efforts to make land available to all Guatemalans as communist in nature and feared such a "communist pattern" would weaken elite landownership and strengthen communist tendencies within the Guatemalan government itself (Rabe 2016). The US government had already extended its paranoid anti-communist Cold War to Guatemala and the rest of Latin America by the 1940s, looking for any signs of ties with Moscow. By the early 1950s, the Decree 900 agrarian reforms only intensified US concerns and heightened the Truman administration's hostility toward Guatemala (Rabe 2016; Schlesinger and Kinzer 2005). Fearing that Guatemala would become a stooge of the Soviet Union and pressured by US interests in the country, President Truman approved the US Central Intelligence Agency (CIA) "Operation PBFORTUNE" plan, which was designed to overthrow Árbenz in 1952; however, the plan became compromised and, ultimately, was quashed (Rabe 2016).

Shortly after US President Eisenhower took office in 1953, he authorized a new operation to overthrow Árbenz called "PBSUCCESS." The operation orchestrated a covert invasion of Guatemala on June 18, 1954, via a supposed "Guatemalan" military coup. Just ten days later, Árbenz was forced to resign, handing over his presidency to Colonel Enrique Díaz (García Ferreira 2013; Rabe 2016). *La Primavera* was over and an elitist military regime took hold of Guatemala, ushering in a new era of democratic decline and burgeoning violence (Guillén 2007; Jonas 2000; McPherson 2006; Schlesinger and Kinzer 2005).

OUTBREAK OF THE INTERNAL ARMED CONFLICT

The post-*primavera* epoch from 1954 onward marked an era of vast decline in economic and social conditions for most of Guatemala's citizens, but especially for majority Indigenous populations. With the liberating reforms of the Arévalo and Árbenz administrations, poor (mostly Indigenous) masses had finally gained access to land and more suitable living conditions. However, the 1954 presidential overthrow erased any gains made during *La Primavera* by swiftly reversing land distributions achieved during that period and reestablishing a government focused primarily on protecting the interests of Guatemalan elites, as well as those of US interests (Booth, Wade, and Walker 2010; Schirmer 1998).

With land and their means of subsistence stripped away from them, rural farmers were forced to return to *fincas* to work under miserable conditions and were often resigned to forms of debt peonage and incessant poverty. Those small-scale farmers who were able to maintain their land owned parcels far too small to provide adequate subsistence for their families. With limited access to resources and living in deplorable economic conditions, poor rural inhabitants (the majority of them Indigenous) experienced extensive malnutrition, unsanitary living conditions, lack of healthcare, and physically demanding work, resulting in exponentially increased mortality rates and malnourishment of children with 75 percent of Guatemala's children gravely undernourished by the early 1970s (Handy 1984, 212).

The 1976 earthquake caused even further devastation for poor citizens in both rural and urban areas. In less than forty-five seconds, more than one million people instantly became homeless (Arias 1990, 243; Levenson 2002, 60). Poor rural farmers lost what little they had and fell more susceptible to illness and disease (Campaign for Peace and Life in Guatemala 1999). Even worse, approximately 22,545 people were killed and 70,000 were wounded, although those numbers were likely higher since counting victims and wounded peoples at the time was difficult (Levenson 2002, 60). Most victims and survivors of the earthquake were disproportionately poor, rural Maya Indigenous farmers (Arias 1990, Woodward 2008).

Increased military tyranny and violence at the time also weakened social conditions and created an unstable landscape infested with terror and angst. In 1960, the Guatemalan military launched an internal armed conflict that was billed as a counterinsurgency campaign against a small but growing group of Marxist-inspired Leftist guerrillas who had established base camps in the western highlands region. Soon thereafter, the military's strategy to wipe out the insurgents quickly expanded to include terrorizing, annihilating, and disappearing unarmed, noncombatant rural highlands civilians as well, most of whom had no affiliation whatsoever with the Leftist movement. Amnesty International reported that, between 1966 and 1976 alone, over 20,000 Guatemalans became victims of covertly sanctioned murders or disappearances (1976, 1). And this was just the beginning. Guatemalan peoples were about to enter one of the darkest periods in their postconquest history (CEH 1999; REMHI 1998; Zur 1998).

THE PERIOD OF *LA VIOLENCIA* (1978 TO 1983)

In 1978, the internal armed conflict intensified, and full-scale genocide erupted, resulting in disproportionate, long-term consequences for Guatemala's majority Maya Indigenous populations (Davis 1988). The dark period of full-scale genocide, *la violencia,* began in May of 1978 when a group of between 500 and 700 Maya Q'eqchi' *campesinos* (rural farmers) began demonstrating peacefully for land rights in the village of Panzós, located in the Department of Alta Verapaz (Grandin 2011, 1; Jonas 1991, 127). Many of the *campesinos*, who had been farming the area land, had been displaced due to increased mineral exploitation in the area and land seizures by wealthy cattle ranchers through land transfers sanctioned by the National Institute of Agrarian Transformation (INTA) (Grandin 2011; May 2001; Sanford 2008). In the 1961, INTA—a corrupt, military-controlled bureaucratic institution managing land affairs in Guatemala—granted unused public lands in remote rain forests of the Petén and Alta Verapaz regions to nongovernmental organizations and the Catholic Church to resettle *campesinos* in farming cooperatives to help alleviate some of the agrarian land shortages occurring in the highlands at the time (Grandin 2011). Land granted in the region of the *Franja Transversal del Norte* (Northern Transversal Strip), in particular, was rich in oil and minerals. Soon many high-ranking military officers and wealthy elites began claiming land there for their own, destroying crops and seizing parcels from *campesinos* who had already been farming them (Garrard-Burnett 2010; Grandin 2011; May 2001).

In a desperate attempt to maintain their rights and lands, Q'eqchi' *campesinos* organized a public demonstration to call attention to their quest to obtain official legal titles from INTA for the parcels of land that they had already been farming (May 2001, 65). The protest was quickly squelched, however, when military soldiers were brought in by local elite landowners and fired on the crowd, resulting in a brutal massacre (Amnesty International 1998; Jonas

2000; Saavedra 2001). In the massacre, over fifty-three Q'eqchi' peoples (including women, children, and elderly) were killed and more than forty-seven were wounded (CEH 1999a, 157). Similar massacres in nearby rural villages, as well as local urban centers, soon followed.

One notorious urban massacre occurred in response to the 1980 occupation of the Spanish Embassy by a small delegation of Maya Indigenous *campesinos*. Driven by desperation, the *campesinos* occupied the embassy to protest recent land seizures by military officers and to draw attention to growing human rights abuses throughout the country (CEH 1999a; Garrard-Burnett 2010). Governmental response to the protest was brutal and horrifying. Guatemalan troops, under orders from President Romeo Lucas García (a former general), simply lit the embassy on fire and burned the entire group of Indigenous *campesinos* alive, along with Spanish diplomats, embassy staff, the Guatemalan foreign minister, and a former vice president, killing thirty-seven people in the fire. One *campesino* (rural farmer) initially survived and was brought to the hospital, but was subsequently kidnapped, tortured, and killed some hours later by "unknown" men (CEH 1999a, 190). His lifeless, burned, and disfigured body turned up hours later on the University of San Carlos campus where it was presented as a warning to anyone considering participation in public dissent. Lucas García made his message clear: he would not tolerate dissent and would use whatever means necessary to decimate even the slightest threat of opposition or public organization against government land seizures during his administration (Guillén 2007; May 2001).

Lucas García, who had won the 1978 presidential elections via fraudulent means, was a major landowner in Alta Verapaz in the area where the initial Panzós demonstration and subsequent massacre took place (Jonas 1991; Saavedra 2001). Lucas García became intent on stifling any Indigenous movements protesting against government land seizures. Because of his previous military rank, Lucas García was powerfully placed within the military and was not afraid to use military might to violently enforce his agenda. He used his presidency to carry out a ruthless campaign of terror, murder, and genocide that gave rise to the bloodiest period of Guatemalan postconquest history (Casaús Arzú 2008; CDHG 1991; Grandin 2011). Under the Lucas García presidency, Guatemalans with any potential links to any type of reform activity or organizing such as trade unions, university students, teachers, lawyers, journalists, and opposition politicians were swiftly annihilated (Garrard-Burnett 2010; Schlesinger and Kinzer 2005). In fact, individuals from those sectors were murdered at the rate of five or more a day during Lucas García's presidential term, from 1978 to 1982 (Handy 1984, 176). Students and academics were especially targeted by the military because Lucas García publicly portrayed and accused them of subversive ideologies and activities (CEH 1999; Luján Muñoz 2018; May 2001; REMHI 1998). From March to September of 1980 alone, 127 university teachers and administrators, along with 50 university students, were murdered by military forces for their supposed participation in subversive practices (Handy 1984, 178; Simon 1987, 72).

The Guerrilla Army of the Poor (*Ejército Guerrillero de los Pobres,* or EGP) responded to the increased state violence against unarmed, noncombatant civilians and community organizers by recruiting more *campesinos* into its ranks (Garrard-Burnett 2010). In the early 1970s, remnants of previous guerrilla movements came together under the new leadership of the EGP (May 2001; Stolen 2007; Woodward 2008). The EGP began to rally after the 1976 earthquake to respond to increasing military control of all forms of rural organization. The government's "scorched earth" campaign aimed at fully controlling rural villages provoked the guerrilla contingent to mobilize at full-force (Jonas 2009). They began to gain new momentum as relatives, friends, and colleagues of murdered victims joined their ranks in the struggle against overt military oppression (May 2001). Tracing the lineage of their movement back to resistance efforts developed to counter the 1954 CIA-backed presidential overthrow campaign, the guerrillas continued to not only fight against the military's counterinsurgency campaign but also against the situation of all-out Indigenous oppression and land reform that had worsened in the late 1970s (Smith 1990d). According to a World Bank report, a mere 10 percent of the population (mostly consisting of the oligarchic elite) possessed over 80 percent of all land in the country at the time (1978, 9). The increasing loss of land and basic human rights abuses, along with intensified military monitoring and control, fed burgeoning public discontent and tensions that ultimately erupted into violent conflict.

Conflict between the military government and Marxist-inspired Leftist guerrillas rapidly escalated in the highlands in the late 1970s and early 1980s (Jonas 1991; Stolen 2007; Woodward 2008). Travel in the highlands became dangerous as a result, causing the tourist industry to significantly decline (Simon 1987). Long-time US American residents sold their homes and left the country, as did wealthy Guatemalans who desired to escape the unstable environment of their home country (Handy 1984). Foreign capital also rapidly diminished in Guatemala as foreign interests perceived Lucas García's administration as having limited control over the growing guerrilla movement. To retaliate against the loss of wealthier residents and foreign capital, Lucas García sent additional troops into villages in the highlands where the military suspected that guerrillas had temporarily set up camp (CEH 1999; REMHI 1998; Saavedra 2001). When the military troops arrived, the guerrilla forces would be long gone. However, the military would retaliate against the rural inhabitants of the village anyway, leaving behind a bloody trail of terror and violence. These retaliatory tactics actually worked against the military. Instead of stifling the guerrilla movement, Lucas García's brutal tactics inflicted on unarmed, noncombatant village civilians drove increasing numbers of them to support and join the guerrilla movement as it began to gain a hold on some portions of the highlands (Garrard-Burnett 2010).

Lucas García attempted to quash the escalating guerrilla movement by appointing his brother, General Benedicto Lucas García, as the new defense minister in 1981 (CEH 1999; Garrard-Burnett 2010; REMHI 1998; Schirmer 1998). General Lucas García intensified the counterinsurgency campaign by executing vicious attacks primarily on any rural, Maya Indigenous villages he believed to be sympathetic to the guerrillas. He also feigned a civic-action program aimed to assist villages with local construction projects as a means of monitoring residents. Central to his scheme was the hidden objective of forcing highlands *campesinos* to abandon their remote, scattered communities and to relocate to concentrated villages that the military could more easily control. This was a policy and tactic similarly followed in both Vietnam and Algeria (Grandin 2011). With his brother's backing, President Lucas García launched and supported this grueling campaign of forced relocation to "model villages" near the end of his presidential term, yet he did not remain in office long enough to see it through (CEH 1999a; Simon 1987).

Growing discontent with President Lucas García's government began to strain his presidency. The US government, disappointed with his regime, determined Lucas García could not control the Leftist guerrillas, which the US government viewed as a direct threat against foreign investments (Dill 2009; Jonas 1991). With the increasing pressure of the nearby Leftist insurgency in El Salvador and a revolutionary government in Nicaragua, US President Ronald Reagan's administration quickly intensified its strategic concern with Guatemala in the early 1980s (Jonas 1991; Luján Muñoz 2018). In addition, a myriad of international reports announcing that human rights violations and murders had taken place during Lucas García's regime caused the US Department of State, normally an ardent supporter of Guatemala's military governmental administrations, to issue a travel advisory, recommending that US citizens avoid traveling to Guatemala except for "essential visits" (Simon 1987, 73). This travel warning had dire consequences for Guatemala's tourism industry, one of the leading industries in the country at the time. Lucas García countered international reports of human rights violations and the subsequent travel warning by asserting that the repression was not caused by his administration. However, other independent organizations abroad investigated the situation and found that the Lucas García administration was, indeed, responsible for thousands of questionable deaths at the time (CEH 1999a, Grandin 2011; Simon 1987). While the US under the presidency of Jimmy Carter had already officially withdrawn military aid to Guatemala in 1977 because of reported human rights abuses, it continued to demand greater military control of the guerrillas. At the same time, the US government sought further disassociation from human rights violations occurring in Guatemala and, as a result, completely withdrew all forms of support of the Lucas García regime in 1981 (Dill 2009; Jonas 1991).

As Lucas García was completing his initial presidential term, it became apparent that he had maintained little support at home and abroad. In 1982's fraudulent elections, Lucas García lost to General Aníbal Guevara, who was "hand-selected" by a military clique and Lucas García, himself, to serve the next presidential term. Despite his appointment, however, Guevara never actually took office. Many top military officers and elite feared Guevara (a member of Lucas García's party) would only continue the military incompetence and inadequate tactics for crushing the guerrilla movement that they believed characterized Lucas García's administration (CEH 1999a). Consequently, a group of junior military garrison commanders quickly organized to carry out a military coup to overthrow the Guevara presidency. One of those commanders was General Efraín Ríos Montt, who would go on to commit some of the worst atrocities of Guatemala's entire thirty-six-year internal armed conflict and genocide (Garrard-Burnett 2010; Guillén 2007; Woodward 2008)

The Brutal Reign of General Efraín Ríos Montt

On March 23, 1982, junior military garrison commanders led a successful revolt to overthrow the Guevara presidency and to install General Ríos Montt at the helm (Garrard-Burnett 2010; Schirmer 1998). By this time, guerrilla forces in the highlands had grown substantially[3] and had significant influence in control of several regions (Schirmer 1998, 22). In addition, three major guerrilla organizations (the EGP; *Fuerzas Armadas Rebeldes,* or FAR; and *Organización Revolucionaria del Pueblo en Armas*, or ORPA), along with the national communist party (*Partido Guatemalteco del Trabajo*, or PGT), had joined forces in early 1982 to form a broader and more united front called the *Unidad Revolucionaria Nacional Guatemalteca* (or URNG) (Guillén 2007; Jonas 2009; May 2001).

To smother the expanding and newly united Leftist insurgency movement, Ríos Montt further intensified General Benedicto Lucas García's counterinsurgency program. Ríos Montt was determined to eliminate "subversives" and their supporters at all costs and without hesitation. The result was operation *Victoria 82* (Victory 82), which was designed to ensure that villages in the highlands were occupied by military or civil patrollers at all times, and that all rural *campesinos* even remotely suspected of being subversive were either killed or forced to flee to refugee camps. The *Victoria 82* plan called on the military to carry out additional massacres and step up their "scorched earth" campaign aimed at annihilating thousands of unarmed, noncombatant supposed "subversive" Maya Indigenous civilians in the highlands (Garrard-Burnett 2010; Sanford 2008).

In accordance with Ríos Montt's military strategy, army soldiers viewed any civilian population, especially those in primarily Maya Indigenous communities, as indistinguishable from the guerrilla movement (Montejo 1999). Out of fear, many *campesinos* tried to flee as soon as the military entered their villages. However, the military captured, tortured, and killed hundreds of thousands of unarmed, noncombatant civilians and justified their actions by stating that those who were truly not guilty of subversion would not have run from the military (Sanford 2003; Stolen 2007). The military also instilled terror in villages by dumping disfigured corpses along roadsides or hanging them from trees, serving as a warning to others (Falla 1994; Garrard-Burnett 2010; Warren 1998). Many villagers who survived by fleeing their communities fortunately found temporary relief in refugee settlements in Mexico and Belize (Manz 2004). By the end of 1982, an estimated 150,000 Indigenous peoples had fled to Mexico and approximately one million had fled or were internally displaced from their homes altogether (CEH 1999d, 38). In addition, the military carried out 246 massacres, murdered over 10,000 people, and orchestrated the disappearances of 833 people during Rios Montt's 17-month presidential term alone (CDHG 1991, 35). Ríos Montt's counterinsurgency campaign ruthlessly eliminated innumerable unarmed, noncombatant civilians, razed countless communities, and engendered seemingly limitless military control and monitoring of daily life. Along with soldiers, civilians were involuntarily enlisted to support military maneuvers as part of Ríos Montt's expansion of the civil patrol program, called the *Patrullas de Autodefensa Civil,* or PAC. Together, soldiers and civil patrollers carried out Ríos Montt's campaign of terror.

The civil patrols soon became central to the army's strategy. The civil patrols consisted of male residents of highlands villages and hamlets who were between the ages of fifteen and sixty. They were forced into the civil patrol, which was under the authority of a local army commander (Amnesty International 1998; Schirmer 1998). Civil patrol members were given weapons and told to defend the highlands against the guerrillas and any potential subversive actions. As such, these men, as involuntarily conscripts, were required to provide unpaid service in their village areas for eight to twenty-four hours every four to fourteen days. By 1982, nearly one million men, most of whom were Maya Indigenous, were involuntarily incorporated into the civil patrol program (CEH 1999c, 80). Using these men as another force against the guerrillas and a source of local surveillance and control, the military gained a stronghold over the highlands region. Consequently, civil patrols became both a first line of defense against the guerrillas and an effective mechanism of terror used to assert control over the majority Indigenous populations (Garrard-Burnett 2010; Saavedra 2001; Sanford 2008). According to the military, the civil patrols were a primary factor in drying up guerrilla support among highlands inhabitants. Using the civil patrols to obtain extensive control of the poor, Ríos Montt's military campaign cemented the state's stranglehold on the highlands, thereby achieving the primary objective of his counterinsurgency program (Garrard-Burnett 2010; Sanford 2008).

Ríos Montt's campaign to destroy the guerrilla movement and subdue "subversive" *campesinos* was brutal. Army attacks on villages included beating children to death on rocks and slicing open *campesinos* with the ends of bayonets. Soldiers also commonly burned crops, homes, and entire villages. The rape of women, individual torture, and massacres of entire populations also occurred in increasing numbers (CEH 1999; REMHI 1998). In his account of a military attack on his natal highlands village, Montejo remarks, "With the rise to power of Efraín Ríos Montt, all remaining human rights were abolished, and the army became the sole arbiter over the lives of Guatemalans" (1987, 113). Few people in Guatemala were exempt from the terror. Using covert tactics, such as "death squads" that were comprised of former security force personnel operating in plain clothes and acting under orders from military or national police officials, Ríos Montt was even able to order the murders of elite individuals in opposition and politicians who would have been untouchable under any other regime.

While Ríos Montt gained considerable control over the country in a relatively short period of time, a bitter conflict between two powerful factions of the military began to ignite and threaten his regime (CEH 1999; Garrard-Burnett 2010; Schirmer 1998). A divide had grown between junior garrison officers who had initially supported the 1982 coup and Ríos Montt. The *fusiles* and *frijoles* (rifles and beans) campaign of Ríos Montt, which consisted of eliminating support of the guerrillas by destroying civilians' fields, homes, and possessions (*fusiles*) and placing them in resettlement camps where their needs would be provided for (*frijoles*), had grown into inconceivable, brutal violence. Having witnessed the brutality, many junior officers began to oppose the heinous acts committed in Ríos Montt's counterinsurgency campaign. A group of junior officers, concerned with the brutality, waning US military aid, and corruption in the Guatemalan military, responded to the heightened violence by formally presenting a petition calling for less brutality. The petition did little to convince Ríos Montt to diminish his gruesome tactics. Attempting to navigate the sudden treacherous division between junior and senior military officers, Ríos Montt found that he could not satisfy either side of this divide (Schirmer 1998).

Ríos Montt's economic policies also began to alienate business leaders, large landowners, and a sizable portion of the middle class. The economy during Ríos Montt's rule was seriously depressed due to a worldwide recession, an archaic tax structure that was insufficient to support governmental needs, poor external investments, lack of sufficient investment capital, and the severe decline of the tourist industry (CEH 1999a). The international community also began raising awareness of violence and human rights violations carried out under Ríos Montt's administration. Major flight of capital from the country soon followed, which made it nearly impossible for Ríos Montt's regime to purchase additional arms or to support the national economy (Calvert 1985; Garrard-Burnett 2010; Simon 1987). Efforts by Ríos Montt's administration to impose new taxes, to ration foreign exchange, and to renew agrarian reform also proved unsuccessful in supporting and improving the national economy.

Ríos Montt's economic policies were further hindered by his religious fanaticism, which obliged him to stock his regime with fellow members of the conservative evangelical Church of the Word, based out of Eureka, California. His fervor as a religious zealot rapidly grew to become indistinguishable from his politics (Garrard-Burnett 2010; Simon 1987). Recognizing Ríos Montt's inability to improve Guatemala's economic conditions and having been passed over for positions that instead were given to Ríos Montt's church cronies, government officials and military officers began to craft a plot to remove him from office (Saavedra 2001; Schirmer 1998). On August 8, 1983, his presidency was terminated by a military coup that was supported by a majority of the military command. Ríos Montt was physically forced out of office and his Minister of Defense, General Oscar Humberto Mejía Víctores, took over as President and remained in the position until 1986 (CEH 1999a). Although the Mejía Víctores administration was hardly the democratic engine it had proposed to be, it did end the brutal genocidal legacy of Ríos Montt's government, diminishing the dark period of *la violencia* (Saavedra 2001; Tierney 1997).

La violencia, especially during Ríos Montt's reign, was one of the most tragic periods in all of Guatemala's history (Booth, Wade, and Walker 2010; Guillén 2007). Handy (1984) notes that the violence and suffering of Guatemala's impoverished majority Maya Indigenous populations in the early 1980s, in particular, far surpassed that which was experienced in the early days of the Spanish conquest. Although the military overthrow did not bring immediate peace to Guatemala, it did significantly reduce the violent military tyranny in which both Lucas García and Ríos Montt orchestrated all-out genocide against unarmed, noncombatant civilians, the vast majority of whom were unaffiliated with the Leftist movement. The brutal period of *la violencia* resulted in hundreds of thousands of mostly Maya Indigenous peoples becoming victims and survivors of such an unjust military tyranny that Garrard-Burnett terms the Guatemalan genocide the "Mayan Holocaust" (2010, 7). Although Ríos Montt's reign of terror ended, it forever stained the nation's history and left behind countless victims and survivors.

VICTIMS AND SURVIVORS OF GUATEMALA'S INTERNAL ARMED CONFLICT AND GENOCIDE

The massive slaughter carried out during the thirty-six-year internal armed conflict and genocide took its toll on the entire Guatemalan populace (Green 1999; Jonas 1991; Montejo 1999). Actual battles between the army and the guerrillas did not result in massive casualties. Instead, the vast majority of victims were civilians, not combatants in guerrilla groups (CEH 1999d, 27). The Guatemalan state, through its military and paramilitary groups, was responsible for 93 percent of all human rights abuses and violent acts registered by the CEH and carried out during the armed conflict and genocide, which increased with grave intensity during *la violencia*. Guerrilla forces were responsible for three percent of all human rights abuses and violations, while four percent were unknown (CEH 1999d, 42). All told, through its "scorched earth" operation, the military murdered and disappeared 200,000 individuals, carried out over 626 massacres, and razed 440 villages (CEH 1999a, 73; CEH 1999c, 256; Sanford 2003, 14). In addition, over one million people were displaced internally with many forced to leave their home communities indefinitely (CEH 1999d, 38). An estimated 150,000 Guatemalans fled as refugees to Mexico (CEH 1999d, 38). Those who remained in Guatemala and survived the slaughter were seriously traumatized and forced into submission under the ongoing tyranny and oppression of the government (CEH 1999; REMHI 1998).

The Guatemalan government's campaign to stamp out Marxist-inspired Leftist guerrillas went far beyond its scope by killing and terrorizing hundreds of thousands of unarmed, noncombatant civilians. Hardly a person living in Guatemala at the time went untouched by the armed conflict and genocide. Yet the hardest hit populations unquestionably were Maya Indigenous peoples who suffered and died in some of the most gruesome ways imaginable. According to the CEH truth commission report, 83.3 percent of the victims and survivors of human rights abuses and violent acts were Maya Indigenous peoples, most of whom had nothing to do with either the military or the guerrilla struggle (1999b, 321). Roughly 45,000 women were widowed with some scholars contending that the number may be as high as 80,000 (Green 1999, 4; Gugelberger 1999, 50), and 150,000–200,000 children were orphaned (CITGUA 1989, 18; WOLA 1989, 1). The majority Maya

Indigenous populations bore the brunt of the armed conflict and genocide even though numerous unarmed, noncombatant *ladino* civilians also became victims and survivors. Unfortunately, the vast majority of victims and survivors[4] were caught in the middle of ideological struggles between competing Western philosophies (i.e., capitalism, communism, and democracy) and suffered immensely as a result (Fischer and Maxwell 1999).

THE OFFICIAL END OF THE THIRTY-SIX-YEAR INTERNAL ARMED CONFLICT AND GENOCIDE

While the end of Ríos Montt's bloody reign slowed much of the all-out genocide in the country, it did not completely cease the politically-driven violence. Right-wing candidate Jorge Serrano Elías won the presidency in 1991 and political violence continued under his administration despite his supposed desire to advance a peace settlement. Against a backdrop of increasing opposition of labor and other mass organizations, Serrano sought to extend his control over the military and rising opposition by disbanding the congress and all political parties in 1993 (Jonas 2000; Woodward 2008). Predictably, massive popular protests ensued, and the legislature demanded Serrano's resignation rather than disbanding per Serrano's dictate. Serrano begrudgingly resigned on June 1, 1993, and Ramiro de León Carpio was elected interim president in 1993 by the congress. Ríos Montt sought to run for president in 1990 but was denied based on a stipulation in the new constitution that disqualified any individual who participated in a previous attempt to overthrow the government from running for president. He instead was elected to the congress in 1990 and became president of the congress in 1994 (Schirmer 1998; Woodward 2008).

In January 1996, Álvaro Arzú took office and sought to establish peace with the guerillas as part of his agenda. After a series of agreements in Oslo, Mexico, and Madrid, representatives of URNG and the Guatemalan government, under President Arzú, signed the formal peace accords on December 29, 1996, which officially ended the thirty-six-year internal armed conflict and genocide (Schirmer 1998).

Ríos Montt continued as president of the national congress in May 2000, affording him legal immunity from prosecution of any crimes related to the armed conflict and genocide. Just three years later, he was allowed to run for president after a constitutional court initially forbade him from running. Fortunately, he only received eleven percent of the vote and lost any chance of regaining the presidency. However, Ríos Montt did continue to serve in the congress, enjoying full legal immunity from any prosecution of charges of genocide and crimes against humanity (Bowen 2019; Gunson 2018; Kinzer 2018).

SEARCHING FOR JUSTICE AND RECONCILIATION

Regrettably, the signing of peace accords in 1996 did not foster immediate justice or reconciliation for most of Guatemala's population. The peace accords did allow for the return of hundreds of thousands of refugees who had fled to Mexico and Belize and ended extensive militarization, especially in the rural highlands. However, efforts to derail truth reports and investigations, corruption, and impunity of high-level military officers and leaders made justice and reconciliation efforts increasingly challenging, if not fleeting, in post-conflict Guatemala (Little 2004; McAllister and Nelson 2013).

One of the first attempts to bring about justice and reconciliation after the signing of the peace accords was marred by the April 26, 1998, murder of Guatemalan Bishop Monsignor Juan Gerardi Conedera. Gerardi was murdered following the release of the truth 1998 report, *Guatemala: Nunca Más,* created by the REMHI project that he had helped spearhead. He had been appointed Auxiliary Bishop of the Archdiocese of Guatemala in 1984 and was charged with overseeing the creation of the Human Rights Office of the Archdiocese of Guatemala (ODHAG) in 1989. After years of ODHAG collecting information via interviews with survivors throughout the countryside who detailed horrific events and identified perpetrators of the internal armed conflict and genocide, Gerardi publicly presented the REMHI findings on April 24, 1998. The findings were particularly damning to the military and national police as survivors overwhelmingly identified them as the primary perpetrators of the armed conflict and genocide (Holiday 2001; Molina Mejía and McSherry 2001). Two days after his public presentation of the findings, Gerardi was murdered in his own home, which was viewed as an attempt to send a message of terror to anyone who would seek justice in and truth of what happened during the armed conflict and genocide. After years of tampered investigations, intimidation of judges and witnesses, and other lengthy unnecessary delays, three former military officers were convicted of Gerardi's murder in 2001 and sentenced to thirty years in prison. One convicted perpetrator has since died and the other two received reduced sentences (twenty years instead of thirty) in 2005 (GHRC 2019; Molina Mejía and McSherry 2001; Woodward 2008).

While some consider Gerardi's murder and the REMHI project a key test of impunity, both also helped lay important groundwork for further truth and reconciliation efforts. One of the agreements in the peace accords, established through the Oslo Accord (1994), called for the establishment of the United

Nations supported Historical Clarification Commission (CEH) in Guatemala to investigate human rights abuses and other violations that occurred during the internal armed conflict and genocide (CEH 1999a, 15; Manz 2008; Oglesby and Ross 2009). Work began in 1997 with the election of three commissioners: two Guatemalans and one international expert. Over the next two years, a staff of over 300 people collected over 8,000 first-hand witness testimonies while also gathering information from the REMHI project database, declassified US government documents, key witnesses, and other organizations (Ball and Price 2018; Oglesby and Ross 2009). This immense effort resulted in a twelve-volume report entitled *Guatemala: Memoria del Silencio* (*Guatemala: Memory of Silence*) that was presented publicly to representatives of the Guatemalan government, URNG, and the United Nations Secretary General on February 25, 1999. The report explicitly reveals that the military and its agents had committed ninety-three percent of the documented abuses and that the state clearly had committed acts of genocide between 1980 and 1983 (CEH 1999; Oglesby and Ross 2009). The Guatemalan government refused to accept the findings, however, casting a long shadow of impunity over justice, reconciliation, and necessary changes to deal with the country's dark period in the twentieth century (Holiday 2001; Sanford 2003).

The shadow of impunity was further extended by failure of the May 1999 referendum on constitutional reforms that had been agreed upon in the 1996 peace accords and that were to be implemented within the first year following the signing of the peace accords (Holiday 2001). Failure of the referendum meant that agreements established in the peace accords, such as limiting the role of the military and revising the constitution to be more inclusive of the country's multiethnic and multicultural populations, would not be ratified and institutionalized. Interestingly, just two months before the failed referendum, US President Bill Clinton apologized for US involvement in supporting the violence and repression of the internal armed conflict and genocide in Guatemala (Broder 1999; Gibney and Warner 1999; Sanford 2003).

Despite failure of the referendum, the CEH findings did spur a group of individuals, including Nobel Peace Prize laureate Rigoberta Menchú Tum, to bring forth, by the end of 1999, an official complaint to Spain's legal system. The complaint was argued under the principle of universal jurisdiction, which is grounded in Spain's Organic Law of the Judicial Branch. The group officially filed the complaint in the Spanish *Audiencia Nacional* (National High Court) because both legal immunity and impunity in Guatemala protected perpetrators, such as Ríos Montt, from legal prosecution of charges of genocide and crimes against humanity. In Spain, however, legal immunity would not be recognized (Oglesby and Ross 2009; Ross 2016). As a result, the *Audiencia Nacional* accepted the official complaint and charged eight prominent Guatemalan leaders with genocide, terrorism, torture, summary execution, and unlawful detentions perpetrated against Maya Indigenous peoples and their supporters in Guatemala during the 1970s and 1980s (Avakian 2018; Roht-Arriaza and Bernabeu 2008). Spanish Organic Law specifically allows for prosecution of particular crimes, such as genocide and terrorism, by non-Spaniards outside of Spain. After the complaint was accepted, an open investigation was agreed upon on March 27, 2000. After years of appeals, determining procedures, gathering witness and expert testimonies, and a myriad of legal setbacks, the case slowly made headway despite the added challenge of the Guatemalan government refusing to extradite Ríos Montt to Spain for the case (Oglesby and Nelson 2016; Roht-Arriaza and Bernabeu 2008). While the case had various setbacks, it did serve as what Ross calls an "incubator that developed the Guatemalan genocide case" (2016, 362).

In late 2010, Claudia Paz y Paz Bailey, a scholar and human rights activist who helped lead the analyses for the CEH report, was appointed as Guatemala's attorney general, opening up new legal avenues to pursue indictments of leaders within Guatemala itself (Ball and Price 2018; Brett 2016; Ross 2016). Paz y Paz Bailey removed prosecutors with ties to the military or who were simply nonperforming and made human rights abuse cases a top priority (Avakian 2018; Brett 2016). Just two years after Paz y Paz Bailey took over as attorney general, Ríos Montt finally lost his seat in congress, as well as his immunity from prosecution. Subsequently, he was indicted by a Guatemalan court for genocide and crimes against humanity specifically committed in the Ixil region between 1982 and 1983 (Brett 2016). Ríos Montt was put on house arrest in January 2012 while he awaited his trial, which was scheduled to begin on March 19, 2013 (Ball and Price 2018; Doyle 2012; Oglesby and Nelson 2016).

The trial against Ríos Montt and his former director of military intelligence, General José Mauricio Rodríguez Sánchez, was presided over by a three-judge tribunal panel and involved 100 Maya Ixil eyewitnesses of torture, death, and rape (Oglesby and Nelson 2016). The case was directly supported by the CEH (1999) report that clearly linked Ríos Montt to genocidal massacres during his presidency and by secret records that anonymously surfaced in 2009. The records, referred to as *Operación Sofía*, consist of 359 pages of military documents and communiques from the Ixil region that covered the period of 1982 until the end of Ríos Montt's reign. They explicitly show that the army intentionally carried out brutal attacks as part of a counterinsurgency strategy that blanketly targeted rural, Maya Indigenous populations, deemed the "internal enemy" (Avakian 2018; Oglesby and Nelson 2016).

After almost two months of eyewitness and expert testimonies, the trial concluded on May 10, 2013, with the three-judge panel finding Ríos Montt guilty of genocide and crimes against humanity, including the murder of

1,771 civilians, the torture of 163 individuals, sexual violence against 41 women, the bombing of 15 communities, forced concentration of 1,383 people, and the forced displacement of 29,000 mostly Maya Ixil peoples (Brett 2016, 293). He was sentenced to 80 years in prison (50 years for genocide and 30 for crimes against humanity), while Rodríguez Sánchez was acquitted of all charges since his work with military intelligence was not viewed as part of the operational chain of command (Burt 2016; Oglesby and Nelson 2016). Just ten days after Ríos Montt's conviction, however, the Guatemalan Constitutional Court threw out the genocide conviction and prison sentence, citing procedural errors unrelated to the testimonies. Ríos Montt was sent home on house arrest and the Court demanded a new trial (Avakian 2018; Ball and Price 2018; Oglesby and Nelson 2016).

A new trial was set to begin in January 2015, but Ríos Montt's lawyers attempted to argue that he was physically and mentally unfit to stand trial due to dementia. The forced departure of attorney general Paz y Paz Bailey in May 2014 added to the struggle to legally prosecute Ríos Montt in Guatemala in 2015. Yet by August 2015, a new trial was set to begin in early 2016. It was stipulated that the trial would take place behind closed doors and would not require Ríos Montt to be physically present given his deteriorating health condition. Essentially, the new trial court ruled that Ríos Montt would be required to face a retrial, despite his dementia diagnosis, through the proxy of his lawyers. The new trial court also stipulated that there would be no criminal sanctions such as jail time should Ríos Montt be convicted (Ball and Price 2018; Oglesby and Nelson 2016). Despite these stipulations and the January 2016 start date, the trial was suspended once again to resolve outstanding legal petitions (Ball and Price 2018). The trial eventually did restart on October 13, 2017, but the case against Ríos Montt was dismissed just five months later due to his death on April 1, 2018. The case against Rodríguez Sánchez continued (Burt and Estrada 2018). On September 26, 2018, the court unanimously found that the Guatemalan military, indeed, had committed genocide and crimes against humanity against Maya Ixil peoples during Ríos Montt's *de facto* government. Rodríguez Sánchez, however, was acquitted of all charges. The split two-to-one decision was based on lack of evidence that Rodríguez Sánchez explicitly gave orders to commit the atrocities (ibid.).

A Long Road to Justice and Reconciliation

The signing of the 1996 peace accords clearly did not lead to a peaceful period of post-conflict justice and reconciliation in Guatemala. While various cases have been brought forward and prosecuted, Guatemala continues to be an "impunity state" that overwhelmingly leaves violence and crimes unpunished (Bowen 2019). Persistent impunity in Guatemala has been further perpetuated and advanced by the more recent shut down of the United Nations backed *Comisión Internacional contra la Impunidad en Guatemala* (International Commission Against Impunity in Guatemala, or CICIG). CICIG was established in 2007 at the request of the Guatemalan government to independently investigate high-profile crimes and to then hand over cases to local prosecutors as a means of working to dismantle networks of criminality and corruption deeply embedded in the country's institutions (Beltrán 2016, 64; Bowen 2019, 137). The autonomous anti-corruption commission successfully brought down many of the country's elite, including President Otto Pérez Molina—a retired general who was directly involved in the internal armed conflict and genocide—and his vice president, Roxana Baldetti. Both were charged with illicit association, customs fraud, and bribery (Beltrán 2016; Green 2019). The subsequent President, Jimmy Morales, along with his family, also came under investigation for allegedly accepting illegal campaign funds. However, he shut down CICIG in September 2019 to his advantage despite polls showing seventy percent of Guatemalans supported the commission (Green 2019; Schwartz 2019). The forced presidential termination of CICIG stalled important anti-corruption efforts and is likely to undercut future efforts to prosecute government officials and oligarchic elites complicit in the armed conflict and genocide, among other crimes.

Unfortunately, growing impunity is not the only post-conflict strife in Guatemala today. Production and clandestine exportation of illegal drugs to the US, organized crime, transnational gang violence, relentless poverty, militarized mineral extraction, food insecurity, gender-based violence, a deteriorating economy, and massive migration are just some of the overwhelming challenges that Guatemalans face in a nation-state that has yet to come to terms with its brutal past (Burrell 2013; Levenson 2013; Weisbart 2018; Woodward 2008). Without a system in place to address deeply rooted racism and what Holiday (2001) refers to as one of the most inequitable economic structures in the hemisphere, the road to justice and reconciliation in Guatemala will likely continue to be elusive for years, if not decades, to come.

NOTES

1. I recognize that the historical overview presented in this chapter lacks Indigenous peoples' perspectives via inclusion of their own historical accounts and oral histories, which are imperative for a full, accurate account of Guatemalan historical processes, structures, systems, and events. The need for Indigenous perspectives in Guatemalan history is substantiated by historian David Carey who notes, "Most *ladino* and Western scholars' presentations of Guatemalan history fail to incorporate

Mayan historical perspectives and values. These ideas are important to an understanding of Mayan past, present, and future" (2001, 274). While space limitations did not allow me to include extensive Indigenous historical accounts and oral histories in this chapter, I do hope the chapter gives readers a sufficient general overview of the historical development of processes, structures, systems, and events that led to the internal armed conflict and genocide and, ultimately, to participants in my research project having been orphaned. I also hope it inspires readers to seek additional resources on Guatemalan history that do include extensive Indigenous historical accounts, oral histories, perspectives, and voices (e.g., Carey 2001; CEH 1999; Cojtí Cuxil, 1997; Manz 2004; Montejo 2021, 1999; Otzoy 2017; REMHI 1998).

2. The New Laws of 1524 were developed to regulate and further entrench Crown control over the wealth of precious metals and agricultural exports in the area while simultaneously casting stricter control over the ample and much desired supply of Indigenous laborers (Castillo Méndez 2008, Luján Muñoz 2018; Kramer 1994).

3. Jonas notes that the number of members in the guerrilla movement may have reached as high as 6,000–8,000 individuals at its peak, from 1980 to 1981 (1991, 138).

4. The term "victims" in this book denotes individuals who died as a result of the armed conflict and genocide, while the term "survivors" signifies those who continued to live after surviving atrocities.

Chapter Two

Destroying the Seed

Truth commission reports and publications clearly reveal that the internal armed conflict and genocide in Guatemala resulted in the death, disappearance, and victimization of hundreds of thousands of unarmed, noncombatant civilians of all ages (CEH 1999; REMHI 1998). Valiant efforts to collect and publish personal accounts of civilian victims' and survivors' experiences have been and continue to be underway, offering valuable insights into the truth and scope of what happened. Uncovering what occurred and how it has affected survivors is imperative; however, most research has focused on the lives of survivors who were adults during the most brutal period of *la violencia* (e.g., Green 1999; Zur 1998). Yet many of the victims and survivors of that horrific period were children at the time. Disproportionately fewer studies in contemporary research focus solely on child survivors' specific experiences, especially those of children orphaned because of the murder, disappearance, or death of one or both of their parents. Given that the estimated number of children orphaned during that time period ranged from 150,000 to 200,000 (CITGUA 1989, 18; WOLA 1989, 1)—and in reality is likely even higher than reported because of the large number of adults murdered and disappeared who presumably would have had more than one child—the lack of research centered on this particular group of survivors is surprising and has not gone unnoticed by orphaned child survivors themselves. This is demonstrated by a child survivor reacting to a description of my research project who asked, "Seriously? Someone is finally going to write about what happened to us?" Her response illustrates child survivors' desire to have their stories told and heard. Their struggles and adversities are also deserving of attention because they, as children, were deliberately targeted by their own government. In fact, the Guatemalan military explicitly targeted children as part of their military strategy to "destroy the seed" (mainly Maya Indigenous children) so that Maya Indigenous families, and any chance of future descendants, would be eradicated. That Guatemalan children, as well as children of other genocides, were deliberately targeted should be a major focus of

61

research and a primary call for the global community to prevent such future atrocities. In this chapter, I discuss the deliberate targeting of children in Guatemala and elsewhere, and discuss how human rights treaties and conventions have failed to protect them.

THE GUATEMALAN MILITARY'S DELIBERATE EFFORTS TO "DESTROY THE SEED"

The REMHI (1998) truth report corroborates that Guatemalan children as their own distinctive survivor group have been deeply affected by violence and political repression resulting from the internal armed conflict and genocide. Based on over 5,400 eyewitness testimonies collected through the REMHI project, the report provides clear evidence that violence against children at the hands of the military was deliberately enacted as a means of "destroying the seed" (1998, 29–31). The military sought to destroy mainly Maya Indigenous children, whom they viewed as "bad seeds," directly through murder and disappearances and indirectly through various means. For example, children who survived mortal attacks commonly suffered indirectly at the hands of the military by witnessing violence, death, and other traumatic events firsthand (ibid., 29). Tens of thousands of children were forced to flee their communities and country, living in precarious conditions in Mexico or Belize with their families as refugees. The report also substantiates that children were abducted by soldiers and covertly sold to "adoptive" families in urban areas, many of whom were perpetrators of the violence against the children's families (ibid., 38). Furthermore, soldiers forced some children to witness brutal murders and torture so that they would report what they saw to other surrounding villages (Garrard-Burnett 2010; REMHI 1998).

The CEH (1999) truth report concludes that 4,249 (or 18%) of 23,313 reported human rights violations against individuals reported in their project were committed against children during the harshest years of the genocide. In other words, nearly one-fifth of victims and survivorswas a minor between the ages of zero and seventeen years (CEH 1999c, 58). Among the reported human rights violations committed, children also comprised 20 percent of victims of arbitrary executions, most of which were carried out during massacres that largely took place in rural Maya Indigenous communities between 1980 and 1983 (ibid., 59–60). According to eyewitnesses, children in the first five years of life, in particular, were executed with extreme cruelty. These young children often had their heads bashed against tree trunks, rocks, walls, and floors. Others had their heads severed with machetes (ibid., 62–64). Pregnant women and their unborn babies were also tortured and murdered with particular cruelty. Eyewitnesses tell of soldiers repeatedly stomping on the belly of a pregnant mother to kill her and the fetus. Others recount events such as soldiers cutting open a mother's womb with a knife and burning the fetus (ibid., 61–62). Such cruel and violent acts demonstrate the lengths to which the Guatemalan military would go to "destroy the seed" so that Maya Indigenous families could not continue their biological bloodlines and their cultural lifeways in the future.

Among the total number of child survivors identified who remained alive, fourteen percent survived torture and cruel, inhumane treatment (ibid., 59). In some cases, these children were tortured by military forces under the auspices of "obtaining information" about guerrilla forces, regardless of whether the children actually held knowledge. Most child torture, however, was carried out purposely to instill terror among suvivors' families, communities, and social organizations (Garrard-Burnett 2010; REMHI 1998). Terror-inducing torture took both psychological and physical forms such as witnessing the execution of loved ones and being left with physical scars and ailments as a constant reminder to survivors and others of their torture and the continuous looming threat of military brutality (CEH 1999c, 68–70). These terror-inducing methods were designed to further "neutralize" (or pacify) the mass populations by reducing the likelihood of an uprising and quelling any tendency to support guerrilla insurgents.

Forced disappearances also directly affected Maya Indigenous children in Guatemala during the armed conflict and genocide. The CEH report indicates that eleven percent of forcibly disappeared victims, particularly between 1979 and 1986, were children. Roughly eighty-eight percent of child disappearance cases was committed by state forces, the military, and members of the civil patrols (ibid., 66). According to eyewitness testimonies, some of the disappeared children were kidnapped while in school; others were captured and disappeared following massacres in their villages or while out searching for their disappeared parents. Many disappeared children were likely executed, but there may also be a number of disappeared children who survived, are living with unrelated families mainly in urban areas, and are unaware that they were kidnapped from their families and natal communities during that time period (ibid.).

As with forced disappearances, forced displacement had often fatal consequences and specifically targeted children as well. According to the CEH report, 60 percent of victims who died during forced displacement were children, meaning that well over half of the victims who were forced to flee their home communities and died as a result were minors (ibid., 59). Forced displacement had a disproportionate effect on children, as they were more susceptible to illness, starvation, and injury-related deaths given their physical vulnerability. For those children who survived, many suffered from emotional and physical distress because of the dire conditions endured by their families while fleeing their villages and in the subsequent months of unstable living conditions (ibid., 65).

Children, especially girls, were also deliberate targets of rape perpetrated principally by military soldiers. The CEH report reveals that 27 percent of all rape cases reported from over 11,000 eyewitness testimonies involved girls under the age of seventeen, with some victims and survivors as young as infants (ibid., 58–59). Among all child rape victims and survivors, 8 percent were five years old or younger, 22 percent fell between the ages of six and twelve years, and 70 percent between thirteen and seventeen years old (ibid., 66). Many child victims were then tortured and murdered after being raped. While most cases involved girls, reports of boys as rape victims and survivors emerged as well, although specific statistics on the rape of boys are not presented in the truth report. For those who survived, rape was used by the military as a form of torture to humiliate and dehumanize children because the military considered them "the enemy." Rape was also used as a terroristic tactic to instill fear among Maya Indigenous populations more generally, especially in rural communities (ibid., 67–68).

Many children also suffered unlawful detention and deprivation of liberty during the armed conflict and genocide. The CEH report establishes that 16 percent of survivors who were deprived of their basic liberty, especially between 1979 and 1986, were children under the age of seventeen. State security forces, soldiers, commissioned officers, and civil patrollers were responsible for 96 percent of the cases (ibid., 70–71). Children were deliberately detained because of presumed involvement in social or political activities that military considered "subversive," or that supported the guerrilla movement. In such cases, child detainees were not given special consideration simply because of their minor status and suffered much of the same torture and abuse that adult detainees experienced. Young students were often detained for dubious reasons. Some child detainees were murdered while in detention, while others were used as bait to lure their parents to a military detachment for swift capture. Others were kept against their will in the detachments and held as servants for the soldiers (ibid., 71).

Some children deprived of their liberty ended up as domestic servants. This form of servitude was especially connected to massacres and "scorched earth" operations during *la violencia*. Following a massacre or the razing of a village, state security forces would often kidnap child survivors and place them in their own homes or homes of other families where they were forced to work as the families' domestic servants (ibid., 71). In some cases, the children were subjected to systematic abuse and exploitation, suffering a range of psychological and physical abuses that led to ongoing trauma and fear. In other cases, child survivors were raised as members of the family with whom they were placed. These child survivors may not even know now that they are not biological members of the family, or that they were kidnapped from their natal communities. The economic exploitation and physical and psychological abuse of children kidnapped during the genocide led to not only loss of liberty but also loss of cultural identity, Indigenous languages, physical and psychological integrity, and familial and natal community ties (ibid., 71–72).

A final area of deliberately targeted child rights violations addressed in the CEH truth report is the forced recruitment of minors into the military and civil patrols. At the time of the armed conflict and genocide, constitutional law in Guatemala called for obligatory military service for males but only those eighteen years of age and older. However, eyewitness testimonies reveal that boys under the age of eighteen were often forcibly conscripted into the military for the purposes of the military counterinsurgency strategy, which was an illegal mechanism for exploiting the labor of minors (ibid., 78). Similarly, boys under the age of eighteen were forcibly recruited to serve as civil patrollers. Prior reports from the ODHAG and other institutions concluded that children between the ages of ten and fourteen constituted two percent of the civil patrol members. Membership in the civil patrols reached as high as 1,000,000 in 1989 (ibid., 80), which means that at least 20,000 children (or 2% of the total) were under the age of fifteen when forced into the civil patrols. Explicitly involving children in military-driven surveillance and operations violates a multitude of national and international laws. Yet the Guatemalan military's own strategic operations plan, dubbed "*Firmeza 83,*" overtly called for the direct recruitment of children into the civil patrols (Ejército de Guatemala, 1983, 50). Such recruitment was an audacious and flagrant disregard of established national and international laws protecting minors.

The deliberate targeting of children by the Guatemalan military formed part of an explicit strategy aimed at "destroying the seed." This deliberate targeting of children was heinous and cannot be viewed as unavoidable "collateral damage" resulting from armed conflict. To understand why the Guatemalan military callously targeted children in its counterinsurgency campaign, it is important to examine how their blueprint developed, which was strongly influenced by the US Phoenix program in Vietnam.

The Phoenix Program in Vietnam: A Blueprint for "Destroying the Seed" in Guatemala

The US CIA launched its Phoenix program on December 20, 1967 (Andradé 1990, x). Named for the Vietnamese mythical bird of royalty and power, *Phung Hoang,* and translated into English to the closest analogue of the mythical bird that rises from the ashes, the Phoenix program was developed to rejuvenate intelligence efforts to "neutralize" (or pacify) the Vietnamese population more effectively, removing any threat of civilian support of the Vietcong and the North Vietnamese army (Andradé 1990, 72–73; Jones 2005, 107; Miller 2017). The CIA and US military identified the Vietcong Infrastructure (VCI) as civilian intelligence sources suspected of supporting Vietcong and North Vietnamese soldiers (Valentine 1990, 13). These civilian intelligence sources mainly consisted of noncombatant women, men, and children who were not part of a military organization and were living in villages throughout South Vietnam at the time (Andradé 1990, x). To "neutralize" the VCI, the Phoenix program called for killing, capturing, or converting to US allies any civilian individuals, regardless of age, who were believed to be part of the VCI. As both an intelligence sharing program and an action program directed at mainly noncombatant civilians, the Phoenix program unarguably became one of the most controversial elements of the US war in Vietnam (Miller 2017).

Some proponents and participants in the Phoenix program contend that it was merely an intelligence coordination, not an assassination program (Andradé 1990; Cook 1997; DeForest and Chanoff 1990; Rosenau and Long 2009). Other analysts and scholars, however, argue that the program did, in fact, utilize elite US and trained Vietnamese paramilitary troops to carry out assassinations, kidnappings, torture, and intimidation as techniques of terror against the civilian population of South Vietnam (Miller 2017; Turse 2013, 189–90). In his review of the incident summaries and sworn statements of veterans collected in the Vietnam War Crimes Working Group files, Nick Turse (2013), a US Pentagon task force charged with investigating alleged atrocities by US troops against South Vietnamese civilians, notes that what occurred in Vietnam under the auspices of the Phoenix program neither fits squarely with what US Americans saw on the nightly news during the war nor with the postwar narrative. A significant number of innocent civilian Vietnamese peoples of all ages, including children, were deliberately kidnapped, tortured, and killed, and the Phoenix program was used to call for and justify those atrocious acts (ibid., 190). Even proponents of the Phoenix program who claim it was not an assassination program openly admit that abuses did occur and often went unpunished (Andradé 1990, 283).

The Phoenix program's techniques of terror carried out on noncombatant civilians—kidnappings, torture, interrogations, extortion, surveillance, intimidation, and killings—became the primary techniques taught by CIA instructors to Latin American military officers in the 1970s at the infamous US Army's School of the Americas, or SOA (McSherry 2002, 43; Monbiot 2001). SOA training manuals explicitly drew from the Phoenix program to teach Latin American military officers methods of torture such as electroshock, sensory deprivation, drugs, and hypnosis, as well as other forms of brutal interrogation, with no regard for an individual's age or civilian status.

Assassination and intimidation methods were also included as part and parcel of the SOA program (ibid.). Ultimately, over 60,000 Latin American graduates of the SOA program were trained how to brutally create climates of fear and carry out egregious terroristic methods. Such training *en masse* resulted in some of the worst human rights abuses in history and children were not safe from any of these methods, as evidenced in Guatemala (Kepner 2000, 476; McSherry 2002, Monbiot 2001).

Genocide and State-Sponsored Terror in the Guatemalan Highlands

Directly influenced by the US Phoenix program with its methods taught directly to Guatemalan military officers who attended the SOA, the military counterinsurgency campaign in Guatemala explicitly used state-sponsored terroristic strategies that involved "the most extreme displays of disregard for human life" (REMHI 1999, 7). The aim of these strategies was to terrorize and severely intimidate the majority (mainly Maya Indigenous) population so that they would become "neutralized," or simply too frightened to either support guerrilla insurgents or participate in any sort of mass uprising against the terror-wielding state (Garrard-Burnett 2010; REMHI 1999). To achieve this aim, the military implemented its "scorched earth" strategy to "drain the pond" (or eradicate the Maya Indigenous populations, including children) to get at the "fish" (the Marxist-inspired Leftist guerrillas), which would have long-lasting psychological ramifications for a majority of Guatemalans (CEH 1999; Garrard-Burnett 2010; Sanford 2003).

The Guatemalan military's overt terroristic strategies involved arbitrary terror and destruction to create a culture of fear that not only permeated daily life during *la violencia* but also persisted well beyond that time period (Afflitto and Jesilow 2007; Garrard-Burnett 2010; Green 1999; Zur 1998). This culture of fear quickly expanded and intensified during the regime of General Ríos Montt who executed his military blueprint *Victoria 82*. Under the first phase of *Victoria 82* and in line with training received at the SOA, the military murdered any unarmed, noncombatant villagers even remotely suspected of supporting the guerrillas, destroyed their belongings, and forced as many remaining survivors as possible into military-controlled settlements. Through these tactics, the military fully established and intensified the culture of fear that persists in the country even today (Garrard-Burnett 2010; Sanford 2003). Recognizing this culture of fear as a military strategy, Davis notes,

> Most observers are in agreement that the purpose of the Guatemalan army's counterinsurgency campaign was as much to teach the Indian population a psychological lesson as to wipe out a guerrilla movement that, at its height, had

probably no more than 3,500 trained people in arms. In essence, the purpose of the campaign was to generate an attitude of terror and fear—what we might term a "culture of fear"—in the Indian population, to ensure that never again would it support or ally itself with a Marxist guerrilla movement [1988, 24].

For highlands inhabitants who remained living outside of militarized model villages, the army used an array of terror-inducing tactics to instill deep-seated fear and ensure submission to the state. These tactics were not only perpetrated by the military itself but also by individuals from within the community who, as civil patrollers, were forced to carry out horrendous acts against their own community members. In essence, the military's ideology of violence spread well beyond its very own ranks into the communities it infiltrated, turning communities against themselves (CEH 1999; Sanford 2003; REMHI 1998). Violence and threat from perpetrators *outside* of the community were simultaneously fortified by violence and threat carried out by perpetrators *within* the community itself. Both sources of terror deserve further examination.

Terror from Outside

As noted in chapter one, the military carried out over 626 massacres in which 440 entire villages were razed (CEH 1999c, 256; Sanford 2003, 14). These massacres were designed not only to "drain the pond" but also to produce overwhelming anxiety in civilians from surrounding villages and hamlets. Key to spreading the terror of massacre beyond the targeted community was leaving behind a few survivors as witnesses who were used to spread the message of terror to other communities by warning them about what they had seen (CEH 1999; Falla 1994; REMHI 1998).

Less public than massacres of entire villages but equally terrorizing was the military's creation and use of clandestine death squads. The death squads served as unpredictable, autonomous right wing terrorist groups. They carried out some of the most heinous acts of violence and terror in the highlands, indiscriminately murdering and kidnapping villagers, making mass arrests, and publishing ominous death lists (Garrard-Burnett 2010; Jonas 1991). The death lists, known as "black propaganda," were published both locally and nationally in print media, distributed in the streets, and posted in public spaces. The lists contained the names of individuals whom the death squads and the military designated as *condenados a muerte* (condemned to death) (CEH 1999b; Figueroa Ibarra 1991). Wanted posters of innocent individuals whose names were randomly added to the death lists were also posted around communities in the highlands, as well as in local newspapers. The military and its death squads deliberately used these highly publicized death lists and wanted posters to intensify the growing climate of terror, as most peoples feared their names would randomly appear on the lists at any moment, which was often the case (Garrard-Burnett 2010; Jonas 1991).

Equally blatant but more individually-focused, torture-filled detentions and public displays of tortured bodies became commonplace during the military's "scorched earth" offensive. Torturous detentions were used to extract information from villagers about guerrilla or other community activities considered "subversive" in nature (Amnesty International 1998; Manz 2004). For survivors who survived the torture, the psychological effects were devastating, not only for them but also for their families and the communities to which they returned. Public displays of tortured and murdered victims evoked further fear among local populations (Aguilera Peralta and Beverly 1980; Falla 1994). Afflitto and Jesilow explain,

> Corpses are left in visible, public places for a reason. The more horrific and spectacular the death and subsequent display of annihilated political opponents, it is arithmetically argued, the more pronounced the deterrent effect for opposition activities. The sensationalistic nature of the violence maximizes the terrorist actor's message of apparent omnipotence, invincibility, and surety of victory [2007, 24].

Though the myriad ways in which dumped bodies showed signs of torture are too heinous to detail here, it is important to note that the state-sponsored terroristic tactic of torture and public displays of torture victims added exponentially to the culture of fear mounting in the highlands, especially during and in the wake of *la violencia*. Such horrific displays of violence terrorized survivors, both young and old, in ways that continue to have lasting effects for survivors even today (Green 1999; Montejo 1999; Zur 1998).

As commonplace as torture had become during the armed conflict and genocide, it was not the only means used by the military to destroy bodies and psychologically terrorize unarmed, noncombatant individuals as mentioned previously. For thousands of women and girls in highlands communities, the military reserved a particular form of violence and threat: rape. The military used rape as a warning to their relatives of future disappearances of family members; as an expression of military punishment and domination; as a means of interrogation to solicit information about potential guerrilla supporters; and as a way of generating even greater fear throughout the highlands (Amnesty International 1998; Manz 1988; REMHI 1998). The military also used rape to "destroy the seed" (or children) of supposed guerrilla supporters by literally inseminating women and girls with the "seed" of pacification and forcing their submission to the military-driven state (*Consorcio Actoras de Cambio* 2006; *Museo Comunitario Rabinal Achi* 2003). Many soldiers, either voluntarily or under threat of death, raped women and girls while their commanders commended them for dispersing the military "seed" of subjugation. Victims of rape were often subsequently murdered, and their violated bodies were also left in public spaces to warn and horrify others. Those who did survive faced disastrous consequences such as permanent body mutilation, infectious sexually-transmitted infections, decreased physical health, unwanted pregnancies, spontaneous and intentional abortions, infanticide, decreased future fertility, extreme shame, social stigmatization, excommunication from families and communities, and grave psychological suffering (Consorcio Actoras de Cambio 2006; Museo Comunitario Rabinal Achi 2003; REMHI 1998).

Random bus passenger interrogations and night raids were two more terroristic tactics employed by the military to intensify the culture of fear and further drive home the message that anyone could be detained, violated, and killed at any moment. Civil patrollers and soldiers commonly stopped rural buses, forced passengers to get off, and interrogated them to detain anyone they deemed "suspicious." Many innocent passengers were subsequently arrested and disappeared (CEH 1999; Fischer and Hendrickson 2003). Soldiers and other military collaborators also carried out night raids on villagers' homes to instill fear and kidnap individuals whom they later murdered (CEH 1999; Frank and Wheaton 1984; REMHI 1998). To strengthen the effectiveness of these night raids, curfews were put into place throughout the highlands during the period of *la violencia*, forcing villagers to stay in their homes as soon as night fell. Any movement outside of homes past nightfall was viewed as "subversive" in nature and the "perpetrators" (those who simply left their homes at night to buy medicine, visit relatives, feed their animals, etc.) were commonly murdered and disappeared by soldiers or civil patrollers on the spot (CEH 1999; REMHI 1998).

Terror from the Inside

One of the most horrific terroristic measures that the military used during the internal armed conflict and genocide was the forced participation of highlands villagers in the murders, disappearances, torture, rape, and interrogation of their fellow community members via the civil patrols. The establishment of the government-mandated civil patrols in villages was designed to help the army maintain localized surveillance and control of the highlands populations (Garrard-Burnett 2010; Saavedra 2001; Sanford 2008). Villagers had two choices: patrol the village on behalf of the army or be accused of being a subversive guerrilla supporter and die (CEH 1999b; Thompson 2001; REMHI 1998). Faced with such a decision, most male highlands inhabitants had no choice but to carry out surveillance on their neighbors. Soon community members came to fear neighbors and even some relatives who were perceived as *orejas* (ears), or spies. *Orejas* fed information to patrol leadership who often followed by making false accusations or *denuncias* (denunciations or reports of insurgent participation) to clear their own names from suspicion and to receive payment for information they passed on to the military. *Orejas* also fueled malicious rumors that could be transformed into deadly *denuncias* at any moment (Foxen 2007; Green 1999). The fear that *orejas* were everywhere at all times and could be anyone was yet another internal mechanism that contributed to the pervasive culture of fear (Garrard-Burnett 2010; Manz 1988; Museo Comunitario Rabinal Achi 2003).

Responsibilities of the civil patrollers were not limited solely to surveillance. Some patrollers committed murders of fellow villagers in fear of retaliation by the military. Others used their position to ignite old rivalries with fellow villagers by falsely accusing them of being "subversives" and then delivering them to the military for questioning that ultimately led to their demise. These unpredictable actions of the civil patrol members, who were ultimately fellow villagers, caused increasing ruptures in family and community social relations and contributed significantly to the ubiquitous culture of fear proliferating across the highlands (Green 1999; Thompson 2001). Neighbors feared neighbors, trust in community members was lost, and silence became a desperate tactic used by villagers to avoid serious repercussions from the civil patrols in a place where violent death could occur at any moment (Jonas 2009; Moser and McIlwaine 2001).

Highlands villagers also carried out horrendous acts against their fellow community members via their own obligatory participation in the military as conscripted soldiers. During *la violencia*, the military stepped up its efforts by forcing mostly young Maya Indigenous males into the army. The young men were most often randomly and illegally captured in rural villages, tossed in the back of large military trucks, and taken away to military bases where they were forced (often at gunpoint) into military service (CEH 1999; Davis and Hodson 1983; REMHI 1998). Up to as many as 8,000 young Indigenous men from the rural highlands, some under the age of eighteen as mentioned earlier, were rounded up and forced into the military every year until conscription was abolished in the mid-1990s (Zur 1998, 36). The CEH truth commission report confirms that between 1980 and 1985 alone, the number of conscripted soldiers tripled and, by 1985, the number totaled over 50,000 (1999d, 207). During *la violencia*, these young, mostly Maya Indigenous conscripted soldiers were soon forced to murder, rape, and torture their own people in the name of forced military service. Their service caused even greater divide and distrust throughout the region (Taylor 1998; Zur 1998).

Results of the military strategies carried out during the Guatemalan armed conflict and genocide were horrific on multiple levels. Through the use of

cruel, inhumane, and unimaginable terroristic tactics further forged in the
Phoenix program in Vietnam and taught to military officers at the SOA, the
military used whatever means possible to eradicate Maya Indigenous peoples
and communities in the highlands, to further subjugate survivors, and to cultivate a culture of fear resulting in devastating psychological effects that have
lasted well beyond *la violencia* for survivors. Orphaned child survivors who
participated in my research project experienced these terrorist strategies firsthand and their experiences corroborate just how nefarious and long-lasting
the consequences of those strategies have been.

Firsthand Experiences with the Military's Brutality and Terroristic Strategies

Working as a volunteer in Guatemala in the mid-1990s, I heard many stories
of survivors' experiences with military brutality and terroristic strategies
during the internal armed conflict and especially during *la violencia*. When
I returned to officially conduct ethnographic research, I asked several participants in my research project if they felt like sharing their stories of what
they experienced in early childhood and what caused them to come to live at
the residential home for orphaned children in Santa Teresa. I present the following stories[1] from three of the individuals who participated in my research
project and voluntarily and openly spoke about their experiences on various
occasions, including during formal ethnographic research interviews, at informal gatherings, and in follow-up conversations.

Mario

When asked about his earliest recollections of life before living at a residential home for orphaned children in Santa Teresa, Mario (born in 1978)
described his memories as "static snapshots or scenes." Prior to the first of a
series of fateful days that would change his life forever, Mario only recalls
fragmented scenes of his early childhood in which his parents and siblings
were present. His most vivid memory, however, came at around the age of
two.[2] Mario reflected, "Well one of the scenes that I remember from my childhood as if it occurred yesterday was when I lost my mom. I remember that it
was one evening that we were gathered together—all of the family—in the
kitchen of the house when four armed men arrived and from the doorway,
they asked my mom to leave and to go with them." Mario believes that his
mother most likely knew at that moment that leaving the house to go "speak"
with the soldiers would ultimately mean her demise. Mario shared that his
mother stood her ground. He explained, "They were donning ski masks, were
armed and everything and they told her to leave, and she said 'No!' She didn't

want to leave and so she refused to leave the house." So, the four soldiers forced their way into the house. Mario continued,

> just being two years old, it is hard to remember something so clearly. I [remember] it because it was a pivotal moment that I really do not know if I actually spoke [it] or if I just thought it, but what is certain is that I begged the armed men to not take my mom away, and I remember very well that they responded by saying that I shouldn't worry because she was going to return in just a few minutes.

Mario believes that the soldiers became fed up with his mother's resistance. Mario stated, "One of the armed men snatched me from my mom's arms and [thrust] me into my oldest sister's arms." They then seized his mother by the arms and dragged her barefoot and unarmed out of the house. Mario and his siblings were terrified because they knew at that very moment—based on various recent accounts of similar events happening to neighbors and villagers from other areas—that they likely would never see their mother alive again. Mario can still sense the terrified shock he and his siblings felt as they screamed after the soldiers to please leave their mother alone, to no avail.

Meanwhile, Mario's father, who hid himself in a back corner of the house while the soldiers confronted his wife, made what Mario imagined was an incredibly difficult decision. Mario's father was a religious leader in their tiny hamlet and served as a representative of the hamlet at municipal-level meetings in the primary town center in the region, a four-hour walk from their home. Any type of leadership position in rural highlands communities during *la violencia* commonly led to a death sentence carried out by the military because leaders were often falsely equated with "subversives" capable of carrying out a community rebellion against the military (CEH 1999; REMHI 1998). Mario related,

> My dad left [the house] clandestinely because if the men saw him there, they would take him away too because they were killing all of the leaders of the community and he was a leader. He could get out at that moment because there was no electricity there [in the village]. Everything was dark. Inside, there was only a single candle and outside it was completely dark.

Under the cloak of darkness, Mario's father—who Mario imagined must have been deeply conflicted by the situation—made the difficult decision to quietly slip out a back window and flee from the house while the soldiers kidnapped his wife. Mario's father ran for the mountains that evening, where he hid from the soldiers to stay alive and to keep his children from being left with no parents at all.

Having just witnessed their mother's kidnapping, Mario remembered hud-
dling together with his siblings in their house and sobbing uncontrollably
from the torment they had just experienced. Mario's oldest sibling at the
time was his eighteen-year-old brother, who tried in vain to keep his younger
siblings calm. Mario recalled how the hours ticked away slowly that evening
as he stayed close to his siblings, who were overwhelmed and panic-stricken.
He reflected, "We were crying and waiting for [our mom] to return home and
first my father arrived and since that time, we never knew anything more
about [our mom]." Mario continued, "Yes, [dad] escaped that evening and
didn't return until midnight because he was afraid that [the armed men] were
watching the house and would see him enter." Mario's father had to return
carefully in the dark, not making any sounds or using the front door. Mario
and his siblings were relieved to see their father return, yet they felt the
weight of mourning their mother's likely demise.

For the next two weeks, Mario's oldest brother went about the hamlet and
neighboring villages desperately searching for their mother or at least for
answers to what had happened to her. Unfortunately, no one remembered
seeing her or had heard of her whereabouts. Mario shared, "my oldest brother
did everything possible to find her and she was never found. It was as if the
earth had swallowed her up." Overwhelmed by the sadness of their mother's
disappearance, Mario recalled that the family tried to do what they could to
continue living as a family even though it would be painfully hard to do so
without their mother.

Exactly fifteen days after his mother's disappearance, Mario's father, who
had been so careful to stay home and out of view from any soldiers in the
area, made a much needed trip to sell fruit and vegetables at a market in a
town some distance away from their tiny hamlet. That particular Sunday,
Mario's father set out to sell the produce he had just harvested from their
land such as oranges, limes, avocados, and *jocotes* (a small, sweet, plum-like
fruit common in the area). According to Mario, his father loaded the sacks
of fruit onto his horse in the early hours of the morning just before dawn and
headed out on foot down the mountain path that would take him to the market
several hours away. Mario and his siblings stayed behind, as they typically
did, to care for their animals and home. In the evening, however, Mario's
siblings instantly knew that something was wrong. Mario explained, "[My
dad] always took the horse along to carry all of the fruit that he brought [to
the market] and in the end, only the horse returned because he knew the path
to the house. That day, they had grabbed not only [my dad] but others who
also were traveling on the same path."

Seeing the lone horse, Mario's older siblings frantically looked for their
father. Shortly after they had begun their search, word came from other hamlets that soldiers donning ski masks were seen on the path that day. People

had witnessed firsthand the soldiers abducting people on the path. Mario reflected that he and his siblings were sickened with fear because they just knew at that moment that their father likely had been kidnapped and disappeared because of his leadership position in their tiny hamlet. They realized that day that they would probably never see their father again and would be all alone without parents. Mario's oldest brother was now in charge and had no choice but to try to make it as the head of household for a family of orphaned children.

Tending the crops, caring for the animals, and looking after their youngest siblings, Mario's oldest brother and two older sisters became the primary caregivers for their two younger brothers. Mario's sisters were just twelve and ten years old at the time, but together, they took care of all the household duties and of their two youngest siblings, Mario (age two) and his second brother (age three). Mario shared that the task of carrying on as a family was difficult. It was 1981 and the "scorched earth" offensive was at full force (CEH 1999; REMHI 1998). Just barely one month after their father's disappearance and hoping that the worst of the violence was over, Mario and his siblings would undergo yet another horrifying event that would forever change their lives.

The hamlet where Mario's family resided became one of the hardest hit in the highlands region during the genocide (CEH 1999; REMHI 1998). It was located in a primarily Maya Kaqchikel area that consisted of rich agricultural land. The families who lived in the hamlet had been farming the area for centuries and were able to make a somewhat successful living due to high quality volcanic soil and weather conditions. During *la violencia*, however, the hamlet became an often contentious physical battleground between military and guerilla forces because it was situated near the frontlines of the fighting factions (ibid.). As a result, the military suspected and treated everyone in the area as a potential "subversive," or guerrilla supporter. This assumption was consistently used to justify military-led disappearances and murders of unarmed, noncombatant civilians who wanted nothing to do with either side of the armed conflict. For Mario, the situation came to a devastating head when nearly one month after his father had disappeared, the military descended upon their hamlet and began to massacre its denizens (ibid.).

Amid the panic of the ensuing chaos, Mario's siblings fled from their house and headed to the surrounding mountains to hide along with other villagers. Mario's oldest sister, just twelve years old at the time, grabbed Mario in the scuffle and hurriedly tied him on her back with a *revoso* (traditional shawl often used as a sling), which is a common way that Maya Indigenous women carry infants and toddlers in Guatemala. With Mario secured to her back, his sister made a run for the nearby mountains while her siblings took off in other directions. Mario described the atmosphere as chaotic because the military had opened fire on the fleeing community members. Mario's oldest brother relayed to him much later that in the chaotic mad rush for the mountains, some people were toppled by gunfire, while others scrambled over fallen bodies. Mario recalled, "Yes, all of the people [of the village] were trying to save themselves by fleeing to the mountains. Some were successful, but the majority of them died." Meanwhile, Mario's sister ran as hard as she could in the pandemonium. Mario claimed that he can remember feeling his sister's body suddenly jolt forward several times in rapid succession. She was just twelve years old and was shot multiple times in the back by soldiers, instantly falling to the ground. Mario could not recall the next sequence of events, but miraculously he had not been hit or even grazed by the gunfire even though his sister was carrying him on her back. Mario reflected, "they murdered her with so many bullets and from that moment on I believe that God showed me his love by allowing me to live. In reality, it was a miracle because it just was not possible that she was killed by so many bullets in the back . . . she was running away [from the gunfire] and she was carrying me on her back . . . it is so unexplainable." Mario's survival of this massacre was truly remarkable.

The following few days proved to be an extraordinary series of events for Mario. He had managed to wiggle out of the *revoso* his sister was carrying him in when she had fallen. Just a toddler at the time, he somehow managed to climb up into the hillside without getting shot, toppled, or injured in the massacre. He continued to wander up and off into the mountains for three days all alone and with nothing to eat or drink. Unbeknownst to him, Mario faced potential dehydration, starvation, attacks from area mountain lions, and further persecution by military soldiers. His life truly hung in the balance at that point in his early childhood.

Meanwhile, Mario's brothers and youngest sister made it back to the family home. The military had departed the area a day after the massacre, which allowed most families to return to their homes several days following the attack. Mario and his oldest sister, however, were nowhere to be found. Mario explained, " . . . my brother . . . was searching for me and asking families near the hamlet and around the mountains where my sister was fleeing to [when she was killed]." Mario continued, " . . . according to what they say, I was alone in the mountains for three days, hungry, cold, and exposed to animals and who knows what else. . . . I was lost for three days in the mountains and some men found me when they were going to work [in the fields] and they heard the cry of a baby and that was me." According to his brother, the men who found Mario immediately brought him to their home where one man's wife cleaned Mario up and fed him. The man and his wife decided that they would care for Mario until they could figure out where he belonged. In the meantime, they sent word around to neighbors and relatives that they had found an abandoned child in the mountains. Fortunately, Mario's brother came upon a villager who told of a farmer who had found a lost toddler. Mario's brother rushed to the farmer's home hoping it was Mario. Mario shared that his oldest brother told him years later that he remembers think-ing it would be impossible to find Mario, similar to his attempts at finding his mother, but his perseverance made all the difference. After their reunion, Mario and his oldest brother returned to their family home that same eve-ning, joining their surviving sister and three-year-old brother to salvage what remained of their family.

Mario recalled that for the next three years his older siblings tried their best to maintain their home and to sustain their family. It was a lot of work for all of them. As Mario explained, "we always went to work with our old-est brother, helping in what little way we could. We did not have much time to enjoy our early childhoods because we were always working." It also remained dangerous in the area. Mario reflected, "[We lived] in the house because there was no other place to live during the day and in the evenings, many people fled to the mountains because it was then that [soldiers] would arrive at the house and kidnap or simply kill the people." Indeed, most of the inhabitants of the hamlet spent the daytime in their homes and the evenings camped out in the mountains to stay alive. Other residents left the area alto-gether and went to live in far-reaching villages and towns where *la violencia* was not as intense such as the Pacific coast (CEH 1999; REMHI 1998). But Mario's family did not have relatives in other villages with whom they could stay, and they did not have the money to completely relocate to a new place. With no other options, Mario's siblings simply stayed together and tried their best to maintain the family home and land.

Mario's oldest brother, in particular, did the best he could to keep his sib-lings together, but despite the help of his younger sister, who was just eight years his junior, it was becoming increasingly difficult to find work, tend the crops, maintain the household, and care for his younger siblings. Mario and his second brother were also reaching school age, and Mario's oldest brother had no idea how he would pay for their educations. Concerned about his youngest sibling's future, Mario's oldest brother decided that he would enroll Mario in the permanent residential home for orphaned child survivors in Santa Teresa, which he had heard about through word-of-mouth. Mario shared, "For [my brother] it was very difficult to support all of us and he had heard about the [home for orphaned children] and wanted to enroll both of us, but afterwards he didn't want to leave [Julio] there because to be left without both of us, well [Julio] was older than me and he could help out more than I could." Once he made the final decision, his oldest brother told Mario one morning that the two of them were going to go on a small field trip that very day.

Mario was beside himself with excitement. Except for his three-day wandering in the mountains (which he did not recall), he had never been further away from home than a nearby village. He imagined that getting out of the hamlet to see other areas would be so wonderful and he had a hard time containing his excitement for the trip. He remembered eagerly waiting for his older brother to gather up a few things so that they could head out together. Hand in hand, Mario and his brother walked for some time to the main dirt road that linked the smaller hamlets to the municipal town center. Once on the road, they waited for a passing truck to catch a ride into town. From town, Mario got to ride a local bus for the first time. The bus, with its brightly painted colors on the outside and the loud *ranchera* music blaring within, was an incredible first-time experience for Mario. He recounted, "I was so content to be on a trip with my brother and to see the world around me that I hadn't known before." Mario was overjoyed as the bus packed with people and animals chugged along the winding mountain road, working its way toward the town of Santa Teresa, the next major stop on the bus route.

Juliana

Juliana (born in 1977) has joyful memories of her father that are further reinforced by the stories her older siblings have shared with her about him over the years. Juliana was just three years old when her father was taken away from their family home. The family never saw him again. They also lived in an area of the highlands that was especially persecuted by the military during *la violencia* (CEH 1999; REMHI 1998). Like Mario's father, Juliana's father was considered a leader in their small hamlet because he served as a vocational instructor who taught other community members masonry and agricultural skills necessary for sustaining their families. Juliana, the youngest of seven children, vividly recalled her father providing community instruction. She remembered him working in the fields and taking care of the animals together with his children. Juliana fondly described their family home, noting that "it was a cozy little house with two rooms, and it was in the second room that our [entire] family slept." Juliana characterized her family as close-knit at that time in her early childhood, "We shared everything from working together to playing together. We were very close." Unfortunately, the unity and tranquility found within Juliana's family home would not remain.

Late one evening in 1982 under the cloak of darkness, a group of armed men entered Juliana's family home. She was in the bedroom sleeping with her older siblings when they heard a violent stir in the kitchen. Juliana described, "Yes, I was sleeping and when I awoke, they were already hitting him. . . . The [armed men] went to grab my father from where we were sleeping. One of my brothers went to defend him when they were tying [my father] up and they beat [my brother], wounding him in his foot." Juliana noted that her brother's foot injury kept him from walking for days. Meanwhile, her mother hysterically pleaded for her husband's release. The pleas made no difference as the men continued to beat her father and began to drag him out of the house. Juliana elaborated, "And my dad told [my mom] not to cry because he no longer wanted to continue to struggle [with the men] because he hadn't done anything to anyone." She expressed that her father likely feared that his wife's crying and pleading could have made it appear as if he was guilty. Juliana explained that as the men dragged her father from their home, "they said that [my dad] would return home in five years and up until now, those five years still have not come to pass." Her father simply disappeared. No remains were ever found, and no information whatsoever about what happened to him has ever been revealed.

According to what Juliana's mother told her some years later, when she was old enough to understand the situation, the men who had kidnapped her father were armed members of the civil patrol unit in the area. Juliana and her family members consider themselves direct victims and survivors of the civil patrol's violent power and impunity. Once her father was detained and dragged from their home, Juliana noted,

[The civil patrollers] accused [my dad] of belonging to the group that opposed the soldiers. . . . so, yes, they brought [my dad] to the municipal center [that evening] to face the mayor at the time to be judged and [the mayor] found no evidence or any guilt whatsoever.

Despite no evidence against her father, he was detained in the municipal building rather than lawfully released. According to Juliana, "He spent the night detained in [the municipal building] and the next day, [the civil patrollers] brought him to where the soldiers were living and from that moment on, we never knew anything more of him." That day, Juliana's father became one more among the over 200,000 unarmed, noncombatant victims murdered and disappeared during the internal armed conflict and especially during the heightened and most violent years of *la violencia* (CEH 1999a, 73). His murder was devastating for his family and added to the collective trauma that Maya Indigenous communities in the highlands faced both then and now.

Juliana's family strongly believes that it was her father's position as a community educator and advocate that led to the false accusations against him, ultimately resulting in his death. Juliana shared, "He was working to get electricity in the hamlet. He wanted a hamlet cooperative. He wanted to raise chickens. He wanted to succeed and that's what he fought for. He wanted to be self-sufficient, in other words." Based upon her father's position and more recent evidence that the family has obtained from organizations helping surviving family members find their loved ones' remains, Juliana revealed, "And just a short while ago, we found out that they killed [my dad] solely because of envy."

With her husband kidnapped and disappeared, Juliana's mother was left to pick up the pieces. Unfortunately, civil patrollers had not only detained Juliana's father but had also destroyed the family property. Juliana recalled, "In that moment, we had nothing because they killed all of the animals or took some of them and the harvest, well . . . there had been no harvest later that year [either] because nothing was planted because they burned the house and the fields . . . " Juliana's mother and siblings had to work especially hard that first year after her father's disappearance just to try to survive from one day to the next. Everyone in the family did what they could to find wage-paying work. Juliana elaborated, " . . . I only remember that we had to work so hard with my mom . . . I remember that she did every kind of work possible and not only in the fields." Her mom did not have formal education beyond elementary school, which was typical of Maya Indigenous women of her age at that time. Without little, if any, education, many widowed Maya Indigenous women were relegated to working in agricultural fields, washing laundry by hand for other families, and engaging in other domestic work, all of which required hard work and long hours for very little pay. Having lost their property, animals, crops, and their primary wage-earner (her father), Juliana's family faced extreme poverty extending well beyond the year following her father's kidnapping and disappearance.

For the next four years, Juliana's mother and siblings worked hard to stay together and to try to make it as a family, even though their family would remain forever fragmented because of the disappearance of their father and the subsequent disappearance and presumed murder of her oldest brother as well. By working diligently both at home and at various wage-paying jobs, Juliana's mother was barely able to sustain her family. Recognizing how hard their mother was working, then nine-year-old Juliana and her ten-year-old brother began looking for work or educational alternatives that would allow their mother to work fewer hours and would simultaneously provide an education for her youngest children.

Juliana and her brother heard from a cousin about a potential opportunity for the two of them. Their cousin had been enrolled in the permanent residential home for orphaned children in Santa Teresa after both of his parents were disappeared during *la violencia*. Juliana and her youngest brother also talked to two other local children who had just returned to her small hamlet after staying at the same residential home for a short time. The two children reported that Juliana's cousin was doing quite well there. Juliana and her brother further learned from the other two children that the residential home not only provided food, housing, and clothing but also offered formal and vocational educational opportunities. It was 1987, and both Juliana and her brother hated to see their mother work so hard despite the efforts of all her siblings to help economically sustain the family. With this in mind, Juliana and her brother approached their mother one evening with the idea of enrolling the two of them in the residential home, which was less than a day's travel away from their hamlet.

Juliana confided, "[My mom] didn't want us to go, but we insisted on going." According to Juliana, her mother had worked so hard to keep her family together that letting two of her children go to live in some strange place must have been hard to fathom. Seeing how much her children were beholden to the idea, however, Juliana's mother eventually conceded, and shortly thereafter, the local Catholic priest agreed to transport Juliana, her brother, and mother to the residential home where Juliana's mother would sign over legal custody to the Catholic sisters in charge. Juliana's mother signed the legal forms with the understanding that she could regain custody of her children at any time, which is the general policy at the residential home. However, at this point in Juliana's life, her mother agreed to enroll Juliana and her brother to support their wishes and to help them access education and other vital resources that she simply could not provide them with at the time.

Susana

Susana (born in 1980) was barely a year old when her father was disappeared, and her family faced the grave devastation that had become all too common for families throughout the rural highlands, especially during *la violencia*. When asked about that early period of her life, Susana remarked, "No, no I don't remember anything. The only thing I can recall is that my mom always cried whenever she spoke about what had happened. She always talked about how much it still frightened her because she thought that the [armed men] would come back again." Susana's family underwent a situation similar to that of Mario and Juliana. Her family was asleep one evening when armed men charged into their tiny home looking for her father. According to what Susana's mother has told her, the men were hard to identify. Susana explained, "It was hard to tell. They were men dressed in green, according to what my mom says, but it was nighttime and there was no electrical lighting, so you couldn't distinguish who they were." After the men forced their way into Susana's family home, a few of them quickly worked to detain her father, while the other men threw Susana and her youngest brother (just three years old at the time) under the only bed they had in the home. The men then began beating her two oldest brothers (seven and five years old at the time) who had been standing idly by in the chaos. One man also punched Susana's mother, who was nine months pregnant, in the breast. Susana claims that her mother still deals with incessant breast pain, which she attributes to the beating she took that evening. With her father's hands tied behind his back, the men made their way to the door and dragged him out of their home. Susana related, "Yes, [my dad] was disappeared because we never knew anything more of him. After the night that they [dragged] him away . . . we never knew anything more of him. . . . we never found his body."

Unfortunately, like so many unarmed, noncombatant victims of the genocide, Susana's father—who also had nothing to do with the military or the guerrilla movement and was not a community leader—was kidnapped and presumably killed, his remains never found. Susana's family has no idea why her father was kidnapped and murdered. Susana assumed it was because he was a hard worker and owned land that others may have wanted. With her father disappeared, Susana, her siblings, and mother also had to immediately flee from the house, which was located in a tiny hamlet on the far-reaching outskirts of the town of Santa Teresa. Susana shared, "[T]hey took everything and they burned down the house . . . they took our food—the corn, the beans, the plates we used." With no other place to go, Susana's mother ran with her children to a neighbor's home to seek refuge and to hide. According to what she tells Susana, her mother was afraid the men would return to kill them all, so she had to find somewhere else to hide her children to keep them alive.

Desperate for a place of safety, Susana's mother spent the next few days trying to figure out what to do. Susana's paternal grandfather had died of natural causes some years earlier and her paternal grandmother was too old and too poor to help financially support Susana's family. With no other alternative, Susana's mother asked for help from the Catholic Church in Santa Teresa. Susana's family had been members of the church for some time and with her father gone, her mother had to find help wherever possible. Susana explained, "Yes, we lost everything. Some people from Santa Teresa who belonged to the Catholic Church helped us build a tiny house and the Catholic nuns provided us with clothing, food, etc." Through the assistance of other community members, Susana's family was able to build on the property of a *ladina* woman who had a large parcel of land near the town proper and for whom her father had once worked. The woman lived full-time in Guatemala City but had family ties in the area and held onto a piece of land that she had inherited from her family. Recognizing the immediate need of Susana's family and in appreciation for all that Susana's father had done in taking care of her land, the woman gave Susana's mother permission to construct a small house on her property, which was closer to the town center of Santa Teresa and provided a much more secure location during *la violencia* than in Susana's more isolated natal hamlet. Although Susana's mother had to pay a small fee to build on the woman's land, it was greatly reduced from what others in the area would have charged. Susana's mother was grateful for the offer, especially since her own widowed mother, Susana's maternal grand-mother, was just too poor and lived too far away to offer her assistance.

With a simple tin roof over their heads and some food and clothing secured for her family, Susana's mother set out to find employment. During the day, Susana's mother was forced to leave her two youngest children at home while she went to work in the fields with her two oldest children. Susana reflected, "What was [my mom] going to do? She had few options because our dad was disappeared and there was no other person to earn money for the family." Fortunately, Susana's mother found local farmers who needed help with their crops and could pay her and her young boys a small fee for their labor. Susana explained, "My mom had to work, and they didn't pay her very much [but] that's how she was able to feed us." Susana's mother worked in the local area so that she could return home for lunch to check on her children and feed them. In the evenings, Susana's mother left her two oldest boys in charge of the younger ones and went to perform other domestic chores for local fami-lies (e.g., cleaning, cooking, washing clothes by hand, etc.). Despite the great efforts Susana's mother made, earning enough money to feed and sustain her children was difficult. What made life even more challenging for Susana's mother at the time was that she had given birth to her youngest child just two weeks after her husband's disappearance. She took the baby with her to the fields and to her other various jobs, but the stress of working so much and the distress of losing her husband made Susana's mother lose her appetite. Susana shared, "At six months [of age], my baby brother died of malnutri-tion because of the limited milk my mother could produce. She wasn't eating because of her sadness." Susana's little brother, Armando, was laid to rest and for the next few years, her mother continued to work extremely hard to maintain and provide for her children.

Three years after her husband's disappearance, Susana's mother found a more permanent wage-paying position with the Catholic parish house in the town of Santa Teresa. The same group of Catholic sisters who had generously provided her with food and clothing just a few years earlier had offered her a job as a domestic caregiver for the parish. Her duties included cooking, clean-ing, and washing clothes for the Catholic sisters and the parish priest while they carried out their daily work in the town proper and in the various hamlets and settlements throughout the municipality. *La violencia* had caused much destruction and devastation in areas outside of Santa Teresa, and the Catholic sisters found themselves spending countless and long hours working with people in distant villages, leaving little time to prepare their meals, wash their own clothes, etc. The Catholic sisters also were fully aware of the predica-ment of Susana's family and wanted to help her mother in whatever way pos-sible. Hiring Susana's mother to help out in the parish would benefit everyone involved, and Susana's mother eagerly accepted the position. In addition, the

Catholic sisters were very open to having Susana (four years old at the time) accompany her mother while she worked so that Susana did not have to stay home all alone while her brothers continued to work in area fields.

The new employment position was a perfect fit for Susana's mother. She now had consistent employment and decent pay and could return home in the evenings to care for her children. The Catholic sisters also appreciated the skills and dedication of Susana's mother. After working for them in the parish house for a year, Susana's mother was asked by the Catholic sisters if she would be interested in continuing her work with them as they had decided to open up a permanent residential home for orphaned children that also would be located in the town of Santa Teresa, not far from the Catholic Church. The Catholic sisters were dedicated to finding a way to care for the growing number of orphaned children they encountered in their daily work in the local area and the highlands generally, so they moved quickly to establish an innovative residential program to meet the needs of scores of orphaned children in the region. Susana's mother graciously accepted the position and went to work at the residential home as soon as it opened. According to Susana, "The truth is that when the home started . . . there were only ten children . . . There was just one house, House One. There was no other construction [on the site]." Susana's mother was among the first caregivers, or *tías*, hired by the Catholic sisters to provide daily care for the orphaned children enrolled.

For the next two years, Susana's mother took care of orphaned children daily. Susana recounted, " . . . my mom was working [at the residential home] and I went with her, and we stayed there working—this happened for several years—arriving early at 6 a.m. and returning home late." She also explained that while her mother was working at the residential home during the day, Susana was charged with running home to cook lunch for her brothers and then washing their clothes before returning to the residential home to continue helping her mother. Susana was only five and six years old at the time and clearly recalled cooking beans and making tortillas for her brothers' lunch, a task that required cooking skills she had learned from her mother. Fortunately, just two years after starting her employment, Susana's mother was invited by the Catholic sisters to enroll her own children in the residential home so that they would not have to labor like adults and would have the chance to go to school. Recognizing the increased opportunities that this offer would create for her children's future, Susana's mother gratefully agreed. Accordingly, Susana (age seven at the time), her three older brothers, and her mother all came to live permanently in the residential home in 1986, allowing them to live and share their experiences with other children whose parents were also kidnapped and disappeared during *la violencia* and who faced an equally challenging future as orphaned child survivors of the armed conflict and genocide.

Struggling to Survive

The experiences shared by Mario, Juliana, and Susana further illustrate the brutality of the internal armed conflict and genocide in Guatemala. They reveal how the military explicitly kidnapped and disappeared men as a specific means of destroying families physically, emotionally, and financially, a practice that greatly affected the lives of children living in the highlands. Left without the principal breadwinner of the family, widowed Maya Indigenous women struggled to keep their children alive. Their experiences also reveal how mothers were kidnapped and disappeared as well, leaving many children who survived the violence to struggle on their own. Finally, the experiences of all three orphaned child survivors underscore the deliberate targeting of children in the Guatemalan genocide. In Mario's case, his sister was purposely shot in the back; given that she was carrying her little brother on her back, the bullets were meant to strike and kill him as well. In Susana's experience, two of her brothers were intentionally beaten by the masked men who kidnapped her father, and her pregnant mother was physically attacked, likely with the sole purpose of fatally harming her baby. The trauma Susana's mother endured in the attack and from the loss of her husband directly affected her ability to sufficiently feed her infant son after he was born, which resulted in his death. While Mario, Juliana, and Susana were fortunate to have survived, they were targets of a larger military effort to "destroy the seed," whether directly in the murder of children, or indirectly via killing parents and destroying property to create nearly insurmountable conditions in which children could survive. Unfortunately, the deliberate targeting of children in armed conflicts and genocides was not a new state or military strategy executed only in Guatemala. It has been a long-standing strategy in many armed conflicts and genocides throughout history and around the world.

DELIBERATE TARGETING OF CHILDREN IN OTHER ARMED CONFLICTS AND GENOCIDES

Military leaders and perpetrators of genocide have commonly used the metaphor of children as "nits" (lice eggs) in their rhetoric and justification for deliberately targeting and annihilating children. For example, in 1641 in an overt drive to destroy not only Irish men and women but also children, English Commander Sir Charles Coote justified his abhorrent attacks on children by asserting, "Kill the nits and you will have no lice" (Kiernan 2007a, 606). The same "nits make lice" slogan would reemerge, both in the Australian outback and the western region of the US in the nineteenth century. In 1864, for instance, a former Methodist minister and commander of the Third Colorado

Volunteer Cavalry Regiment, Colonel John Milton Chivington, announced that his intention was to kill all "Indians" he came across, including the most elderly and infirm as well as newborn infants because, as he similarly proclaimed, "Nits make lice" (Rensink 2009, 14). The Nazis also used the "nits" metaphor, likening Jews to lice and using the metaphor to rationalize the brutal extermination of children of all ages (Kiernan 2007a). Such heinous crimes committed against children are incomprehensible, and as Holocaust scholar and survivor Nechama Tec reflects, " . . . are the most shocking and least understood injustices against humanity" (Heberer 2011, xxi). To explore the explicit targeting of children in genocides further, I turn to the following overview of just some of the many unfortunate cases in which children were deliberately targeted either directly via murder or indirectly by creating harsh living environments ultimately and cruelly intended to lead to children's demise. My aim is to illustrate that targeting children in armed conflict and genocide was not unique to Guatemala. Rather, it has been a long-standing global issue that the case of Guatemala further illuminates, calling for greater international attention and action to adress what has happened and to prevent such atrocities in the future.

Native Children in the United States

Native children in what is now considered the US have long been a target of military forces that sought to destroy Native peoples for well over five centuries. Starvation, famines, land removal, forced relocations, epidemics, and state-sanctioned mass killings have been just some of the strategies used to annihilate Native peoples, including children (Chalk and Jonassohn 1990). These strategies nearly were successful, drastically reducing the total Native population in what is now the continental US to a meager total of 237,196 by the time of the 1900 US census (US Bureau of the Census, 1937, 2; Madley 2015, 356).

Similar to Maya Indigenous communities in Guatemala, Native children in the US were not simply "collateral damage" in the campaign to destroy Native peoples and take their lands. During the initial conquest period, for example, English leaders offered forty pounds for a male Native's scalp and twenty pounds for not only a female Native's scalp but also for the scalp of any male Native child under the age of twelve years old (Mato Nunpa 2014, 100). By the late 1800s, the bounty for scalps of Dakota peoples of any age or gender in Minnesota, for example, would rise to $200, which was equivalent to an annual salary at the time (ibid.). The drive for extermination of both Native adults and children is further exemplified in the 1864 massacre of at least 150 mostly unarmed and peaceful Southern Cheyenne and Arapaho peoples at Sand Creek in southeastern Colorado (Green and Scott 2004, 4;

Madley 2015, 142). Among the dead were the most vulnerable: the elderly, women, and children. The notorious Colonel Chivington led the attack and ordered his troops to eradicate Native peoples at Sand Creek under his policy to "kill and scalp all, little and big" (Rensink 2009, 10). Such cold, heinous attacks on Native peoples regardless of age demonstrate the callousness with which colonizers have carried out efforts focused on eliminating Native peoples, including children.

One of the indirect, yet deliberate strategies for eliminating Native children was their forced transfer from their Native families and communities to government-run boarding schools. The experimental off-reservation boarding school program for Native children was founded in 1879 by Colonel Richard Pratt, whose deadly pronouncement to "Kill the Indian, and Save the Man" would have dire repercussions for Native children and families for many decades and generations to come (Pratt 1973, 261). The boarding school program's central aim was forced assimilation that ultimately would eliminate Native peoples by erasing Native identities especially among their children and creating a future socioculturally devoid of any Native peoples and lifeways. If the state could not eliminate Native peoples through death, it would destroy them socially and culturally.

The Carlisle Indian School in Pennsylvania, founded in an unused cavalry barracks, was the first boarding school to open with Colonel Pratt as its first superintendent. The aim of the school was to force replacement of language and culture through full immersion of Native children into the dominating European American society, thereby destroying any vestige of their Native identities (Stout 2012, xii–xiii). Many native families were forced to hand their children over, and those who initially resisted were often intimidated by officials who often withheld rations and annuities until the families relinquished their children to the boarding school program (Child 2012, 123).

At boarding schools, Native children experienced daily physical punishment, forced labor, torture, starvation, and sexual abuse (Child 2012; Stout 2012). A core part of the boarding school experience was the "outing program" created by Colonel Pratt. The program required Native children to spend half the day in the classroom and the remainder of the day performing often grueling manual labor in and around the school, which had detrimental effects on the children's physical and mental well-being (Child 2012, 124). Soon, the environment at the schools would become even more deadly, especially for children whose physical health already had been compromised. Based on per capita funding, boarding schools depended on increased enrollment for additional funding for salaries and school operations. Consequently, schools sought to maximize enrollment and with such high density populations of students living so closely together, epidemic diseases such as trachoma and tuberculosis plagued boarding schools (ibid., 131). Many children died as a result (Stout 2012, xiii). At Carlisle Indian School alone, 186 Native children from 50 Native groups or communities died and were buried on the grounds (Fear-Segal 2010, 157). Those who did survive commonly experienced irreparable ruptures in their families and cultural experiences. In the end, tens of thousands of Native children for nearly a century were essentially incarcerated[3] in such boarding schools. The last one closed in 1972, but devastating social, cultural, and psychological repercussions continue to torment many Native peoples and communities even today (Campbell and Evans-Campbell 2011). As with Native children, the deliberate targeting of children is also evidenced in other early twentieth century genocides such as in what is now Namibia, Africa.

Herero Peoples of South-West Africa (Namibia)

In 1904, Herero peoples in what is Namibia today rose up against German colonization and the grave mistreatment they had experienced at the hands of colonizers. German forces brutally responded to the uprising and within just seven years the population of Herero peoples plummeted from 80,000 to 15,000. While 1,000 Herero peoples successfully fled to British territory, roughly 65,000 perished in the German genocidal attacks (Chalk and Jonassohn 1990, 231). Herero children were as equally targeted by German soldiers as adults and were among the tens of thousands who had been exterminated in a mere seven years. German General Lothar von Troth, who oversaw the squelching of the Herero rebellion, had ordered the Herero people to leave the territory voluntarily or by force. He proclaimed, "I shall not accept any more women and children. I shall drive them back to their people—otherwise I shall order shots to be fired at them" (Chalk and Jonassohn 1990, 243). Likely thousands of children died as a result and girls were regularly raped and then bayoneted to death (Jones 2016, 166). Unfortunately, the genocide carried out against the Herero peoples only foreshadowed the deliberate targeting of children in genocides of the twentieth century yet to come, such as the Armenian genocide.

Armenian Genocide

The Armenian genocide was carried out by the Young Turks during World War I. Between 1915 and 1923, over one million Armenians of all ages were murdered (Jones 2016, 200). Those who were not instantly slaughtered by Turk forces became deportees under an enforced "Temporary Law of Deportation." The law was imposed on hundreds of thousands of Armenians, including children, who were forced to march to supposed "safe havens" in the wastelands of the Deir el-Zor desert in distant Syria (Bloxham 2003,

141). The marches were, in fact, a method of annihilation purposely meant to decimate people along the way as deportees were subjected to exhaustion, exposure, episodic massacres, mass drowning, serial rapes, disease, epidemics, and being burned alive (Dadrian 2003). Such overt acts of brutality were especially devastating for the most vulnerable among the population: the elderly, infirm, and children (Kiernan 2007a). Children and adults who were able to survive the grueling deportation death marches and reach refuge overwhelmingly arrived on the verge of death from starvation, wounds, and exhaustion (Jones 2016).

Child survivors during the marches also faced high risk of being abducted by local villagers or bands of violent convicts along the way. Once abducted, some Armenian children were converted to Islam and raised as "Turks," while others were forced into domestic servitude (Jones 2016). Abducted Armenian boys were most often put into orphanages or military schools (Ekmekcioglu 2013, 529). Survival in the orphanages was perilous at best. In one incident, 500 Armenian orphaned children from Agn, Khapert province, were gathered and poisoned *en masse* by a local pharmacist and physician. In another incident, the police chief of Deir Zor ordered 2,000 Armenian orphaned children be bound by their hands and feet and thrown into the Euphrates River two by two to drown (Armenian Genocide Museum-Institute, AGMI, 2020). Images and information about what was happening in Armenia at the time were published regularly in US and other international newspapers and there was strong public outcry against what was happening (Armenian National Institute, 2020). Yet due to diverted attention to World War I battles and international inaction, atrocities continued for eight years, and global lessons learned from Armenia failed to stop the genocidal horrors that came just sixteen years later in the Holocaust (Adalian 2009).

The Holocaust

The Holocaust is perhaps the most known genocide in history among the general population. Over six million Jewish peoples were systematically murdered by the Nazi regime and among them were as many as 1.5 million children (US Holocaust Memorial Museum, 2020; Jones 2016, 318). Many Jewish children died under Nazi ghettoization where they succumbed to starvation, forced labor, disease, and destitution. The children who survived the grave ghetto conditions were frequently some of the first to be deported to concentration camps (or kill centers) for "liquidation" as Nazi authorities viewed Jewish children as "useless eaters" (Heberer 2011, 68, 108–109). Once at the concentration camps, children had the lowest rate of survival (US Holocaust Memorial Museum, 2020). Jewish infants and toddlers almost always were sent directly to the gas chambers along with their mothers or caregivers. Young children not directly sent to the gas chambers rarely survived the harrowing conditions of the camps. Adolescents had the best chance of survival as they could blend in with the adult population and were less physically vulnerable to the stark camp conditions than younger children, yet many still perished (Heberer 2011, 151).

Some Jewish children did miraculously survive the Holocaust outside of the concentration camps. Between nine and ten thousand children survived because they were safely transported to Great Britain via the *Kindertransport* (children's transport) rescue efforts of public and private organizations between 1938 and 1940 (Heberer 2011, 73). Many thousands of children were also saved because—much like Mr. Holten described in the foreword of this book—they were successfully hidden by non-Jewish families in Nazi-occupied territories during World War II (US Holocaust Memorial Museum, 2020). Despite these valiant efforts, the number of Jewish children killed during the Holocaust is staggering. An estimated 1.6 million Jewish children lived in the areas that fell under Nazi control at the start of World War II in September 1939. With 1.5 million children killed, that meant that only an estimated 100,000 children survived, which is a "kill rate" of ninety-four percent (Heberer 2011, 347). In addition to Jewish children, scholars estimate that Nazi forces and their allies killed between five and ten thousand German children with disabilities who were living in institutions and tens of thousands of Romani children during the war (US Holocaust Memorial Museum, 2020). The Holocaust left a horrific stain on humanity. Global response to the Holocaust was one of horror and disgust, leading to the popular phrase "Never Again" that called for the prevention of such atrocities in the future. Despite the international recognition of the horrors of the Holocaust, however, genocides continued to occur even in the post-World War II era, such as in Cambodia.

Cambodian Genocide

When the Khmer Rouge tried to socially reengineer Cambodian society from 1975 to 1979, it resulted in the murder of nearly two million people who faced firing squads, mass executions, torture, forced labor, and starvation (Chalk and Jonassohn 1990, 402). In just four years, over one-quarter of the total Cambodian population was annihilated, including children (Jones 2016, 402). Under the leadership of Pol Pot, the Khmer Rouge took power in 1975 and declared that same year "Year Zero" (Jones 2016, 400). In their aim to create a classless agrarian utopia, Pol Pot and his Khmer Rouge leaders, under the guise of anti-urbanism, redefined Cambodian society by deporting people from urban centers to the countryside. The deported urbanites were deemed the "new" people, while the peasantry was considered the "base

people." As a result, the Khmer Rouge targeted wealthy bourgeoisie professionals and anyone who was pro-US, anti-Vietnamese, or of Chinese and
Muslim Cham descent as "new people" to be annihilated or forced into labor
camps (Jones 2016, 400). They also targeted children and used the slogan
"chik smav trauv chik teang reus" (to dig up the grass, one must also dig up
the roots) as justification to annihilate children or force them into separate
labor camps (Jones 2016, 406).

The Khmer Rouge considered some children potential clean slates that
could be molded into the reengineered society that Pol Pot and his contingent
envisioned. For them, children no longer were considered to belong to their
parents. Instead, children belonged to Angkar, the Khmer Rouge's "organization" (Mam 2006; Shapiro-Phim 2002). Therefore, many children were
separated from their parents and placed in labor camps where they were fed
one daily bowl of rice water (Kiernan 2007b; Pran 1999). Children were also
expected to behave like adults, working as forced labor in the killing fields,
serving as armed militia, spying on families, and serving as executioners
(ibid., xvii). Kiernan notes that it is difficult to determine the death toll of
children during the Cambodian genocide, but there is no doubt that they were
among the nearly two million murdered and the six million survivors who
witnessed the decimation of their families (ibid., xvi). Clearly the rallying
cry of "Never Again" did little to prevent the atrocities in Cambodia. In just
five years, one-quarter of the national population had been wiped out while
the world looked the other way, despite worldwide knowledge that it was
happening. Today, the Cambodian population continues to grapple with the
social, cultural, and psychological scars from that period and likely will for
generations to come (Jones 2016). Among the population are likely countless
child survivors whose plight only recently has come to light. Their stories and
struggles necessitate further attention and acknowledgment both nationally
and internationally, as do those of Sudanese child survivors.

Sudan's Second Civil War and Genocide

Not long after the genocide ended in Cambodia, Sudan would begin struggling with both civil war and genocide. Sudan's second civil war between the
Arab north and Black Christian and Animist south lasted from 1983 to 2005
and resulted in the death of an estimated two million people (Parkhurst Moss
2008, xvi). One of the most tragic aspects of the war and genocide was the
targeting of young Sudanese boys from the south. These boys were among the
five million people displaced during the war and ranged in age, on average,
from seven to seventeen (US Office of Refugee Resettlement, 2014).

The boys from the south who became deliberate targets of the genocide
were mainly from Dinka and Nuer communities. Sudanese government

forces from the north viewed them as fodder to be used in battle zones or to walk through minefields to detonate mines so they would not kill government forces. The forces worried that these boys would eventually become revolutionary soldiers once they reached adulthood. Under direct threat from military forces, the boys feared they would be forced to serve as combatants or be outright killed. Recognizing their precarious situation, over twenty thousand Sudanese boys fled their homes in the late-1980s and made the long, arduous walk for three months across dangerous desert terrain with no provisions to refugee camps in Ethiopia (Hazard 2017; US Office of Refugee Resettlement, 2014). They faced dehydration, starvation, and attacks by lions and other wild animals along the way and many perished as a result. The group of boys came to be referred to as the "Lost Boys," referencing fictional characters in the story of Peter Pan. For the Lost Boys of Sudan who reached the refugee camps, life was precarious with few resources, and, in 1991, the fall of the Ethiopian government forced them to set out yet again, walking back to Sudan and then onward to a refugee camp in Kenya (US Office of Refugee Resettlement, 2014). By the time they reached the Kakuma refugee camp, only half of the original twenty thousand boys had survived (Hazard 2017).

The conditions faced by the Lost Boys, as well as other Lost Girls, led to the demise of thousands. Those who did survive lived out their remaining childhoods in the instability of refugee camps and, in some cases, the uncertainty of relocation to foreign countries. Much like Guatemalan child survivors, Sudanese child survivors experienced traumatic disruption in their lives during their most formative years of childhood. Also similar to the Guatemalan case, the Sudanese government sought to eliminate them simply because they were viewed as potential future threats against the government even though there was no way of knowing if that would ever actually happen. Sadly, the genocide case in Sudan adds to the growing evidence that children have not simply been "collateral damage" in armed conflicts and genocides. They are unquestionably and unfathomably deliberate targets.

Insurmountable Evidence of Deliberately Targeting Children

The cases presented above regrettably are but some of the many cases of armed conflict and genocide in which evidence of deliberately targeting children is glaringly ample and clear. These children's annihilation was premeditated, planned, and explicitly executed in the same way it was in Guatemala. Such atrocities against children are unfathomable, yet they continue to happen time and again even into the twenty-first century. Prior to the Holocaust, there were few, if any, international human rights instruments or entities established to identify, address, or monitor the egregious targeting of children in armed conflicts and genocides. In 1945 following the Holocaust, the UN was formed. Since that time, the UN has established human rights instruments and collective measures to try to prevent and remove threats to peace and equal rights, such as genocides and crimes against humanity. Yet these instruments have largely failed to protect millions of victims and survivors of armed conflicts and genocides—including children—since World War II (Cole 2015; Gegout 2013). Some of the failure has occurred because the same actors who have committed atrocities and genocides hold veto power within the UN. In addition, actual implementation of human rights instruments and the establishment of related policies have been slow at best. To gain a general understanding of why and how international human rights instruments have failed to protect children, I now turn to a brief overview of specific treaties and conventions that explicitly recognize and address children's rights.

HUMAN RIGHTS TREATIES AND CONVENTIONS AND THEIR FAILURE TO PROTECT

The UN charter was signed on June 26, 1945, and ratified on October 24, 1945, bringing the international organization fully into existence on the heels of World War II and the Holocaust. In 1946, the UN Commission on Human Rights began working on the Universal Declaration of Human Rights (UDHR) to establish fundamental human rights as universally protected for the first time in history (UN 2020a). Within the UDHR, several key articles proclaim to protect the human rights of individuals generally and to children specifically. For example, Articles 2, 3, 5, and 9 focus on the rights to freedom, life, liberty, and security of person, as well as to the right to not be subjected to torture, cruel, inhuman, or degrading punishment or treatment and to arbitrary detention or exile. Article 25 specifies that childhood is entitled to special care and assistance and that all children shall enjoy the same social protection (UN 2020b).

The UDHR was followed by a series of important UN conventions that further delineated human rights and included specific acknowledgment of and protections for children as their own distinctive group. The Convention on the Prevention and Punishment of the Crime of Genocide, ratified by the UN General Assembly in 1948, specifically established the right to protect children in several of its articles. For example, Article II (e) recognizes the forcible transfer of children from one group to another as a form of genocide and, thus, as a direct threat and failure to protect children (UN OHCHR 2020a). Article 10 (3) of the International Covenant on Economic, Social and Cultural Rights (ICESCR), adopted by the UN General Assembly in 1966, acknowledges that special measures of protection and assistance should be taken on behalf of all children and young persons without any discrimination

(UN OHCHR 2020b). The International Covenant on Civil and Political Rights (ICCPR), also adopted by the General Assembly in 1966, addresses the needs of children in Article 24, calling for their right to measures of protection (UN OHCHR 2020c).

The UN treaty that most directly and fully addresses the rights of children as their own distinctive group is the Convention on the Rights of the Child (CRC), which was adopted by the General Assembly in 1989 and entered into force in September of 1990 (UN OHCHR 2020d). The CRC fully views children as individual rights-holders who are entitled to the same human rights and fundamental freedoms as any other human being. As such, these provisions have afforded children increased visibility in political and legal systems both nationally and internationally by officially acknowledging children as a distinct group with their own special entitlements and rights (Liefaard and Sloth-Nielsen, 2017, 1). Among the CRC's 54 comprehensive articles, Articles 38 and 39 specifically address armed conflict and call for the protection and care of children affected by it (UN OHCHR 2020d). To date, there is only one country in the world that has not signed and ratified the CRC: the US (Liefaard and Sloth-Nielsen, 2017, 1).

The UN is not the only international entity to adopt and ratify treaties addressing the rights of children and the need to protect them as a specific group, especially in times of armed conflict and genocide. The Protocol Additional to the Geneva Conventions (Protocol II) was entered into force by the Diplomatic Conference on the Reaffirmation and Development of International Humanitarian Law in December of 1978. The protocol centers on protecting survivors of non-international armed conflicts, and Article 4 (3) explicitly addresses children's right to be provided with the care and aid they require (UN OHCHR 2020f). The American Convention of Human Rights, adopted in Costa Rica by the Organization of American States (OAS) in 1969, also recognizes children as their own group and with the right to protection in Article 19 (OAS 2020). Article 16 of the OAS Additional Protocol to the American Convention on Human Rights in the Area of Economic, Social and Cultural Rights (Protocol of San Salvador) similarly calls for the protection of children from family, society, and the state (OAS 2020). The Additional Protocol was adopted by the OAS in November of 1988.

Despite all these international instruments put into place since 1945, the deliberate targeting of children in armed conflicts and genocides has continued. In the case of Guatemala alone, the state continued to deliberately annihilate and target children even though the government had signed and ratified three of the above mentioned instruments—the ICCPR, CRC, and American Convention of Human Rights—within the very period of the thirty-six-year internal armed conflict and genocide itself. Especially egregious is the fact that the Guatemalan government, having signed the CRC in 1989 and ratified it in 1990, continued to target children for another six years until the 1996 signing of the peace accords. For example, even when I was a volunteer in Santa Teresa from 1994 to 1996, the military continued to round up young men and boys in trucks and forcefully conscript them into the military.

International human rights instruments have been an important step in identifying and proclaiming human rights around the world, but the instruments essentially have no teeth. There is no enforcement arm of the UN. Instead, states that sign and ratify the instruments are expected to respect the obligations presented in the instruments by putting into place their own domestic measures and legislation to provide the principal legal protection to respect, protect, and fulfill human rights (UN OHCHR 2020g). Left to their own efforts, however, many states have operated with impunity for human rights violations and international crimes, which has largely been the norm since the founding of the UN (Van Schaack, 1999). Few leaders who have committed human rights violations have ever been brought to justice in a national court. In the case of Guatemala, even when General Efraín Ríos Montt was actually convicted of in a national court for genocide and crimes against humanity, his conviction was swiftly overturned by the Guatemalan Constitutional Court (Oglesby and Nelson 2016).

In the 1990s, the UN established *ad-hoc* criminal tribunals for the violations of human rights and genocide in Rwanda and former Yugoslavia. It also financially supported the development of the Extraordinary Chambers in the Courts of Cambodia designed to prosecute senior leaders of the Khmer Rouge (Van Schaack, 1999). The challenge for these entities is that they depend on domestic enforcement and civil redress. In response to the limitations of the *ad-hoc* criminal tribunals, the UN Diplomatic Conference of Plenipotentiaries on the Establishment of an International Criminal Court (ICC) took place in Rome in June of 1998 and signed the Rome Statute to establish the ICC, which was ratified in 2002. The ICC acts in circumstances where national legal systems are unable or unwilling to exercise jurisdiction, prosecutes only the most serious crimes of concern to international communities as a whole, and operates within the realm of customary international law (Arsanjani 1999; Gegout 2013).

While the ICC is an important first step toward a legal mechanism for addressing impunity of human rights violations and international crimes, it is hampered with limitations. For example, the ICC cannot prosecute retroactively. It can only investigate crimes that occurred after July 1, 2002, when the Rome Statute came into force. Also, some states have yet to accept its legitimacy and politics can overpower an investigation. Furthermore, the ICC has tended to be selective in its cases, can only deal with two or three cases each year, and has only indicted Africans to date, demonstrating potential bias regarding the countries and individuals that actually undergo prosecution

(Gegout 2013). Powerful countries such as the US, Russia, and China opted not to be parties of the Rome Statute and so cannot be investigated. Finally, the ICC depends on state cooperation and cannot fulfil its mandates without that cooperation. Hindered by these limitations, the ICC has limited scope and currently does not effectively prevent potential or indicted criminals from perpetrating serious crimes in the present or the future, including genocide and crimes against humanity (Clark 2011; Gegout 2013). These crimes continue to occur in our world today and unfortunately, are not likely to abate any time soon.

THE NEED TO UNDERSTAND THE CONSEQUENCES OF THE DELIBERATE TARGETING OF CHILDREN

Children, as their own distinct group, are particularly vulnerable to the brutality of armed conflicts and genocide. Young children, for example, do not have the same physical strength as healthy adults to withstand grave bodily harm and precarious living conditions. There is overwhelming evidence, both in the case of Guatemala and other armed conflicts and genocides around the world, that children were deliberate targets despite their known vulnerability. As my own research and the other cases of genocide presented in this chapter clearly illustrate, children who have fallen victim or survived armed conflicts and genocide were not simply "collateral damage" caught in the cross-fire of battle. They were explicitly targeted because of their age, ethnic identities, and potential future threat (whether real or imagined) as combatants or revolutionaries. The negative consequences of their targeting have been fatal for millions of child victims and life-long for child survivors. Given the masses of children who have been and currently are deliberately targeted, the trauma and long-term consequences that child survivors have endured deserve further examination apart from the experiences of adults. With this in mind, chapter three further explores the trauma and loss experienced by child survivors who participated in my research project.

NOTES

1. I wrote the participant stories in this chapter and the chapters that follow based on different pieces of information participants shared with me on various occasions. As I wrote the stories, I followed up with each participant if further clarification or missing information was needed. The stories are presented in chronological order to give readers a sense of what happened in relation to the historical timeline of Guatemala, specifically during *la violencia*. Therefore, the format and order in which

the information in the stories is presented may not be how participants, themselves, would have presented their own stories. My hope is that one day the political conditions in Guatemala will improve to a level that will allow participants to present their own stories in their own format and order, while keeping them and their families safe from any kind of retaliation from the Guatemalan state and those who carried out the internal armed conflict and genocide.

2. Readers may question whether Mario, at age two, could truly remember this event. Recent work in developmental psychology demonstrates that individuals can remember events that happened when they were as young as two years of age, especially if they are traumatic ones (Jack, MacDonald, Reese, and Hayne 2009). In Mario's case, whether his early childhood memories are solely his own recall or whether they are a combination of his own recollection and his siblings' retelling of the events is irrelevant. This is Mario's story as he told it to me and as he remembers it today. Therefore, I do not call into question the veracity of Mario's earliest childhood memories.

3. I recognize that Native American boarding school experiences were not bad for some individuals. Having worked in various Native communities in the US and with Native colleagues, I have heard various stories of Native family members who had a positive boarding school experience. However, I believe that such experiences were not the case for the vast majority of Native children who were enrolled in boarding schools and both scholarship and data support that position.

Chapter Three

Trauma and Loss

Child survivors in my research project have experienced more hardships, distress, and emotional struggles in their childhoods than most individuals do in a lifetime. Many of them watched in horror as their parents were kidnapped by masked soldiers. Others saw their villages ransacked and community members massacred, while even more were forced to flee their homes and live precariously in the mountains to avoid death or persecution by the military. Some observed their parents' self-destruction via alcohol or suicide and deem it an indirect consequence, but a consequence nonetheless, of the armed conflict and genocide. For those who were too young to recall witnessing such heinous acts, the peril they experienced from the repercussions of losing one or both of their parents may have caused such distress that it, too, exacerbated their experiences of trauma and loss associated with the internal armed conflict and genocide. For all child survivors, regardless of having been witnesses or not, the sense of trauma and loss they experienced from the armed conflict and genocide involved not only the pain of losing their parents and other family members but also of losing their homes, economic resources, and familial and natal community ties, fomenting for many an ever-increasing sense of instability in their young lives.

What child survivors were forced to face as children, both emotionally and physically, is hard to imagine. The life experiences of Mario, Juliana, and Susana presented in chapter two illustrate just some of the horrors that child survivors faced during the armed conflict and genocide. Yet their trauma and loss did not end with the last act of military brutality against their families or communities. They would continue to experience trauma and loss throughout various stages of their childhood because of their orphan status and the heightened difficulties that their status presented as they faced transitioning to different living contexts. This chapter examines their lived experiences but starts with a general overview of the psychological suffering and culture of fear that permeated the highlands region to give a sense of the context in which child survivors and their families were living, especially during *la violencia.* The chapter then turns to the personal experiences with trauma and loss of child survivors who participated in my research project, examining not only the trauma and loss they faced in the aftermath of losing one or both parents but throughout the remainder of their childhoods and even as they transitioned into adulthood.

PSYCHOLOGICAL SUFFERING AND THE CULTURE OF FEAR IN GUATEMALA'S HIGHLANDS

Recorded by health workers and scholars in the immediate aftermath of *la violencia*, survivors' testimonies revealed that they suffered from sadness, anxiety, and helplessness, all conditions they considered a direct result of the terror they experienced during the armed conflict and genocide. Survivors often described feelings of despair manifested in symptoms such as headaches, stomach aches, chest pain, gastric problems, and sleep disturbances, as well as traditional cultural categories of illness such as *tristeza* (sadness) and *susto* (shock) (Falla 1988; Foxen 2007; Green 1999; Zur 1998). Health workers and scholars also note that trauma, paranoia, grief, depression, anxiety, alcohol abuse, and suicide were commonly reported experiences among survivors. Thus, these experiences reveal that the military was ultimately "effective" in their aim to psychologically terrorize the masses in its counterinsurgency campaign, especially during *la violencia* (Davis and Hodson 1983; Manz 1988).

The two primary truth reports also demonstrate that *la violencia*, in particular, has left deep psychological wounds among individuals and families, as well as in Guatemalan society overall. Both reports reveal that survivors continue to experience ongoing conflict- and genocide-related fear and trauma even after the armed conflict and genocide officially ended (CEH 1999; REMHI 1998). For example, survivors often express unsettled, prolonged emotional pain and guilt for not being able to both bury their disappeared loved ones, in accordance with burial customs, and properly mourn their deaths because they do not know where their loved ones' remains are located. Torture survivors speak of experiencing low self-esteem, anxiety, lapses in memory, interrupted sleep, nightmares, mistrust, lethargy, irritability, disorientation, and depression. Testimonies of rape survivors are commonly infused with feelings of shame, guilt, stigma, nervous tension, insecurity, and the decreased will to live. Those forced into the civil patrols or the military speak of intense feelings of guilt, shame, sadness, helplessness, and anxiety because of their forced participation in the killing and terrorizing of their own people (ibid.).

Testimonies presented in the REMHI and CEH truth reports additionally reveal a host of physical symptoms experienced by survivors, including blurred vision, insomnia, gastrointestinal problems, ulcers, chronic headaches, migraines, loss of appetite, and fatigue. Additionally, survivors experience longstanding and continuing mental health problems such as apathy, panic attacks, general anxiety, addiction, uncontrollable rage, isolation, depression, and suicidal ideations (CEH 1999; REMHI 1998). While the data presented in the truth reports is vital, most of it was culled from the experiences and testimonies of adults. Experiences of specific population segments, such as children, often can vary drastically in both form and content. Rather than assuming that Guatemalan child survivors' experiences merely reflect those of adult survivors, it is important to explicitly acknowledge and explore their distinct experiences independently. Such an approach allows a more comprehensive understanding of the extent and magnitude of the consequences of the armed conflict and genocide for child survivors both in the wake of trauma and loss and beyond the signing of the 1996 peace accords as they began to navigate adulthood. To gain a better understanding of those consequences, I now present the particular experiences with trauma and loss of child survivors who participated in my research project.

TRAUMA AND LOSS EXPERIENCED BY CHILD SURVIVORS IN MY RESEARCH PROJECT

At a young age, Mario, Juliana, and Susana faced the traumatic loss of one or both of their parents. Chapter two featured their recounting of how one of their parents had been taken from their house at night by masked men, a common tactic used by the military to kidnap and disappear mostly unarmed, noncombatant Maya Indigenous civilians whom they falsely deemed a threat to the counterinsurgency campaign. These were small children who either witnessed the kidnapping first-hand or learned of it from their siblings and surviving parent after it happened. Unfortunately, such experiences were commonplace for child survivors who participated in my research project. The following details several of their first-hand accounts of witnessing the kidnapping and disappearance of parents.

Trauma and Loss Associated with the Kidnapping and Disappearance of Parents

Sheni (born in 1979) remembers only some of the events that led up to her father's kidnapping and disappearance. She is the second of three children born in a small highlands village during *la violencia*. Her parents were living in their father's family home when the house was raided by masked soldiers, and their father was dragged away. They never saw him again. As her paternal relatives could no longer afford to support them, Sheni's family was forced to find a new place to live. Sheni elected not to go into further detail with me about her father's disappearance or the events that she witnessed as a small child because she wanted to focus on less traumatic events in her life. However, she did share her opinion about the effects *la violencia* has had on child survivors, noting that many of them continue to be traumatized because of what they witnessed in the flesh.

Natalia (born in 1976) also recalled some of the events that led up to the massacre that ocurred in her village in the Ixil region and resulted in her parents' kidnappings and disappearances. Though she does not remember in vivid detail her parents being detained and dragged away, she does remember being transported to a military base in a helicopter. She was kept at the military camp from the ages of four to eight and was cared for by one of the women who cooked for the soldiers at the camp. That same woman, whom Natalia came to call her foster mother, eventually snuck Natalia out of the military camp four years after she had arrived and brought her to live in the residential home in Santa Teresa where she could go to school and live in relative peace. In our interview, Natalia declined to go into greater detail about her early childhood experiences with the *la violencia* partly because we had talked about it many times before and partly because she did not want to revisit those memories, a decision I respected. However, when asked what type of effect *la violencia* has had on her life, Natalia responded that, in addition to trauma and emotional distress, the loss of family and a home has been devastating for her.

Others speak about having been too young to remember specific details about the actual kidnappings and disappearances of their parents, even though they were present at the time. Instead, their early childhood memories are of the consequences that immediately followed for their families. These memories are vivid and equally distressing for them as child survivors.

Debora (born in 1980), for example, never knew her biological mother. She was just ten months old when her mother became one of the many kidnapped and disappeared victims of the armed conflict and genocide. With no memories of her mother, Debora learned from her father later that her mother had been kidnapped and disappeared one evening in early 1981. The family was eating their evening dinner when a small group of armed men came into the house and grabbed her mom. The armed men began to strike members of her family, but her dad managed to get Debora and her two siblings out of the house quickly. The soldiers were attacking villagers all around their small highlands hamlet that evening. In the chaos of the moment, her father (just in his early twenties at the time) was able to make a run for the mountains with his three children, hoping that they could hide from the soldiers there in the darkness of nightfall. He ran with Debora in his arms and dragged her three-year-old sister by the hand. Her seven-year-old brother ran alongside them, but in an instant, he turned around to run back for their mom. Debora's father shared with her some years later that he imagined his son suddenly realized their mother was not with them and went back to the house to get her, ignoring his father's pleading shouts for the child to come back. No remains were ever found of either Debora's mom or brother. Debora acknowledged that Maya Indigenous peoples in the area where her family lived were especially targeted during *la violencia.* She, her older sister, and her father never returned to their tiny hamlet or home. For the next several weeks, they lived clandestinely in the surrounding mountains.

Sofia (born in 1979) was also still an infant when her father was murdered and has no memory of the actual event. According to her mother, Sofia was not quite two years old when a group of masked soldiers stormed her family home after dark one evening late in 1980. The soldiers demanded that Sofia's father accompany them to a nearby military post. Her father knew that going with the men meant his death and so he refused to go. Sofia's parents had heard from neighbors that other villagers had been detained in this same way under the auspices of taking them to the nearby military post, only to be kidnapped and disappeared along the way or at the post itself. No details of their deaths were ever released. Angered by the unwillingness of Sofia's father to cooperate, the soldiers violently dragged him out of the house that freezing cold evening. Sofia's mother quickly followed behind the soldiers with Sofia holding on to her *corte* and her younger infant daughter in her arms. Her mother pleaded with the soldiers to let her husband go because he had done nothing wrong. He simply was a farmer in their tiny village and had no ties to the guerrilla movement whatsoever. The soldiers falsely retorted that her husband was a "communist subversive" and ignored her pleas.

The soldiers began beating Sofia's father once outside the house, throwing him to the ground and threatening to kill him. Her mother screamed and pleaded, telling the soldiers that if they killed her husband, they would have to kill her too. Hearing the scuffle occurring on the patio in front of Sofia's family home, her extended relatives came running to help. A family member scooped up Sofia, prying her hand loose from her mom's *corte*, and grabbed her younger sister out of her mother's arms. Her mother refused to leave, but the family members worked frantically to convince her otherwise, lest she, too, be killed. Sofia's mother finally relented and wept inconsolably as her relatives rushed her and her girls down the hill and away from the home. When they reached the bottom of the hill, a gun shot rang out and echoed across the small valley. Sofia's father was shot point-blank in the back of the head and died instantly. Sofia does not remember anything from that evening, but memories of her mother's suffering following the event are vivid and ever-present. Her father, his brother, two brothers of her mom, and several distant relatives had all been murdered by soldiers during that period of *la violencia.* Without their primary wage earner, Sofia's mom struggled to provide for her daughters. Asking about her experience, Sofia reflected, "I saw other children who had parents and they were content. I didn't have a dad. I didn't have toys. I couldn't spend time with my dad, and that has resulted in a lot of resentment, which has greatly affected me." Both the economic and emotional strain that resulted from the murder of Sofia's father is something that has impacted her entire life experience.

Like Debora and Sofia, Oscar (born in 1978) was too young to remember the actual events that led to his father's kidnapping and disappearance. He was only three years old when his father was dragged from their home one evening by men in uniforms and ski masks. One of six children, Oscar remembered how his family struggled after his father, the primary household wage earner, was kidnapped and disappeared. He recalled some of the days leading up to his father's kidnapping but does not recall the actual kidnapping itself. When his father was kidnapped, his family was forced to abandon their home. His mom and her six children stayed in a make-shift shelter for about two years or so. Oscar always stayed home with his sister and another brother while his mom and three oldest brothers went to work in the fields for area farmers to make what little money they could. He noted that it was extremely difficult to make ends meet during that time and it was often overwhelming for his and his entire family's health and emotional well-being.

Many child survivors in Guatemala have either witnessed their parents' kidnapping first-hand or have experienced the devastating consequences of losing their parents in the immediate aftermath of their kidnappings and disappearances. They frequently speak about how their families were left with nothing—no material goods, no home, and no sense of security. They also talk about the grave impact that the kidnappings and disappearances had on their surviving parent and siblings. In Debora's case, her father soon turned to alcohol to cope with the crushing weight of having lost his wife and son and trying to save the lives of his little girls. For Susana, the pressure of her mother's and older brothers' working hard to maintain her family was distressing not only for her but also for her siblings, who simply had to work to support the family even though they were still small children, which meant they had no opportunity to go to school. Trauma and loss for child survivors who lost parents via kidnappings and disappearances was devastating. It also was devastating for those who lost parents in ways they, themselves, identify as indirectly related to the internal armed conflict and genocide.

Death of Parents Indirectly Related to the Internal Armed Conflict and Genocide

While some child survivors who grew up in the permanent residential home in Santa Teresa witnessed or experienced the deep repercussions of one or both parents having been kidnapped and disappeared during the armed conflict and especially *la violencia*, others lost parents who died because of alcoholism, suicide, or illness. They also view their trauma and loss as a consequence of Guatemala's internal armed conflict and genocide, albeit indirectly.

For example, Esteban (born in 1979) was initially raised in a distant highlands region in Guatemala. Underlying tones of suffering and disappointment infuse Esteban's account of his earliest memories. He can recall his dad playing with him and his mom washing clothes on the days they were sober. Those were the happy times he tries to remember. However, alcoholism for both of his parents tainted the family environment and history. Esteban's father had served in the military in the mid-1970s as a low-ranking foot soldier. Esteban believes that military service had severe negative psychological consequences for his father. He insists that his father developed a certain hatred and anger from serving as a military soldier that made him, as Esteban asserts, a "rashly impulsive person".

After his stint in the military, Esteban's father fell in love with a young woman who lived across the street from his family home. This young woman would become his wife and Esteban's mother. Despite feuds between his parents' families, who did not approve of the relationship, Esteban's parents married and had three children; Esteban is the middle child. Both Esteban's mother and father began to drink more and more *cuxa* (a locally-distilled corn alcohol) as their ongoing family conflict and tensions intensified. Alcoholism had increased exponentially in Esteban's small village, especially during *la violencia*. In fact, both of his maternal grandparents died of alcohol-related cirrhosis of the liver within months of each other. The culture of fear and overwhelming distress in this intensely targeted distant region of the highlands likely played a role in increased alcohol consumption. Esteban's father was also riddled with extreme anxiety, which Esteban thinks is most likely associated with undiagnosed post-traumatic stress disorder from serving in the military during the heightened years of the genocide coupled with jealousy over his wife's business of selling *cuxa* out of their house to local village men.

One day, after telling his wife that he was heading out to plant corn (it was not the right time of year to plant), Esteban's dad headed into their small, rustic family kitchen. Esteban's mother looked perplexingly at Esteban and asked him to follow his father. Just six years old at the time, Esteban did as he was told and watched in puzzlement as his father climbed on top of the brick *pollo* and tied a rope around one of the wooden beams in the ceiling. Esteban was confused, but he knew something was not right and immediately ran to get his mother. She rushed back to the kitchen with Esteban in tow, only to find her husband hanging from the wooden beam. His father was already dead.

Esteban's mother had a hard time coping with her husband's suicide. Esteban remembers his mother living like what he termed "the walking dead." Distraught and traumatized, she drank more intensely and became overwhelmingly oblivious to her children's needs. Esteban explained,

> [My sisters and I] spent so many days and nights hungry because my mom simply forgot to feed us . . . every once in a while our grandma would give us something or maybe some aunts or uncles, but most of the time we were alone and just went hungry for many days.

Experiencing the loss of his father was difficult, but his mother's inability to help her children cope with the loss added even more distress.

Within a year of his father's suicide, Esteban's mother was diagnosed with an unidentified blood condition that caused paralysis in one of her legs. The paralysis spread quickly to her other leg, and soon she was unable to walk. She began taking medication to treat the condition. Esteban recalled, "I remember my mom yelling in agony from the pain. She was in so much pain and I can remember it very well. She knew she was going to die." He was keenly aware of his mother's impending demise at the time despite his young age and the memories of her in pain are vivid for him.

To make matters worse, Esteban's mother could no longer work because of the paralysis. Despite continued medical treatment, her condition did not improve. Esteban's relatives contend that his mother's intense alcoholism interfered with her medical treatment and essentially voided any benefits the treatment would have had for her. Against medical advice, Esteban's mother continued to drink heavily to help cope with the pain she was experiencing and with mourning her husband. Esteban and his older sister now believe that the combination of their mother's drinking and the potent medication that she likely was taking led to the lethal blood poisoning that eventually took her life. Just over a year after his father completed suicide, relatives called Esteban to his mother's bedroom and told him to ask his mother for forgiveness for any wrongs he may have committed because she likely would not live through the night. Esteban clearly remembers his mother's deep cries of agony from her painful condition during the weeks leading up to her death. Her legs hurt so badly that all she could do was cry out in pain. However, she refused to stop drinking because she believed, in Esteban's estimation, that alcohol was the only way to dull the pain both physically and emotionally.

Esteban elaborated on that evening, "I asked my mom to pardon me for anything I ever did wrong in life or any sins, then I hugged and kissed my mom and went off to bed as my relatives told me to do. However, at three o'clock in the morning, I was awakened by my family members who were crying hard because my mom had just died. It was so hard!" He was terrified to hear the crying and wailing in his house because he knew that it meant his mother had died. Sitting alone in the dark, Esteban came to the cruel realization that it was now only just his two sisters and him. He searched for answers to the sudden barrage of questions that swarmed his mind. He shared, "I kept asking myself: How could my mom leave us alone? What were we going to do? Who would care for us? Where would we live? What did mom's death mean for our futures? It was so hard! What were we going to do?"

Esteban explicitly identifies his father as an "indirect victim" of the armed conflict and especially *la violencia* and considers his mother's death as loosely connected but still associated as well. Esteban's parents may not have died directly in kidnappings and disappearances, but the traumatic distress and sense of loss that their indirectly related deaths caused are still significant for him and made his early childhood experiences extremely difficult.

Esteban's older sister Noemi (born in 1973), who also participated in my research project, similarly remembers her childhood before living in the residential home in Santa Teresa as one imbued with trauma and loss. As a child, she felt a bit neglected because of her mother's struggle with alcoholism. She believes she had to mature faster because, as the oldest, she felt compelled to care for her two younger siblings. Once her mother died, Noemi not only took on head of household duties at the age of fourteen, but she also sold some of the *cuxa* they still had on hand in the house and bought vegetables and meat to make the funeral meal for her mother's wake and burial. Additionally, she took several wooden planks from the walls of their house and additional wood from their basic furniture to build a box in which to bury their mother since they did not have the money to buy a coffin. From their mother's death forward, Esteban and his older sister had no idea where they would go or how they, along with their little sister, would survive.

Cris (born in 1981) is another child survivor who lost his father to an illness. The official enrollment records of the residential home in Santa Teresa indicate that Cris was brought there because his father had died of cirrhosis of the liver and his mother had abandoned him sometime later. The Catholic sisters at the residential home think that his father's illness could have been caused by alcoholism and perhaps was related to consequences of the armed conflict and genocide, but no further details were provided by relatives when Cris was enrolled in the residential home. From their work within various highlands communities, however, the Catholic sisters note that alcoholism became all too common, especially during and immediately following *la violencia. The*

Catholic sisters contend that they witnessed numerous adults using alcohol to anesthetize themselves to the pain of losing family members and of suffering from the terror and culture of fear of those times. Consequently, a number of children were sent to live in the residential home because one or both parents died of alcohol poisoning or cirrhosis of the liver. While Cris cannot confirm whether his father's death was directly or indirectly related to the armed conflict and genocide, he does know that his father's death has left him with many unanswered questions. He still does not really know his extended relatives today and was simply too young to remember anything of his father. He shared, "Sometimes I think about it and wonder, 'What was his name?' Maybe he died in the violence . . . nobody will tell me about it." Cris has asked his mother many times about his father, but she never tells him anything. Perhaps it is because she does not want to convey any genocide-related trauma, or there is a deeper secret she is keeping. Regardless, Cris's life has been profoundly difficult without having a father and knowing so little about him. While his father was not directly kidnapped and disappeared during the armed conflict and genocide, Cris's experience of having lost his father during that time was trying for him and his sense of loss was shared by many of his fellow alumni of the residential home in Santa Teresa.

Nidia (born in 1980) lost her mom to an illness during the height of *la violencia* as well. Like Cris, Nidia has no idea whether her mother's illness had any direct connection to the armed conflict and genocide, and her surviving relatives have provided no further clarification. The official records of the residential home reveal that her mother died of a colic attack. Though an actual diagnosis of her mother's fatal illness remains a mystery, Nidia can recall her mother's death. Because she was five years old at the time, she can vividly remember the details and explicitly characterizes her memories of the death as traumatic. After her mother died, Nidia went to live with her grandmother for a time even though her father was still alive. He worked in the fields and in various jobs, making it nearly impossible to simultaneously take care of a little girl of Nidia's age. Her grandmother was extremely poor and everything they had in the house was scarce and carefully-rationed. As noted in previous chapters, the heightened brutality of the armed conflict and genocide at the time exacerbated living conditions and villagers' abilities to earn wages to obtain much-needed goods, adding to the already stressful living conditions of impoverished highlands inhabitants at the time.

Additional participants in my research project were orphaned during or immediately following *la violencia* because they were abandoned by parents for a variety of reasons that may have been directly related to the genocide. For example, Lina (born in 1979) was just a little girl when she was abandoned by both of her parents. According to the Catholic sisters in the residential home, Lina was left at a small highlands hospital, with no further information regarding her family or natal community provided. She became a ward of the state, which transferred custody of her to the residential home where she arrived in 1986. The residential home's enrollment records indicate that she was probably born in a small hamlet in the highlands that was located directly in the path of the most intense "scorched earth" campaign during *la violencia*. The Catholic sisters maintain that her parents most likely were threatened or murdered—she may have been handed over to the hospital by unrelated community members at the time—and that she was brought to the hospital to save her life. Lina has no idea why she was abandoned and still feels the pain of not having parents. She has no memories of her parents whatsoever and still wonders today what happened to them. She only knows that she was left in a hospital and then brought to the residential home where she was raised and cared for during and in the aftermath of *la violencia.*

Miguel (born in 1974) was already thirteen years old when he was enrolled in the residential home. His father had abandoned his family just a year prior to Miguel's enrollment. One of six children, Miguel remembers his father, but does not understand why his father suddenly abandoned him, his five siblings (including an infant sister), and his mother. With their father gone, Miguel's family had no place to go. Their father's family was poor and could no longer support them, especially since they resided in one of the hardest hit regions during *la violencia*. Miguel's mother took all her children with her as she tried to find wage-earning work in the highlands, but it was difficult because she had no formal education or wage-paying work experience. After nearly a year of searching and not being able to meet her children's basic needs, Miguel's mother finally found employment with the residential home in Santa Teresa. Fortunately, she was allowed to bring her youngest four children along with her to live in the residential home. All four were severely malnourished by the time they arrived and were happy to have immediate access to food and clothing. For the youngest, however, the care and resources provided in the residential home came too late. Her malnourishment was just too severe, and she died as a result. Miguel came to the residential home for the wake, and that is when the Catholic sisters saw that he and his older siblings were also severely malnourished. Thus, they were immediately invited to stay and live in the residential home as well.

Child survivors clearly suffered trauma and loss that they associate both directly and indirectly with Guatemala's internal armed conflict and genocide. Some were old enough to remember the traumatic events such as the kidnapping and disappearance, suicide, or illness of their parent. Others simply were too young to recall the event, but clearly recall suffering from the consequences of those losses, which became a vivid memory for many. Unfortunately, these traumatic events were not the end of their emotional distress and suffering. For many orphaned children during *la violencia* and in its immediate aftermath, living situations became precarious, unpredictable, and unstable at best. For most of those who participated in my research project, yet another dramatic shift in family life and living context would lead to even more trauma and loss in their young lives. That shift was transitioning to living in the permanent residential home in Santa Teresa.

Trauma and Loss Related to Transitioning to Living in the Permanent Residential Home

Unlike their peers who mostly grew up with their families in their natal communities such as Santa Teresa, child survivors in my research project were brought to and enrolled in a permanent residential home where most lived for the remainder of their childhoods. Even their peers from Santa Teresa who had lost a parent in the armed conflict and genocide were able to stay in their natal communities or family homes with their surviving family members, including both immediate and extended relatives. Child survivors in my research project, on the other hand, were brought to a strange and initially intimidating place that, for many, was located a great distance from their natal communities. The initial transition to living in the residential home was difficult for most, and the distress of that transition remains vivid in their memories. Only three of twenty participants remember the transition to the residential home as a relatively happy, or non-distressing event, which I detail first. The majority, however, identify the transition as a traumatic one that deepened their sense of loss.

Esteban was ecstatic to arrive at the residential home. After his father's suicide and his mother died of a lethal combination of alcoholism and blood poisoning, he went to live with his paternal grandmother who had agreed to take him in only because he had the potential to become a useful laborer for her when he grew a bit older. She refused to take in his sisters, however, and extended family members were mostly indifferent to their plight. Esteban's oldest sister, Noemi, astutely sent word to an aunt, her godmother, living in the capital, notifying her that she and her little sister had nowhere to live. Their aunt had heard of the residential home in Santa Teresa and made the day-long trip to Esteban's distant natal village to collect the girls and their meager belongings. She then brought the girls to the residential home where she knew they had the best chance of being well taken care of and of getting a good education, something she was not in a financial position to provide them at the time. For Esteban, however, it would be two more years before he would be reunited with his sisters and would see his fate drastically improve.

After his mother's death, Esteban's paternal grandmother, who had agreed to take him in, was unconcerned with his well-being and hardly looked after him at all. Esteban remembers roaming barefoot at the time and going from house to house in the tiny village looking for any food anyone was willing to give him. Sometimes he slept in his grandmother's house in some corner, and other times he would stay with another relative for the night or find some warm spot in the village where he could sleep. He remarked, "I really was a street dog with no shoes."

Esteban had no permanent place to live and call his home, and none of his relatives seemed to care much about him, likely a result of the ongoing family feud between his parents' families. The few articles of heavily-used and soiled clothing he did have were hand-me-downs from cousins who no longer wanted to wear such rags. Esteban did not mind because he had nothing. In his opinion, a ripped, dirty pair of pants was better than nothing at all. He excitedly recalled, "I once got a pair of rubber boots from a cousin who had outgrown them. I was so excited to have a pair of boots. I hadn't had any shoes for a long time. I couldn't believe I actually had a pair of shoes to wear and especially rubber boots!" He remembers wearing those boots until there was absolutely nothing left of them. Meanwhile, Esteban continued to live in the streets until his older sister received word of his situation. Looking back, he believes that his relatives agreed to keep him only so that they could have him work in domestic servitude once he was old enough. Concerned about her little brother, Esteban's older sister spoke with the Catholic sisters at the residential home and pleaded with them to take her to her natal community to find her brother and bring him back to live with them in the residential home. The Catholic sisters agreed, and Esteban's sister, accompanied by staff members of the residential home, made her way back to her natal village and collected her brother. After arriving at the residential home, Esteban remembers his excitement at being with his sisters once again and having received his first pair of his very own new shoes. He also recalls how exciting it was to suddenly have lots of kids to play with and to have his very own bed. For him, the transition to living in the residential home was not a traumatic one, but an immensely positive, life-changing opportunity that he still values today.

Susana, featured in chapter two, also had an easier transition because her own mother was already working in the residential home, and she had been accompanying her mother on a daily basis, helping her with chores there. However, the very first day that Susana arrived to help her mother, she remembers fearing the place. At first, she did not want to speak with the other children. She was too afraid, but by the second day, she began to play with the other children and became familiar with the residential home environment. By the time she and her three older brothers actually came to live in the residential home two years later, she was fully comfortable with the other children and the living environment, making the transition a relatively easy one. Susana reflects that coming to live in the residential home was a beautiful experience, especially since she is the only girl among her siblings in her family, and she wanted to play with other girls, not just her big brothers. For her, the residential home allowed her to have new companions and to be around what she identifies as "good people."

Carlos (born in 1979) provides yet a third and final example of a child survivor whose transition to living at the residential home was fairly positive. After his father died of an unknown illness, Carlos and his mother were left with no home, money, or belongings, and lived precariously on the streets. Recognizing that her son deserved to live in a healthy environment where he could go to school and have his basic needs met, his mother enrolled him in the residential home. Carlos recalled that it had been difficult living in the streets even though it meant he could be with his mom. Arriving at the residential home seemed like a whole different world. The transition was not all sad and, in fact, he was happy to have other children to play with, let alone having access to food, clothing, stable housing, and education.

Though Esteban, Susana, and Carlos mostly experienced a happy, or at least not a traumatic, transition to living in the residential home, the overwhelming majority of child survivors in my research project found the transition extremely distressing. Most reported having had a crushingly difficult time adjusting not only on the first day that they arrived but also in the days and months that followed. Mario, for example, described the transition as an extremely sad one. On the day he arrived, he was excited to be traveling on a colorful bus with his brother. He had no idea of what was about to happen. Mario and his brother got off the bus in a strange town where its residents spoke Kaqchikel, but it had a different sound than the Kaqchikel that Mario had learned in his small natal hamlet. Mario remembers first soaking in all that he saw as he headed off with his brother to some unknown destination. He was certain the purpose of their visit would be something marvelous, intriguing, or fun as the day had proven to be so far. He was a bit stumped, however, when his brother led him into a small compound of houses in the town where a large group of children was playing. Mario's brother asked him to wait in the courtyard because he had to speak with someone. Mario nervously watched the other children as they laughed and played. He was just too shy to join in.

Mario's brother returned after a short while and explained to him that he would now be living in this new place where he could go to school and have a better quality of life. Mario recalls becoming instantly confused. This was supposed to be a fun field trip with his brother. Why was his brother leaving him? What had he done wrong? Mario had so many questions and no answers. He became deeply sad and morose. Mario vividly remembers his brother leaving the residential home and disappearing as he walked into the distance. Mario only spoke Kaqchikel and could hear a strange language, Spanish, in this new place. He felt so alone and abandoned by his big brother, who had become like a father to him. Those first few days in the residential home were especially devastating for five-year-old Mario. He was given the nickname *pollo triste* (sad chicken) in the residential home because he cried constantly the first few weeks. He was just too sad and shy to make friends easily. Other children had arrived around the same time and seemed to make friends within days. For Mario, it took much longer because he was so grief-stricken and did not have the courage or strength to break out of his shell, make friends, and learn Spanish. In fact, it took him nearly a year to eventually make friends. Fortunately, one friend became Mario's defender. He was a little older and came from a similar situation as Mario. He stood up for Mario if other kids tried to pick on him. With his friend's help, Mario eventually established friendships with most of the other children and became more involved in the daily life and sense of community in the residential home, but that transition was traumatic and devastatingly slow.

Debora was an infant when her father brought her to live with her grandmother while he and his oldest daughter, who was just three years old at the time, continued to live clandestinely in the mountains. Debora was just too small to survive the precarious living conditions in the mountains and without milk. For the next three years, Debora lived with her grandmother and other extended family members. Debora's father never came to visit her for fear that military soldiers would look for him there and then would kidnap and disappear him, leaving his little girls with no parents at all.

When Debora was four years old, however, her father received word that she was being abused at his mother's home. Debora does not know how her father found out about the physical abuse of his youngest child, which was perpetrated by an uncle. Fortunately, her memory of that abuse is foggy. However, the notification that she was being physically abused must have been unbearable for her father because he furiously returned to his mother's home despite the constant military presence in the area. He collected Debora to live with him in the mountains even though it meant living in rough conditions. For the next year, Debora and her sister lived day to day, uncertain from where the next meal or form of shelter would come. Some of Debora's earliest childhood memories consist of times they spent together in the mountains, which she remembers fondly. While she has warm memories of mealtimes with her father, she recalls that their time in the mountains also marked a turning point for him. Her dad was plagued with extreme despair because of everything that had happened, and he started drinking heavily. She noted, "My father drank because he felt so alone, and he missed my mother so much."

Debora's father eventually moved with his two daughters to the outskirts of a larger village to have what Debora presumes was increased access to alcohol. The larger village was also a main military target area during *la violencia*, but her father moved them to the village outskirts, nonetheless. After settling in this new location, she and her older sister tried to keep themselves occupied while their father heavily drank day and night. Debora remembers wandering the streets with her sister. She believes that people in the town saw the two little girls and became concerned about their welfare. She remembers that some Catholic nuns came to them and invited them to participate in a daycare program free of charge. Both girls agreed and spent the next couple of months attending the daycare during the weekdays, receiving daily meals, some clothing, and occasional preschool-type education. In the evenings, however, they would try to find their father, often ending up alone. Debora shared, "We slept in the street and people saw us and gathered us up. We slept in some [random] house and in the day, they would bring us to the daycare. In the evening, we would return to the street again, but the [villagers] would not leave us to sleep in the street."

Debora's father continued to drink more and more. Concerned about the girls' well-being, the Catholic nuns running the daycare decided to ask Debora's father for permission to send the girls to live in the residential home in Santa Teresa some distance away. Her father was reluctant at first; however, he knew it was in the best interest of his daughters since he was unable to provide them with a stable living environment. The next day, the girls and their father got into a large truck that happened to be going in the direction of the residential home. Debora remembers the day they got in the truck, but at the time, she had no idea what was about to happen.

Arriving at the residential home, Debora remembered seeing the other children for the first time. Her dad left her and her sister to play with the other children while he went to speak with the Catholic sisters in charge of the residential home, but the girls were just too timid to join the other children. Debora and her sister stayed huddled together watching the others while they waited for their dad to return. Fortunately, Debora did not fear the Catholic sisters she saw when arriving at the residential home—she had become familiar and comfortable with religious nuns at the daycare—but she was anxious around the new children. After what seemed a long time for Debora, her father returned and explained that she and her sister would now be living in this "home" for orphaned children. She vividly recalls watching her father leave the residential home grounds and the Catholic sisters closing the gates to the property behind him, enclosing her and her sister inside. Debora explained, "Oh! It was so sad! They locked us in so that we wouldn't run after our father. . . . He came to see us to say goodbye and we wanted to go with him. And they locked us in so that we wouldn't follow him." When asked to describe her first memories of the residential home from that day forward, Debora indicated that it was difficult from the very beginning, especially if a child is shy. She felt there was nothing she could do but cry even though the other children tried to console her. She was so sad to no longer be with her father. She elaborated, "It was so difficult for me because despite his drinking, I loved him very much." Debora imagines that the transition was even harder for her older sister who had lived for a much longer period of time in the mountains with their father following the kidnappings and disappearances of their mother and brother. Debora was fortunate that she was enrolled in the residential home with her sister, but the transition was still difficult for both of them.

For Juliana and her brother Juan, the possibility of living in the residential home was something they first approached their mother about after hearing that a cousin had already been enrolled there. As mentioned in chapter two, Juliana and her brother were saddened to see their mother work so hard and thought that being enrolled in the residential home would relieve some economic pressure. Though their mother did not like the idea at first, she eventually relented.

Juliana remembers her excitement the day they travelled to the town where the residential home is located. She arrived feeling happy. She was excited about the new opportunities the residential home would afford her and her brother and was especially thrilled that her mother could now work much less. Juliana's excitement turned to instant fear and sorrow, however, when she arrived at the residential home and the reality of the permanency of the move set in. She immediately wanted to return home with her mother and give up the idea of living in the residential home. However, her mom is, as Juliana describes, "a very just woman" and had already signed the legal documents, making it now more difficult but not impossible for Juliana to return home with her. Juliana suddenly became petrified of her new situation. To make matters worse, she had to contend with the issue of language. Most of the children in the residential home and in the local community spoke Spanish as a common language, but Juliana could not speak Spanish. She was also apprehensive about the presence of soldiers who had marched through the town various times in the first few days that she was living in the residential home.

Over a short period of time, however, Juliana found herself adjusting to daily life in the residential home. In fact, she adapted relatively quickly to life there and within a month, could speak a bit of Spanish and understood it fairly well. She also made new friends rather rapidly with the other girls. She recalls them bubbling with excitement that there was a new girl to play with when she arrived. Juliana saw the girls from the town as equally friendly and accommodating. She related, "They treated me well . . . they said to me, 'Oh, how cute! She doesn't speak Spanish.' And they taught me [Spanish], really, the girls from the town. I love them so much." Juliana's newfound friendships were especially helpful in her transition to living in the residential home even though she characterizes the initial transition as traumatic and distressing.

Many other child survivors' reflections on their initial arrival and subsequent weeks of adjustment to life in the residential home reveal similar trauma and distress. For Oscar, he described the day he arrived at the residential home as the saddest day of his life. He was among some of the first children to be enrolled in the residential home, and he never forgets those first few days and weeks. Oscar did not want to stay there even though he was with his three siblings. He recalls being so miserable that he did not want to eat for several days. For Nidia, the first night in the residential home was especially difficult. She had always slept with her grandmother and when she arrived, she felt completely alone, which was exacerbated by the fact that in the resedential home she suddenly had her own bed in which to sleep. Nidia shared that she felt so uncomfortable and scared as a result. Cris, too, found the residential home a strange place on the day he arrived. He had never left his own family home or traveled anywhere before arriving there. The town also seemed so strange to him. He remembers the oddity of it all, which made the transition so distressing, especially since the residential home and town were so far from his family. Lina similarly found the transition incredibly difficult. She had been abruptly abandoned by her parents, becoming a ward of the state. She was then transferred to the residential home where she did not know anyone. She already felt disconnected and unmoored, and the initial transition to the residential home only intensified those feelings.

Most child survivors say today that they understand why they were enrolled in the residential home. They recognize that surviving family members simply did not have the economic resources at the time to be able to raise them once one or both of their parents had been kidnapped and disappeared, murdered, died, or had abandoned them. However, the drastic shift to new living circumstances as orphaned children was already difficult for most and the transition to a residential home itself added yet another distressing dimension to their experiences with trauma and loss. Even after they had adjusted to their new living conditions in the residential home, the armed conflict and genocide persisted in the highlands following *la violencia* and continually threatened their emotional and psychological well-being. Waves of military confrontations and attacks in the highlands were commonplace, especially in the first few years following the residential home's founding. The Catholic sisters, *tías*, staff, and volunteers, despite their best efforts, could not offer enrolled child survivors complete solace from the terror and threat of the armed conflict and genocide that continued to envelop the region, making the adjustment to living in the residential home a challenge and another distressing experience for child survivors.

Adjusting to Residential Home Life amid the Ongoing Internal Armed Conflict and Genocide

Most child survivors who enrolled in the permanent residential home within the first four years of its founding (1985 to 1988) originated from some of the most devastated areas of the highlands during *la violencia.* Coming to live in the town where the residential home was located, however, did not necessarily equate to living in complete absence of violence or fear-inducing threats, although it was relatively calmer than most of their natal communities. The penetrating culture of fear continued to permeate both the community and the residential home itself, especially since the majority of *tías* and staff members were women widowed in the armed conflict and genocide when their unarmed, noncombatant civilian husbands were kidnapped and disappeared.

Even though Santa Teresa was not a regular hotbed of combat or counterinsurgency activities, a long single line of soldiers frequently filed through the town to tout the military's omnipresence and to intimidate townspeople. When foot soldiers were not considered intimidating enough, the military drove a tank or two down the small main road leading through the center of town during the middle of the night. Such events occurred throughout the remainder of the armed conflict and genocide. Even when I was a volunteer in the residential home, just two years prior to the signing of the 1996 peace accords, such overt military intimidation persisted. On at least two different occasions during my volunteer term, tanks loudly rumbled through the town in the middle of the night, while guerrilla forces supposedly blew up telecommunication towers in the neighboring town just five kilometers away. It is uncertain if that was truly the case or just more military propaganda since there were never any official reports or news reporting on those purported events.

In one particular incident in 1995, the residential home director received word from fellow community members that the military had threatened to enter the town that evening to "weed out" any guerrilla forces sabotaging the regional telecommunication towers. Even though local residents had not seen or heard any guerrilla forces anywhere near the town of Santa Teresa at that time and the towers were located some distance away, the military persisted with its threat to enter and occupy Santa Teresa. Within minutes of receiving word of the impending military presence and intimidation, the residential home director immediately mobilized the Catholic sisters, *tías*, staff, and volunteers to evacuate four of the small houses in the complex. Within fifteen minutes of receiving notification, we had all fifty-three children who lived on the west side of the complex evacuated and camped out in two of the classrooms located in the main concrete building on the east side of the complex, which was better protected from outside threat due to its concrete construction and lockable gates. For a 36-hour period, the residential home was in complete lock-down and we (Catholic sisters, *tías*, staff, and volunteers) stayed with the children in the classrooms, comforting them, while also watching over the children who remained in the protection of the small grouping of houses located on the east side of the complex. The Catholic sisters kept vigil outside of the main building, but behind locked gates, to watch for any impending threat of attack. Fortunately, the military never entered Santa Teresa that evening or the next day, and a day and a half later, the children returned to the west side houses and resumed their regular schedules, including going to the local elementary and junior high schools. However, the event was extremely distressing for the children, and it was a poignant reminder of just how invasive the military's terror-inducing tactics and resulting culture of fear could be even years after the heightened period of *la violencia* had ended. While the residential home did offer at least some semblance of safety, structure, and consistency for child survivors over time as they grew into adolescents and in events such as that described above, it could not spare them from yet another often traumatic transition: the transition to adulthood alone and without a safety net.

Transitioning to Adulthood Alone and Without a Safety Net

With over one hundred orphaned children enrolled in the permanent residential home by the mid-1990s, it was impossible for the Catholic sisters to continue financially supporting the children once they turned 18 and were no longer in the legal custody of the residential home because of their adult status. Consequently, all child survivors left the residential home with nothing more than their formal education, vocational training received in the residential home, and a few personal belongings (e.g., clothing, books, school supplies, etc.). They had to head out on their own to establish themselves independently as adults without any kind of economic, familial, or emotional safety net. The process of leaving the residential home was particularly onerous and often a traumatic one for child survivors because of the loss of one or both of their parents and the destruction of familial property during the armed conflict, and especially *la violencia.* Those losses presented child survivors with several long-term economic constraints that their non-orphaned peers did not face.

First, most child survivors literally had no home to return to and had to find their own form of housing upon leaving the residential home. Nearly all had no inheritance rights or access to familial land, which would have at least provided them with valuable property on which to build a home or with a tangible asset that they could have sold to help support themselves financially in early adulthood. Lacking surviving family members' financial support also burdened their transition to adulthood. Surviving family members, who had been too poor to support them economically in their childhoods, mostly remained poor in the years following *la violencia* and were not in a position to provide economic support for child survivors once they left the residential home. With no other source of economic support, child survivors had to search frantically for gainful employment after leaving the residential home to support themselves against a backdrop of increasing poverty, under-employment, and the rapidly rising cost of living in Guatemala during the late 1990s and early 2000s (Stern 2005; Tierney 1997; Woodward 2008).

Most also lost ties to their natal communities, meaning they were bereft of access to the economic support commonly found between natal community members. Natal communities in the highlands of Guatemala often have functioned not only as a locus of connection to a particular physical place but also as a tie to an extensive social network consisting of extended kin (e.g., grandparents, aunts, uncles, first cousins, etc.), distant relatives (e.g., third, fourth and fifth cousins, etc.), and other community members who often serve as fictive kin (such as godparents). This important social network allows individual community members to attain various forms of emotional, moral, and economic support when needed. For example, in natal communities individuals often seek economic assistance from other members through activities such as planting fields, harvesting crops, building homes, providing food for events, and offering to help with childcare. Individuals within the community also benefit from having connections with fellow community members who may know about and have influence in accessing economic opportunities such as employment positions, bargains on products, inexpensive forms of transportation, and access to land. It is also common in such communities for members to offer economic assistance in the form of free housing, employment, harvest surpluses, or personal cash loans to individual community members who are struggling financially to make ends meet (Adams and Hawkins 2007; Eber 2000; Zur 1998).

Child survivors who participated in my research project lost their important connections to natal communities, depriving them of an important social network to access once they left the residential home and were on their own. This is not to say that they did not feel like they were part of community life in Santa Teresa during their enrollment in the residential home. However, participation in community life in Santa Teresa was considered secondary because community members did not view children of the residential home as having primary kinship ties to the community in the way that individuals born into or who moved to Santa Teresa as a family did. This lack of critical kinship and community ties added yet another layer of economic loss and challenge to child survivors' already arduous transition into early adulthood, which is demonstrated in their reported experiences.

After Mario turned eighteen and completed his junior high school program, the time had come to focus on furthering his education by selecting a career-specific high school program, which was a typical educational progression in Guatemala. Most high school programs in the country were career-focused, and all were private schools, which meant that high school education was costly. During his teenage years in the residential home, Mario became enthusiastically involved in music, singing in the residential home choir and developing a close mentorship with the choir director, a young man from a neighboring town who showed a lot of passion for music and teaching. Mario was mesmerized by the choir director's efforts early on and asked if he would give him acoustic guitar and piano lessons. Through hard work and dedication, Mario learned both instruments quickly and soon played them for the residential home choir during weekly Sunday mass at the Catholic Church in Santa Teresa. Having developed a profound love for music, his selection of a high school career path was clear to him.

Mario wanted to study music formally like his mentor and began investigating music programs; however, he found that only two national high school programs for music existed: one in Guatemala City and the other in the city of Quetzaltenango, which is located on the western edge of the highlands, a multi-hour bus ride from Santa Teresa. When it came to selecting which program to apply for, he was far more restricted by financial concerns than the actual program curriculum itself because he had no source of financial assistance. Fortunately, an Irish volunteer in the residential home at the time personally agreed to raise money from family and friends in Ireland to support Mario's high school education. With a "scholarship" secured, the next concern was figuring out where Mario could live while attending music school. He could not return to his natal community to live with his oldest brother and family because it was even farther away from the schools than Santa Teresa, making the daily commute nearly impossible.

After some thought, the Irish volunteer asked Mario's carpentry teacher if there would be any way that Mario could live with the teacher's older sister who had a house in Guatemala City. The volunteer assured the teacher that Mario's scholarship would pay for room and board at the house. The carpentry teacher, who was close to and supportive of Mario, spoke with his sister, who already knew Mario because she had worked for a short time in the residential home as well. She instantly agreed to have Mario live with her.

With a scholarship in hand and a safe place to live, Mario made the big move to the capital to embark on his musical career. He wanted to make something of his life and was content with his decision to begin the music program in Guatemala City. The program specifically trained students in musical instruction so that they could teach music at elementary and junior high school levels anywhere in the country. Mario knew that he wanted to become a music teacher just like his mentor. Moving to the capital, however, was a scary prospect for him, especially since he had grown up in small, rural Santa Teresa where there had been one single telephone and few vehicles during his childhood. He shared, "I tell you that it was very difficult because I was not used to it—it was a way of life totally different. I had to travel every day by bus to study, but afterwards, I got used to it. Thank God I have always been very independent, and I think that helped me a lot." He was also fortunate to have been able to move into a caring family home that provided him with a safe and supportive environment. Even though he already knew the carpentry teacher's sister somewhat before he moved into her home, living with her and her family strengthened their relationship, and they became a real family for him.

Unlike Mario and starting at around the age of fifteen, Esteban's transition was much more difficult. At the time, his behavior changed drastically (something that I witnessed first-hand while living in the residential home as a volunteer). He related, "I don't remember exactly an event or something happening in particular that caused me to change my attitude, but I started making rough and bad decisions." One of those decisions involved sneaking alcohol into the residential home grounds and secretly drinking with a few buddies who were also enrolled there. Additionally, Esteban became increasingly sarcastic with *tías* and staff, who expressed their frustration with not being able to control his behavior or effectively discipline him. He explained, "Internally, I was suffering a lot, and I even thought about committing suicide like my dad did to end all of my pain." Esteban's grades in junior high began to bottom out. He was not doing his homework and often skipped school altogether.

During one particular episode, Esteban snuck out of the residential home and went to hang out at a friend's house in a neighboring town for the night. The Catholic sisters were panic-stricken when they could not find him. The country was still in the midst of the armed conflict during this time even though the intense period of *la violencia* had subsided. Unidentified troops still roamed the countryside at night, randomly killing people whom they encountered and whom they often falsely claimed were "communist subversives." The Catholic sisters immediately began a frantic all-night search for Esteban. He was gone for hours and when the Catholic sisters finally found him in the morning at his friend's home, they simply scolded him and advised him on how what he did was not acceptable. At their wit's end, however, the Catholic sisters reached a consensus the next day and decided to contact his extended family members in his natal village with whom he had no contact since arriving at the residential home ten years prior.

Because of Esteban's growing rebelliousness and their inability to work effectively with him, the Catholic sisters made the difficult and atypical decision to transfer his legal custody over to his paternal uncles, even though he had no contact or relationship with them. Having turned eighteen a few years earlier, Esteban's older sister had already left the residential home and was living in Guatemala City where she was working as a secretary, but the Catholic sisters did not feel that she was yet mature or financially stable enough to legally support Esteban at the time. Legally releasing Esteban, who was still a minor, to his extended biological family members and to his uncles, in particular, seemed like the only realistic option. Therefore, the residential home social worker accompanied Esteban on a long rural bus ride back to his natal community the next day and officially transferred custody over to his uncles via legal documentation. He was seventeen years old at the time and was essentially kicked out of the residential home, the only real and stable home he had ever known for the majority of his childhood. He had a few marketable job skills but lacked a future direction, having only finished the second of three years of junior high school. He reflected, "I thought my life had already ended. I had not even one idea of what I was going to do. I didn't really know my uncles or my relatives. I didn't want to go back to my village. It just made me feel worse inside . . . so lost."

At the time that he was expelled and sent back to live with his extended relatives, Esteban had not lived in his natal community or with his extended family members for most of his life. Much had changed since he left with his sister years prior. For the next six months, he lived with his paternal uncles. He explained, "It was the most difficult time for me because I did not know what to do out there [in the world]. I did not know how to make a living despite having learned sewing/tailoring skills in the home." Realizing his fate and the gravity of the situation caused by his rebellious behavior, Esteban felt the weight of a life that was going nowhere. For those initial six months, he stayed with his uncles, who treated him like a stranger and domestic servant. He could not find gainful employment to support himself. With no other real options, he contacted his older sister in Guatemala City. Once again concerned with her brother's life direction, Esteban's older sister arranged for him to move to Guatemala City to live with some new friends who owned a store. He would not only live next to the store but also would work with the family at their store as well. Esteban, in utter desperation, decided to take that opportunity and dedicate himself to making something of his life. With arrangements confirmed, he packed his small bag with the few belongings he had, boarded a rural bus, and headed to the capital, uncertain of his future.

Unlike many of her companions in the residential home, Juliana was fortunate to have been able to maintain a close relationship with her mother throughout her time there. Her mother lived less than a day's travel away from Santa Teresa and was able to visit her two youngest children nearly once a month or even more frequently, depending on her work responsibilities and financial situation. Juliana recalled, "I don't judge my mother because she came [to visit] whenever she could, when she had the money for bus fare, whenever she had bits of change [saved up], she came to see me." The ongoing visits from her mother helped sustain Juliana's familial connections, as did her relationship with her brother who remained in the residential home until he turned eighteen. When he became a legal adult, he returned home to help support his family financially by working and sharing his earnings with his mom and siblings.

Juliana remained in the residential home for another year after her brother left, completing the third and final year of junior high school in the neighboring town. She was a promising student and had hoped to continue her education through high school, at the very least, if not all the way to the university level. She had dreams of attaining a college education. However, in her final year of junior high, just as the academic year was ending, Juliana's life would change drastically. She had been informally dating (something the Catholic sisters did not know about or permit) and found out that she was pregnant. Terrified, she went to tell the Catholic sisters, who were still her legal guardians. They were extremely upset, especially since they had taken such great measures and care to keep the children enrolled in the residential home safe. The home's policies, for example, dictated that all *tías* and staff members lock the property gates every night at 6:00 p.m. and during the day whenever there was a perceived threat (e.g., soldiers entering the area, reported thieves in the town, sightings of potential gang members, people with false legal documents trying to take one of the children, etc.). Therefore, Juliana's pregnancy was a shock for everyone because we were all trained to keep the children safe on the grounds and no one was allowed to leave the area unsupervised in the evenings. It became an even greater shock when Juliana revealed that the father of the baby was a fellow child survivor enrolled in the residential home, Miguel, who was also about to begin his high school career training.

Both Juliana's and Miguel's mothers were summoned to the Catholic sisters' quarters the day after Juliana's announcement to discuss what should be done in response to the pregnancy. Within just a few short hours of deliberations, the Catholic sisters and two mothers decided that it was best for Juliana and Miguel to immediately marry and leave the residential home that same day. In a quickly organized ceremony, Juliana (age seventeen) and Miguel (also seventeen) were married by the justice of the peace in the middle of the day on a workday in one of the residential home's classrooms, with the rest of the children, Catholic sisters, *tías*, staff, and volunteers attending the event. Once the vows had been hastily and solemnly exchanged, the mothers of Juliana and Miguel spent the next forty minutes publicly scolding the couple in front of those assembled and warning other child survivors of the negative consequences of an unplanned teen pregnancy out of marriage.

As a *tía* employed in the residential home, Miguel's mother was particularly ashamed of the situation and was placed in a difficult position. I happened to be living and working as a volunteer in the residential home when the wedding occurred in late 1994 and remember the stern warnings the mothers gave. The warnings were followed by more scolding and warnings by the Catholic sisters themselves. The hasty wedding ceremony was a somber event. Once the angry, punitive scolding subsided, we all had some sweet bread and soda in a not-so-joyous celebration of the marriage. With the ceremony and small "celebration" complete, Juliana and Miguel were swiftly brought to the social worker's office where the Catholic sisters signed the legal paperwork to turn custody back over to their mothers since neither of them was yet eighteen. After a few gingerly-placed signatures, Juliana was cast off to embark on the next phase of her life with her new husband. For Juliana, this phase was infused with intense and growing uncertainty, distress, and anxiety as she faced a new marriage and motherhood instead of continuing her education and enjoying the freedom that late teenage years were already offering her peers from the residential home and from Santa Teresa as well.

With no place of their own, Juliana and Miguel decided to move to a city where they could rent a small, simple home and where Miguel hopefully could find employment. One of the drawbacks of the unexpected pregnancy was that Miguel's mother was asked to leave the employ of the residential home as well since she was considered "irresponsible" in the residential home's milieu for letting a pregnancy like this happen, especially when it involved her own son. His mother had given up her hereditary rights to her family's properties when she married, and her husband's family had forced her off their familial property after their separation. Thus, Miguel's mother no longer had a home or land to which she could return after being dismissed from employment. In an effort to try to make something of her life while supporting her son and his new family, Miguel's mother chose to move to the city with Juliana and Miguel, sharing their tiny, rented space. Together, the family was determined to do their best to create and sustain a strong family home, something they all fervently desired, especially as they were about to bring a child into the world. Miguel's four siblings were given permission to remain in the residential home until each reached the age of eighteen, unless they chose to stay in the residential home to finish their high school educations if they turned eighteen before they graduated.

In a somewhat similar circumstance, Debora also experienced a difficult transition to adulthood. She had completed junior high school in the town of Santa Teresa and next chose to enroll in a two-year high school program, located in the colonial city of Antigua, that offered a career emphasis in tourism and hospitality. Because of its small size and meager government funding, the town of Santa Teresa did not have a high school. In fact, most towns throughout the highlands region did not have high schools in that time period (Menéndez 2002). As mentioned previously, most students at the time had to move to larger cities if they wished to continue their formal education beyond junior high. After the first big wave of child survivors had reached high school age, the Catholic sisters decided to procure a small rental home for several of those who were studying in and around Antigua, but who still were under the legal custody of the residential home. The sisters rented the small house as a means of lowering their educational expenses as travel costs had been increasing. For the first year, Debora proved herself as a student and did well in school. She also helped prepare meals and carry out daily chores in the rented home she shared with the other child survivors and one of the *tías* from the residential home who was assigned to care for them. By her second year, however, most child survivors with whom she had lived in Antigua had graduated. In an effort to save money, the Catholic sisters consolidated and moved all minor child survivors who were pursuing high school education to the capital to live in one single rented house. Debora then had to commute to Antigua daily by bus (a one-hour ride each way) in her second year to complete the program. Fortunately, she studied hard and graduated from high school on time, a huge achievement for her and her family as her older sister, who was enrolled in the residential home with her, never continued her education and barely completed junior high school. Debora would have liked to have continued her studies at the college level, but the Catholic sisters could barely afford to financially support child survivors through their high school level of education. Without further financial support, she had no choice but to instead look for full-time employment after her high school graduation since she was already eighteen at the time.

For the first six months after graduation, Debora went to work for the Catholic sisters in their *Casa Madre* (mother house, or central administrative center) in Guatemala City. Fortunately, she developed the technical skills required for an open position within their central administrative office. With a new job secured, Debora had to find a place to live. She did not have any family members with whom she could live in the capital. Her sister was already married and living with her in-laws near Santa Teresa, so living with her was not an option either because there was no space and the daily commute would have been cumbersome. Fortunately, one of the other alumni of the residential home, Adriana, had been living in the capital with her paternal grandparents after leaving the residential home. Realizing Debora's situation, Adriana humbly asked her grandparents if Debora could also live with them and help pay rent. Adriana's grandparents agreed, and Debora, with the few simple belongings she had, moved in with Adriana and her grandparents in Guatemala City.

After six months of living and working in the capital, Debora decided to move back to Santa Teresa and live with her boyfriend, Alex, in his parents' small home. She initially met Alex in the town of Santa Teresa while attending junior high school. Even though she eventually went off to high school in Antigua, the couple had decided to maintain their relationship even from a distance. In fact, when Debora finished her high school program, Alex enrolled in a high school program in the western region of Guatemala to focus specifically on auto mechanic training. His enrollment meant extending their long-distance relationship another two years because Debora would remain working with the Catholic sisters in the capital while Alex attended school on the opposite side of the country, a four-hour bus ride away. However, Debora soon found out that she was pregnant. Even though she had only worked for six months with the Catholic sisters, she decided it was best to move back to Santa Teresa to live with Alex at his parents' home so they could raise their baby together. This also meant that Alex had to drop out of his high school program. Debora and Alex never legally married, which is not uncommon in Guatemala—expense and bureaucratic complications often make legal marriage a challenge. Yet they committed themselves to each other in a common law union and soon afterward welcomed their first child, a son. Debora's transition to adulthood was difficult at times and the unexpected pregnancy was challenging, but she was determined to create the family she always had wished for when she was growing up.

Susana went on to study bookkeeping for her career-specific high school program after graduating from junior high. She began her studies in the neighboring town, which was closer to Santa Teresa and familiar to her as it was where she attended junior high school. After she completed her first year, however, Susana decided to attend a much more intensive and higher quality accounting program in Guatemala City. It also helped that several of the other child survivors were about to begin their high school training programs in Guatemala City as well. Susana and the group of other high school child survivors, with the support of the Catholic sisters, came to live together with one of the residential home *tías* in a rented house that offered a supportive environment within the capital. The rental home allowed child survivors to support each other academically and emotionally throughout their high school careers, while they gradually learned how to adapt to living in an urban center. After just two years of studies, Susana masterfully completed her intensive bookkeeping/basic accounting high school program, and with a degree in hand, set out to find work.

Susana returned to the town of Santa Teresa to look for work so that she could help support her mother who was still working as a *tía* in the residential home. Her oldest brother had just constructed a small house in Santa Teresa, so Susana was able to live there rent-free in exchange for helping with the upkeep of the house (at the time her brother was working and living full-time in the capital) and taking care of their mother. Susana worked odd jobs until she, like her mother years earlier, had the good fortune of being invited by the Catholic sisters to work part-time in the residential home itself. They needed help in their administrative office as the number of children enrolled had grown to over 125, necessitating greater fundraising and bookkeeping efforts. Susana was appreciative of the opportunity and worked hard for the Catholic sisters, whom she viewed as always taking good care of her and her mother. Like Debora, Susana would now officially work with the Catholic sisters and sought to provide them with excellent bookkeeping services, a skill Susana adeptly acquired through their support of her high school career program.

Mario, Esteban, Juliana, Debora, and Susana demonstrate that the transition to life as adults, outside of the residential home, often was not an easy one. Susana was fortunate that her older brother had finished his studies some years earlier, secured gainful employment, and was able to build a small home in Santa Teresa that he could offer to her and their mother. However, most child survivors had no familial home to return to because soldiers destroyed their families' homes and property, especially during *la violencia*. In other cases, their surviving mothers lost their inheritance rights to their land at the moment that their husbands were murdered or died from illness because the land was initially the property of their husbands' paternal relatives. Overall, only two child survivors of twenty in my research project were able to maintain their familial inheritance rights since the parcels of land on which their original familial homes were constructed remained in the hands of their surviving family members who were willing to keep the properties for them. However, the location of the land was far too remote to accommodate their education and employment locations and lacked any viable access to public transport for daily commuting. Thus, the two child survivors who actually had access to humble familial land could not feasibly take advantage of that access.

Most child survivors also did not have access to familial financial support at the time they left the residential home and transitioned to adulthood. All who participated in my research project lost most of their connections to their natal communities and the economic support those communities could offer. Even the two who report having access to familial land in their natal communities recognize that they have lost their connections to the social network of their natal communities and to the reciprocal obligations commonly found in such communities. Because these two grew up in the residential home in Santa Teresa, they believe that natal community members generally do not know or trust them, and consequently, do not recognize them as genuine fellow community members with whom they still have communal ties.

The added financial struggle, distress, and hardship that child survivors have had to endure while transitioning to adulthood remains vivid in their memories and life experiences. For example, Susana noted, " . . . it's more difficult, as you know. If I hadn't been left an orphan, perhaps my dad would have helped me build a house. Instead, I was left with nothing." Medelin similarly reflected, "For example, those who are not orphans, they have family to help them. Their family helps them get ahead, whereas I have to struggle alone." Oscar further explained, "One who has their parents cannot even compare themselves to the situation of an orphan because a person who does not have parents doesn't have the moral support and also doesn't have economic support. Imagine that! Not having moral and economic support is so tough!"

For child survivors, experiences with trauma and loss did not end with the kidnapping and disappearance, or death of one or both of their parents. They continued to experience trauma and loss repeatedly when they were enrolled, commonly out of dire necessity, in a permanent residential home for orphaned children in an often distant and strange town far from their extended relatives and natal communities. The transition proved difficult for nearly all of them. Even those who had sought out the opportunity to enroll, such as Juliana and her brother, still found the initial transition to the residential home isolating, intimidating, and frightening, leading to additional emotional distress and exacerbating their already challenging struggles with trauma and loss. After years of adjusting to life in the residential home, child survivors would, once again, face an arduous transition and set out on their own as young adults without an economic, familial, or emotional safety net to support them. Their initial experiences with trauma and loss were further compounded by their orphan status, a status forced upon them by Guatemala's military and its armed conflict and genocide carried out under the facade of a counterinsurgency campaign. Given child survivors' experiences, I believe that it is not enough to just examine their experiences with initial trauma and distress related exclusively to the death of their parents and other family members or their abandonment. Rather, I argue that researchers and practitioners must recognize that orphaned children who survive armed conflict and genocide are apt to experience sequential traumatization and loss throughout childhood and adulthood explicitly because of their orphan status, which demands greater attention than limited contemporary research has thus far provided.

LIMITATIONS OF CONTEMPORARY RESEARCH

Important efforts have been made in research over the past four decades to identify, examine, and understand the distinct experiences of child survivors who have dealt with ongoing trauma and loss stemming directly from armed conflict and genocide around the world. Some of the earliest studies were conducted with child survivors of the Holocaust, yet those studies did not begin until nearly forty years after the end of World War II (Durst 2003). Essentially, it took almost four decades for researchers to work specifically and independently with child survivors of the Holocaust. Thus, it was in the 1980s that Holocaust child survivors were finally recognized as their own distinct survivior group with unique experiences worthy of attention separate from those of adult survivors (Robinson, Rapaport-Bar-Sever, and Rapaport 1994).

German-Dutch child psychologist Hans Keilson (1979) conducted one of the earliest and most influential studies with Holocaust child survivors. He used, for the first time, the phrase "sequential traumatization" to recognize and analyze the full scope of child survivors' experiences with trauma and loss prior to, during, and following the Holocaust. This was imperative for fully examining the long-term effects on their later lives. Keilson's work ushered in a new era of research, spurring a host of important studies and publications specifically centered on Holocaust child survivors (Durst 2003, 502).

Holocaust child survivor and psychiatrist Robert Krell—influenced by his own experiences with lingering recollections of danger and terror—began documenting survivor eyewitness accounts in the early 1980s as well. Krell understood first-hand that child survivors clearly were robbed of childhood and denied basic conditions necessary for normal development, such as sufficient nourishment, parental nurturance, stability, and a sense of security (1985, 397). He wondered how those losses and challenges would impact child survivors over their lifetimes. To gauge their long-term experiences with trauma and adaptive and coping strategies, Krell compared child and adult survivor experiences by centering on the role of memory, coping methods, and long-term adaptation.

Krell found that adult survivors retained a sense of pride in survivorhood and placed more emphasis on personal initiative in survival, while child survivors found little pride or dignity in survivorhood. Instead, they felt humiliated by Christian children who made them feel different as survivors. Knowing that they were forcibly given away or separated from their families to survive contributed to their lack of pride in being a survivor. Krell also discovered that adult survivors retained a legacy of pre-war memories, whereas child survivors had few, if any, pre-war memories upon which to establish an early foothold in life. Additionally, adult survivors coped with their experiences in the post-war era by banding with other adult survivors and sharing experiences, whereas child survivors were scattered in the post-war period and did not live within survivor communities. Child survivors also did not wish to live in survivor communities later because they desired to be "normal" (ibid., 399). Krell's work has been imperative in validating Holocaust child survivors' unique experiences. He also was instrumental in demonstrating they continue to experience the effects of long-term, sequential traumatization. At the same time, he found that they exhibit resilience via their abilities to attain higher education, build successful careers, and establish healthy families of their own despite their earlier childhood experience (ibid.).

A range of additional studies with child survivors of the Holocaust continued through the mid-1980s and the next three decades that followed. For example, Moskovitz (1985) interviewed twenty-four child survivors of the Holocaust living in England and found that adaptability, appeal to adults, and assertiveness were three primary factors contributing to their vulnerability or resilience. Robinson, Rapaport-Bar-Sever, and Rapaport (1994) interviewed 103 child survivors of the Holocaust in 1992, more than fifty years after the start of World War II. Most of them continued to suffer from survivor syndrome—or feeling guilty for having survived when family members and others perished—and their suffering has been positively correlated to the intensity of trauma suffered in childhood. Moreover, survivors reported symptoms of suffering even more severe at the time of the interviews than immediately following the war. At the same time, however, they demonstrated high abilities in coping and adjustment likely related to their intense urge to give meaning to their lives. They built strong families of their own and integrated socially and professionally into society. In their study, Robinson et al. (1994) further confirmed that child survivors of the Holocaust who suffered massive, prolonged trauma in childhood may reveal post-traumatic stress disorder for many years, while simultaneously exhibiting positive coping skills and resilience in their daily lives.

In a more recent study, Lev-Wiesel and Amir (2000) worked with 170 Holocaust child survivors who were born after 1926. They specifically set out to compare four distinct survivor living experiences during the war: in Catholic institutions, with Christian foster families, in concentration camps, or hiding in the woods and/or with partisans. Child survivors who lived with foster families scored the highest on several psychological distress measures, while those who hid in the woods and/or with partisans had the highest level of well-being (ibid., 453). Their study was important in further distinguishing child survivor experiences, showing that even within a group of child survivors of the Holocaust itself, there are differences in trauma intensity and prolonged effects for child survivors depending on their living context in childhood. This study was followed by a comparative analysis between thirty-four Holocaust child survivors and forty-four adults who did not experience the Holocaust but had lived in other countries that had not been involved in the war. Unsurprisingly, Holocaust child survivors had higher post-traumatic stress disorder symptoms scores, as well as higher scores on other psychological distress measures, than the comparison group. They also experienced prolonged traumatization and suffering, which can place them in a vulnerable position in late adulthood (Amir and Lev-Wiesel 2003, 298).

Focusing on the youngest Holocaust child survivors, van der Hal-van Raalte, Van IJzendoorn, and Bakermans-Kranenburg (2007) worked with a non-convenience sample of 203 child survivors who completed questionnaires pertaining to their survival experience and several inventories on current physical health and psychological well-being. Those child survivors who had been orphaned dealt with more separations and numerous adjustments than those who were not orphaned. However, inadequate childcare arrangements following the war for any child survivor, orphaned or non-orphaned, resulted in lower well-being for participants sixty years later (van der Hal-van Raalte et al. 2007, 519). At the same time, child survivors have shown resilience by living successful lives, achieving success in their professional careers, and building families of their own. Van der Hal-van Raalte et al. provide clear evidence that adequate childcare during and in the aftermath of armed conflict and genocide is imperative to child survivors' abilities to cope with and even counter some of the long-term effects of sequential traumatization throughout their lifetimes.

Studies conducted with Holocaust child survivors, such as those presented previously, offer vital insights into the long-term sequential traumatization that child survivors face over their lifetimes. Not only did these children lose parents and most semblance of childhood during the Holocaust but they continued to experience loss and psychological distress well after the end of the war (Durst 2003, 515). At the same time, they have shown remarkable coping skills and resilience even sixty years later. Holocaust child survivors initially were lumped in with adults when analyzing survivor experiences. However, studies have unquestionably demonstrated the distinct experiences of child survivors are fully deserving of analyses in their own right. Thus, an examination of both long-term psychological distress and resilience is imperative for understanding the long-term consequences of trauma and loss resulting from armed conflict and genocide not only for Holocaust child survivors but also for child survivors of more recent armed conflicts and genocides (Barel, Van IJzendoorn, Sagi-Schwartz, and Bakermans-Kranenburg 2010).

Studies examining child survivor experiences with trauma and loss stemming from more recent armed conflicts and genocides have been limited in scope. Most studies have focused more centrally on assessing psychological distress and trauma while survivors are still in childhood, which is vital and offers important initial findings (e.g., Dyregrove, Gupta, and Raundalen 2002; Kravić, Pajević, and Hasanović 2013; Thabet and Vostanis 2000). Other studies have centered on trauma assessment of those child survivors who became child refugees and lived as adolescents outside of their home countries at the time of assessment (e.g., Geltman et al. 2005; Papageorgiou et al. 2000; Sack, Seeley, and Clarke 1997). Such work has explicitly recognized the sequential experiences with trauma and loss that orphaned children, as a distinct group of survivors, have endured. These studies reveal that as adolescents, survivors often have to contend with taking on adult responsibilities in their child-headed households, living in poverty, and experiencing sexual and physical abuse (e.g., Ng, Ahishakiye, Miller, and Meyerowitz 2015; Reddy 2003; Whetten et al. 2011). While most studies to date have focused on the short-term or immediate aftermath of armed conflict and genocide, a few have begun to conduct longitudinal analyses with child survivors, though such longitudinal work remains temporally-limited to either adolescence or early adulthood (e.g., Betancourt et al. 2015; Munyandamutsa, Nkubamugisha, Gex-Fabry, and Eytan 2012).

Research focused on the long-term consequences of trauma and loss for child survivors of post-Holocaust conflicts and genocides as they enter their thirties, forties, and beyond remains limited. In some cases, sufficient time simply has not passed to provide greater longitudinal data. In other cases, such as Sudan's second civil war, Cambodia, or Guatemala, child survivors are precisely at the stage in adulthood that would allow for rich and illuminating research. Such research is imperative for fully understanding child survivors' experiences, as has been demonstrated eloquently in research conducted with Holocaust child survivors. Child survivors of armed conflict and genocide in the last half of the twentieth century are equally deserving of such attention, which can contribute tremendously to expanding research and praxis. It is through this work that we can genuinely establish best practices in helping mitigate the prolonged effects of traumatization for present and future child survivors. One critical first step in that process, however, is fully recognizing and substantiating the entirety of trauma and loss experienced by child survivors of armed conflict and genocide, including acknowledgment of both their trauma and their resilience.

RECOGNIZING THE ENTIRETY OF CHILDHOOD TRAUMA AND LOSS FOR CHILD SURVIVORS

Contemporary research with child survivors of armed conflict and genocide tends to focus more narrowly on the immediate experiences of trauma and loss following armed conflicts and genocides. Yet these horrific events set in motion a whole other chain of traumatic events and loss for child survivors. Those who participated in my research project had to deal not only with immediate trauma brought on by the armed conflict and genocide but also with traumatic transitions in living contexts in their childhoods, adolescence, and into early adulthood, all resulting from their orphan status. While research immediately following single harrowing events is extremely important, the scope of research with child survivors must expand to include the full range of survivor experiences with sequential traumatization.

Working with child survivors over the long-term and more fully expanding the scope of analyses to include their sequential traumatization allow for a more holistic approach to understanding their experiences. Not only will such research shed light on the prolonged and sequential suffering and trauma among child survivors but also will validate their experiences, which is critical to recovery and reconciliation (Minow 2010). At the same time, child survivors' abilities to effectively cope with their sequential traumatization and build resilience should not be denied and offers another fruitful area of research and praxis. Denying their successes, resilience, and strengths belittles their experiences and presents only a partial view of who they are today. By looking at both trauma and resilience, we gain a broader and more integrated understanding of child survivors' life journeys and of who they have become despite experiencing and witnessing some of the most heinous acts known to humankind. Trauma and resilience are not simply two sides of the same coin or two opposing points on a single unilineal spectrum of well-being. They can and often do co-exist in an individual's experience. Child survivors are no exception. Such complex experiences oblige researchers and practitioners to explore and analyze child survivors' distress *and* resilience when examining the whole of their childhood trauma and loss and the subsequent long-term effects in their lives. For participants in my research project, trauma and resilience are both part of their life experiences and, as such, are explored in chapter four.

Chapter Four

Trauma and Resilience

Trauma experienced by child survivors who participated in my research project was not limited to losing one or both parents in the internal armed conflict and genocide. As demonstrated in chapter three, these survivors continued to suffer traumatic transitions throughout their childhoods and into early adulthood. Some of the effects of the sequential traumatization they experienced were already evident by the time they were entering their adolescence, which I witnessed firsthand. When I arrived at the residential home in Santa Teresa in October of 1994 to begin my two-year volunteer service, it soon became apparent to me that many child survivors were suffering from psychological distress well beyond what could be attributed to typical teenage angst. Even within my first month there, and despite my limited Spanish language skills at the time, I could see that many of these survivors were deeply struggling with memories and emotions born of their earlier traumatic experiences.

Through daily observation during my first full year as a volunteer, I came to recognize that many child survivors experienced especially difficult emotional days on the anniversary of their parents' deaths. Others experienced heart-wrenching sadness on special days like their own birthdays or school events such as Parents' Day because their deceased parents or other family members could not be present. Furthermore, it was all too common on any given day to encounter at least one child survivor who was facing emotional challenges because of the lingering aftermath of the consequences of the armed conflict and genocide. More often than not, signs of emotional distress persisted throughout the year.

In one example, sixteen-year-old Julio would often nervously wring his hands over and over while he spoke quickly and rocked back and forth at an anxious pace, seemingly trying to soothe his anxiety with repetitive motion. Julio (whose father was kidnapped and disappeared when he was a young child) would work himself up into such an anxious state that we, the Catholic sisters, *tías*, staff, and volunteers, often had a difficult time calming him down. He likely was experiencing panic attacks, but no official diagnosis was ever made since mental health services were still limited in rural Guatemala at the time. We, as untrained personnel, would try our best to help calm and comfort him by talking with him and assuring him that everything was okay and that he would always be supported by the residential home community. However, Julio's anxious episodes continued to occur frequently and more intensely during his enrollment in the residential home, especially during his teenage years.

In another instance, seventeen-year-old Lucia would frequently begin hyperventilating for unknown reasons, often escalating to the level of nearly passing out. Uncertain of what specifically would provoke her attacks, the *tías* and staff would quickly jump to her aid, offering her home remedies and eventually a brown paper sack to breathe into and restore normal respiration. Lucia's attacks would often come on the tail-end of some sort of general experience such as talking with adults, arguing with other child survivor girls about some small general disagreement, or generally describing some past event. Thus, it was not always obvious what triggered her responses.

One of the most poignant moments that will forever remain in my memory is when we, the volunteers, took a group of teenage girls to Guatemala City in 1995 to stay in the Catholic sisters' *Casa Madre*. We decided to organize a fun weekend retreat for the girls to work with them on positive issues of self-esteem and future aspirations because it had become apparent that whenever we had the teenagers all together, both female and male, together in an activity in the residential home, the girls would background themselves and never fully participate or speak up in front of the boys. All was going well the first day of the girls-only retreat until seventeen-year-old Carmen left the room during one of the art sessions in which we were addressing what the girls felt were their strengths and talents. She went to sit on a set of stairs adjacent to the outdoor classroom and began to rock back and forth incessantly, staring blankly into the distance. The other girls alerted us immediately that something was wrong because Carmen would not respond to them when they called out to her. When we rushed to check on her, Carmen's eyes rolled back into her head, and she passed out cold. We spent the next ten minutes trying everything to bring her back to consciousness. In a panic, we took her to a hospital that fortunately was just a block down the street. After several hours, she regained consciousness, but the doctors had absolutely no explanation for why she had passed out. Even after a panel of blood tests, there was no answer. The doctors simply stated that she likely suffered from some emotional trauma brought to the surface by our retreat activities.

Carmen's diagnosis remains a mystery; however, her circumstances left a lasting impression on me. At the time, I was only remotely aware of what child survivors had experienced as children since I had only been living in the country less than a year. Over time and as my Spanish language skills improved, however, they spoke more openly with me about their past experiences related to the armed conflict and genocide and the ongoing psychological distress they experienced from the trauma and from the initial transition to living in the residential home. These conversations eventually developed into an ongoing dialogue that has lasted now for nearly thirty years. In the process, I have gained a much deeper sense of and appreciation for what this group of child survivors has lived through not only during the armed conflict and genocide but also following that period and even into adulthood. By virtue of the relationships we forged in their adolescence and maintained for nearly three decades, child survivors have taught me about how they have experienced trauma and its often lingering effects. At the same time, many have achieved unparalleled academic and career success and have shown resilience in many aspects of their lives. Drawing from qualitative and quantitative analyses in my research project, this chapter further examines the sequential traumatization that child survivors have endured and highlights their resilient responses to the long-term consequences stemming from it. To begin, I discuss the utility and justification for using the concept of "trauma" as a framework for understanding child survivors' experiences.

UTILIZING THE CONCEPT OF
TRAUMA AS A FRAMEWORK

In the summer of 2005, I returned to the residential home in Santa Teresa to conduct preliminary research for a five-week period. I had two goals during that phase of research. The first was to determine if the child survivor alumni of the residential home would be interested in participating in a research project focused on their life experiences. The second goal was to begin gathering reflections on the childhood experiences from those interested in participating, which helped guide my research design. After meeting and talking with several of the alumni, I realized that they were not only enthusiastic to participate in my research project but also were excited to help me advance what they perceived were my academic studies.[1] In light of these positive responses, I decided to go ahead and conduct preliminary interviews with nine individuals whom I randomly selected from the residential home alumni database. Through the preliminary interviews, I asked open-ended questions to solicit whatever themes the nine child survivors deemed most pertinent to their life experiences. Preliminary interview questions were general in nature, and I purposely avoided using any type of terminology or labels that could have skewed their responses or influenced their own use of terms to categorize their experiences. I was especially interested, therefore, when child survivors almost immediately used the specific term "trauma" to

define their early childhood experiences with psychological distress and feelings of loss. "Trauma" was one of the terms I purposely avoided using to not
force what can often be construed as too "Western" of a psychological term
or framework[2] on child survivors' own perspectives of their experiences. Yet
during the preliminary interviews, use of the term "trauma" arose in several
contexts across almost all nine participant interview responses. One of the
questions I asked in the preliminary interviews was: Do you think that *la
violencia* continues to affect you in some way today? Even though each child
survivor was interviewed separately at a different time and location, several
explicitly used the term "trauma" in their responses. For example, Eva (born
in 1980) responded, "Yes, because the trauma and violence continue. The fear
is still here." Sofia shared, "It affected me a bit. Sometimes I feel traumatized.
Sometimes, when I am at home, I think about the things that have happened,
and I get sad and begin to cry."

In another preliminary interview question, I asked all nine child survivors:
In your opinion, how has *la violencia* affected the lives of orphaned child
survivors? Again, I was intrigued when several child survivors explicitly
used the term "trauma" in their responses. Nidia, for example, reflected, "In
the fact that they were left without parents and those who lived through this
era, the trauma of having seen how their parents were murdered or abused."
Cristina (born in 1982) similarly noted, "The orphans of *la violencia* suffered
a lot. . . . they saw their parents murdered and family members murdered in
front of them, and they were left with nothing. That affects them in the long
run because they are left with a trauma inside of them . . . "

Use of the term "trauma" also came up in informal conversations with
other child survivors whom I did not formally interview during that summer
research period. Thus, the term was clearly a concept that resonated with child
survivors and proved useful in understanding their experiences with psychological distress. Consequently, I decided to include the term and concept in
my full research project initiated just two years later, for which I employed
both qualitative and quantitative research methods. The following presents
the findings culled from the qualitative portion of my research project.

QUALITATIVE ANALYSIS OF TRAUMA

I returned to Guatemala in 2007 to conduct mixed-method (qualitative and
quantitative) research, including a designated section of analysis focused
solely on assessing child survivors' perspectives on and experiences with
trauma. I also elected to include a comparative element of trauma research
by including a cohort of peers from Santa Teresa in my research project.
Children, regardless of orphan status, who had grown up in the highlands

region during the armed conflict and genocide were exposed to brutal acts of violence and the culture of fear that permeated the region. By utilizing a comparative approach, I sought to distinguish and better understand the particular experiences of orphaned child survivors relative to those of children of the same age and region more generally.

I developed six open-ended trauma-focused questions in a qualitative ethnographic interview conducted individually with the twenty child survivor participants and the randomly-selected group of twenty of their peers from Santa Teresa. The questions were designed to directly solicit participants' reflections on how trauma has affected them generally both in the short-and long-term. I also asked participants about their own experiences with trauma but did not ask them to provide specific details. My aim was to avoid placing participants in the uncomfortable and vulnerable emotional position that revisiting memories of past violence can cause.[3] The findings culled from the responses to the trauma-related portion of the ethnographic interviews are presented below and begin with those provided by child survivors, followed by those of their peers.

Child Survivor Perspectives on and Experiences with Childhood Trauma

The six open-ended trauma questions that I developed for the ethnographic interviews came toward the end of each full interview, following a series of questions focused on participants' basic demographic background information and perspectives on their overall life experiences and perspectives on contemporary politics and economics. It was telling, however, when the use of the term "trauma" frequently came up in child survivors' responses to the initial interview questions not specifically focused on trauma. For example, Nidia responded to a question regarding what *la violencia* signifies in the political history of Guatemala by stating, "Well, in reality it was a very difficult period, very difficult for the people because at the time, it created a lot of psychological trauma, a lot of emotional fear. . . . " In another instance, Mario replied to the question of whether he thinks *la violencia* and general politics in Guatemala had affected his childhood in any way by reflecting, "There was family disintegration, deaths, murders of my family members, and in other cases, traumas that still in this moment one cannot overcome, right? So, yes, yes, it affected me."

Further along in the interviews but prior to the trauma-related section, I asked participants: How has *la violencia* affected the lives of orphaned child survivors in general? Again, several participants explicitly used the term "trauma" in their responses. For example, Sheni shared, "Those long and gloomy histories of their pasts affect them in their behavior. They are timid, rebellious. They have suffered from trauma caused by images of the past." Brandon similarly reflected, "Many of them remain traumatized because they saw it in the flesh, whereas in my case, it was a little less intense because I was younger, and we didn't understand much of it."

When asked whether child survivors thought that that armed conflict and especially *la violencia* generally continued affecting some of their other companions from the residential home in some way even today, several again utilized the term "trauma" to conceptualize distress. For example, Brandon remarked, "I imagine that they have lost contact and still have problems over-coming the trauma of their childhoods." Oscar imparted, "Yes, really there are psychological traumas that they are never going to leave behind. They are never going to be able to separate themselves from them. . . . it's incredible because they are things one can never forget." Nidia, who specifically refer-enced one of her fellow child survivors from the residential home, asserted, "So, yes, it was a very difficult trauma . . . and [she] was traumatized in this sense. . . . and she is now a lawyer and notary."

Child Survivor Responses to Trauma-Related Ethnographic Questions

Noting that the term "trauma" remained a meaningful and salient concept for conveying and understanding child survivors' perspectives and life experi-ences with genocide-related psychological distress, I concluded each inter-view with the six open-ended questions focused directly on trauma. Attentive to participants' emotional well-being, I started with an open-ended question that asked if they thought they had been affected in any way by one or more traumatic experiences as a child and, if so, in what way they believe they had been affected. I did not ask for details but instead sought a general sense of what they felt they had experienced.

The overwhelming majority of child survivors affirmed that one or more traumatic experiences had affected them when they were children. As pre-sented in chapter three, Sofia noted that just seeing other children who had their dads, who gave them love and bought them little toys, was hard for her because she lost not only her dad but also her uncles. Sheni reflected that just seeing soldiers was frightening when she was a child, while Mario shared that having to eventually leave his remaining siblings to live in the residential home was challenging.

A few child survivors did not feel that they experienced trauma, per se, in early childhood simply because they were too young to remember actual events. However, they did recognize that they experienced trauma a little later in childhood because of having lost family members who were kidnapped and disappeared. The loss of family members resulted in the consequent loss of property and caused the extreme poverty that many were forced to live in as children. Only two child survivors responded that they did not recall feeling traumatized during early childhood because they lost a parent due to illness or were abandoned by a parent whom they never knew.

Following up the question regarding general childhood experiences with one or more traumatic events, I next asked participants if they believed that one or more experiences with childhood trauma was still affecting them in some way today. Half of the child survivors immediately stated that they did, indeed, feel that their childhood trauma still affects them. For example, Cris revealed that his trauma is linked directly to the loss of his father. He shared, "I keep thinking about him and asking questions. What was he like? Why did it happen?" Esteban responded that his childhood experience with trauma affects him quite a lot by reflecting, "I have experienced so much, and it still affects me in that it is hard for me to have relationships with other people. I don't have a lot of confidence. . . . Sometimes I am affected by emotional problems that even affect my job." Sheni noted that her childhood trauma still affects her as well, especially when seeing a big group of men passing by because they remind her of the soldiers who terrorized her community and kidnapped her father at gunpoint. Juliana similarly suggested that her child-hood trauma is most triggered when she, too, sees soldiers today: "I just see their uniforms and it frightens me, just seeing their weapons."

Interestingly, among child survivors who felt they are still affected by experiences with childhood trauma today, one responded affirmatively even though he answered negatively to the question of whether he suffered any traumatic childhood event in the first place. Kike, the respondent, explained, "Well, what affects me is not having a father because his kidnapping, I did not see what happened. I didn't see anything." Kike's response provides a glimpse into the complexity of child survivors' experiences with sequential traumatization both as children and as adults. Not witnessing brutal atrocities committed against their parents and family members in no way insulates child survivors from the ongoing psychological distress that those events produce.

Among the ten child survivors who expressed no longer being affected by childhood trauma, five did not identify themselves as experiencing child-hood trauma in the first question. The remaining five contended that they did experience childhood trauma but reported that they no longer feel affected by it today because they have had to overcome it, exemplified by Nidia, who reflected, "No. Not anymore because you have to adapt after that." Similarly, Yohana remarked, "I have already overcome it. If I would remain stuck in those memories maybe, but not anymore. I don't want to think about it because it makes me sad, so it's better not to."

To better understand child survivors' experiences with childhood trauma and to attempt to separate that trauma from more recent traumatic experiences they may have had, I next asked about general experiences with trauma in adulthood. My aim was to determine whether there was any link between those who continue to suffer from childhood trauma and those who suffered from trauma that occurred in their adulthood. Without soliciting any specific details, I asked participants if they thought that they had experienced one or more traumatic events in adulthood that they view as still affecting them in some way today. Only two child survivors responded that they have suffered from a traumatic experience as an adult. The first has had a difficult marriage involving violent domestic abuse, bitter confrontations with in-laws, and custody battles over her two small children. She shared that her marriage has felt like an illusion and that her hopes and dreams of finally having a home and a family have not turned out the way she had planned. The second was Esteban. His experience with trauma as an adult directly stemmed from a near fatal situation in which he was robbed and shot in the street in Guatemala City. He explained, "It affected me greatly, the accident, the assault I experienced. They shot me. That affects me every minute. Believe me . . . I don't like to think of it because I'm alive, but I almost died."

Broadening the scope of questions focused on childhood psychological distress overall, I continued interviews by asking whether child survivors felt that the armed conflict, in general, or the especially brutal period of *la violencia,* in particular, still affected them psychologically in some way today. Nearly half of the participants responded that it did. They directly linked the armed conflict and genocide with the psychological distress of losing family members. For example, Mario shared that he still feels affected because of the actual kidnappings and disappearances of his parents. Some child survivors explicitly noted that losing connections with surviving family members because of their parents' deaths was also a major contributor to their psychological distress. For example, Kike asserted that he is still affected because his father is no longer alive, and he missed out on the opportunity to live together with his mom and brothers. In addition, several child survivors identified lingering fear as contributing to their sense of ongoing, long-term psychological distress. As Sheni poignantly reflected, "The fear remains but little by little, it's not that we are erasing it but that we are setting it aside."

I next posed the question of whether participants thought Guatemalan orphaned child survivors, in general, had experienced childhood trauma. My aim was to extend the scope of inquiry by assessing how child survivors who grew up in the residential home in Santa Teresa perceive other orphaned child survivors' experiences and reactions to the terror of the armed conflict and genocide. Intriguingly, all twenty participants responded affirmatively, even though not all of them reported having experienced childhood trauma themselves. This discrepancy likely results from a few participants reporting that they simply were too young to remember the actual traumatic events such as kidnappings and disappearances of their parents but assuming that others, generally, were likely to have witnessed such atrocities firsthand.

Participants' tendencies to link general orphaned child survivors' distress directly to the trauma of witnessing brutality was evident in their responses. For example, Noemi asserted that orphaned child survivors are traumatized from feeling alone and seeing the death or disappearances of their parents. Cris similarly viewed trauma for orphaned child survivors resulting from seeing people die, which leaves an indelible imprint on their memories. He explained, "And they were there, and they were left thinking, 'I want to harm someone!' They are stuck with that in their minds. Death, seeing blood, seeing all that they had to see, sure, it remains in their minds." Mario distinguished between those who witnessed atrocities and those who did not. For him, the trauma-related distress especially affected older orphaned children because he believes those who were younger were not cognizant of what was happening. He added, "It really affected those who saw how their parents died, how they were killed. Yes, that was so hard. I never wanted to go through that." Juliana used her brother as an example and conveyed that he struggles a lot today because of the trauma he suffered in childhood. As she explained, "He falters and falters, but thank God, he has a wife who understands him, and I have a spouse who understands me."

Other participants referenced separation from family members, uncertainty, and general consequences of the armed conflict and genocide, such as other violence, exploitation, and abuse, as some of the primary underlying sources of trauma for orphaned child survivors in general. Oscar responded that being separated from loved ones has been the biggest trauma for orphaned child survivors. Nidia similarly identified separation from loved ones as a source of childhood trauma. She reflected that even after realizing they had been separated from families, they came to accept their situations in the end, though the pain of it remains. Yohanna referenced child exploitation by a surviving parent or other family members as a primary source of trauma. She asserted that some orphaned child survivors were forced to work odd jobs and obliged to bring money home: "If they didn't bring anything, they were beaten. It was child abuse more than anything."

In the final trauma-related question posed in the ethnographic interviews, I asked whether participants thought that orphaned child survivors' experiences with childhood trauma overall were different than those of other Guatemalans of the same age. Nearly all participants answered affirmatively. Again, they identified witnessing parents' murders and losing close family members as contributing to the difference in experiences. They also referenced simply living through the period of *la violencia* and its subsequent aftermath as major factors distinguishing orphaned child survivor experiences from those of other child survivors more generally. As Oscar elaborated, "The traumas are very distinct, or it's that they have different magnitudes, more elevated magnitudes . . . " Kike explained that those who have suffered see life differently in that they value it more: "Those who haven't lived through it, they believe that everything is just fine because it has always been fine." According to Medelin, orphaned child survivors do not have the support of family to help them get ahead in life the way that others of the same age do. Lastly, Sheni reflected that orphaned child survivors deal with more fear even though they try to move beyond it.

Interestingly, a few participants viewed experiences with childhood trauma for both orphaned child survivors and peers of the same age as equally distressing and without distinction. They referenced common suffering, general violence, loss of parents, and individual differences in taking responsibility for overcoming childhood trauma as factors that negate any trauma distinction between orphaned and non-orphaned survivor experiences. Cris explained, "I think that not just them, not just the orphans, but all of those who lived with their parents as well, all of us have experienced trauma, I believe." Yohana likewise saw no distinction between the experiences of orphaned child survivors and their peers. She claimed that it has been the same for everybody because children who lived through the internal armed conflict and genocide have become somewhat intimidated. She furthered added that typical children who had nothing happen to them have not lived through the same type of experience and did not experience trauma. Yohana concluded, "A normal child only thinks about being treated well, whereas the poor children who had to flee or run away with their parents from place to place so that nothing would happen to them, that was horrible."

These qualitative interviews conducted with child survivors who had lived in the residential home in Santa Teresa provide important insights. Through their responses, participants offered firsthand perspectives regarding childhood trauma and the resulting psychological distress these experiences have caused them and other child survivors, both in the aftermath of the armed conflict and genocide and beyond. To further gauge and distinguish their experiences from those of non-orphaned children, I also conducted individual ethnographic interviews with the group of twenty peers who remained living with their parents, siblings, and extended family members throughout childhood. Peers were asked the same open-ended questions posed to child survivors, and their responses provide an important comparative framework for better understanding child survivor trauma stemming from the armed conflict and genocide.

Peer Perspectives on and Experiences with Childhood Trauma

Assessing and understanding peer experiences generally in childhood and specifically with respect to childhood trauma first requires exploring the community in which these children grew up amid the internal armed conflict and genocide in the highlands region of Guatemala. Even during *la violencia*, inhabitants of the town of Santa Teresa characterized their community as *tranquilo* (peaceful) in comparison to the towns and villages in the surrounding regions that experienced numerous violent events. Santa Teresa—one of the smallest municipalities in the highlands—has never had its own police force or official means of enforcing laws. Instead, townspeople have worked together for generations to try to keep their community safe by monitoring who passes through town and keeping an eye on each other's properties.

Santa Teresa is a relatively small town (fewer than 5,000 residents) and comprises a network of several families who have known and interacted with one another for generations. During much of the armed conflict and genocide, the townspeople of Santa Teresa were able to maintain some sense of stability even amid the chaos of the counterinsurgency campaign when it was in full-force in the surrounding mountains and valleys. Perhaps due to its small size, its location just a few kilometers off of the Inter-American Highway (making it more difficult to serve as a "hiding" place for military soldiers or guerrilla combatants), its relative lack of resources as an impoverished municipality, or some combination of all of these elements, Santa Teresa was not a heavily targeted town by either the military or guerrilla forces. Thus, the relative safety of the town provided some stability in peers' childhood experiences; however, peers were not completely free from exposure to traumatic events, which they conveyed in their interviews when they shared their perspectives on growing up in the town.

Peer Perspectives on Growing Up in Santa Teresa

Peers who went to school with and in many cases were childhood friends of orphaned child survivors from the residential home fully acknowledge the general security and peacefulness that existed in their community during the especially brutal years of *la violencia*. Out of the twenty peers interviewed in my research project, nearly all agreed that the town was relatively safer and calmer than most towns in the highlands. For example, in answering the question of what was advantageous about growing up in Santa Teresa, Otto (born in 1974) responded that the townspeople were united and living in closer proximity to each other, which offered greater protection, whereas rural hamlets and distant parcels of land left people more vulnerable to attacks. Marco (born in 1974) reflected that the town always seemed peaceful, partially because the townspeople did not allow the national police or army to establish a police substation or military encampment there; instead, the townspeople established their own community-driven security that has kept it a peaceful place.

A few peers revealed that Santa Teresa, in fact, was not their original natal community. Rather, their parents made the deliberate decision to move to the town. Having originated from some of the hardest hit areas in the highlands at the time, they sought to bring their children to a place where they could live without the constant threat of murder, kidnappings, and other atrocities happening elsewhere. In one example, Olivia (born in 1974) shared that her family initially lived in constant fear. They were afraid that their house would be attacked, a family member would be killed, or one of them would be kidnapped and disappeared. Her brother and brother-in-law eventually were violently dragged from their house and killed in front of family members. Olivia explained, "In an instant, they killed them both. . . . they paid no attention to who they killed. They took people. They kidnapped them and they never reappeared and oh, you would be so afraid, and you would think, 'They are going to kill me!'" Andrea (born in 1972) also recalled the violence in her natal community. One morning her family awoke to find a death wreath hanging on their house, signifying they were targeted by the military to be killed. Other houses in the community similarly had death wreaths hanging on them that same morning, which was a clear threat and induced great fear in the community. Andrea also remembered being in the local market when soldiers entered and started randomly shooting people while townspeople shouted, "Save yourselves if you can!" She shared, "Everyone ran from one side to the other. I always remember it because it was so difficult . . . we lived through it and that's why my dad brought us here [to Santa Teresa]."

Peers who moved to Santa Teresa did, indeed, find it a relatively peaceful community both during and following *la violencia*, especially when compared with their natal communities. Moving to Santa Teresa gave their families reprieve from the most brutal horrors of the armed conflict and genocide. As Olivia reflected, "[T]his is a peaceful town. Thank God you never hear of anything bad. God has blessed it. . . . here is a town that is small, but it is a happy place." Teresa (born in 1971) also emphasized the relative calm found in the town: "It was joyful for me. It was joyful because I came here to live. There wasn't any fear. There wasn't any violence. It wasn't like our other hamlet where there was so much violence. When I came here to live. . . . I was no longer fearful."

In accordance with the experiences of peers presented above, literature centered on the period of *la violencia* reveals that the town of Santa Teresa and its adjoining hamlets did, indeed, remain relatively safe during the armed conflict and genocide, having never experienced a massacre, an all-out night raid by the military, or any public hangings (CEH 1999; REMHI 1998). Several peers and other townspeople talk about how they could often hear gunfire in the distance in the evenings, but that direct combat never occurred on community terrain. Nonetheless, Santa Teresa's inhabitants were not completely insulated from the armed conflict and genocide. Nearly half of the peers I interviewed had one or more immediate family members who were kidnapped and disappeared during *la violencia*. Though I did not ask peers directly[4] about whether they lost a family member in the armed conflict and genocide, several of them voluntarily spoke about what happened. For example, Otto revealed that he had an older brother who was a teacher in a nearby hamlet. One day, military soldiers entered the small school and violently detained his brother and three other male teachers. The soldiers falsely accused the teachers of being communist guerrillas and dragged them off to an unknown destination. Word immediately reached family members about the detainments, and Otto's father headed out with other male community members to the local road where they knew the soldiers would have to pass to leave the area. Otto's father saw his son and the other three teachers being marched down the road. Otto recalled, "My dad saw my brother's face when he shouted, 'Save me!'" Three days later, the local news reported that several dead bodies had been found in the area. Otto's father went to the site and found that the bodies had been burnt beyond recognition. It was only through dental records that they received confirmation that Otto's brother was, in fact, one of the burnt bodies. He was only thirty years old when he was viciously kidnapped and murdered.

Among the twenty peers interviewed in my research project, sixteen also lost family members who were kidnapped and disappeared, often in other towns and hamlets, during *la violencia*. Family members included grandfathers, brothers, aunts, uncles, and cousins. Thus, while the number of kidnapped and disappeared victims in Santa Teresa may have been small in comparison to other regions and the town was commonly characterized as relatively peaceful by its inhabitants, the armed conflict and genocide still affected residents of Santa Teresa and their children both directly and indirectly.

In addition to loss of their own family members, most peers who grew up in Santa Teresa were exposed to the terror of armed conflict and genocide via violent threats and events that occurred in the surrounding area at the time. The threats and events included occasional kidnapping and disappearances and murders of neighbors, military detentions, destruction of property, and nearby gunfire. In one example, Julietta (born in 1976) recalled that a male adult neighbor was detained by military soldiers and his dead body was later found lying in some tall weeds in the nearby mountains. Elena (born in 1971) remembered when soldiers arrived at her house one evening when she was helping make dinner for her family. The soldiers asked for some tortillas and said that they would not harm them. The family reluctantly and in great fear opened the door and gave the soldiers a small bundle of tortillas. As the soldiers turned and were leaving through the door, someone outside shot two of them. Elena shared, "We didn't move. We were so afraid. We didn't do anything. I was so scared." Otto added that he remembers a day in school in Santa Teresa when soldiers entered to kill one of their teachers just as they had killed his brother and colleagues in one of the schools in a nearby hamlet. He explained, "It was a period when the government wanted to eliminate people they considered to be the creators of good things."

Inhabitants of Santa Teresa and its adjoining hamlets experienced somewhat peaceful community stability during the most intense and brutal years of *la violencia*. However, as the peers' recollections presented above attest, the town did not go without incident and was not completely free from the reach of the ever-present and expanding culture of fear created by the military during the armed conflict and genocide. Local murders, disappearances, military detention, death threats, destruction of property, and gunfire all contributed to the expansive and persistent culture of fear that permeated the highlands. Growing up in a culture of fear became a common experience for many children in the highlands not only during the period of *la violencia* but also in the immediate years that followed and beyond.

Peers who grew up in Santa Teresa also recalled being frightened by public displays of dead bodies, the presence of soldiers, the threat of being monitored, food rationing, and military conscription of mostly young, Maya Indigenous males. These types of events continued to happen even after *la violencia*. Fatima (born in 1975) remembered, "We once went to the municipal center and saw a lot of dead people because they had gone to the mountains to bring them back and it was something frightening for us." Laya (born in 1980) also vividly recalled the culture of fear that reached Santa Teresa: "In that time, they came to kidnap, to murder . . . because I remember I was about the size of my little girl when the soldiers passed through and my siblings said, 'They're coming to get us and take our lives!' And we hid in the *temazcal*."5 Teresa described how families had to lock themselves in their homes at night and not leave until the morning for fear that they would be killed in the streets. Her family and many in the town simply did not venture out at night especially during *la violencia*. She explained, "During that time, after six in the afternoon and onward, we had to shut off the lights and to eat . . . we ate by candlelight. We had to measure the food because if there was too much, they would say that perhaps we were giving food to the guerrillas or to the soldiers."

For peers, as with orphaned child survivors, fear often became inextricably linked with memories of their childhoods, a fear that has persisted well beyond *la violencia*. Nina (born in 1970) conveyed how fear was a common experience for children and adults in the town by sharing, "Well here the only effect was fear. . . . Cars passed and the next day everyone was frightened because they took away someone who disappeared. So, it was in this type of moment that I felt a little distressed." Dario (born in 1976) similarly clarified that people, generally, lived in fear because of mistrust and the terror that they could be murdered just like the teachers who had been killed. He asserted that people were afraid to leave their homes, so they did not have a way to earn money for food and more poverty resulted: "It is awful to live in fear. Everyone lived in fear. When I was going to school . . . I saw gunfire and we, with my dad, worked up in the fields at that time and my mom worked in the school, and she would always come home with such fear that something awful would happen." Josue (born in 1978) also found that there was much fear and terror in that period. He acknowledged the long-term effects that fear and terror have had on people by describing how people who lived through *la violencia* have a hard time eating meat unless it has been well-cooked. He continued, "[W]hen they see the meat and it isn't well-done and there is a little bit of blood, it disgusts them, and they can't eat it . . . there are people who can't see blood because it still very much distresses them."

Nearly all orphaned child survivor and peer participants in my research project characterized Santa Teresa as having been a relatively more peaceful community during the armed conflict and genocide than most highlands municipalities at that time. While Santa Teresa did not see large-scale combat or massacres, especially during *la violencia*, residents did lose family members, witnessed violent events, and lived in the persistent culture of fear that had become all too common throughout the highlands region. The terrifying experiences that peer participants had as children with the armed conflict and genocide and the culture of fear that permeated the town did affect their childhoods and continue to remain etched in their memories. Based on peers' experiences, it is evident that children as a group, in general, did suffer psychological distress, especially during and following *la violencia,* even in areas that were relatively more peaceful at the time. For orphaned child survivors, however, that childhood distress was further exacerbated by their no longer living with family members or remaining in their natal communities. Instead, they lived in a residential home often quite distant from their family homes and natal communities. An analysis of peer responses to the trauma-related questions posed in the individual ethnographic interviews offers further distinction between their experiences with long-term childhood trauma and those of child survivor participants.

Peer Responses to Trauma-Related Ethnographic Questions

Following the same format as the ethnographic interviews conducted with orphaned child survivors, I asked the same six trauma-related questions of peer participants at the end of each individual ethnographic interview. Responding to the first question, half of the twenty peers confirmed that they suffered from one or more traumatic experiences when they were children. The experiences were especially difficult for the four peers whose families fled their natal communities and moved to Santa Teresa in search of a more peaceful living environment. While the number of peers who identified as suffering childhood trauma was less overall than the number of child survivors participants, the fact that half of the peer group acknowledged experiencing some childhood trauma further confirmed that many children in the highlands, regardless of orphan status, were exposed to distressing violence and terror. Several peers answered the question emphatically, immediately referencing the loss of family members. For example, Otto referred to the kidnappings and disappearances of both his brother and grandfather. Teresa shared that soldiers kidnapped and disappeared her mother and killed her three nieces in front of her, while Laya noted that her grandfather's kidnapping and disappearance was a deeply-traumatic experience for her.

Among peers who reported that they did not experience any childhood trauma, most did not lose an immediate family member in the armed conflict and genocide. Thus, they did not view themselves as having been deeply distressed by a particular horrifying event in childhood. The families of these peers remained mostly intact, especially during and following *la violencia*. Two peers who did not identify themselves as experiencing childhood trauma did lose a distant family member in *la violencia*. However, they did not see the actual kidnapping and do not report feeling traumatized by the loss. A final peer who did not experience childhood trauma but did lose relatives simply stated that he was just too young to remember anything regarding his uncles' kidnappings and disappearances.

I next asked peer participants whether they felt that experiences with childhood trauma still affected them in some way today as adults. Only five responded affirmatively. One of the five peers, Laya, who lost her grandfather stated, "Yes, I still think of my grandfather and what a good person he was!" The remaining four peers who responded affirmatively to the question are the same four who witnessed and experienced violence in their natal communities before their families relocated to Santa Teresa. Julietta responded, "Me? Yes! Yes, it affects me because, go figure, at least if [my dad] was still alive, I wouldn't be going through so many hardships along with my children." Olivia explained that her childhood trauma has affected her a lot, especially when she got together with the father of her children. Fortunately, Olivia has been getting emotional support from a good friend who helps her through her difficulties. Yet she affirmed that her childhood trauma experience remains in her mind, and she tries to forget it by putting her faith in God. Greatly affected by her own childhood trauma, Teresa feared that the violence would start up again, especially when she heard of a recent murder: "How that frightens me because it's as if it is all going to start up again and all that has already happened to me because I saw it all. That's why I have problems with *nervios.*"6

Like orphaned child survivor experiences, peers generally reported experiencing little trauma as adults overall. When asked if they felt they had experienced trauma now in adulthood, only two reported that they did. One of the two peers attributed his adult trauma to his journey north. Josue (born in 1978) made his way to the Mexico/US border in the late 2000s and crossed without legal documentation under harrowing circumstances. After successfully crossing the border, he was detained and held in slavery-like conditions by men (human smugglers called *coyotes*) who had helped him cross. The men had Josue locked up in the evenings over several months until he worked and earned enough money to pay their exorbitant "crossing fee." Josue explains that he had planned his trip to the US for over three years, and when he finally got word on a Thursday that he could make the trip with a group the following Tuesday, he did not waste any time. However, once he made it across, he could not pay the full forty thousand Quetzales[7] they were charging at the time. Thinking of his children, Josue worked every job he could get so that he could pay off the fee and leave the distressing confines of the nightly lock-up.

The second peer who reported experiencing trauma in adulthood has had a tumultuous relationship with her spouse. Olivia had four children with her husband, but her husband left her and their children for a mistress in a distant village after her youngest child was born. Olivia was left with no home, few personal belongings, and four children to raise on her own. The experience has been extremely distressful for her. Without providing details, Olivia simply answered the question regarding adult trauma by stating, "Well, yes, because of the problems I have had with the father of my children."

When next asked about whether the armed conflict and genocide have had lasting psychological effects on their lives, less than half of peer participants responded affirmatively. A few mentioned under-achievement and loss of trust in others as causes of some continued psychological effects that persist in adulthood. The majority who answered affirmatively, however, identified persistent fear caused by state-sponsored terror and genocide as the underlying source of continued long-term psychological effects in their lives. For example, Marisol (born in 1974) stated, "Yes, it chills you as if you were bathing in cold water. You tremble from fear because it frightens you." Manuel (born in 1977) explicitly likened the genocide to a permanent scar: "*la violencia* is a scar that you can't get rid of. . . . I remember some of what happened and those older than me remember even more. . . . I believe the memories are still with us." Olivia responded that she still lives in fear of being assaulted or killed. Dario also referenced the constant fear of being targeted and killed stemming from the era of *la violencia*. He claimed that ex-soldiers and ex-guerrillas are now drug traffickers, so the same violence continues despite the signing of the 1996 peace accords. He explained, "You watch television and there are only dead people and more dead people. . . . Just dead people. Yes, only blood."

When peers subsequently were asked if they believe orphaned child survivors, in general, experienced childhood trauma, all but one responded affirmatively. The one peer who responded negatively simply answered "no" without further elaborating. All remaining peers identified orphaned child survivors witnessing their parents' murders and remembering those harrowing events as the underlying causes of their childhood trauma. Julietta, for example, explained, "Yes, because some of them have told me that they saw when their parents were shot or dragged away or when they cut them right there in front of them. . . . Whether they want to or not, it is hard to forget it." Elias (born in 1982) also referred to child survivors seeing what happened when their parents were kidnapped and even seeing them murdered in their own houses. Otto similarly reflected, "Some saw, and others didn't see but perhaps the problem with them is that there wasn't any protection or help. There wasn't any moral security or economic security because they didn't have parents to provide that." Peers also identified the overall loss of parents and family members as root causes of orphaned child survivors' trauma. Melvin (born in 1974) believed that because orphaned child survivors do not have parents, they have experienced trauma. Laya similarly referenced the loss of parents as a source of continued suffering, while Fatima (born in 1975) specifically identified *la violencia* and the regime of Ríos Montt as sources of childhood trauma for orphaned child survivors. She further reflected, "Oh, how they murdered! Yes, trauma and because of living in an unknown place. They have trauma because they are not with their families. It still hurts them at times."

In the final trauma-related question, I asked whether peers thought orphaned child survivors' experiences with childhood trauma differed from those of other Guatemalans of the same age. Nearly all agreed, indicating that orphaned child survivors' childhood trauma was more intense overall. Loss of parents, witnessing violent events, loss of connection to natal communities, and decreased socialization skills were the primary reasons peers gave to explain the difference in childhood experiences with trauma. For Laya, the fact that orphaned child survivors lost their parents and had to live with other people appeared difficult. Miguel referenced mass murder as a source of orphaned child survivors' more intense level of childhood trauma: "Yes, because they became orphaned after all of it because here it wasn't like in the hamlets where their parents were thrown into big pits.[8] Those things remain recorded in the mind. Thank God I didn't have to experience that!" Elena suggested that the distress of losing a parent clearly contributed to orphaned child survivors' traumatic experiences. She elaborated, "But as an orphan, who can you confide in? To be with a family member, a cousin or sibling just isn't the same. An orphaned child does not have the love of a father, of a mother." Fatima, on the other hand, focused more on orphaned child survivors' abilities to socialize, noting that "Sometimes they have difficulties communicating with others or lack the ability to communicate because they may say, 'Oh, I just can't talk with them.' They developed this lack of ability because of what happened to them."

Only two peers responded that there was relatively no difference between peer and orphaned child survivors' experiences with childhood trauma. Understandably, the two women who responded negatively to this question are two of the four women whose families were forced to flee their natal communities and relocate to Santa Teresa to stay alive during the armed conflict and genocide. Both women experienced *la violencia* firsthand and suffered significant trauma and distress as a result. As Teresa confirmed, "Yes, the experiences were the same because we all were afraid of what was happening." Andrea likewise explained, "I think that everyone has had very different experiences, very different and it is something that even the youngest child can always remember with great fear what had happened. It is an experience you can never forget!"

Interpreting the Qualitative Findings

Findings culled from the ethnographic interview questions that focused specifically on trauma provide compelling insight into both orphaned child survivor and peer experiences with childhood trauma caused by the armed conflict and genocide. These findings first demonstrate that many child survivors and their peers used the term "trauma" on their own to describe psychological distress brought on by the terror of the armed conflict and genocide, thus establishing that trauma is a personally meaningful and salient concept for identifying, conveying, and understanding both child survivor and peer childhood life experiences with psychological distress. With respect to trauma experienced by participants, these findings also clearly reveal that the overwhelming majority of child survivors and half of their peers did, indeed, report experiencing trauma, especially in their early childhoods. Those who did not experience trauma pointed to their young age, other family circumstances, and the fact that they did not lose a close family member as mitigating the psychological effects of the armed conflict and genocide in their childhood experiences. For those who did experience childhood trauma, half of the child survivor group and only five peers felt they continue to be affected in some way by their childhood trauma today in adulthood. Loss of parents and other close family members, traumatic memories, persistent fear, and enduring sadness were some of the factors that participants indicated as causing long-term trauma in their life experiences today. At the same time, some child survivors and peers who identified as experiencing childhood trauma no longer felt they were emotionally affected by it. In fact, those child survivors explicitly asserted that they have purposely overcome their childhood trauma, while peers offered no explanation other than to say they simply no longer feel affected.

Turning to adult experiences with trauma, only two orphaned child survivors and two peers identified themselves as having experienced trauma now as adults. Domestic violence committed by spouses, a random shooting, and difficulties after crossing the Mexico/US border as an undocumented adult are the underlying causes of adult trauma for these individuals. When asked if their experiences in childhood with the armed conflict and genocide have had lasting psychological distress other than trauma now in adulthood, almost half of the child survivor group and a few of their peers affirmed so. Losing parents, living apart from surviving family members, lingering fear, loss of trust in others, and under-achievement were identified as contributing to the other long-term psychological effects brought on by the armed conflict and genocide.

Findings from the trauma-related questions also revealed that all child survivors and almost all their peers believe that orphaned child survivors, generally, have experienced childhood trauma. Child survivors and peers specified witnessing parents' murders and other violent events, remembering the tragic events, and experiencing violent acts directly as contributing to childhood trauma. They also identified being separated from family and experiencing grave uncertainty, exploitation, and abuse as additional underlying sources of childhood trauma for Guatemalan orphaned child survivors overall.

Finally, almost all child survivor and peer participants responded that orphaned child survivors, in general, have had more exposure to tragic events and consequently, have experienced more intense and frequent childhood trauma than any other Guatemalan peers of the same age. Witnessing parents' murders, losing immediate family members, losing connections with natal communities, and just living through *la violencia* are some of the primary factors participants recognized as causing greater levels of childhood trauma among orphaned child survivors in comparison with their age mates in Guatemala.

Based on child survivor and peer participants' experiences and perceptions, it is evident that children, as a distinctive group, did comprise a significant portion of the victims and survivors who have endured psychological distress and trauma as a result of the armed conflict and genocide, as well as the culture of fear that the military deliberately promulgated. Consequently, investigation into child survivors' distinct and unique experiences as a group is fully warranted. As participants in my research project attest, the effects of earlier childhood experiences with trauma did not necessarily dissipate with time or the onset of adulthood. Half of the child survivor group and five peers reported still feeling affected by childhood trauma today in adulthood. In addition, almost half of the child survivor group and a few of their peers reported experiencing other general long-term psychological distress caused by the internal armed conflict and from the especially brutal period of *la violencia.* Relationships between childhood trauma and adult psychopathology have been firmly established in psychological research (e.g., Bolstad and Zinbarg 1997; Breslau, Chilcoat, Kessler, and Davis 1999; Kulkarni, Pole, and Timko 2013; Philippe, Laventure, Beaulieu-Pelletier, Lecours, and Lekes 2011) and give cause to further assess such experiences via quantitative measures.

QUANTITATIVE ANALYSES OF PSYCHOLOGICAL DISTRESS, TRAUMA, AND RESILIENCE

To further explore the long-term effects of childhood trauma and other genocide-related psychological distress on child survivors and their peers, I incorporated three psychological assessment instruments in my research project. My aim was to quantitatively assess whether there was an experiential difference between child survivors and their peers reporting long-term effects of trauma and the presence of resilience and to then compare those results with my qualitative findings. Full and extended discussion of my quantitative methods and findings is available in Heying et al. (2016); however, the following overview provides a general synopsis of the instruments used and how the results they yielded actually dovetailed with the qualitative findings of my research project.

Under the guidance of faculty of the Department of Psychology at the University of New Mexico and following the completion of graduate coursework on trauma, along with reading additional extensive cross-cultural literature of trauma and trauma assessment, I selected three psychological assessment instruments for quantitative analysis based on their cross-cultural efficacy. These were the Revised Civilian Mississippi Scale, or RCMS (Norris and Perilla 1996); the Symptom Checklist 90 Revised, or SCL-90-R

(González et al. 1989); and the Post-traumatic Growth Inventory, or PTGI (Weiss and Berger 2006). Each is a Spanish version, empirically-tested psychometric measure that has been used with a wide array of Spanish-speaking ethnic and cultural groups, including Indigenous populations in Mexico and other regions of the world. I administered these self-reporting instruments at the end of each ethnographic interview with the forty participants in my research project.

The first instrument, the RCMS, is a thirty-item psychometric instrument that measures self-reported symptoms of post-traumatic stress in a civilian population. The Spanish version was developed by Norris and Perilla (1996) and requires respondents to rate thirty items on a five-point Likert scale from one (*nada cierto/*not at all true) to five (*extremadamente cierto/*extremely true) in response to questions regarding a traumatic event such as: *I feel like I cannot go on; I enjoy the company of others; and Since the event, I have been afraid to go to sleep at night.* Items in the RCMS Spanish version are grouped based on the diagnostic criteria used for post-traumatic stress disorder (PTSD) presented in the Diagnostic and Statistical Manual of Mental Disorders, Fourth Edition, or DSM-IV (American Psychiatric Association 1994).

Findings from the RCMS revealed no significant group differences between child survivors and their peers regarding self-reported post-traumatic psychological distress now present in adulthood. However, eight child survivors and eight peers did meet the criteria that indicate a potential likelihood of PTSD. Thus, the findings revealed a potential PTSD rate of 40 percent among the child survivor group and 40 percent among the peer group. While there is no norm group with which to compare child survivor and peer responses for the RCMS Spanish version, 40 percent suggests that a sizable number of child survivor and peer participants reported experiencing, at the time of assessment, trauma-related symptoms that are potentially diagnosable as PTSD. Furthermore, eight child survivors who reported a likelihood of PTSD via the RCMS were among the ten who responded in the qualitative data presented earlier that they felt they were still affected today by their childhood trauma or general psychological distress caused by the armed conflict and genocide. Similarly, the eight peers who reported a likelihood of PTSD included all five peers who responded in the ethnographic interviews that they still felt affected by childhood trauma. The remaining three peers with potential PTSD were among the nine who responded affirmatively to the question of whether the internal armed conflict and especially *la violencia* still affects them psychologically in some way today. The RCMS findings also reveal that even though more child survivors than peers reported in the ethnographic interviews that they still felt affected by childhood trauma and general psychological distress stemming from the armed conflict and genocide, there was no significant difference between groups regarding potential self-reported PTSD symptoms at the time of the interviews.

The second instrument, the Symptoms Checklist 90 Revised (SCL-90-R) Spanish version (Derogatis 1983), is a widely-used assessment instrument that measures the overall psychological functioning and distress of a population (Bermejo-Toro and Prieto-Ursúa 2006; Derogatis 1977; Güell et al. 2006; Pedersen and Karterud 2004). It consists of a ninety-item, self-report symptom inventory that requires respondents to rate items on a five-point Likert scale from 0 (*nada*/not at all) to 4 (*mucho*/extremely) in response to the frequency of symptoms experienced in the seven days prior to completing the assessment instrument. Symptoms include headaches, nervousness, lack of appetite, feeling trapped, sudden fright, and feeling low energy. The ninety items comprising the SCL-90-R Spanish version are grouped into nine primary symptom dimensions: somatization, obsessive-compulsivity, interpersonal sensitivity, depression, anxiety, hostility, phobic anxiety, paranoid ideation, and psychoticism. The instrument also measures three global indices of distress: the Global Severity Index (GSI), the Positive Symptom Distress Index (PSDI), and the Positive Symptom Total (PST). The GSI reflects current level or depth of psychological distress and is used most frequently when a single summary measure of distress from the SCL-90-R is required. The PSDI targets symptom intensity, and the PST targets symptom breadth experienced by each respondent in the week leading up to the day they completed the assessment. By measuring levels of distress in the nine areas of symptom dimensions and in the global indices overall, the SLC-90-R Spanish version determines individuals' current point-in-time psychological symptom status (Derogatis 1983).

Results from the SCL-90-R Spanish version for child survivors and their peers reveal that each group continued to experience various general psychological symptoms in adulthood. Neither group, however, was necessarily highly symptomatic or pathological in any one symptom dimension, or in the level of overall psychological distress. As with the RCMS Spanish version findings, results from the SCL-90-R Spanish version are consistent with what child survivors and peers revealed in their responses to the trauma-related questions posed in the ethnographic interviews. Almost half of the child survivor group and a few of their peers responded in the qualitative interviews that their childhood experiences have had other lasting psychological effects in general even in adulthood today, yet they did not talk about those effects as currently debilitating or causing high levels of current distress. Therefore, the quantitative findings culled from the SCL-90-R Spanish version corroborate the findings from the qualitative ethnographic interviews.

The third and final psychological assessment instrument is the Post-traumatic Growth Inventory (PTGI) Spanish version. In contemporary psychology, a

growing area of literature suggests that there are individuals who may perceive some benefit and growth following even the most traumatic of events
(Burt and Katz 1987; Tedeschi and Calhoun 1996; Veronen and Kilpatrick
1983). Recognizing this more recent area of growing research, I became
interested in analyzing the potential for post-traumatic growth among my
own research participants because of trends I noticed in conversations and
through my own eye-witness observations. I found that despite having experienced trauma in childhood, participants commonly and consistently focused
on positive growth in their lives rather than on solely negative repercussions.
Therefore, I felt that examining the potential for post-traumatic growth would
offer yet another lens with which to examine the long-term effects of childhood trauma and distress on child survivors and their peers in adulthood.

The PTGI was originally designed by Tedeschi and Calhoun (1996) to
gauge the degree to which individuals perceive benefits following adversity.
The PTGI Spanish version includes thirteen items that require individuals
to rate changes in their life experiences following traumatic events utilizing
a six-point Likert scale from zero (*no cambio*/no change) to five (*muy alto
grado de cambio*/high level of change). The thirteen items include statements
such as: *I am capable of improving my life, I have discovered that I am stronger than I thought,* and *I have changed my priorities about what is important
in life.* These items ultimately map onto three factors: Factor I (*philosophy
of life*), Factor II (*self/positive life attitude*), and Factor III (*interpersonal
relationships*). In administering the PTGI, I asked each participant to rate the
thirteen items in accordance with thinking about their earlier experiences with
childhood trauma and general psychological distress resulting from the armed
conflict and especially *la violencia* and how they feel today.

Findings from the PTGI revealed significantly higher post-traumatic
growth in the child survivor group compared to the peer group on two of the
three factors of the PTGI Spanish version: Factor II (*self/positive life attitude)*
and Factor III (*interpersonal relationships*). In addition, the child survivor
group trended toward significantly higher post-traumatic psychological
growth than their peers on Factor I (*philosophy of life).*

The PTGI was especially useful in further elucidating child survivors' and
peers' life-long experiences with childhood trauma and distress because it
revealed information not otherwise explicitly captured in the ethnographic
interview questions focused on trauma. Overall, child survivors perceive
themselves as having grown psychologically from their experiences with
childhood trauma and general psychological distress at a rate significantly
higher than their peers. These findings are particularly interesting as the twenty
child survivor participants had the additional distress of being orphaned and
having grown up in a permanent residential home away from their families and natal communities. It is possible that child survivors' significant

post-traumatic growth reflects the fact that they experienced a higher rate and severity of childhood trauma than their peers, constituting more potential for post-traumatic growth (i.e., those who suffer greater trauma necessarily have a longer way to go to return to a "normal" state of psychological well-being and, thus, report more growth). The correlation between greater trauma and post-traumatic growth has been noted as a potential limitation to the PTGI assessment instrument (Tedeschi and Calhoun 1996). However, it is difficult to conclusively determine how rates and severity of childhood trauma currently factor into the PTGI results presented here. What is particularly interesting regarding the results, however, is that child survivors appear to have psychologically overcome, to some extent at least, often intense childhood adversity and now actually perceive themselves as having benefited in some ways from those experiences. The potentially greater rate and severity of childhood trauma and general psychological distress experienced by child survivors may factor into how they now perceive greater benefits and growth from those experiences than their peers. However, these findings do corroborate child survivors' perceptions of their abilities to overcome childhood trauma as presented in the qualitative data drawn from the ethnographic interviews and clearly reflect their resilience, which may have been fostered by several important factors during their childhoods.

FACTORS CONTRIBUTING TO CHILD
SURVIVORS' RESILIENCE

After an extensive literature review regarding psychological trauma and institutional care for orphaned children in diverse contexts around the world, I identified three primary factors that likely contributed to child survivors' not reporting significantly higher rates of psychological distress than their peers on the quantitative instruments (Heying et al. 2016).

The first factor involves the relative safety that the residential home in Santa Teresa offered child survivors during the armed conflict and especially during *la violencia*. Catholic sisters, *tías,* staff, and volunteers went to great lengths to make sure the residential home was a safe environment. The physical structure of the residential home complex consisted of sturdy cement walls and fencing, as well as security doors and gates. Children enrolled in the residential home were accompanied in public by Catholic sisters, *tías,* staff, and volunteers to ensure their protection from outside threats. Distractions via fun activities, movie nights, games, and daily routines in the residential home purposely diverted child survivors' attention away from perceived threats on the few occasions when soldiers were near the town, or when news spread that guerrilla fighters were spotted in the area. In contrast, peer participants in my research project lived mainly with their families in Santa Teresa and may not have felt the same level of security. Various studies have demonstrated that perceived safety amid war and violence correlates with alleviating persistent post-traumatic distress for orphaned child survivors from other areas of the world such as Sri Lanka (e.g., Fernando and Ferrari 2013) and Rwanda (e.g., Dyregrov, Gupta, Gjestad, and Mukanoheli 2000; Schaal and Elbert 2006). It is likely that the permanent residential home in Santa Teresa offered child survivors a sense of relative safety that may have buffered some of the distress, anxiety, or fear associated with their childhood trauma. It may also explain why orphaned child survivors today do not report higher post-traumatic distress scores than their peers even though child survivors lived in institutionalized care for the majority of their childhoods (Heying et al. 2016).

The second factor pertains to the fact that many child survivors lived with surviving family members for some portions of their early and even middle childhoods before coming to live in the permanent residential home in Santa Teresa. The common age at time of enrollment in the residential home for child survivors in my research project ranged from six to fourteen. Consequently, many were able to live and develop in a more typical interpersonal family environment during some of their most formative years before being enrolled in the residential home. Various studies have found that children who come to institutional enrollment at a later age are likely to experience lower rates of persisting social and behavioral problems and are also more likely to experience improved well-being in childhood (e.g., Julian 2013, Whetten et al. 2009).

The third factor includes child survivors' enrollment with siblings. As demonstrated in cases such as Juliana, Susana, Esteban, and Debora, many child survivors came to live in the residential home along with their siblings. This likely afforded them some consistency in family relationships. A number of studies on children's emotional well-being underscore the importance of keeping sibling groups together in alternative care settings when living outside of family homes (e.g., Gong et al. 2009; Washington 2007).

In addition to factors that may have contributed to child survivors not reporting significantly higher rates of psychological distress than their peers, I was also curious what factors may have contributed to their reporting significantly higher levels of post-traumatic growth relative to their peers. Such reported post-traumatic growth differences are intriguing, especially given child survivors' experiences with trauma and distress and with living in a residential home compared to their peers who remained living with family members during childhood, adolescence, and early adulthood. I identified four factors of likely influence.

First, the quality of care that child survivors received in the residential home in Santa Teresa generally, and low caregiver-to-child ratios specifically, may have contributed to their post-traumatic growth in important ways. Intentionally designed to replicate a typical family home structure from the region, the residential home consisted of eight small homes with similar spatial configurations to other local family homes, offering a familiarity of place and space. Within the eight homes resided small family-like groups (e.g., a small group of children of various ages and genders living together with several *tías*). The small child and adult groupings resulted in more intensive quality of childcare fostered by loving, nurturing, family-like relationships between child survivors and their caregivers (Heying et al. 2016). Regardless of specific type of care (family versus institutional care), quality childcare in and of itself that includes loving, nurturing relationships is vital for positive child development (e.g., Betancourt and Khan 2008; McCall 2011; Whetten et al. 2009). Furthermore, literature on child resilience and post-traumatic growth suggests that close ties with caregivers can help diminish psychological distress resulting from war, violence, and other disasters (e.g., Bragin 2007; Calhoun, Tedeschi, Cann, and Hanks 2010; Ungar et al. 2007).

A second factor is the self-disclosure and emotional expressiveness that the residential home fostered among child survivors (Heying et al. 2016). Catholic sisters, *tías*, staff, and volunteers encouraged child survivors to share their experiences with each other and offer each other support. Being able to share their experiences with other child survivors may have helped those enrolled in the residential home make sense of their traumatic experiences and build strong peer attachments. Sharing experiences and building peer attachments have been shown to strengthen child survivors' critical emotional and social support systems (e.g., Johnson et al. 2009; Mota and Matos 2013). Having the opportunity to share personal stories and emotions through self-disclosure can help child survivors develop coping skills and create strong connections with others, facilitating post-traumatic psychological growth (Calhoun, Cann, and Tedeschi 2010; Tedeschi and Calhoun 2004). Other studies with child survivors of genocide, in particular, have also shown similar positive correlations between strong peer attachments and increased well-being. For example, Dyregrov et al. (2000) found that Rwandan orphaned children who grew up in institutionalized care were more likely to feel accepted and to develop camaraderie with others by sharing with each other their experiences with psychological distress and loss related to genocide. Likewise, Schaal and Elbert (2006) found that Rwandan child survivors who were raised in institutional care may experience feelings of greater safety and acceptance because they grew up knowing that they were not alone in their sorrow and suffering.

A third factor involves the perceived stability that living in the residential home may have afforded child survivors, especially amid the internal armed conflict and in the wake of the brutal period of *la violencia*. The Catholic sisters deliberately established routinized schedules for the child survivors in the residential home. Daily routines included attending school, participating in vocational training, receiving tutoring help, attending study sessions in the home, helping with household chores, engaging in cultural activities, and practicing Mayan language skills. Studies confirm that restoring and maintaining formal education and other vocational training offer children a sense of security and predictability even during times of war, violence, and conflict, which, in turn, can instill a sense of hope that may improve mental and social outcomes (e.g., Betancourt and Khan 2008). Literature on post-traumatic growth further demonstrates that routine involvement in cultural practices, formal education, and vocational training can help children develop skills that foster their sense of both self-reliance and self-confidence, which are important for post-traumatic growth (Calhoun et al. 2010; Tedeschi and Calhoun 1996).

A fourth and final factor concerns improved access to economic resources afforded by the residential home. Many child survivors and their families were forced to live in dire poverty following the kidnapping, death, or abandonment of one or both of their parents and the destruction of property by military soldiers. Coming to live in the residential home meant that child survivors instantly had access to sufficient and healthy food, clothing, and school supplies. They also could go to school throughout the entire time they were enrolled in the residential home because of scholarships and financial support that the Catholic sisters secured for them. Peers from Santa Teresa, on the other hand, often grew up with limited economic resources. Consequently, some peers were not able to continue their education past elementary or junior high school. Lastly, child survivors had access to medical care that many of their peers did not, which could have added to their overall sense of well-being. Having consistent access to various resources, formal education, and medical services may have furthered child survivors' sense of stability and well-being, helping foster their post-traumatic growth (Heying et al. 2016). However, future examination of the relationship between increased economic resources and post-traumatic growth is needed and should involve various child survivor groups in residential settings around the world.

A MORE COMPREHENSIVE AND HOLISTIC
EXAMINATION OF TRAUMA AND RESILIENCE

There is much to learn from Guatemalan child survivors about facing and even overcoming, or at least positively coping with, the effects of the tragedy and trauma caused by the armed conflict and genocide. Both orphaned child survivors and their peers were forced to endure childhood hardships, distress, and loss unfathomable for many people. Orphaned child survivors faced even greater adversity because they lost one or both of their parents and were brought to live in a residential home for orphaned children located for most in an unfamiliar environment far away from surviving family members and their natal communities. Child survivors and peers recognize that growing up amid the chaos of genocide, terror, and a persistent culture of fear generated complex challenges that were further exacerbated by child survivors' orphan status. Yet as my qualitative and quantitative findings reveal, child survivors and their peers have managed to positively confront childhood trauma and, in the process, ameliorate some of their suffering demonstrated by the fact that they do not report or exhibit extreme levels of debilitation or psychopathology in adulthood. This is especially apparent and poignant for child survivors as they have not only overcome the trauma of their childhoods to some extent, both in the short-and long-term, but also perceive those experiences as having contributed to their own personal growth and adaptability to life challenges now in adulthood. Positively dealing with and overcoming such horrendous experiences with childhood trauma, especially sequential traumatization, to become resilient, well-adapted adults despite having lost their parents, homes, and familial and natal community ties is a remarkable testament to child survivors' resilience.

Resilience is generally defined as the ability to return to and maintain psychological and physical equilibrium following a traumatic event or events (Bonanno 2004). However, the experiences with childhood trauma for participants in my research project and their abilities to generally rise above that trauma in adulthood necessitate expanding the definition of resilience to further reflect their unique life experiences. For Guatemalan orphaned child survivors, effectively engaging in resilient behaviors means that they have the "capacity for adapting successfully and functioning competently despite experiencing chronic adversity or following exposure to prolonged or severe trauma" (Cicchetti 2010, 524; see also Masten, Best, and Garmezy 1990). This definition of resilience reflects more than just a "return to equilibrium" by recognizing that individuals respond to traumatic circumstances and events often by establishing positive, creative, and constructive ways to adapt and function. Child survivors' capacities to adapt and function competently are evident in their abilities to simultaneously recognize the childhood trauma they faced and to background associated memories so they can move forward with life in a positive, constructive manner. Such sentiment is apparent in Sheni's assertion that she and her fellow child survivors are not "erasing" what happened in their early childhoods, but rather are "setting it aside." Sheni's statement demonstrates that, in general, child survivor participants' aim is not to forget or to erase what has happened in their earlier childhoods. Instead, they opt to focus on their potential and on their abilities to mobilize their positive capacities in constructive ways to become resilient, well-adapted adults despite their traumatic and distressing pasts and the lingering consequences associated with them.

Orphaned child survivors in Guatemala are not alone in their remarkable ability to not only rise above the debilitating effects of childhood trauma but also grow in positive, constructive ways from it. This underlying theme of resilience strongly resonates with other anthropological research similarly conducted with Guatemalan survivors of the armed conflict and genocide. For example, anthropologist Ricardo Falla's early work in the 1980s with Maya survivors living in refugee camps in Mexico and in resistance groups hiding within Guatemala highlights the destructive effects of the armed conflict and genocide on these communities and individual members but also demonstrates that survivors are "psychologically resourceful agents" who cannot be portrayed as mere victims (1994, 192). Falla notes that the scars from mass terror likely will not fade from collective memory, and yet Maya Indigenous communities have found ways to not just survive but also to actively resist, escape, and readjust. Maya Indigenous communities have displayed remarkable survival and resilience (ibid., 192).

In a similar vein, Montejo (1999) found resilience and hope among fellow Jakaltek refugees with whom he lived and worked in Mexico. Having experienced the armed conflict and genocide firsthand and having similarly been forced to live in exile, Montejo shows that these refugees managed to adapt to their situations and to develop a strong sense of community, both testaments to their resilience. His research has revealed the persistence and courage of refugees whose determination and endurance underscore the strength of their culture and give him hope for their future (1999, 25).

Research conducted with Maya widows of the internal armed conflict and genocide in Guatemala reveals encouraging signs of hope and resilience among another distinctive population of survivors who were devastated during the armed conflict and genocide, as well as in the aftermath that followed. Judith Zur (1998) worked with Maya widows to explore how they talked about and explained their experiences with violence and the persistent culture of fear that infiltrated their daily lives. She found that Maya widows have utilized creative survival strategies to reconstruct their lives on both a physical and psychological level. Despite ongoing physical and psychological suffering, Maya widows actively formed social groups and cooperatives within their communities to construct a sense of themselves as widows, daughters, and mothers of the dead and disappeared (ibid., 179). By sharing their painful memories of the violence and "remembering" in these social groups and cooperatives, the women have found new possibilities for action, for reworking their identities, and for asserting new positions in society. Through their participation in development projects and community organizing with each other, Maya widows have taken an active and public stance in dealing with the negative consequences of the genocide, in forming strong social ties with other widows, and in calling for justice by prosecuting the brutal crimes committed against them, their families, and their communities. Maya widows' participation in the social groups and cooperatives demonstrates their abilities to actively engage in resilient behaviors that directly address the horrific events and conditions in which they have been forced to live. As Zur writes, "They have learnt to adapt, to survive; some have begun to 'work' for justice . . . " (1998, 30).

Anthropologist Linda Green (1999) also found resilient practices among a group of Maya widows of the armed conflict and genocide in an undisclosed area of the highlands. These women similarly used the creative practice of coming together to work on development projects, share experiences, and raise their awareness of the ways in which their suffering had been shaped by gender, class, and ethnicity. Finding a niche within development projects, Maya widows came to rework their identities by incorporating their experiences as widows and Maya women. This allowed them to call greater attention to and, in some cases, confront their marginal positions as Maya women in post-conflict Guatemalan society (ibid., 108). They have also found much needed emotional respite from the "culture of fear" that continues to plague Guatemala in the post-conflict era. Identifying and recognizing the underlying sense of resilience found among even the most physically, psychologically, and economically devastated of survivors, Green reflects, "Some widows of Xe'caj constructed alternative forms of community in the midst of their suffering that speak powerfully to the resiliency of the human spirit" (ibid., 171).

Resilience has emerged as such a strong underlying theme in the life experiences of survivors of Guatemala's internal armed conflict and genocide that also is highlighted in the truth reports. Both the REMHI (1998) and CEH (1999) truth reports fully explore the negative consequences and suffering caused by the armed conflict and genocide, but they also explicitly underscore survivors' own creative and resilient responses to the terror. Both reports emphasize that survivors have actively participated in forms of resistance to and coping with the terror that has infused their daily lives. According to the REMHI report, for example, "The strategies people have used to cope with the effects of violence are an important facet of their experience. Many individuals and groups assumed a very active posture despite the risk involved" (1999, 51). From testimonies collected in both truth reports, the majority Maya Indigenous highlands populations created and participated in organizations, movements, and activities designed to legally denounce human rights violations, to search for the disappeared, to report massacres and other acts of violence, and to create support networks for survivors. These rural activist organizations and activities demonstrate that highlands inhabitants were not just passive, vulnerable victims of the armed conflict and genocide, withering away and disintegrating into the backdrop of the harrowing aftermath. Instead, many have become active and resilient individuals who continue to work diligently to reconstruct their lives, restore their dignity and human rights, and repair the social fabric that have bound their families and communities together for centuries. This is not to say that the armed conflict and genocide has not left indelible emotional, psychological, and physical scars in the lives of survivors. Rather, the REMHI and CEH reports further corroborate the creative, resilient ways in which survivors have responded to trauma and distress, which must be brought to light to better understand the complexities of survivors' life experiences.

While child survivors who participated in my research project were too young to engage in activist organizations and community activities when they were children, they nonetheless formed a strong sense of resilience that has allowed them to adapt to life as orphaned child survivors who are now adults and to function positively despite living without the moral and social support of one or both parents. Most child survivors I interviewed acknowledged having experienced childhood sequential traumatization, yet not one of them identified their childhood trauma as causing life-long debilitating or pathological effects. Instead, they deliberately focus on positive events and aspects of their lives. This is particularly evident in the quantitative post-traumatic growth results, which indicate that child survivors view themselves as having grown from their experiences with childhood trauma in ways that exceed the experiences of their peers. Failing to recognize child survivors' creative, adaptive abilities and resilience by instead only focusing on the negative consequences they have endured offers only a partial view of their lived experiences. The complexities of child survivors' experiences require a more comprehensive and holistic examination of the sequential nature of their childhood trauma, of the distress their trauma has caused *and* the resilience they have developed along the way. Any lesser examination belittles their struggle and demeans their resilience. As my research reveals, child survivors deserve more concerted efforts to understand the full breadth and depth of their experiences.

NOTES

1. During the two years that I was a volunteer in the permanent residential home, one of my primary duties was to provide homework assistance to child survivors. Several child survivors remarked that by participating in my research project, they could finally "return the favor" for me helping them with their education when they were in elementary school and junior high by now helping me with my "education."

While I assured them that their assistance in that way was not necessary or required, they remained enthusiastic and proud to participate, nonetheless.

2. I took graduate courses in trauma at the University of New Mexico, Albuquerque, in which we analyzed many articles from scholars across various disciplines who strongly caution that conceptual constructs such as "trauma" used to categorize psychological distress and the utilization of psychological assessment instruments created in "Western" societies to measure for the effects of "trauma" (such as PTSD) may not accurately or genuinely capture the essence of human responses to psychological distress across diverse groups of peoples and societies (Bracken 2001; Desjarlais and Kleinman 1994; López and Guarnaccia 2000; Summerfield 2000). Therefore, I was acutely aware of not assuming and applying terms in my own research, such as "trauma," that may not have had meaning or been useful for participants in conveying their own personal experiences with psychological distress.

3. In addition to specifically avoiding questions regarding any details about particular events associated with childhood trauma, I also provided participants with contact information for a local counselor and a psychologist in the capital who agreed to assist them with psychological therapy free of charge if any experienced distress during or following the interviews caused by the questions or content.

4. I chose not to ask direct questions regarding the death or kidnapping and disappearances of family members to avoid causing research participants distress during and/or following the interviews. If the participants brought up such events while describing what they felt *la violencia* meant within the context of Guatemalan history, I recorded it and asked follow-up questions only if the participant said it was okay to do so.

5. A *temazcal* is a traditional Maya Indigenous sweat bath that locals use for bathing. It is typically a small, dome-like adobe structure roughly three feet tall in the middle that is located outside of the house and is warmed with heated stones (Groark 1997).

6. *Nervios* (nerves) is defined as "powerful idiom of distress used by individuals from a variety of Caribbean, Central and South American countries. It is a way through which people express concerns about physical symptoms, emotional states, and changes both in the family and in the broader society" (Guarnaccia and Farias 1988, 1223).

7. At the time that Josue left for the US in 2005, one Guatemalan Quetzal was worth roughly US$0.13. The total cost of his passage (45,000 Guatemalan Quetzales, or Q45,000) would have been equivalent to US$5,894. This amount was more than twenty-three times the average monthly salary of Q1,891 (or US$245.83) for individuals living in the Santa Teresa region in 2005 (Ministerio de Trabajo y Previsión Social 2010).

8. Manuel is referencing the clandestine graves that the military used throughout the highlands to bury mass numbers of victims.

Chapter Five

Born Indigenous, Die Indigenous

Child survivors in my research project experienced severed ties with families and natal communities as a consequence of the internal armed conflict and genocide. These severed ties meant that child survivors experienced major shifts and disruption in centers of early influence that are critical for identity formation in childhood (Holland, Lachicotte, Skinner, and Cain 1998). Families and natal communities typically serve as primary sources of socialization and enculturation for children, and, as such, are directly linked to identity formation. For children in the Guatemalan highlands, where the majority of most residents identify as Maya Indigenous peoples, families and natal communities have been especially central to ethnic identity formation (Carey 2001; Montejo 2004).

The Guatemalan state and its military have long recognized the importance of familial and natal community ties in Indigenous identity formation and deliberately sought to destroy those ties through explicit annihilation and assimilation policies and practices. Such policies and practices were used in attempts to wipe out Indigenous identities altogether under the guise of the state's nationalist identity-making project. Yet their annihilation and assimilation efforts were largely unsuccessful as Indigenous peoples have continued to perceive and express ethnic identity in their own dynamic and complex ways (Green 1998; Falla 1994; Montejo 1999). In fact, not only did the state's forceful efforts to annihilate or assimilate all Indigenous peoples largely fail but such efforts also came to be replaced by what Hale (2006) suggests are new openings in contemporary Indigenous and *ladino* relations. As dicussed in the introduction of this book, Hale argues that these new openings have shifted *ladino* political sensibilities whereby most *ladinos* now cautiously advocate for multicultural equality.

Persistence in Indigenous identities and shifts in *ladino* political sensibilities have contributed to a more "multicultural," though still largely discriminatory, social context in Guatemala today (Hale 2006). For child survivors in my research project, long-term consequences of the state's annihilation and assimilationist agenda related to various aspects of their ethnic identity remain in effect. They recognize that they have lost certain aspects that they associate with ethnic identity (e.g., Mayan language skills, Maya Indigenous traditions or *costumbres*, the use of traditional clothing, etc.). At the same time, however, they neither exude nor report any sense of overarching "identity loss" or "identity crisis" whatsoever in their own personal experiences.

Despite having lost certain aspects they associate with their Maya Indigenous identities, child survivors featured in this book perceive themselves as maintaining a strong sense of ethnic identity continuity and are adamant about asserting that continuity. At the same time, they also recognize that they engage in creative and transformative practices regarding ethnic identity to adapt in positive, deliberate ways to the long-term consequences brought on by their severed familial and natal community ties. These practices, relatively novel when compared to perhaps overarching experiences of Maya Indigenous peoples of the same age or older in Guatemala, include attaining advanced education, achieving professional careers, and working as lawyers to help litigate for human rights issues in the country, to name just a few. Drawing from both a deep sense of continuity and their own novel practices, child survivors have forged a deeply rooted and strong sense of ethnic identity. This is encapsulated in one survivor's poignant proclamation, "I was born Indigenous. I will die Indigenous." In this chapter, I elaborate on how child survivors have forged their strong sense of ethnic identity and belonging against a backdrop of armed conflict and genocide. I also reveal how these survivors view ethnic identity and belonging today as they help their own children develop a similarly strong sense of ethnic identity and belonging in Guatemala's post-conflict context. To achieve this aim, I begin with a discussion of Guatemalan state efforts to carry out ethnocide, which provides context for understanding the challenges child survivors faced when forming their sense of ethnic identity in childhood.

GUATEMALAN STATE EFFORTS TO CARRY OUT ETHNOCIDE

For centuries, the Guatemalan state has imposed its nationalist identity-making project on the whole of its heterogeneous, majority Indigenous populations for the specific benefit of a small group of non-Indigenous oligarchic elite. As part of its hegemonic endeavors, the state enacted explicit assimilationist policies and practices such as prohibiting men's use of traditional dress while in the workplace and forcing Spanish as the only permitted language in public schools (Becker Richards and Richards 1996; Otzoy 1996). Through these intentional efforts, the state sought to replace Indigenous identities with a single, unified national *ladino*identity as a means of achieving the ethnically homogeneous nation-state it long desired (Smith 1988). However, the *ladino* identity-making project has continuously failed, especially as ideological hegemony, because the mass populations have not bought into the state's nationalist identity-making agenda. Ideological hegemony occurs when the masses voluntarily give consent to the ruling elite's way of thinking without resisting or questioning it or the elites' actions via the state (Gramsci 1957, 10). In Guatemala, that did not happen. The mass populations continued to question the state's ideology and actions. Recognizing its failed hegemonic efforts, along with burgeoning public discontent and popular organizing taking place throughout the country in the 1970s, the Guatemalan state turned to violent coercion as a way of forcefully implementing its nationalist identity-making project on the masses (Smith 1988).

Assimilation to the Guatemalan state's nationalist ideology by means of violent coercion was a central goal of the counterinsurgency campaign, especially during the period of *la violencia* (Schirmer 1998; Smith 1988). The state, through its forced assimilation policies, characterized Indigenous identities in largely essentialist terms, or as a list of static, autochthonous traits (e.g., language, dress, beliefs, religious practices, traditional customs, etc.), and deliberately sought to target and destroy those traits and related institutions that it perceived as central to Indigenous identities in Guatemala (Garrard-Burnett 2010; Hale 2006; Watanabe 1992). Jennifer Schirmer (1998) further illuminates the state's explicit goal of forced assimilation established in the counterinsurgency campaign by discussing the content of military documents published during *la violencia*. In these documents, the state explicitly calls for the "ladinization" of (or the imposition of *ladino* identity on) Indigenous populations by ordering the military to force Indigenous peoples to abandon their language and traditions, and to repress the use of Indigenous dress and other forms of external displays of ethnic identity that would continue to differentiate Indigenous from *ladino* citizens (ibid., 104).

The REMHI (1998) and CEH (1999) truth reports further corroborate that, through its military actions, the state sought to strategically eliminate Indigenous identities by explicitly destroying and disrupting Indigenous communities, autonomous systems of governance, social customs, traditional lifeways, belief systems, Mayan languages, and traditional clothing. Military operations also aimed to destroy Indigenous communities by massacring and razing villages and forcing entire populations to abandon their communities altogether. They also cause major upheaval in the social fabric of communities via civil patrols that instilled fear and hostility among community members and, thus, weakened central Indigenous community ties (CEH 1999; REMHI 1998). Physical destruction of Indigenous communities and erosion of the social networks within them were deliberate acts carried out by the state and its military explicitly to decimate Indigenous identities. The REMHI report reflects both the frequency and intensity of community destruction by revealing it was one of the most commonly identified effects of the armed conflict and genocide reported in survivor testimonies, with one out of five testimonies mentioning it (1999, 40).

Along with both physical annihilation and destruction of the social fabric of communities, the military also specifically carried out state orders to eliminate traditional autonomous systems of governance particularly common in Maya Indigenous communities in the highlands communities (CEH 1999c; REMHI 1998). The military achieved this goal by first killing local community leaders and authorities and then imposing external military authority over all aspects of community governance. Consequently, traditional community governance based on centuries-long Maya Indigenous beliefs, ethics, moral principles, and convictions used to regulate social life and resolve conflicts was decimated as the military exercised full and unjust authoritarian control with greater ease over Maya Indigenous community members (ibid.). The REMHI report specifically reveals that the military often forcefully changed, replaced, or subordinated community leaders to military authorities, who then imposed foreign values and customs on communities and abused their power (1999, 43).

Military strategies to wipe out Indigenous identities also involved eroding social customs. Considered dangerous by the state, social customs, such as marriages, kinship systems, and obligations, and extended social relationships within and among Indigenous communities were interrupted, discouraged, and deemed as direct threats to the state. Constant surveillance of community and social life by military soldiers and civil patrollers made community members fear participating in traditional social and cultural customs. As a result, most customs were downplayed or avoided altogether, especially during *la violencia* (CEH 1999c; Manz 1988; REMHI 1998).

The state considered traditional lifeways, such as subsistence farming, another form of direct threat to its nationalist identity-making project. Along with the persistent economic crises of the 1970s and 1980s, the counterinsurgency campaign made subsistence farming no longer economically viable for most Maya Indigenous families in the highlands at the time. Subsistence farming had been the primary Maya Indigenous lifeway for centuries and was considered a marker of Indigenous identity by the state. To further erode and eradicate Indigenous identities, therefore, the military forced families off their lands, prohibited the cultivation of traditional crops (e.g., maize, black beans, etc.), burned planted crops, killed and plundered livestock, destroyed and stole farming implements, and identified subsistence farmers as potential "communist subversives" simply because of their occupation. As a result, subsistence farming as a traditional lifeway decreased substantially, challenging not only Indigenous families' sense of ethnic identity but also their fundamental survival (CEH 1999c; Manz 1988; REMHI 1998).

Indigenous belief systems similarly were identified as threats against the state and its assimilationist agenda. Religious beliefs, also perceived by the state as particularly central to Indigenous identity, were deemed " communist subversive" doctrine and a major obstacle to nationalist ideology. The growing popularity of Liberation Theology and its tenets that called for societal transformation via empowerment of the poor and oppressed gave the state further motivation to attempt to also eliminate Catholicism among the masses (Garrard-Burnett 2010; Gutiérrez 1988; Jonas 1991; Schirmer 1998). To rid the highlands of both Liberation Theology and traditional Indigenous spiritual belief systems, the state charged military personnel and civil patrollers with the task of prohibiting all Catholic and traditional Maya religious ceremonies and rites, as well as forbidding the sale of ritual materials such as candles, incense, and other religious accouterments needed for religious practices. Military and civil patrollers also destroyed religious and cultural symbols, objects, and sites as an explicit strategy in its counterinsurgency campaign. Symbols and objects were commonly shattered or were used in disturbing ways by soldiers and civil patrollers to pervert their meanings (CEH 1999c; REMHI 1998). Traditional sacred sites and Catholic churches were frequently closed off, destroyed, or desecrated by the military. Murders, torture, and raping of Indigenous victims and survivors were often executed by the military on such sacred sites or in churches where temporary military posts had been installed. In addition, religious leaders were killed and tortured, pastoral work was banned, and the public profession of Catholic or Indigenous religious beliefs was strictly forbidden. In place of Catholic and traditional Maya beliefs, perceived as central to Indigenous identities, the state instead sought to instill fundamental evangelical doctrine that directly supported its nationalist identity-making project through espousing anti-communist sentiment, cultural assimilation to *ladino* lifeways, and social control (Manz 1988; Zur 1998).

Indigenous languages became another target of the state's forced assimilationist practices. With twenty-two distinct Mayan languages within its borders, the Guatemalan state perceived Mayan language use not only as a marker of Maya Indigenous identities but also as a major hindrance to its national assimilationist aims. Therefore, the military and civil patrollers enforced the prohibition of Mayan language use among Maya Indigenous populations, despite the fact that Mayan languages were not only the first language for many in these populations but also their only language at the time. Individuals heard speaking their native language were often immediately accused of being guerrilla supporters and commonly shot and killed. This unjustified and errant stigma that the military created especially surrounding Mayan language use, in which speaking a Mayan language was often considered an automatic signal that one was a guerilla, caused many native speakers to abandon their Mayan languages altogether during the heightened years of the genocide. Kay Warren has noted that in that time period, survivors often switched from speaking their Mayan language to Spanish so strangers and outsiders could understand that their conversations were nonpolitical in nature (1993, 48).

Mayan languages were further challenged in refugee settlements and for those forced to serve in the military. Villagers who were displaced, either internally or externally, had little choice but to learn Spanish to communicate with other refugees who spoke other Mayan languages they did not understand and with citizens from host countries in which they sought refuge such as Mexico and Belize (CEH 1999c; REMHI 1998). Similarly, the military required that new soldiers and civil patrollers, most of whom were young, conscripted Maya Indigenous males, speak only Spanish in their service to counterinsurgency operations. The intent, once again, was to force Spanish as the unified language of the nationalist identity-making project. Thus, through military coercion, the state forcefully prohibited and stigmatized the use of Mayan languages in the effort to replace those languages with Spanish, working to further erode Indigenous cognitive frameworks associated with Indigenous language use (Adams 2001; Manz 1988).

Finally, the state sought to prohibit and stigmatize Indigenous *traje*. Colors, patterns, and styles reflected in Indigenous *traje* traditionally represent the wearer's connection to her or his community of origin (Hendrickson 1995; Nelson 1999; Otzoy 1996). The state perceived *traje* as symbols not only of specific Indigenous community connections but also of Indigenous identities and traditions more generally; *traje* constituted a visible marker that distinguished and, thus, separated Indigenous citizens from their *ladino* counterparts. The use of *traje* was particularly forbidden in military resettlements. It was outwardly stigmatized as soldiers and civil patrollers were trained to frequently equate the use of *traje* with the identification of a "communist subversive" or guerrilla supporter. Fearful that they would be falsely denounced as a guerrilla or guerrilla supporter simply because of wearing *traje*, many Maya Indigenous peoples, especially women, quit using *traje* altogether or used *traje* from some other unrelated community to conceal their actual community of origin. Furthermore, displaced populations who were forced to abandon their homes fled with only the *traje* they were wearing at the time. Trying to find or purchase the materials necessary to weave new *traje* with their particular community designs while in refugee camps was a near impossibility, especially given the poor economic conditions of life within the camps. Whether as a survival strategy or an economic consequence, the use of *traje* did wane during *la violencia*. The state hoped that eliminating *traje* use would help advance its nationalist agenda and contribute to the effectiveness of its often violent coercive efforts to assimilate its Indigenous citizens into the single, unitary national *ladino* identity that it desired (Becker Richards and Richards 1996; Montejo 1999; Zur 1998). However, these efforts would prove fruitless as Indigenous survivors not only resisted forced assimilation but also responded to the state's calculated assimilationist efforts in creative and transformative ways.

Indigenous Survivor Responses to the State's Assimilationist Agenda

The Guatemalan state made concerted and often violent attempts during the armed conflict and genocide to force assimilation on the majority Indigenous masses. However, the state's attempt to eradicate Indigenous identities over-whelmingly failed. As during most of Guatemala's postconquest history, many Indigenous peoples continued to resist and reject the national assimila-tionist project even during the most extreme violence and coercion that con-stituted *la violencia*. In doing so, many Indigenous peoples actively refrained from dissolving into the nationalist ideal of a singular *ladino* identity (Brown, Fischer, and Raxché 1998; May 2001; Montejo 2005; Smith 1990b). In fact, many countered assimilationist attempts by stepping up their own efforts in popular organizing and politico-scholarly activism surrounding issues of Indigenous rights, identities, and citizenship in the highlands and in urban centers (Fischer and Brown 1996; Warren 1998).

By the mid-1980s, Maya Indigenous activists began to engage in cultural revitalization, beginning with projects addressing linguistic issues that were viewed as less political in nature and, therefore, perhaps less dangerous to undertake at the time. As a result of these initial efforts, Indigenous activists produced various works such as standardized Mayan language dictionaries and grammars (Brown 1996; Fischer 2004a; Lopez Raquec 1989; Montejo 2005). Warren (1998) characterizes these initial efforts as constituting a form of nationalist essentialism that has the potential of overshadowing the complex, dynamic processual nature of ethnic identity formation. However, activists soon expanded their activities beyond what were viewed by some as essentialist aims. For example, some Maya Indigenous activists and orga-nizations began to focus on a variety of issues that were bolder in scope and substance, such as demanding political reforms aimed at promoting ethnic equality within Guatemalan society (Fischer 2004a, 89–90). Under the guise of a new Pan-Maya movement, these activists and organizations united to form the *Coordinadora de Organizaciones del Pueblo Maya de Guatemala*

(COPMAGUA) and were invited to participate in the 1996 peace accords to represent Maya Indigenous interests at the negotiating table (Hale 2006; May 2001; Montejo 2005).

COPMAGUA played a key role in the peace negotiations by helping to develop the Accord on the Identity and Rights of Indigenous Peoples, the first ever official document to formally recognize Guatemala as a multicultural, multiethnic, and multilingual nation-state. The accord was subsequently ratified by government, military, and guerrilla leaders in March of 1995 as part of the peace negotiations that ended the thirty-six-year internal armed conflict in 1996 (Hale 2006; Jonas 2000; Konefal 2010). While a popular referendum in 1999 failed to officially approve constitutional changes related to and officially mandated by the 1996 peace accords, Pan-Maya groups did come to wield political clout in Guatemala (Fischer 2004a, 92). For example, Maya Indigenous leaders, scholars, and activists have since attained unprecedented electoral power from municipal to national levels. Notably, by the year 2000, fifteen out of 113 self-identified Indigenous congressional deputies successfully secured several important ministerial positions within the national government (ibid.). Increased Maya Indigenous involvement in politics helped further foster Indigenous unity and established a base for political and economic power and efforts to attain greater social equality within the state. This move to involve more Indigenous peoples directly in politics is imperative for advancing postcolonial dialogues in Guatemala. It can also help advance the conservation and resurrection of various Indigenous cultural elements that Pan-Maya activists identify as vital to cultural revitalization (Montejo 2004; Warren 1998). Additionally, it is also imperative for formally and legally acknowledging Indigenous peoples' rights to form and express their own complex notions of identity, which is critical to ending the state's self-serving national assimilationist identity-making project (May 2001; Watanabe and Fischer 2004).

For the most part, majority Indigenous populations in Guatemala have succeeded in resisting and rejecting the state's far-reaching coercive assimilationist impositions, while persevering under some of the harshest conditions (Montejo 2005; Nash 2004; Smith 1990b). Many Indigenous peoples have not only survived genocide but also have brought about a resurgence of Indigenous pride, activism, and participation in the very state apparatus that sought to destroy them (Fischer 2006, 2004a; Montejo 2004; Warren 1993). Such resurgence among adult survivors of the genocide, evident in historical and academic accounts published over the past three decades, indicates persistence, assertion of Indigenous identity, and a strong sense of belonging for many adult Indigenous survivors of Guatemala's internal armed conflict and genocide. However, less is known about what long-term effects the coercive assimilationist agenda of the counterinsurgency campaign has had on the sense of ethnic identity and belonging experienced by survivors who were children during the armed conflict and especially during *la violencia.* Furthermore, little is known about how ethnic identity and belonging are subsequently perceived and expressed today by grown orphaned child survivors, most of whom had ties with their families and natal communities permanently severed. This currently limited area in research literature can now begin to be addressed by exploring the specific experiences and perceptions of ethnic identity and belonging among those who participated in my research project. To do so, I start with a focus on aspects of ethnic identity that they feel they have lost because of their distinct experiences as orphaned child survivors who were raised in a permanent residential home, often distant from their families and natal communities for most of their childhoods.

CHILD SURVIVOR EXPERIENCES WITH LOST ASPECTS OF ETHNIC IDENTITY

Most child survivors in my research project recognize that they lost important ties to their extended families and natal communities in early childhood because of the armed conflict and genocide. Compounding the situation is the fact that this particular group of orphaned child survivors spent the majority of their childhoods growing up in a permanent residential home located in a predominantly Maya Kaqchikel town that was unfamiliar to most of them. Estranged not only from their families and natal communities but, in many cases, also from their natal Mayan language and cultural groups, these child survivors continued to form their identities in a setting much different from that of their surviving family members and of their peers who grew up in their family homes in Santa Teresa. Consequently, child survivors are fully aware that they have lost certain aspects they associate with Maya Indigenous identities while growing up at the residential home, and they recognize those losses as a direct consequence of the armed conflict and genocide.

Child survivors most frequently identified language as a common lost aspect of identity. For example, when I asked him directly about ethnic identity, Mario lamented that he had lost most of his Kaqchikel language skills after arriving at the permanent residential home, even though the home is situated in a majority Kaqchikel community. He shared with me that although he can understand it perfectly, he can only respond with a few words. He further explained that he has forgotten certain words and how to conjugate verbs, which makes maintaining a fluent conversation difficult. Mario explicitly stated in his interview that language is part of Maya Indigenous identities and that he lost that aspect because he left his family to try to live a better life via the residential home. Thus, he asserted that in exchange for bettering his life, he simply was not able to maintain that aspect of his ethnic identity.

Esteban also identified language as a primary lost aspect of his Maya Indigenous identity. His case is demonstrative of the often complex nature of ethnic identity in Guatemala. Esteban's father identified as K'iche' and his mother as Uspanteka. According to Esteban's recollection, each parent was fluent in their own Mayan language but made the deliberate decision to speak only Spanish with their children so they could fully participate in the Spanish-speaking world around them. Subsequently, Esteban had little to no K'iche' or Uspanteka language skills when he first arrived at the residential home. However, his Spanish language skills were excellent, which may have made the transition somewhat smoother for him than others who arrived with no Spanish skills whatsoever. He continued to speak Spanish in the residential home but also began learning the local Kaqchikel language, both from the caregivers in the residential home who originated from the area and from other community members. When asked to describe how the armed conflict and genocide changed the way he perceives and expresses his ethnic identity today, Esteban explained, "Well, I would say that it affected it greatly because now I am not K'iche' or Uspanteko. I am practically Kaqchikel, but my identity as an Indigenous person was not affected because I am Indigenous." His older sister, Noemi, similarly only learned Spanish at home and continued to speak it when living in the residential home. Unlike her brother, however, she did not acquire any Mayan language skills, such as Kaqchikel, along the way. Interestingly, their younger sister, who had no previous Mayan language skills, studied linguistics in the university. She is now fully immersed in Mayan language revitalization and has engaged in Mayan language learning at the university level as an adult.

Wearing traditional *traje* and engaging in traditional customs and practices are also aspects of ethnic identity that child survivors in my research project feel they have lost because of severed ties with families and natal communities. Debora's experiences exemplify these losses. In addition to almost completely losing her Kaqchikel language skills, she ceased wearing *traje* and does not participate in any traditional customs or practices. However, she fully asserts her Maya Indigenous identity, stating, "I feel very happy to be Indigenous." For Debora, being Indigenous "is a tradition that one has . . . that is passed down."

Esteban never wore traditional *traje* on a regular basis in early childhood before arriving at the residential home and, subsequently, did not engage in that practice for the remainder of his childhood or in adulthood. As mentioned earlier, it was not uncommon for men to wear non-traditional clothing when Esteban was a young child, as state policies long forbade *traje* use in the principally male-dominated workplace (Becker Richards and Richards 1996;

Montejo 1999; Zur 1998). While Esteban did not specifically identify the loss of wearing *traje* as a lost aspect of his identity, he did miss engaging in other traditional Maya Indigenous customs and practices. Like Debora, he did not practice Maya Indigenous traditions, but he does not see that as necessarily weakening or eroding his ethnic identity: "I don't do any of this, but I am Indigenous, and I can't change that. I can't deny something that I am physically. I can't deny myself."

The overarching sense of pride and connection to their Maya Indigenous identities was a common theme in the interviews when I discussed lost aspects of ethnic identity with child survivors. Most child survivors lost some, if not all, connections to surviving family members and their natal communities. For example, Debora has long since lost contact with her father, sister, and extended relatives. She also has not been back to her natal community since her family fled so many years ago. Yet she takes great pride in her Maya Indigenous identity. Mario also never returned to live full time in his community because it is simply too far away from the capital where he has found steady employment and has established himself as an adult. However, he still feels generally connected to his natal community because he sees it as part of his Maya Indigenous cultural heritage. He further added that ethnic identity for Maya Indigenous peoples comes from their kinship connections to natal communities. He asserts that even if they act or speak differently, they are still Indigenous: "An Indigenous person knows where they came from, knows their parents are Indigenous, and so cannot appear to be from some other culture. Being Indigenous comes from within you and you can't change that."

Unlike most child survivors who grew up in the residential home, Susana was able to maintain both her familial and natal community ties. She was born in a small hamlet near Santa Teresa. Therefore, even though she came to live in the residential home, she continued to see her relatives in the town on a regular basis. Her mother also worked in the residential home, permitting Susana to maintain a close relationship with her own mother and to continue speaking Kaqchikel with her and her relatives. Consequently, Susana believes she was able to maintain most aspects she associates with her ethnic identity. Much like her child survivor cohort, she proclaims a strong connection to her Maya Indigenous cultural heritage, stating, "You can change the way you look, but you continue being Indigenous from the inside. You carry it inside . . . in your blood."

The concept that Maya Indigenous identity is situated within oneself and, thus, permeates one's entire being—often connected with blood in a general, not race-as-biology, sense—repeatedly surfaced in nearly all of my interviews and conversations with child survivors. For example, Esteban explained why he identifies as Maya Indigenous despite having lost certain cultural aspects he associates with it by asserting, "You can't stop being Indigenous because you carry it in your blood." Noemi also emphasized blood when talking about being Indigenous: "I am proud to be who I am, and it is something that is in my blood and as such, I can't just stop being who I am." Time and again, child survivors in my research project talked about ethnic identity as being internally rooted and often associated with one's blood. I believe that their internalized sense of ethnic identity and its relationship to blood differs from the concept of blood quantum or DNA that more commonly arise in discussions of Indigenous identity and "race" in places such as the US and Canada. Rather, child survivors' perceptions of the connection between ethnic identity and blood seem to involve a broader internal conceptualization, necessitating further elucidation.

The Connection between Ethnic Identity and Blood for Child Survivors

In both interviews and informal conversations, child survivors consistently asserted a strong sense of Maya Indigenous identity conceptualized as being situated internally within them and often within their blood generally. This conception fosters an internal, unbreakable sense of continuity and profound rootedness in ethnic identity, reflected in child survivor statements such as "I was born Indigenous, and I will die Indigenous" or "Even if you change your looks, you continue being Indigenous inside." The notion of ethnic identity continuity related to Maya Indigenous identities in Guatemala has similarly been observed in anthropological research conducted by scholars such as Montejo (1999) and Walter Little (2004).

Montejo (1999), for example, similarly demonstrates that Maya refugees living in exile in Mexico have a strong sense of continuity related to ethnic identity. He argues that Maya refugees reaffirm this sense of continuity by referencing their strong connections with the past and by working to maintain their traditions and to revive certain aspects of their Maya cultures despite the changing conditions of exile in another nation-state (*ibid.*, 198). Little (2004) also contends that the notion of continuity in ethnic identity is important for Maya Kaqchikel vendors with whom he works in Antigua, Guatemala, and he argues that it derives from their community connections. For Little, "place and identity, localized specifically as community, continues to be one of the more prominent ways that Mayas conceive of their identities" (2004, 1890). Similar to the work of scholars such as Montejo (1999) and Little (2004), I also found that for child survivors in my research project, continuity is an important aspect of their experiences and perceptions of ethnic identity. However, my understanding differs slightly from that of various contemporary scholars with respect to where child survivors in my research project, in particular, derive their sense of continuity.

These child survivors did not report or demonstrate that they participated in reviving certain aspects of their cultural heritages in the way or on a scale that refugees in Montejo's (1999) research have. Most have not been able to maintain ongoing social interactions with their primary centers of socialization from early childhood onward. Little (2004) emphasizes the continuity and the centrality of community connections in Maya Indigenous identities, which he believes must be sustained via ongoing social relations with the place and people of one's community of origins. He notes that people who have left their communities of origin "are not considered part of the home community if they do not maintain regular social relations" (ibid., 188). Little's assessment is no doubt reflective of the particular experiences of the group of Maya Kaqchikel vendors with whom he worked. However, it does not help elucidate why child survivors in my research project, most of whom were not able to maintain ongoing social relations with extended family, communities of origin, or natal community members, still feel a profound sense of continuity in their ethnic identities.

Despite severed ties, I believe that continuity in ethnic identity perceived and asserted by child survivors in my research project derives from a deeply internalized sense or feeling of general connection with family and natal communities via a broader sense of Maya cultural heritage. By sensing or feeling an ongoing, indestructible, internalized connection with past relations that may no longer physically remain or with a place they no longer visit, child survivors perceive their ethnic identities as deeply rooted within their being. This group of survivors asserts that others cannot harm, erase, or destroy those roots, which allows them to sustain their sense of continuity in ethnic identity despite the ruptures they experienced during their formative years of identity formation.

Child survivors often assert that their sense of indissoluble continuity regarding ethnic identity is centrally located or grounded within themselves and reference blood generally. Such grounding of continuity within the self and in relation to blood does not seem to reflect a race-as-biology conceptualization of ethnic identity as they do not refer to blood as an actual physical distinction that separates people based on biological features or the physical mixing of bloodlines. It also does not seem to convey a race-as-social construction conceptualization either. When talking about continuity in ethnic identity as being located within one's being and one's blood, child survivors most frequently reference their individual, internalized, and indestructible feeling and experience of Maya Indigenous identity without necessarily considering social hierarchies, ethnic differences, or other forms of external relations.

Continuity, for these child survivors, simply is an internal, indestructible feeling of connectedness to their Maya cultural heritage and to their ancestral past. This is not to say that social constructions of "race" do not factor into how child survivors perceive their ethnic identities today; social constructions of "race" have long influenced notions of ethnic identity in Guatemala and throughout the world. Rather, I contend that their internalized sense of continuity, despite having lost important familial and community ties, provides a perspective on Maya Indigenous identities that deserves further investigation. This is particularly imperative in an era when increasing numbers of Maya Indigenous Guatemalan peoples are relocating to urban centers and foreign countries. Certainly, the massive movement of Maya Indigenous peoples out of natal communities and the country may make the family and community relations that scholars have long argued are central to Maya Indigenous identities much more difficult to maintain. Yet it will not necessarily result in "identity loss" or "identity crisis," as the experiences of child survivors in my research project illustrate.

Child survivors' sense of indestructible continuity in ethnic identity is remarkable considering their childhood experiences. Certainly, they made efforts on their own to forge a strong sense of ethnic identity, but they also had the support of Catholic sisters, *tías*, and staff in the residential home who intentionally celebrated, promoted, and encouraged ethnic Indigenous identity formation and preservation in various ways. While it is difficult to gauge the degree of influence that the efforts made by Catholic sisters, *tías*, and staff have had on child survivors' sense of continuity in ethnic identity, these efforts do warrant further exploration, especially as they further elucidate child survivors' experiences and may provide a model for other residential homes and programs working with orphaned children around the globe.

Residential Home Efforts to Foster Ethnic Identity Formation and Preservation

The Catholic sisters who founded the permanent residential home in Santa Teresa were fully aware that the rupture of familial and community ties brought about by the internal armed conflict and genocide would precipitate a dramatic shift in the centers of socialization and enculturation for orphaned children who came under their care. Cognizant that this shift could potentially attenuate child survivors' sense of ethnic identity, initially formed amid earlier familial and community influences for most, the Catholic sisters made deliberate efforts to celebrate, promote, and encourage continuity in Maya Indigenous identity formation. What follows are some of these efforts as they have been described to me by child survivors, Catholic sisters, *tías*, and staff over the years, as well as through my own personal observations made since my first experience living and working in the residential home as a volunteer and up through my most recent return visit.

The Catholic sisters' approach to promoting continuity in ethnic identity formation may be viewed as reflecting a more essentialist notion of ethnic identity. However, when I asked what the residential home staff did to encourage continuity in ethnic identity formation in the residential home, both the Catholic sisters and child survivors identified the following efforts: primary Mayan language maintenance; traditional dress continuity; cultural activities; a positive multicultural environment; religious formation; agricultural training; and maintaining child survivors' connections with their surviving family members whenever possible. Each of these efforts was put forth with a great deal of care, intention, and hope for the future.

The Catholic sisters recognized the importance of maintaining child survivors' diverse primary Mayan language skills while they were enrolled in the residential home, even though it was located in a town where residents speak primarily Spanish and Kaqchikel. The Catholic sisters were concerned that child survivors would no longer be able to communicate with their surviving family members and would feel a loss of connection with their families and natal communities if they completely lost their abilities to speak and understand their Mayan languages. The sisters, some of whom identify as Maya Indigenous peoples themselves and speak a Mayan language as their own primary language, were also concerned about child survivors losing the cognitive framework associated with Mayan languages that they had developed in early childhood.

To help maintain continuity regarding Mayan language use, the Catholic sisters hired mostly *tías* who spoke a Mayan language as their primary language (most spoke Spanish to varying degrees as well). The Catholic sisters also hired women who spoke only Spanish as their primary language to help facilitate and expand the Spanish language skills of the few child survivors enrolled who identified as *ladino* and only learned Spanish from their families. Spanish-speaking staff also helped Maya Indigenous child survivors with attaining and honing their Spanish language skills. In the initial years after the residential home was founded, the *tías* on staff spoke principally Kaqchikel, K'iche', and Spanish, reflecting the languages spoken by the children enrolled at the time. As more orphaned child survivors from other regions were enrolled in the residential home, the Catholic sisters intentionally hired additional *tías* with the particular language skills necessary to match and help maintain newly arrived child survivors' primary Mayan languages. For example, *tías* who spoke Q'eqchi' and Tz'utujil were hired because many newly arriving children spoke those languages as their primary and often only languages. In addition to the *tías*, Maya Indigenous Catholic sisters and staff working in the residential home also spoke their primary Mayan languages, mostly Kaqchikel, K'iche', and Q'eqchi', to help maintain and develop child survivors' language skills and to sustain a multilingual environment that celebrated, promoted, and encouraged diversity and acceptance among children, Catholic sisters, *tías*, staff, and volunteers.

In addition to primary Mayan language maintenance, the Catholic sisters also intentionally worked to ensure that child survivors would maintain the form of traditional dress to which they had been accustomed prior to their enrollment in the residential home. In particular, orphaned girls who identified as Maya Indigenous and who had worn traditional *traje* in their natal communities were provided with their community-specific *traje* throughout the remainder of their enrollment in the residential home. Orphaned boys generally had not used traditional *traje* prior to being enrolled, but often wore it for special events. To achieve continuity in traditional dress especially for Maya Indigenous orphaned girls, the Catholic sisters purchased *traje* every year from each of the girls' natal communities or from nearby communities that sold *traje* in the particular patterns and style of the girls' natal communities.[1] The residential home has received clothing donations from various international and national organizations since its inception. It certainly would have been cheaper and much easier to dress all child survivors in donated non-Indigenous clothing that came mostly from the US and Canada. However, the Catholic sisters recognized that *traje* was another important way in which they could help foster continuity in ethnic identity formation, especially for orphaned Maya Indigenous girls.

The Catholic sisters also organized what they termed "*actividades culturales*" (cultural activities) as part of their ongoing efforts to support and encourage continuity in ethnic identity formation. They identified cultural activities as various events that consisted of traditional dances, skits, plays, and musical performances in which child survivors, Catholic sisters, *tías*, staff, and volunteers all participated. Cultural activities took place throughout the year during holiday celebrations, such as Christmas and Easter, and for special events such as the feast day of the town saint, *Día del Cariño* (Valentine's Day), *Quinceañeras* (15th birthday celebrations for girls in the residential home), *Día de los Muertos* (Day of the Dead) held November 1, and *Día del Niño/a* (Day of the Child) commemorated on October 1. Cultural activities also occurred during visits from various volunteer work groups arriving mainly from the US. The work groups typically stayed in the residential home for a week, assisting with building and maintenance projects, as well as offering various classes such as English, crafts, and art. Cultural activities were usually scheduled for the last night of each work group stay and served as a type of *intercambio cultural* (cultural exchange) between child survivors, Catholic sisters, *tías*, staff, and volunteers of the residential home and visiting group members.

The largest cultural activity that took place during the year, however, was *Noche Cultural* (Cultural Night), held during the anniversary celebration of the residential home. Each year, child survivors,Catholic sisters, *tías*, staff,, and volunteers begin a nine-day celebration of the founding of the residential home, leading up to the feast day of the patron saint of the residential home. The founding of the residential home is celebrated on the feast day of the saint in adoration of her. During those nine days, the residential home held activities such as a soccer tournament, the running of a torch from a distant location to Santa Teresa, two basketball tournaments (one for boys and one for girls), an art contest, foot races, and nightly prayer sessions as part of a *novena* (Catholic nine-day prayer devotion). The largest event next to the festive lunchtime meal prepared on December 12, however, is the *Noche Cultural*, which typically is held on the night of December 11. *Noche Cultural* activities include traditional dances, musical performances, skits, lip-syncing, *dinámicas* (group participation activities), poetry readings, and the presentation of trophies for the various anniversary events (e.g., soccer tournament, art contest, basketball tournaments, foot races, etc.) that take place leading up to the *Noche Cultural*. The *Noche Cultural* is designed to showcase talent and pride in the ethnic diversity of child survivors, Catholic sisters, *tías*, staff of the residential home. It also contributes to the supportive and encouraging multicultural environment that the Catholic sisters have worked hard to establish and maintain in the residential home.

While cultural activities in the residential home provided child survivors, Catholic sisters, *tías,* and staff with ongoing opportunities to showcase their talents and their pride in their various cultural heritages, the Catholic sisters also worked to promote pride in Maya Indigenous heritages on a daily basis by providing what they termed *un ambiente multicultural* (or a multicultural environment). They achieved this by creating a milieu that underscored the equal validity and importance of all groups of peoples in Guatemala, including Maya Indigenous, Garífuna, Xinca, *ladino*, and other non-Indigenous peoples. No group was privileged over another, and the Catholic sisters consistently reinforced the point that all Maya Indigenous child survivors were of equal status with *ladino* children enrolled. Messages of equality were relayed via the positive relationships cultivated between child survivors, Catholic sisters, *tías*, staff,, and volunteers[2] who were of varied backgrounds and cultural heritages themselves. Messages were also transmitted through an intentional focus on equal treatment of all children. Lastly, visual images displayed in the residential home contained messages of equality and pride in child survivors' Maya Indigenous heritages. One particular example is a mural painted in the main administrative and classroom building in the residential home. The mural consists of two small Maya Kaqchikel children with the specific *traje* of the town of Santa Teresa who are holding traditional incense near a cornstalk, both of which are important Indigenous symbols. The children painted in the mural are depicted wearing *traje* from Santa Teresa because it was a way to simply recognize that the residential home is located in the town of Santa Teresa and offer gratitude for its existence, while promoting Maya cultural heritage more generally.

The sisters also used religious formation as a means of supporting and encouraging continuity in ethnic identity formation among child survivors enrolled in the residential home. Most child survivors' families were practicing Catholics, as centuries of Catholic proselytization in the highlands had converted and coerced, often violently, a majority of the population to Catholicism generations, if not centuries, ago. In keeping with child survivors' family religious backgrounds and with the doctrine of Catholic Church as members of a religious order, the Catholic sisters provided Catholic religious formation for all child survivors enrolled. Formation included religion classes held in the residential home that were specifically tailored to each child's age and to their stage in receiving the sequential order of the Catholic sacraments (e.g., baptism, first communion, confirmation, etc.). These religious formation classes were designed to teach child survivors basic religious doctrine and to prepare them for receiving the sacraments. Religious formation also included attending weekly Sunday Catholic mass, as well as additional masses held for Holy Days of Obligation throughout the year such as All Saints Day, Christmas, and Easter. *Novenas*, prayer services, rosaries, scripture readings, and *posadas* (Christmas *novenas*) took place directly in the residential home throughout the year. Only on rare occasions, such as the blessing of the seeds before fields were planted, would elements of traditional Maya Indigenous spirituality be included in the religious formation offered in the residential home. However, lack of regular inclusion of elements of traditional Maya spirituality had more to do with the exclusionary requirements of the Catholic Church and the sisters' devotion to Catholicism rather than with general discriminatory practices against Maya Indigenous peoples or traditional spiritual practices.

Agriculture constituted another intentional effort to help engender continuity in ethnic identity. It was one of the four vocational training areas offered to child survivors in the residential home. In addition to teaching them valuable agricultural skills and to reducing overhead costs by growing half of the food consumed in the residential home itself, the Catholic sisters contended that agricultural training was another means of ethnic identity formation. All children enrolled in the residential home were initially raised in families that depended mainly, if not completely, on subsistence farming. In addition, their families generally came from generations of descendants who were subsistence farmers. Subsistence farming was viewed as an important lifeway and considered part of a family's cultural heritage. Subsequently, agriculture was identified by the Catholic sisters as an important aspect of ethnic identity for-mation and would be included in the residential home's regular activites. To provide some sense of continuity with the lifeways and family cultural heri-tages that child survivors had before being enrolled in the residential home, the Catholic sisters explicitly chose to involve them in various aspects of agri-culture when they were not in school. Besides developing fundamental voca-tional skills, agricultural training was aimed at cultivating and maintaining child survivors' connections with their family backgrounds and lifeways even though it was likely that child survivors would become wage-laborers work-ing outside of the agricultural sector when they became adults. Agricultural training in the residential home included planting, tending, and harvesting crops, as well as animal husbandry with chickens, rabbits, and pigs.

The sisters' final deliberate effort to support and encourage continuity in ethnic identity formation for child survivors involved maintaining their family connections whenever possible. They had an "open door" policy in the residential home in that surviving family members could visit child survivors at any time and as frequently as they desired throughout the year. The Catholic sisters also personally invited surviving family members to important events such as graduations, holiday celebrations, first communions, Catholic confirmations, residential home anniversary celebrations, *quincea-ñeras,* and birthday parties. In addition, they encouraged surviving family members to come to the residential home every mid-December (after the anniversary celebration) to take the children home with them for a short stay so they could spend the Christmas holiday reconnecting with extended family members in their natal communities whenever possible.

Unfortunately, not all surviving family members could afford the time off from work or had the money needed to travel to the residential home to visit their orphaned child relatives. Even fewer could afford to take their orphaned relatives home for the holidays. However, those who could reunite and spend time with their children were encouraged by the Catholic sisters to do so whenever possible. For child survivors who did not receive visits and could not spend the holidays with their family members, Catholic sisters, *tías,* staff, and volunteers planned special activities and field trips over the Christmas break as a way of helping them feel special and recognized even though such activities and field trips could never fully replace spending time with their own surviving family members. Encouraging and supporting ongoing con-nections with family members was an important way in which the Catholic sisters tried to maintain child survivors' ties with their family and community backgrounds and attempted to strengthen continuity in their sense of eth-nic identity.

Despite these deliberate efforts to support and encourage continuity in ethnic identity formation, ruptures between child survivors' familial and natal community ties and survivors' own perceptions of ethnic identity began to appear in their adolescence. By the time that I arrived in the residential home in 1994, the majority of teenage child survivors refused to speak their primary Mayan languages anymore and only conversed in Spanish. Even when Catholic sisters, *tías*, or staff spoke to the teens in Kaqchikel or K'iche', for example, child survivors would only respond in Spanish and conveyed great annoyance at being spoken to in any other language. Often when teens were scolded for not responding in their own Mayan languages, they would become further upset and would mutter under their breath about how it was "*estúpido*" (stupid) to speak a Mayan language. Many teen girls also refused to wear their traditional *traje* on a regular basis. Following trends in clothing at the time from their *ladina* peers from Santa Teresa and in the residential home, many Maya Indigenous girls decided to wear jeans or leggings with T-shirts or polo shirts instead, stating that *traje* was uncomfortable, old-fashioned, or just plain "*estúpido,*" a word that became common parlance of the teens in the residential home in their adolescence, much to our frustration.

Family and natal community backgrounds became another source of curt rejection among many teenage child survivors. Most teens were much less open to talking about their families or natal communities, and often displayed emotions of shame or embarrassment if anyone asked them about their backgrounds. Making matters more difficult, visits from family members had nearly stopped for most child survivors by the time they were teenagers as the cost of travel had increased substantially and surviving family members simply could not take time off from work to make the trek to Santa Teresa (most wage-laborers worked Monday through Saturday schedules, leaving little time for travel). Thus, most child survivors had little if any consistent contact with their surviving family members in adolescence,[3] which further diminished their familial and natal community ties.

The disjuncture between familial and natal community ties and child survivors' own sense of ethnic identity was apparent both in behavior and attitude during their teenage years and, ultimately, became a primary impetus behind my own decision to enroll in a graduate program in anthropology to conduct research specifically examining this issue more formally. Originally, I believed that my research would demonstrate that one of the many long-term consequences of the internal armed conflict and genocide on the lives of child survivors was the loss of a strong sense of ethnic identity typically forged from family and community influences. Based on my own observations as a volunteer in the residential home during child survivors' adolescence, I was certain that they would report little connection today in adulthood with their cultural heritages or earlier childhood ethnic identity formation, especially those who identified as Maya Indigenous. I was ignorantly convinced that I would find that as adults, Maya Indigenous child survivors would come to claim some semblance of a *ladino* identity instead of a Maya Indigenous one, demonstrating that they had *ladinized* (or assimilated from an Indigenous to *ladino* identity). Therefore, I initially set out to conduct research with the underlying assumption that the armed conflict and genocide had, indeed, destroyed child survivors' sense of connection with their specific Maya cultural heritages and with their Maya Indigenous ethnic identities generally. Fortunately, I was completely mistaken. Child survivors now in adulthood demonstrate and assert that they have not only *not* lost their overarching sense of ethnic identity or experienced any sort of "identity crisis" but they also *have* formed a strong sense of ethnic identity and pride that is forged upon simultaneous notions of continuity and creativity. Their strong sense of ethnic identity today illustrates that in place of loss, they actually are upholding and transforming what it means to be Maya Indigenous citizens in the Guatemalan nation-state today.

CHILD SURVIVORS' STRONG SENSE OF ETHNIC IDENTITY IN THE GUATEMALAN NATION-STATE TODAY

During my ethnographic interviews with child survivors, I asked a set of questions about how they perceive ethnic identity as adults in contemporary post-conflict Guatemala. I began by first asking them what they believe distinguishes diverse segments of the general population in the country and how those distinctions relate to ethnicity more generally. Most child survivors conveyed a non-essentialist view when speaking about differences in ethnic identity. They specifically identified culture, ways of living, beliefs, morals, ways of thinking, and personality traits as some of the primary ways in which various groups, in general, are distinctive in contemporary Guatemalan society.

Oscar, who identifies as Kaqchikel, focused on belief systems, perspectives, and acknowledgment of cultural heritage as principal aspects of distinction. He noted that being Maya Indigenous means one is conscious of how their cultural or ethnic group is viewed and of their beliefs, worldviews, and traditions. He further added that a person identifies oneself by having distinct beliefs and being conscious of all one's ancestors. Oscar asserted that *ladinos* are not necessarily distinctive in their physical appearance because the majority are a combination of Indigenous and Spanish descent. In fact, he acknowledged that some are now using the term "*mestizo*" again as a category of ethnic identity that recognizes the mixture of these groups.

Susana and Brandon also spoke of belief systems and worldviews as primary elements that distinguish Guatemala's diverse populations. Susana, who identifies as Kaqchikel, believes having respect for others, not being arrogant, being humble, and sharing rather than being selfish are principal characteristics that distinguish Maya Indigenous peoples from others, especially in relation to *ladinos* generally. She perceives Maya Indigenous peoples as being much more open and likely to share with others than those who identify as *ladinos*. Brandon, who also identifies specifically as Maya Kaqchikel, focused more on one's cognitive framework as a distinguishing characteristic of ethnic identity. He responded that it is simply a form of thinking differently that sets Maya Indigenous peoples apart from *ladinos* and other population segments. Based on their responses, it is clear that child survivors commonly view ethnic identity as differentiated between heterogeneous population groups in the country more by belief systems, worldviews, and the ways in which people comport themselves than by physical characteristics, biological differentiation, or essentialist traits.

I continued to explore ethnic identity distinctions in the interviews by then asking whether child survivors felt that they had to change any form, part, or aspect of their ethnic identities to make a life for themselves as adults in the Guatemalan nation-state today. Interestingly, all child survivors emphatically responded that they did *not* feel they had to change anything about the way they perceive, distinguish, or express their ethnic identities today to get ahead in life. For example, Debora underscored her pride in identifying as Indigenous. She stated that she feels happy to be Indigenous because clothes do not make the person. She acknowledged that she always has known that she is Indigenous and that it is a tradition that comes from long before. Debora similarly asserted that even if she wears pants and a T-shirt, she is still Indigenous. Medelin, who does not identify as Maya Indigenous but specifically as *mestiza,* reflected that although she is not Indigenous, she loves Indigenous traditions. She noted that she is proud to be born in Guatemala and like her child survivor peers asserted, "you are simply born Indigenous, and you die Indigenous."

While child survivors in my research project related that they have not had to change any portion of their ethnic identity whatsoever, several noted that there are others in the country who may feel compelled to do so. They asserted that some individuals change certain aspects of their ethnic identity to make a life for themselves in adulthood, attributing those changes to economic constraints. For example, Esteban argued that many Maya Indigenous peoples especially feel forced to change aspects of their ethnic identity such as women wearing *traje*. He observed that Maya Indigenous women often feel discriminated against in urban centers such as the capital and that those who move to the capital often stop wearing *traje* because of the shame they feel for being discriminated against. Esteban's older sister, Noemi, is a clear case in point. She moved to the capital and immediately stopped wearing *traje* altogether. In addition to trying to avoid discrimination and associated shame, his sister's decision to stop wearing *traje* also had economic dimensions. He stated that it is much cheaper to purchase non-Indigenous clothing in the capital, whereas purchasing *traje* has become increasingly more costly. Esteban's sister similarly acknowledged those external forces as contributing to her decision to stop wearing *traje*, but she did not feel that her decision was forced per se. It simply was her decision, and it helped her family financially. Esteban's younger sister, however, fully embraces wearing *traje*, although she also wears non-traditional clothing at times. Interestingly, neither sister expressed any kind of "identity loss" even though they engage in cultural practices to differing degrees.

To further explore the ways in which participants in my research project differentiate ethnic identity, I next asked them whether they believe that certain aspects of ethnic identity that they had mentioned, such as language, traditional dress, customs, religion, or traditions, are necessary for an individual to perceive, distinguish, and express their ethnic identity, especially Indigenous identity, in contemporary Guatemalan society. I was particularly interested in whether child survivors perceived distinct overt markers as essential to distinguishing or expressing and therefore, maintaining Indigenous identity in adulthood. Consistent with responses to previous questions focused on ethnic identity, all but one child survivor answered that these aspects, while they should be maintained whenever possible, are not essential for distinguishing or expressing Maya Indigenous identity, in particular. Instead, they once again asserted that ethnic identity is perceived as being located within the individual's being and is outwardly distinguished or expressed via connections with Maya cultural heritage and their ancestral past. In one response, Sofia simply replied, "You just feel it." Cris noted that wearing *traje* is not as important, but language is. Yet he relayed that it is what is inside of a person that matters most and that shapes and maintains one's ethnic identity. Mario also reflected that being Maya Indigenous is inside of the person. He acknowledged that a person's Maya Indigenous identity is distinguished from other ethnic identities by originating from one's natal community, from having Maya Indigenous parents, and from having no other culture. Child survivor responses to the question of overt markers and traits of ethnic identity further confirm that they have more of a non-essentialist perspective of ethnic identity. Overall, they perceive ethnic identity as being centrally experienced and rooted *within* the individual.

Extending focus on how child survivors generally perceive ethnic identity and its relationship to particular overt markers or traits, I next used an example to ask whether they felt that a young Maya Indigenous woman who no longer wears *traje*, does not speak a Mayan language, and does not participate in any Maya customs is still considered a Maya Indigenous woman. Almost all child survivors answered that they would consider the woman in the example to be a Maya Indigenous woman despite the changes that have occurred. They referenced blood in a general sense, Maya cultural heritage, and communities of origin as the basic elements of one's identity. They argued that these elements cannot be changed simply because an individual desires to change them. Their responses further corroborate their view of ethnic identity as being centrally rooted within the individual, imbuing a strong sense of continuity. In one instance, Susana unhesitatingly replied that the woman is Maya Indigenous because she carries being Maya Indigenous inside of her and in her blood generally. Brandon replied that the woman may not carry an external marker that communicates the community from which she originates, but she definitely is Maya Indigenous. Mario also noted that she may have lost her ability to show others via her *traje* or language where she is from, but she has not lost her ethnic identity. He emphasized that she knows where she is from, who her parents are, and what her culture is, so she cannot appear as if she comes from somewhere else. Lastly, Miguel offered a particularly profound response to the question: "You never forget your roots, only that which grows above ground, but the roots, no."

Nidia offered another poignant response to the question of whether a Maya Indigenous woman who abandons overt markers of ethnic identity is still Maya Indigenous by retelling a story. The story centered on two young women she had recently encountered in the central municipal building of a larger highlands town. She needed to visit the municipality to process some documents, and while waiting in line, she stood behind two young women who were dressed in non-traditional clothing. Nidia explained that to her, they clearly had a Maya Indigenous appearance and mannerisms. When the girls were called to the counter, they were asked some questions about their ethnicity. Nidia overheard them say that ever since the girls were little, they had been using non-traditional clothing such as basic skirts and pants used by *ladina* women. However, Nidia heard the girls say that they had grandparents and parents who are Maya Indigenous and who originated from Maya Indigenous communities in the highlands region. Yet when the girls were asked by the attendant whether they identified as *ladina* or Indigenous, they looked at each other blankly. Nidia, a teacher always willing to educate others, decided right there and then to get involved. She asked the girls to remember their grandparents. She suggested that they think about what they wore and if they spoke a Mayan language. Nidia shared with the girls that if they could answer these questions, they would have their answer. The girls replied that their grandparents are Maya Indigenous. Nidia responded, "There it is! Because you carry it within you regardless of your clothing that you have on, but you carry it in your blood." She then asked the girls if they spoke two languages, and they answered that they speak Spanish and a little of their grandparents' Mayan language. Nidia proudly and firmly asserted, "There it is! You are Indigenous." Nidia's story offers yet another telling substantiation of how child survivors perceive ethnic identity as internally rooted within the individual where it is preserved, which fosters ethnic identity continuity.

The final question regarding ethnic identity that I posed to child survivors was whether they felt that the way in which people perceive, distinguish, and express their ethnic identities today has changed overall in Guatemala as compared to the past several decades and even past century. Only four of twenty child survivors responded in the negative. They pointed to the decrease in discrimination between groups of peoples, especially between Indigenous and *ladino* groups in general, as primary factors facilitating Guatemalans' abilities to maintain the ways in which they perceive and express their ethnic identities over multiple generations. However, most child survivors conveyed their belief that changes in overt markers and practices such as dress, language, and customs have occurred. Consequently, they believe that these changes connote a change in how ethnic identity is outwardly expressed more generally, but the changes have not affected the internal perception or experience of ethnic identity overall. In one instance, Lina exuded this internal conceptualization of ethnic identity continuity by stating that overt markers and practices certainly have changed because they are different from the past, but from beginning to end, one continues to be Maya Indigenous. Mario used *traje* to further this notion. He shared that *traje* use has shifted with many young women now purchasing *traje* from other communities simply because they like the style, colors, and designs. He further elaborated that young Maya Indigenous women are less concerned with only wearing the designated *traje* that represents their specific natal community. He also affirmed that many young Maya Indigenous peoples have lost their languages, but they continue being Maya Indigenous peoples regardless. For Mario, they do not just quit being Maya Indigenous because it is rooted deep within them.

Several child survivors referenced the shift in relations between Indigenous and *ladino* segments of the population as affecting changes in ethnic identity expression. They noted that economic factors such as higher costs of *traje*, increased access to resources, and opportunities for Maya Indigenous peoples, as well as poverty among *ladinos,* have shifted the ways in which ethnic identity is individually expressed, as well as perceived and accepted, by others. Subsequently, they alluded to a more class-focused rather than ethnicity-focused perspective on changes in external ethnic identity expression and intergroup relations among the heterogeneous national population today. For example, Susana explained that Maya Indigenous peoples in the past were discriminated against if they wore their *traje* in towns or urban centers. She further suggested that *ladino* peoples looked down on Maya Indigenous peoples in *traje*, but today that has changed. Today one feels proud to be Maya Indigenous as people now admire them and say as much. For Susana, some people today decide to change simply because they want to look different, but others do not. She concluded that *traje* now costs so much and has become so expensive that it often is difficult for many poorer families to maintain the tradition of using it.

Oscar also believes that the way in which people perceive and express their ethnic identities today has changed primarily because of the economy. He argued that it is the economy that makes a person accepted or not in contemporary Guatemalan society. He explained that it does not matter if someone is Maya Indigenous or *ladino* now because there are *ladinos* who are also poor, and, at the same time, there are Maya Indigenous peoples who are wealthy. For Oscar, wealthy Maya Indigenous peoples have increased their economic situation, which has allowed them to express their ethnic identities in ways they choose, such as purchasing *traje*, as it is not a problem financially. At the same time, he believes that they are changing how people perceive Maya Indigenous peoples because they no longer fall into past stereotypes of poor, illiterate subsistence farmers.

Overall, child survivors believe that the ways in which ethnic identity is outwardly expressed has generally changed in Guatemala when compared with the past. They noted that changes in overt markers or particular aspects of ethnic identity such as language, traditional dress, and customs account for some of the primary changes in how ethnic identity is now expressed. However, they are more adamant that the ways in which one inwardly experiences and perceives ethnic identity remain constant and unchangeable. Interestingly, child survivors brought up the issue of intergroup relations (primarily between Maya Indigenous and *ladino* groups) as either related to changes that are occurring in outward ethnic identity expression or associated with ethnic identity and change generally. They believe that relations between Indigenous and *ladino* peoples have improved overall. Thus, they view Guatemala's heterogeneous population as being on an increasingly more equal socioeconomic class footing than in the past. Such equal footing, they argue, allows individuals to perceive and outwardly express their ethnic identities in an environment that is less discriminatory and less hostile toward particular groups, especially Maya Indigenous peoples. Therefore, child survivors argue that increased acceptance and respect for and among members of the heterogeneous national population place fewer constraints on how one now perceives or expresses ethnic identity. Yet some constraints remain.

Child survivors did not convey a sense of, or personal experience with, overarching ethnic identity loss in the initial ethnographic interviews and certainly did not exhibit any sort of "identity crisis" in interviews or over the years I have visited them. This was especially intriguing as I had witnessed firsthand their struggles with and defiance of ethnic identity expression in adolescence. Instead, as adults they articulated a strong internal sense of continuity in how they conceptualize and subsequently perceive their ethnic identities. However, I was uncomfortable making such an assertion without further speaking with them about their specific experiences with any sort of ethnic "identity loss" or "identity crisis." Consequently, I sought to expand my research and gain greater insights on child survivors' experiences with ethnic identity by continuing to solicit their perspectives and reflections via several post-fieldwork follow-up questions.

Gaining Additional Insights on Ethnic Identity from Child Survivors

With the help of a Guatemalan research assistant from Santa Teresa, I conducted initial follow-up interviews one and two years after my initial fieldwork with all child survivors who participated in my research project. In the follow-up interviews, I explicitly asked each individual whether they felt they had experienced an overarching sense of ethnic "identity loss" or "identity crisis" and if so, whether they attributed that loss or crisis to the long-term consequences of the armed conflict and genocide. Not surprisingly, all twenty child survivors emphatically answered in the negative. Instead, they asserted a strong and profound sense of ethnic identity. For example, Nidia once again proclaimed, "No! I continue being and will die Indigenous." Carlos similarly answered that he has always known who he is and where he comes from. Kike reported that he is very proud to be who he is and no matter what part of the world he is in, he is who he is. He shared that he likes his *traje,* which he now wears for ceremonial purposes or cultural events and is proud of his people. Reflecting on his recent experience traveling in Europe for a work-related conference and wearing his *traje* then to represent Maya Indigenous peoples in Guatemala, he noted that during his trip, "Indigenous and Guatemalan pride vibrated through my veins."

I next asked child survivors whether they thought that there was any overarching sense of ethnic "identity loss" or "identity crisis" generally among the over 150,000 to 200,000 orphaned child survivors of the armed conflict and genocide. Only four felt that child survivors, as a group, have lost some of their overall sense of ethnic identity, especially Maya Indigenous identity, because of language loss, being distanced from family, and having to adjust to a new way of living after the deaths of their parents. These four, however, reaffirmed that they, themselves, do not feel they have lost any overarching sense of their ethnic identities. The remaining sixteen child survivors responded in the negative. In fact, most noted that, because child survivors have had their ties with their families and natal communities severed, they have worked even harder than most Guatemalans their age at maintaining their ethnic identities via their internalized sense of connection with their Maya cultural heritage. They also asserted that they have worked harder at cultivating their pride in how they perceive and express their Maya Indigenous identities in adulthood.

In one example, Lina illustrated that pride by sharing that she believes that all child survivors are conscious of who they are and are proud to have the Maya Indigenous identities that they have. She asserted that their ethnic identities are something they are born with and are not going to lose. Jacki compared her experiences to her peers' and replied that many people have not suffered in the same way from problems stemming from the armed conflict and genocide. For Jacki, those individuals live with their family yet have less "culture," a term she chose to use, than most child survivors do. Oscar similarly asserted, "We child survivors have learned, with great pain, to not forget who we are or where we come from." Lastly, Mario offered one of the most profound responses to the question by expressing, "I think that we, the victims of *la violencia*, are the people whose bodies and souls are tattooed with the mark of where we have come from and who we are and that tattoo we have made ourselves with dignity and with pride in being Indigenous."

Overall, it is evident from both the initial ethnographic and follow-up interviews that child survivors have not felt a major sense of overarching ethnic "identity loss" or "identity crisis" because of being orphaned during the armed conflict and genocide. As they have so eloquently shared, instead of loss, they view themselves as deliberately having worked harder than others at maintaining the ways in which they perceive and express their ethnic identities, even in the face of extreme adversity. However, child survivors have also acknowledged the loss of some aspects that they associate with ethnic identity such as Mayan language skills, traditional *traje* use, religion, customs, and other traditions. They have also recognized that the early disconnect with their families and natal communities, which had been the primary sources of socialization and enculturation for them in early childhood, challenged their own ethnic identity formation through the remainder of their childhoods. However, they do not believe that the loss of those particular aspects they associate with ethnic identity and the change in early influences on ethnic identity formation are tantamount with overall ethnic "identity loss" or an "identity crisis." Rather, ethnic identity for child survivors entails a consistent thread of continuity passed down from generations before them. That sense of continuity is internally rooted within their being and, thus, is maintained even in the midst of a counterinsurgency campaign explicitly designed to destroy it. Child survivors' notions of ethnic identity also convey ethnic identity as simultaneously dynamic because they do not view it in strictly essentialist terms. Instead, they perceive ethnic identity as encompassing a wider range of non-essentialist aspects such as ways of living, cognition, and moral values that are dynamic, yet rooted within the individual and linked to their Maya cultural heritage. These simultaneous notions of continuity and fluidity regarding ethnic identity are further espoused in responses to a final set of questions that I posed to child survivors. The questions were designed to assess their experiences with belonging, especially those who identify as Maya Indigenous citizens, in the post-conflict Guatemalan nation-state today.

CHILD SURVIVORS AND BELONGING WITHIN THE CONTEMPORARY GUATEMALAN NATION-STATE

While child survivors unequivocally assert a strong sense of ethnic identity as adults, I was curious about their conceptualizations of belonging as ethnically diverse citizens of the Guatemalan nation-state today. To explore this, I posed several questions regarding Maya Indigenous and *ladino* relations because they have been contentious for centuries and have been at the root of discriminatory practices culminating in outright genocide. I first asked child survivors whether they felt that they had the same access to rights (e.g., human rights, civil rights, etc.) as everyone else in the national population given their primarily Maya Indigenous identities. They were split in their responses to the question. A little over half of the group answered in the affirmative. In one response, for example, Oscar offered a hopeful perspective by sharing that as a law student, he has been analyzing Guatemalan legislation. He affirmed that all citizens of the country do, in fact, have the same rights legally, but that it is worth asking if those rights are being upheld. He recognized that while discrimination continues to exist in various forms, other means and resources now have been added, eliminating some of the obstacles to attaining one's rights regardless of ethnic identity. For Oscar, this included increasing one's class position through education and employment. Referencing increased education and employment opportunities for Maya Indigenous peoples, Oscar proclaimed, "I feel that we, as Guatemalan *Indígenas*, yes, we are going to transform this Guatemala and we are going to change it completely."

Several child survivors agreed that they do have the same rights as everyone else, but they state that although those rights are recognized legally "on paper," they are not necessarily recognized in practice. For example, Yohana noted that all citizens have the same rights, but sometimes people simply do not respect them. She contended that people who violate those rights continue to exist. Medelin also felt that everyone has the same rights, but some fail to recognize them. For instance, she related that the government requires citizens to pay taxes, but then pays people poorly for their work. Mario further explained that everyone has the same rights according to the law and to what is written, but that is still not necessarily what is practiced today.

Interestingly, only three child survivors of the group of twenty adamantly claimed that they do not feel that they have the same rights as everyone else given the way they perceive and express their Maya Indigenous identities. For these three individuals, continued discrimination against Maya Indigenous peoples by others and institutional racism are preventing equal access to rights for all the country's citizens. Esteban illustrated this point by explaining that while Maya Indigenous peoples are being given new opportunities within Guatemalan society, deep-rooted discrimination against them endures and contributes to persistent, institutionalized racism. He referenced his work with a governmental agency where he witnesses firsthand the failure to uphold equal rights. Esteban opined that a Maya Indigenous person simply is not going to be appointed as head of the organization, reflecting long-standing racial discrimination particularly in the area of labor. He further added that companies follow a similar pattern in that a Maya Indigenous leader is nonexistent. In his opinion, hiring managers and leaders in the workforce continue to assess someone's appearance and request to see their surname to determine whether they are Maya Indigenous or *ladino*, ultimately giving promotions and leadership positions to *ladino* employees and candidates only.

Broadening our discussion of belonging, I then asked child survivors whether they felt that discrimination between Maya Indigenous peoples and *ladinos* more generally continues to exist. All child survivors agreed but were split in their perceptions regarding the degree to which discrimination continues. Half believed that discrimination continues at the same level it always has, especially within workplaces and schools. Yohana offered an illustrative example based on what she has observed in her position as a teacher in a rural town in the highlands. She shared that school administrators regularly tell the teachers that they should encourage their students not to discriminate against each other, but Yohana asserted that it continues to happen. They try to teach the children from early on to accept each other and to play with all the other kids. Yet the kids continue to exclude poorer children or Maya Indigenous children from their play groups. Yohana thinks this drive to exclude certain children starts early and that parents need to keep teaching their children they should not discriminate against others.

The other half of the child survivor group contended that discrimination continues to exist but that relations between Maya Indigenous and *ladino* peoples certainly have improved. Brandon, for example, answered that relations have improved a lot. He noted that Maya Indigenous peoples can travel in a bus and no longer must get up and give their seat to a *ladino* person. He likened this development to racism against Black peoples in the US. He continued by saying that it has not been more than fifty years since that type of racial segregation was outlawed in the US. Still, he believes one can see a lot of it based on his experiences living in the US for a few years. For Oscar, discrimination between ethnic groups has changed a lot, but it has not been eliminated completely. He argued that there is a percentage of people in Guatemalan society who have accepted the various cultures that exist, but racism persists. Mario was more tempered in his response. For him, discrimination has improved a little bit because people are more accepting, but it still exists, just at a much more subtle level. He explained that laws have helped erase the divisions between various ethnic groups somewhat and led people to accept others more than ever before. Mario also noted that there are more mixed-ethnic couples, which helps to reduce division between groups, but discrimination persists, nonetheless.

In my final inquiry about ethnic relations and belonging, I focused on centers of political and economic power by asking participants who they thought controls and benefits most from the Guatemalan nation-state today. I was curious whether ethnic identity differences, especially between Indigenous and *ladino* peoples generally, would come into play. The overwhelming majority of child survivors replied that the wealthy oligarchic elite control the government for their own economic gains. They also specifically identified the organization known as the Coordinating Committee of Agricultural, Commercial, Industrial, and Financial Associations (CACIF), a powerful business confederation consisting of the country's wealthiest and most powerful businessmen, as controlling the presidency and, thus, the government. Esteban explained in more detail that the government is primarily influenced by the CACIF because they make and unmake the presidency. In Esteban's opinion, the CACIF is behind the government, so government officials cannot make a single decision that the CACIF is not in agreement with because they believe they are most affected by such decisions and have the most to gain. He noted that the CACIF is made up of the wealthiest citizens of the country who have little concern for everyday peoples, yet everything they do affects everyone else. Carlos similarly identified the CACIF as controlling the government and, thus, national decisions such as salary increases and reductions in consumer costs. He emphasized that Guatemalans have lived through biased decisions with all presidential administrations because the CACIF has long controlled government politicians who must ask the CACIF before they can do anything.

Child survivors' perspectives on the relationship between ethnic identity and belonging vis-à-vis ethnic relations in contemporary Guatemala offer important insights. Over half believed that while discrimination based on ethnic identity persists, it does so at a lower level than in the past. However, they were cautiously optimistic and referenced general acceptance, new laws, intermarriage, and shifts in class position as some of the factors contributing to the decrease in ethnic discrimination. Furthermore, nearly all contended that, regardless of the way in which they ethnically identify themselves, they currently have the same legally recognized civil and human rights as everyone else in the country. They asserted that those rights simply were not recognized for the majority Maya Indigenous populations that preceded them. They also argued that the only question remaining is whether those rights are actually being upheld in practice. Lastly, child survivors agreed that the political and economic center of power in Guatemala is not one based solely on ethnic identity (i.e., power is not associated solely with the general *ladino* category of identity) but rather on wealth. They agreed that the wealthy oligarchic elite, especially those who are members of the CACIF, and politicians, more generally, are those currently monopolizing political and economic power within the country. That child survivors did not solely reference *ladino* identity when categorizing the wealthy elite highlights the prominent and ever-increasing role of socioeconomic class issues in Guatemalan social relations today. Examining shifts in class issues both independent of ethnic relations and in relation to them are even more vital now for analyzing and understanding what it means to be a Guatemalan citizen in the post-conflict era today and beyond.

ETHNIC IDENTITY AND BELONGING
IN GUATEMALA IN THE FUTURE

My research with child survivors clearly reveals their strong sense of ethnic identity and belonging despite disruptions in early primary centers of socialization and enculturation. Their strong sense of ethnic identity today in adulthood certainly differs from what I witnessed when they were adolescents still living amid the internal armed conflict and genocide. Juliana shared with me a story that she felt best encapsulates their experiences, especially with continuity in ethnic identity. She began by explaining that a young Guatemalan man who left for the US to find work returned home some years later. The young man asked his father the names in Kaqchikel of some items in their family home, as if he had forgotten the Kaqchikel language altogether. When a piglet suddenly escaped from his father's house, however, the young man acted quickly, grabbed the piglet, and returned it to its pen. Observing his son's actions, the father smiled and reminded his son that although he may have forgotten how to speak Kaqchikel fluently, his quick reaction in easily catching the piglet in the way his peoples have done for generations demonstrated that he still knew how to respond to such events in Maya Indigenous ways. The young man had not forgotten the cultural practices that he was taught as a child. Juliana concluded the story by proclaiming that the son's ethnic identity was deeply rooted within him and in that way, he could never forget or lose it.

While child survivors express profound continuity in their sense of ethnic identity, they also have expanded what it means for them to be Maya Indigenous peoples today. By engaging in creative and constructive practices such as education and professional careers, they have transformed what it means for them to be Maya Indigenous peoples in ways that differ from those of their peers. For example, child survivors have far outpaced their peers from Santa Teresa and most other highlands residents of their age group in both education and income. The majority of child survivors in my research project have attained college educations, while only one peer who participated in my research has. In fact, child survivors pursued higher education at triple the rate of their peers. In addition, several have gone on to earn advanced degrees in law and finance, while none in the peer group has. Because of their college educations and advanced degrees, most of the child survivor group now work in professional careers, including for federal departments, with one serving in the highest judicial branch in the country. Several are also entrepreneurs, operating their own businesses on the side while they work professionally for organizations and companies. Establishing professional careers has led to their increased earning potential, evident in the fact that they far outpace their peers in terms of annual income. Finally, most child survivors came to reside in urban centers, such as the capital, where they could pursue higher education and secure professional employment. Their peers, on the other hand, all remained living with family in Santa Teresa. Losing family financial support when their parents were murdered and their family lands were taken or destroyed forced child survivors to set out on their own as young adults. Living without an economic safety net, most had no other option but to seek a future in urban centers where more educational and employment opportunities are available.

Attaining higher education, working as professionals, and living in urban centers has created new economic openings for child survivors and their children. At the same time, these creative practices have not weakened their strong sense of ethnic identity. On the contrary, such practices have reinforced their desire to instill that same strong sense of Maya Indigenous identity continuity in their children. While child survivors do not have an essentialist conceptualization of ethnic identity overall, they do value teaching their children various aspects they associate with ethnic identity. Child survivors teach aspects that many of them have lost in the hope that it will help foster their children's sense of continuity in ethnic identity and pride. For example, they shared with me that they are ecstatic that their children now can take Mayan language classes in public schools and that schools in Maya Indigenous communities are required by law to be bilingual (operating in both the local Mayan language and Spanish). The shift away from Spanish-only education is vital not only for language revitalization but also for helping child survivors introduce their own children to their Mayan languages (since many have lost the ability to speak it) and for sharing their deep sense of pride in their Maya Indigenous cultural heritage.

Child survivors also actively involve their children in community cultural events, even in the capital, that allow them to dress their children in *traje* for special days. Despite the increasing cost of *traje*, many child survivors intentionally purchase *traje* from their natal communities for their children to use for these special events. In addition, many return to the residential home in Santa Teresa with their families for the annual feast day. They often dress their children in the local *traje* of the town regardless of their actual natal community affiliation as a way of paying homage to their upbringing in Santa Teresa. In this sense, they are working to cultivate their children's connection with other Maya Indigenous peoples, which they hope will foster a sense of unity and pride in being Maya Indigenous Guatemalans today and in future generations.

Lastly, some child survivors in adulthood have tried to reconnect more recently with their natal communities and extended relatives so that they can expose their children to Maya Indigenous lifeways outside of urban centers. For many, returning to natal communities is a long trek from their current homes, so they are not able to make the trip with much frequency. However, they want to familiarize their children with their Maya Indigenous kin and natal communities and further nurture their children's internalized sense of ethnic identity by bringing them to the land of their ancestors, which child survivors perceive as "nourishing the roots" of their Maya Indigenous identity. Child survivors' deliberate efforts to actively instill an enduring sense of ethnic identity continuity in their children, while helping them successfully navigate contemporary society and urban living, is admirable and a testament to their own strong sense of ethnic identity and pride.

UNDERSTANDING CHILD SURVIVOR EXPERIENCES WITH ETHNIC IDENTITY AND BELONGING IN GUATEMALA

The Guatemalan military sought to destroy Maya Indigenous peoples and ethnic identities, once and for all, under the guise of its national assimilationist identity-making project via violent coercion. This was executed as one of the chief military strategies carried out during the internal armed conflict and genocide. Operating under essentialist assumptions regarding identity, the military worked to annihilate Maya Indigenous citizens or assimilate them by prohibiting and stigmatizing the use of overt markers associated with Maya Indigenous identities. The military also destroyed families and communities in an attempt to demolish primary centers of socialization and encultura-tion regarded as especially central to ethnic identity formation among Maya Indigenous children. Despite these efforts, the state's coercive national assimilationist identity-making project largely failed. Far from being assimi-lated, Maya Indigenous adult survivors launched a major resurgence of Maya revitalization, activism, organizing, and political participation. Multiple accounts and scholarly works examining Maya Indigenous survivors' expe-riences during and following the genocide reveal that, rather than falling victims to assimilation, survivors often engaged in creative and constructive practices. These practices helped them to maintain a strong sense of ethnic identity, actively promote diversity, and demand equal rights for Guatemala's heterogeneous Indigenous populations, fortifying their sense of belonging as citizens in the aftermath of the armed conflict and genocide (e.g., Jonas 1991; Montejo 2005, 2004, 1999; Warren 1998).

While there is clear evidence of the failed national assimilationist identity-making project among adult survivors of the genocide, little has been examined regarding how child survivors, especially those who were orphaned during *la violencia,* have responded to the long-term consequences of the military's violent assimilationist strategies in their lifetimes now that they are reaching middle adulthood. My research with individuals who were orphaned in childhood as a result of the armed conflict and genocide helps begin to fill this gap in research. Child survivors in my research project, similar to other survivor groups, have maintained a strong sense of ethnic identity and belonging in the Guatemalan nation-state today. Their abilities to maintain a strong sense of ethnic identity and belonging are particularly intriguing. Having experienced such severe disruption in early centers of socialization and enculturation and being enrolled in a permanent residential home for the remainder of their childhoods in a community with which most were unfa-miliar, these children could have easily experienced an overarching sense of loss in how they would come to perceive and express their ethnic identities in adulthood. However, for twenty child survivors who participated in my research project, that did not occur.

In addition to continuity, child survivors' strong sense of ethnic identity also encompasses the notion of creativity. Contemporary scholars such as Smith (1990a, d), Warren (1998), Montejo (1999), and Little (2004) similarly show that ethnic identity is deeply rooted in Maya cultural heritage while also continually formed, reworked, negotiated, reasserted, redefined, and reconstituted in an ongoing process within a multitude of overlapping local, regional, national, and global systems. Rather than perceiving and expressing ethnic identity, particularly Maya Indigenous identities, within a fixed set of static, autochthonous essentialist traits, child survivors have demonstrated that they, too, perceive ethnic identity in wider, more dynamic terms. The ways in which child survivors perceive and express their ethnic identities also incorporate more creative processes and practices than are utilized by their peers. For example, child survivors have successfully engaged in higher education, professional careers, entrepreneurship, and urban living, while their peers, with the support of their families, have mostly remained living in Santa Teresa working lower-paying jobs. Child survivors have independently established their own novel or innovative academic, professional, entrepreneurial, and living patterns in adulthood, which they view as part and parcel of their lived experiences and strong sense of ethnic identity rather than as a major shift in or detraction from their sense of ethnic identity overall.

Child survivors' participation in creative processes and practices has allowed them to adapt to their situations and contexts both actively and creatively. They have participated in new educational, economic, and social arenas that have spurred openings in Guatemala's social hierarchy. For example, they earn more income overall than their peers, with most child survivors now living somewhat financially comfortably in a more middle-class position than their peers. The upward mobility of Maya Indigenous peoples in the social hierarchy, at least according to socioeconomic class, is a common theme that permeates child survivors' ethnographic interviews. They frequently commented and pointed out that there are now wealthy Maya Indigenous people (indicating upward mobility) and poor *ladinos* (signifying downward mobility).

The overwhelming majority of child survivors have further indicated improved access to the same economic resources and general rights as everyone else in the country today even though they had been in a major economic disadvantaged position in early adulthood because of their orphan status. Their views of improved access indicate that major socioeconomic class shifts are, indeed, occurring in the Guatemalan social hierarchy, transforming what it means to belong as Indigenous, as well as *ladino,* citizens in the nation-state today in an era Hale (2006) terms "neoliberal multiculturalism." Child survivors' perceptions of shifts in the old social hierarchy, one that had been based on an ethno-class conflation for centuries, are further fortified by the fact that several of them are now explicitly working in law and human rights litigation, thereby directly challenging the old social hierarchy crafted by the oligarchic elite for their own benefit. Child survivors' participation not only in creative practices regarding their own identities but also in the

litigation of rights for Maya Indigenous peoples in the country is transforming what it means for them and others to be Maya Indigenous citizens in
contemporary post-conflict Guatemala.

Child survivors are not alone in their experiences with simultaneous continuity and creativity regarding ethnic identity. They also are not unique in their
participation in transformation related to belonging in today's nation-state.
Other ethnographic research with adult survivors of Guatemala's armed conflict and genocide likewise demonstrates continuity and creativity, as well as
transformation, in the post-conflict era. For example, Green (1999), in her
work with widows of the internal armed conflict and genocide, observed that
they perceive and express their Maya Indigenous identities in similar terms.
Green argues that the context of sociopolitical violence and meanings of survival necessitate a reexamination of cultural continuity and transformation
as dialectical rather than dichotomous processes. Instead of cultural continuity conceptualized as a linear replication of static traits and traditions, she
purports that survivors view it as shared history that is passed on to the next
generation and reworked with each subsequent generation via memory and
myth. Green emphasizes that meaning is then constructed out of the present
and of the possible (1999, 19).

Falla (1994) also encountered continuity, creativity, and transformation
in how Guatemalan genocide survivors perceive and express ethnic identity
and view belonging, especially in the immediate aftermath of *la violencia*.
Working primarily with Maya Indigenous Guatemalans from the Ixil area
who were forced to either move to Mexican Lacandón refugee camps or to
establish their own resistance communities during *la violencia*, Falla found
that refugees had to expand their perceptions and definitions of ethnic identity
as a result of their new status as refugees. However, that expansion was not
tantamount to a sense of loss regarding ethnic identity overall. Falla observed
that Maya Indigenous localism has been lost for refugees as they have had
to shift from identifying principally with their natal communities to identifying more generally as Guatemalans. Yet their sense of ethnic identity and the
links they share with others of the same background were not broken. Falla
affirms that ethnic identity of different Maya Indigenous groups was not
lost in the camps despite the heightened consciousness of their nationality
(ibid., 189–190).

Ethnographic research conducted by Green and Falla, as well as by others
such as Susanne Jonas (1991), Carol Hendrickson (1995), Montejo (1999),
and Zur (1998), corroborate that the simultaneously occurring processes
of continuity, creativity, and transformation regarding ethnic identity and
belonging are a common theme for many Guatemalan survivors. What
makes the case of child survivors in my research project particularly interesting, however, is that they were in their most formative years of childhood

socialization and enculturation during *la violencia*. Experiencing such abrupt shifts in core centers of socialization and enculturation brought about by severed ties with families and natal communities certainly could have resulted in an overwhelming sense of loss or crisis regarding ethnic identity and belonging. However, their sense of ethnic identity and pride is stronger than ever. Within their hearts, minds, and senses of being, they know that they were born Maya Indigenous and so, as they state, they will die Maya Indigenous. For child survivors, no one—not even the Guatemalan state—can rightfully deny them their ethnic identity or sense of belonging as Maya Indigenous Guatemalans who are helping to forge a more pluricultural society today and for future generations to come.

NOTES

1. For example, the primary market day in the nearby town was every Thursday. During the Thursday market, it was common to purchase various community-specific *traje* from regional vendors who came from other towns, hamlets, and settlements in the region to sell *traje* representing those communities at the market.

2. Volunteers at the residential home typically originated from countries such as the US, Ireland, the United Kingdom, and Germany. Volunteers served periods of time ranging from one month to multiple years.

3. Even in the period of 1994 to 1996, there was only one telephone in the entire town of Santa Teresa and rarely any telephones whatsoever in any of the rural areas. Thus, telecommunications simply were not an option for maintaining regular contact with family members at the time.

Chapter Six

Making a Future

Guatemalan child survivors in my research project experienced a childhood full of multiple challenges and obstacles. This made their transition to adulthood much more difficult than that of their peers who had the consistency of living with their families in Santa Teresa throughout childhood and into adulthood. Facing adulthood without an economic, familial, and emotional safety net and without further financial support from the Catholic sisters, child survivors often had no choice but to forge ahead alone, working hard to establish themselves as adults. When I asked survivors what motivated them to keep moving forward, a common phrase continually surfaced: *"tiene que"* ("you have to"). In other words, child survivors perceived their situations as one in which there has been no other choice but to just keep moving forward and to strive to make a better life in whatever way possible. As Juliana noted in an interview, "What other choice is there, Shirley? You just have to . . . you have to move on." The phrase *"tiene que"* powerfully reflects child survivors' persistence and resilience, underscoring their ability to achieve remarkable feats despite the long-term consequences of the internal armed conflict and genocide that they have continued to face. This chapter explores their achievements and struggles in adulthood with the aim of more fully depicting the entirety of their life experiences to date and honoring their life accomplishments as well.

GUATEMALAN CHILD SURVIVORS
TODAY IN ADULTHOOD

Once they became adults, graduated from high school (for most), and left the permanent residential home in Santa Teresa, many child survivors had to move to urban centers in search of employment and advanced educational opportunities, since the Catholic sisters simply could not continue to financially support them. The move to urban centers was not an easy one for most survivors, as they were often unaccustomed to urban living and knew few people, if any, who lived there. A small number who remained in Santa Teresa commonly did so because they formed a civil union with a local resident and moved into their in-laws' homes in the town or nearby, or in Susana and Oscar's case, they are originally from the area. Fortunately, those who did move to urban centers were able to secure full-time employment and support themselves within the first several months of moving there, although it was not necessarily an easy process. In what follows, I provide an overview of what transpired specifically in the lives of a number of child survivors once they left the residential home and established themselves in their new living contexts. I begin by centering on several who have been featured throughout this book and then follow with an update from several others who participated in my research project as well. My goal is not only to elucidate key themes from their experiences but also to further underscore and validate the importance of recognizing child survivors as a distinct group of survivors with their own unique challenges, obstacles, and achievements in both childhood and adulthood.

Juliana

After moving to an urban center with her husband and mother-in-law, Juliana gave birth to a little girl who was in perfect health. Juliana and Miguel were elated by their new roles as parents, and Miguel's mother was thrilled to have another grandchild. Within the year, Juliana became pregnant again with their second child, a son. To improve his chances of obtaining a higher-paying job, Miguel enrolled in a high school program that trained students in specific career paths. He chose to learn accounting and auto mechanics in addition to taking general high school courses. He worked multiple jobs simultaneously over the next two years to support his family while attending school full-time. Meanwhile, Juliana had her hands full with two small children, and two years later, she gave birth to another son. Fortunately, she not only had the support of her mother-in-law but could also count on her own mother to occasionally help out with the children. Reflecting on those initial years of her marriage and motherhood, Juliana shared, "When I married, every fifteen days my mom came to see me to see if my husband and mother-in-law were treating me well." She later added, "This is something my mom always said to me: 'I will be with you whenever you need me.'"

After graduating from his high school career training program, Miguel continued to work several jobs to make ends meet and to support Juliana's staying at home to care for their children. In 2000, Juliana gave birth to their fourth child (a little girl), and shortly afterwards, Miguel landed a position with an auto mechanic business located directly on a section of the

Inter-American Highway that passes through a major city. Miguel made such a positive impression that his boss not only hired Miguel permanently but also invited him to bring his own family to live in the large apartment that was located right above the business. After years of renting a tiny, rustic home a kilometer down the road, Juliana and Miguel moved their family, including Miguel's mother, into a beautiful apartment with ample room for their growing family. With a new home, Miguel's steady job, and the older kids now in school, Juliana decided it was time to exercise her own talents to supplement and advance her family's household income.

One of the universities in Guatemala City had recently opened a satellite program in the city where Juliana and her family were living to accommodate an increasing student population that consisted of many young adults living a significant distance from the capital. The university program in Juliana's city was located near their new apartment. For weeks while washing clothes, Juliana observed the students from her rooftop patio and noticed that there were no nearby cafes or stores selling snacks or light food fare to them. She brainstormed an idea of selling homemade snack items (e.g., empanadas, sweet bread, corn mush, tamales, etc.) to the university students who would not necessarily have money to spend on food in costly nearby restaurants. After sharing her idea with Miguel, who was also excited about the possibilities, Juliana prepared some basic snack items and headed to the university satellite site the next day to sell the items and gauge the entrepreneurial potential there. It was a complete success.

Juliana soon expanded her menu to include lunch items (e.g., fried chicken, beef stew, rice, soup, homemade tortillas, etc.) and developed a profitable business. Her thriving business allowed her to exercise her entrepreneurial skills, and flexible work hours permitted her to return home in the afternoon for her school-age children after school. Her business also provided an additional source of income for the family, bringing in enough money to nearly triple their household income. Juliana was proud of her business and success, as was Miguel. Their family was now making greater strides in strengthening their financial future, a future that could support their children's advanced education.

In the early 2000s, Juliana gave birth to their fifth and last child, a son. Juliana and Miguel were thrilled to welcome a new addition to their growing family. However, their newest son began to show signs of illness shortly after his birth. After many doctor's appointments, they still were not able to get a confirmed diagnosis. Even though the entire family helped with the care of their youngest son and carefully watched over him, he died when he was just two years old. The loss was horrific and traumatic for Juliana and Miguel. Juliana was especially devastated and found it extremely difficult not knowing the exact cause of death. She questioned her parenting skills and her level of attentiveness due to her growing business and wondered if it was interfering with proper care of her children, a notion that Miguel quickly dispelled. In time, Juliana found solace in her faith and in her family. She was able to tell me the story of her youngest son without shedding a tear, sharing that "he is among the angels now and is watching over us. We are so fortunate to have our own little angel in heaven who is keeping watch over our family."

Despite the devastating loss of their youngest child, Juliana notes that it brought the family closer together than ever before. While interviewing her, I observed how Juliana showed such loving affection toward her children. The sweet affection between Juliana and Miguel was also admirable. Having participated in their "forced" marriage ceremony nearly two decades earlier, I often wondered how their relationship would turn out years later. I was skeptical of a rushed marriage such as theirs and often wondered if it would last much beyond the birth of their first child. I was amazed, however, to watch Juliana and Miguel tenderly interact with each other eating lunch, laughing, and sharing stories from that past during the nine hours I spent with them. They would often softly touch each other on the arm as they spoke about their lives together. Miguel would kiss Juliana softly on the cheek throughout the meal, and they would sweetly tease each other about their idiosyncrasies. I have never witnessed such an openly affectionate relationship between a husband and wife in Guatemala. They are truly happy together and have been successful in creating a loving and supportive family and home.

I was also amazed at Juliana's inner strength and strong sense of identity. Despite all that she has experienced from early childhood and even into adulthood, she has a resilient and self-assured character. When we were preparing the vegetables for our lunch on the day of the ethnographic interview, Juliana explicitly shared with me that she is proud of who she is as a woman, a mother, and a wife: "For better or worse, these things happened to me, but with God's help, I have been able to become a strong woman who has a lot of love for her family." In a follow-up interview, I asked Juliana what makes her such a strong woman. She responded, "I think I have a lot of insecurities because of the loss of my father and sometimes I think that if I would have had a different life, I would have been more focused, and I would have taken advantage of the opportunities that I could have had in life." She thought for a moment and then added, "Maybe I am strong in some areas, but in others I feel weak, and I promise you that I am going to learn how to work a computer. That is one of my goals. Did I tell you that I took a dance class recently? And I am taking a sewing and cooking course as well. It's good to learn how to cook well instead of burning boiling water!" Juliana and I laughed at her last comment. Her sense of humor remains one of her defining characteristics and strengths.

As I was getting ready to leave Juliana and Miguel's home after our day together reminiscing and conducting the ethnographic interviews, Juliana quickly left the room only to return with something in her hands. She handed me an original publication of award-winning junior high school essays from around the country. The eight national award-winning essays published in the book were chosen among numerous entries from junior high school students from all regions across Guatemala in a particular year in the early 1990s. Juliana's essay was among the eight that had been selected for publication. She told me that her essay was based on the experiences of her family, especially during *la violencia*. I was so proud to discover that she had won such a prestigious award. I told her that I would copy the publication as quickly as possible so that I could immediately return the original to her in excellent condition. I was truly flattered and honored that she would share with me something so important and so personal to her. She had such a gleam in her eye when she showed the publication to me. Later that evening when I returned to Santa Teresa, I sat down to read Juliana's essay while reflecting on her life and the thoughts and reflections she so generously shared during our interview. She truly is a resilient survivor who has made the best out of some incredibly challenging life experiences. I am continuously awed by her.

Debora

Shortly after welcoming their first child, Debora and Alex were faced with a difficult decision. With few job prospects and worsening economic conditions in Guatemala, Alex was desperate to secure gainful employment to support his new family. Because of the arrival of their baby, he never finished his high school degree, which made securing a job even more difficult as high school diplomas had become more commonplace among Guatemala's young adult population in the late-1990s and were becoming a common minimum requirement of many better-paying employment positions at the time. To find steady and better-paying work, Alex made the difficult decision to leave for *el norte* (the US).

Although Debora from the beginning hated the idea that Alex would be leaving her and their son behind, she also understood their financial difficulties. Describing their situation, she stated, "I had no option but to be in agreement with his decision." After three grueling attempts to get across the Mexico/US border, Alex finally made it and settled in Texas where he began working as a construction laborer. Fortunately, with the increasing accessibility of cell phones in Guatemala at the time, Alex was able to call home every day to work at maintaining a healthy, stable relationship with Debora and especially with their son, who was four years old at the time. Debora recalled, "He was so lonely in the United States in the beginning! He called us a lot."

Debora shared his feelings of loneliness. To make it through those early days of separation, she and Alex would often speak with each other multiple times during the day by phone. Debora elaborated, "We believed that it would take about seven years to make enough money so that we could live simply but comfortably here so that Alex could return and continue his studies and find a job. . . . I thought seven years was like an eternity, but at least we had a plan with a return date."

While Alex established himself in the US, Debora and her son continued to live in the home of Alex's parents. They shared a single room with a double bed, a small desk, a basic armoire, a box of toys, an old sewing machine that still functioned despite its age, and a small television that Alex sent money for Debora to purchase for their son. Debora spent most of her days caring for her son, helping her in-laws with chores around the house, and volunteering in her son's various elementary school activities. Alex did not want her to find employment at the time because he preferred that she stay home to take care of their child. Debora would have liked to start studying at the college level while Alex was away, but he forbade it, saying she needed to stay home with their son instead. She shared that he also believes women are not meant to study: "He says that those women who study do it to be with other men. . . . I would like to study, but he won't let me, so I just want to be happy and live like the family that I never had." With no other alternatives, Debora dedicated herself to her son and his education, as well as to overseeing the construction of a second story to her in-laws' home. The second story would serve as Debora and Alex's own home since land parcels were becoming expensive and scarce in Santa Teresa. Alex's parents would keep the first level as their own home. To bring the project to fruition, Debora supervised the second story project and was concentrating on the next phase of construction at the time of our initial interview. The next construction phase would involve laying the cement flooring, constructing the brick walls, and installing the plumbing.

At the time of an ethnographic follow-up interview just a few years later, Debora had reported that Alex had relocated to Georgia in search of better-paying job opportunities. He simply was not getting the work he once did when he first arrived in Texas, which was before the global economic crisis hit in 2008. Despite his move, he was disappointed with the lack of job opportunities in Georgia as well. Debora explained, "He hardly sends us money because he says there isn't much work." Thus, he moved to Georgia to find a better job, but the economy made it less profitable than he had anticipated. Debora's hope at the time of the follow-up interview was that Alex would return to Guatemala as soon as possible, especially since he was no longer making enough money to send home for their future, and her son could only vaguely remember him—often asking what his dad looks like or what kind of person he is generally. Debora confessed, " . . . I have hope in God that this year he will come home because so much has happened already."

For Debora, the loss of her mother and the intense desire to be part of a family were the primary themes when she talked about her life experiences in interviews and informal conversations. When asked in a preliminary research interview what type of long-term impact the genocide has had on her own life, she responded, "A lot because you miss having the advice of a parent to say, 'Don't do this.' Or the advice of a mother who tells you, 'Do this, my daughter, because it is good for you.' It is so difficult when one does not have parents." Speaking about her early childhood and the genocide in the formal research interview conducted two years later, Debora again remarked, "It affects me a lot because it was my mother that they murdered. Even today I still feel the pain because I wish I had someone to go to for advice, but I don't have anyone." Several years after that interview, Debora replied to a question about how she is feeling by stating, "There is always a great emptiness because even as an adult you need a mother's guidance." For Debora, the loss of her mother and the void it has left in her life are permanent reminders of her difficult early childhood, a challenge that remains with her every day even as an adult.

While Debora related that she cannot escape the emptiness she feels because of the loss of her mother, she has done her best to raise her son and to create the family she never had. She hopes her son will be a good person and continue his studies: "The strength in my life is my son because God gave me a person so loving, which is my son." She furthered added that she just wants to "live in harmony and with lots of love," explaining "Sometimes you feel so alone in this life, but then people appear who give you the strength to go on. . . . My great family now is my son." Debora felt strongly about providing her son with the love she says she rarely felt as a child, especially as a teenager in the residential home.

Debora's life experiences reflect a common theme among child survivors. By having lost family members and having no familial "safety net" to support them, they have no other choice but to move forward in life. For example, Debora pointed out that *la violencia* affected child survivors greatly because they were left without a dad or mom. She feels that for many parents, the sadness of losing their spouse caused them to begin to drink, much like her father, and, thus, they left their children with a more responsible caregiver. Many children who came to the residential home were enrolled because, like Deborah and her sister, they were left in the street by a surviving parent who struggled with trauma and loss. Expanding on her own experience, Debora continued, "It is now when I am an adult that I need my mom and my dad. Right now, today, I have nothing." Fortunately for Debora, she has been successful not just in moving forward but also in becoming a strong individual confident in who she is and in creating the family she always hoped to have in her life. Alex eventually returned to Guatemala earlier than they had planned. A declining economy in the US made securing good-paying work increasingly difficult. Debora was happy to have Alex home, and they since have had two more sons. Their home remains unfinished, but she is certain that one day they will complete it and she will have the home of which she has always dreamed. In the meantime, Debora continues to be a generous person who is empathic with others instead of bitter from her earlier life experiences. She is a truly remarkable individual who, despite a myriad of barriers and life challenges, has moved forward and continues to strive for what she desires in life: a loving, supportive family and home.

Esteban

With the help of his older sister, Esteban moved to the capital after living with relatives in his natal community for a short time after being expelled from the residential home. His goal was to get his life back on track. He first moved in with his sister's friends in one of the outer areas of the capital. Esteban explained, "I started working in the store owned by my sister's friends, a couple with children, and I lived with them, paying rent for a small room in their home, which was located right next to the store itself. So, for two years I was fortunate to live with the family and work right there in their store." Through constant encouragement from the mother of the family with whom he lived, Esteban also enrolled in school and took classes on Saturdays to finish the third year of junior high. Managing both school and work was a challenge, but he did well for himself. After completing junior high, he next enrolled in high school and focused on a career track in computer science. Esteban worked hard at his education and completed his high school training in just two short years. After graduation, he decided it was time to focus solely on employment. Thanks to a connection made by the Catholic sisters in the residential home in Santa Teresa, he found a job as a sacristan with a Monsignor of a Catholic church in the city. Esteban remained in the church's employ for two years, taking up residence at the church pastoral house.

All was going well in Esteban's life, and he felt that his life was finally moving in the right direction. His hard work was paying off. One evening, however, Esteban was returning home to the church after running errands when he was robbed at gunpoint. The thieves shot him in the stomach even though he had not put up a struggle, leaving him bleeding profusely in the street. It was a completely random, heinous robbery and shooting, not uncommon even now in the post-conflict era in Guatemala (Benson and Fischer 2009; Goldín and Rosenbaum 2009). After the shooting, he was hospitalized for several weeks and eventually recovered physically from his wounds. Emotionally, he developed a great fear of walking in the streets at night and felt that he continued to suffer from what he, himself, identified as "post-traumatic stress" for quite some time after the shooting.

Determined not to take life for granted and to make something of his life after his near-death experience, Esteban decided to look for a tiny home to rent in the capital for himself and his two sisters. To financially support a small family home with his sisters, he sought various jobs that charted different directions for his career aspirations. First, he secured employment with the Guatemalan National Postal and Telegraph Office in the capital. After a short time, he left the post office and, thanks to his older sister who had connections, landed a better-paying job with the National Museum of History. At the museum, Esteban, who has always had a knack for learning languages including English, worked as a tour guide and with restoration officials in cleaning and preserving various artifacts. One month after accepting the position with the museum, he also took a second job with a national bank to work as a collection agent. The hours for the bank were primarily in the evenings, which allowed him to maintain both the full-time job at the museum during the day and the part-time job at the bank during the evenings. Together, both jobs required him to work over 70 hours a week. Because he was dedicated to making something out of his life and to making a home with his sisters, Esteban did not mind the long work hours. Over the next year, he proved himself to the museum officials and, subsequently, was promoted to work in the museum's administrative offices as an accounting assistant. Working countless hours and with renewed ambition to advance his career and earning potential, Esteban decided it was also time to enroll in a private university that same year, taking college courses on Saturdays and adding yet another commitment to his already busy schedule.

In 2007, Esteban once again was promoted, this time within the Guatemalan Ministry of Culture and Sports Department itself, which is the primary governmental agency that oversees the nation's cultural and sports venues and entities, including the National Museum of History where he had been working. He was promoted to a higher level accounting position within the Ministry offices and moved locations to work downtown near the presidential palace. In his new position, Esteban was a full-fledged accountant for all of the national museums and sports venues within the Ministry. He also continued to take university courses on Saturdays, majoring in business administration. He paid for his education course by course with some assistance from a US family who supported the residential home for years and graciously provided him with a college scholarship and a lot of encouragement. Esteban completed his degree in 2014. When asked about the importance of education in a follow-up interview, he reflected, "I am now very dedicated to education, and I really believe that, yes, I can do something for my community by

providing others with an education . . . by teaching and encouraging others
to go to college."

With a profound passion for education, Esteban next set his sights on
graduate school. He continued working full-time and attending classes in the
evenings and on weekends. In 2015, he graduated with a Master's degree
in human resources. Having achieved his educational goals, he married his
fiancée in 2016. Today, they have two beautiful children and a loving home.
Both Esteban and his wife continue to work in the Ministry of Public Finance
where they first met. In a recent conversation, he shared with me that he
and his wife also plan to continue their educations. His wife aims to earn an
advanced accounting degree in auditing, and he plans to go to law school. His
goal is to become a lawyer and notary who defends the rights of children who
are living in alternative care. He asserted that he does not want children to be
deprived of their rights or to have their families take advantage of them in the
way that his extended relatives did with him. Esteban is adamant that he will
defend and fight for children so that they also can maintain and foster their
ethnic identities and sense of belonging. In addition, he recently established a
side business in real estate valuation that he hopes will cover the costs of law
school tuition, books, and other educational expenses.

Esteban's life has been one filled with challenge, pain, trauma, disappointment, hope, growth, resilience, and success. His father's suicide left an indelible image in his mind—one that he asserts that he can never escape—and
his mother's death was equally traumatic. While his father and mother did not
die directly in combat, via disappearance, or in a massacre, he believes that
his father's death was an indirect result of his military service during *la violencia*. Reflecting on his earlier life experiences in a more recent interview,
Esteban contended, "Yes, the genocide affected me indirectly . . . psychologically I would say . . . psychologically I was affected by the conflict but in
an indirect way, as a consequence of my parents' deaths." Yet he has proven
his resilience time and again. He is also generous and giving. For example,
to assist his older sister with growing financial obligations after her spouse
died unexpectedly, Esteban legally adopted one of her four daughters (the
father of the three older daughters was still alive and able to support them).
He remains dedicated to making sure that his niece-daughter is provided for
both financially and emotionally so that, as he puts it, "she will never know
what it is like to live like a 'street dog.'"

One goal Esteban has not been able to achieve is regaining full legal
ownership of his deceased mother's home, which he lived in when he was a
child. He has the legal title in his possession and has tried to get the house
back through the legal system. Unfortunately, one of his paternal uncles still
argues that the home is his even though the property belonged to Esteban's
maternal relatives and Esteban officially holds the legal title. That same uncle

is currently occupying the house with no intention of ever rightfully returning it to Esteban and his sisters. It will be a long road trying to regain the house both legally and physically, but Esteban and his sisters are determined to get it back as it is the only tangible keepsake and living memory of their parents, as well as of their family and natal community connections. Given Esteban's demonstrated persistence and strength gained from a childhood of obstacles and adversity, it will not be surprising one day to find him happily living in his maternal home with his own family, as well as those of his sisters.

Susana

Susana continued to work hard as a bookkeeper for the Catholic sisters in the permanent residential home in Santa Teresa for several years after completing her high school degree. She was grateful for her employment. However, she also knew that if she was going to get ahead in life, she needed to advance her formal education. Following in the footsteps of her three older brothers—two of whom had started college and were studying to be lawyers at the time—Susana took the national college entrance exams in 2001 and scored so well that she was automatically admitted to the prestigious University of San Carlos in Guatemala City. She decided that she, too, would study law, because of her dad. Her family never knew what the motive was behind his kidnapping and disappearance, and no one sought justice in the case or in the case of thousands of victims from that same period. Susana wanted to study law to make sense of what happened to her dad and to help her community. She recognized that there are many poor people who cannot pay for legal services. A bilingual speaker, her goal was to obtain a law degree so that she could help her community members access important legal services in their native language, allowing them to better understand their legal cases.

Having made a sound decision to study law, Susana became more dedicated than ever to her studies even though it meant a grueling schedule. She explained, "I began college in 2002 and for six years I lived in Santa Teresa and every day from Monday to Saturday I went to classes. Monday through Friday I studied from 2:00 p.m. to 5:15 p.m. and on Saturdays, I studied all day." Her schedule meant that for six straight years she worked in the residential home Monday through Friday from 8:00 a.m. to noon and then had to immediately take the nearly two-hour bus ride into the capital to make her 2:00 p.m. class. She participated in classes all afternoon, took the bus back home every weekday evening, studied until late, and then got up early the next morning to start her demanding routine all over again. Saturdays involved getting to the university by 8:00 a.m. and leaving after 5:00 p.m. Despite the exhausting schedule, Susana did very well in her classes and completed her coursework in late 2006. She then began a paid internship in a nearby city at a small law office, while also initiating the process of studying for the national bar exam.

In the same year that she completed her coursework, Susana terminated her employment with the Catholic sisters in the residential home to be able to fulfill the full-time requirements of her legal internship, which required her to work Monday through Friday, 8:00 a.m. to 6:00 p.m. She also decided to attempt entrepreneurship. She opened a small mercantile-type store in Santa Teresa in 2005. The store allowed her to earn additional income and to hire her mother as the storekeeper, which was a less-demanding employment opportunity than in the residential home. Susana's mother had been working as a *tía* in the residential home for years, but the work was hard, and she was getting older. Susana did not want her mother to work so hard at her advanced age and thought the store would be a better working environment for her.

Susana opened her store on the outer perimeter of her older brother's home and offered a wide variety of products from gumballs to black beans to beauty products. One of my favorite things to do while living in Santa Teresa during fieldwork was to hang out at Susana's store and take the time to see all the items she sold even though the actual floor space was no more than 150 square feet. Her store contained everything. There were hair gels, scarves, Snickers candy bars, purified water, and even Diet Coke (still hard to find in the area at the time and my personal favorite then). I would often stop by Susana's store in the late afternoon to pick up an onion, some beans, a chili pepper or two, some potatoes, and tomatoes—all fresh and ready to be cooked. Susana also diversified and added ready-to-cook chicken meat to her products for sale. Prior to my fieldwork period, I had not seen plucked, cut, and ready-to-cook chicken meat for sale anywhere but in stores in larger towns and cities. Susana explained that as villagers' schedules got busier and most adults increasingly had to travel daily to larger cities for work, the situation was ripe for providing a new product such as ready-to-cook chicken that customers could simply pick up on their way home and quickly cook up for the evening meal. Her mother was in charge of killing the chickens and preparing the meat, which she did three times a week. The meat was then kept in the store refrigerator that Susana had procured from the capital. The chicken meat was a real success with customers, as was Susana's store more generally. Her entrepreneurial skills are amazing, and she has had much success with her store since she opened it. She was also pleased that she was able to bring her mother to live with her in her brother's home and have her work in the store where she could rest in between waiting on customers. In addition, she was glad to have her mother's help not only in the store but also with her new baby girl, who was born in late 2008. Susana had been in a relationship with a fellow alumnus of the residential home for many years, and while they never legally married, they "united"[1] and came to live together in late 2006 in the home of her brother. She was thrilled to take on the new challenge of motherhood while completing her law degree and was happy to have her mother's help.

After her internship in late 2008, Susana began studying even more intensely for the bar exam and scheduled it for February of 2010. In the meantime, she also opened a legal services office with two colleagues in a neighboring town. The legal services she and her colleagues provided include notary services, legal title transfers, and marriage certificates. Her hope was to expand the services to full legal representation once she passed the bar exam. Unfortunately, Susana had to delay taking the bar exam because her oldest brother died in a tragic car accident in 2009, devastating the family. Susana's mother was especially distraught over her son's death. They had made it through so much, having survived genocide and a military raid on their home that led to their father's demise. Given her mother's despair, Susana felt that she had to set her studying aside to tend to her mother. Unfortunately, just when it seemed that life was about to get back on track for Susana and her family, her youngest brother was severely injured in a serious car accident in 2010. The accident nearly killed him, and he was in a coma for a month. It took him many years to recover his memory, some of which he still struggles with today. Susana's mother was by his side daily in his recovery, and Susana felt she had to further delay taking the bar exam to accommodate the immediate needs of her family. When asked what she hopes for in her life, Susana responded, "To always have employment and at the same time, create sources of employment for other Guatemalans." She also hopes to continue studying law and to complete an advanced Juris Doctorate (J.D.), which will qualify her to become a magistrate judge with a particular focus on advancing the human rights of Maya Indigenous peoples in Guatemala.

When I asked Susana what made her so successful, she explained, "It is for necessity . . . I would have liked, at this age, to have attained greater goals, but I have had obstacles such as my oldest brother's death one year ago and my youngest brother's accident. . . . I am now planning on opening a [legal] office in another municipality, to continue with the store, and to finish building my house in Santa Teresa."

Susana purchased a small parcel of land on her own in Santa Teresa several years ago and initiated the first phase of construction in 2010. While she was somewhat dissatisfied with the pace at which she has been reaching her goals, she has been extremely successful, nonetheless. When asked why she thinks that she and her fellow child survivors from the residential home have experienced so much financial and educational success in comparison with their peers from Santa Teresa, Susana contended, "It is out of necessity and not having parents to count on. You have to depend on yourself and if you don't make the efforts, no one will do it for you. You have to make decisions and make plans for the future, thinking about how you can't depend on any-one else." Her comments reflect the *"tiene que"* sentiment that surfaced in so many child survivors' narratives.

Susana is a strong, independent, educated woman who is confident in her abilities to forge her own path in life and who maintains a strong connection to her Maya Indigenous heritage. She identifies herself as Kaqchikel. She also identifies her mother as Kaqchikel, but her mother originated from a neigh-boring municipality and not from Santa Teresa proper. Susana related that her father also identified as Kaqchikel and came from an adjoining hamlet that is part of the municipality of Santa Teresa, which is why they originally lived there. Unlike many of her fellow child survivors who grew up in the residential home, Susana was able to maintain close connections to her natal community because the residential home was located in the same municipal-ity where her family had been living.

As a strong Kaqchikel woman, Susana has made huge strides in her educa-tion. Though she would never brag about her successes and is one of the hum-blest and most generous individuals that I have ever come to know, Susana is a truly amazing person who has achieved so much despite the odds. And yet her primary goal in life today, besides her own educational pursuits, is for her daughter to get an education so that she can achieve something much greater than Susana has. Susana is a clear example of strength, courage, and humility.

Mario

Mario completed the challenging musical education program in Guatemala City in four years, right on schedule. The program is one of the best and most demanding career-specific high school programs offered in the country and requires four rigorous years of academic and musical instruction (most other programs require three years or less). Mario did well academically, while also advancing his core musical skills in piano and guitar. He completed his teach-ing practicum and graduated at the top of his class.

In a stroke of luck, I happened to be in Guatemala during Mario's high school graduation. I was overwhelmed with pride watching him on stage with his cohort as the instructors spoke of their achievements and successes. When the time came to receive their diplomas, each student came up to the podium and waited as their parents joined them on stage, presented their graduat-ing child with a class ring, and together, as a family, accepted their child's diploma. This is a common tradition in Guatemala, but for Mario it posed a particular challenge as his parents had been kidnapped and disappeared in the early 1980s when he was a child, and his siblings could not attend the event. He was thrilled, however, when two other former international volunteers, a group of from the residential home, and I arrived as a surprise before the commencement ceremony. Without hesitation, he excitedly asked if two of us would step in as his "parents" to join him in receiving his diploma. I deferred to the other former volunteers because I did not want to take the great opportunity away from them even though I would have been so honored to be on that stage with him. Instead, I promised to take many photos of the moment.

As Mario's name was called, the two former foreign volunteers came to the stage and proudly accepted the diploma with him while giving him big hugs (not typically a tradition in graduation ceremonies in Guatemala at that time). While parents traditionally give their graduating child a class ring in the moment, there was no class ring to present to Mario as we had no idea that we would be asked to step in for his disappeared parents. But that did not matter to him. He was so rightfully proud of his accomplishment and was simply happy to have people there to celebrate with him. I felt a pang of sadness, however, thinking about how proud his parents would have been and how odd it must have been to have foreigners as proxies for parents. However, Mario was thrilled and not at all embarrassed by us or the fact that an international contingent supported him, as strange as we were for everyone else in attendance (there were many whispers when the two former volunteers went up on stage with him). He was overjoyed with his accomplishment, and this was just the beginning of his success. Mario wasted no time moving on to the next step of his career path.

Within a few months of his high school graduation, Mario was offered employment as a music teacher at two prominent private high schools in Guatemala City. He began offering instruction at one school in the mornings and at the second institution in the afternoons, with a very small break in between. He worked hard, offering both choral and instrumental music instruction. After one year of working both jobs, Mario decided it was time to also add university studies to his plate. He took the national college entrance exams and scored high enough to gain admission to the University of San Carlos in Guatemala City. He began taking courses in the evenings and on the weekends to accommodate his working schedule. He often took five to six courses each semester, while maintaining (and flourishing at) both of his full-time jobs. After the first couple of years of general coursework, Mario decided that he would major in communications. He explained, "I decided that it would be a good idea to combine my present career in music with communications and journalism. I thought it would be a good idea and so, that's what I did." He continued to work and study, and yet his desire to succeed propelled him even further, resulting in his taking a shot at entrepreneurship as well.

In 2006, Mario opened an Internet café in the city where his second brother had been enrolled in a boarding school during childhood. Mario rented the business locale, purchased the most up-to-date computer equipment with his own savings, hired qualified staff, and opened the doors to his new business. Sharing his reasons for opening a business, he reflected,

> I never just wanted to work for someone else or for an institution. I always wanted something of my own and what better than something that also relates to communication. Besides, [Internet services] are a tool that was beginning to take hold in the interior of the country, but with the advances that exist today, I don't think it's as profitable because there is a lot of competition, but thank God, we are still able to compete with the rest.

Working two professional jobs and running his own business while continuing with university courses, Mario completed his college degree in the fall of 2007. Again, I was most fortunate to have been in Guatemala at the time of his college graduation. I could not have been more honored when Mario came one Sunday to Santa Teresa where I was staying during fieldwork. He had the biggest smile on his face. With a gleam in his eye, he proudly handed me the invitation to his commencement ceremony. We both laughed as I recalled the great fortune of having been in Guatemala for his high school graduation some years earlier. With a smile as big as his, I told him that I planned to also be at his masters and then doctoral graduations. "Okay!" Mario excitedly exclaimed, "Sounds great to me!"

Mario's college graduation was one of the stateliest that I have ever witnessed. His smile could not have been larger as I approached him from across the room and saw him in his full regalia prior to the ceremony. He was so appreciative that I was there, but I felt deeply that I was the one who was so honored to be present. After giving him a huge congratulatory hug, I went up into the balcony of the majestic theatre where the commencement ceremony was being held. I watched as the group of about twenty-five graduates filed in and ascended the stage. After hearing from several presenters, the graduates were called up one by one to receive their diplomas. I could not help but think of how much work it had taken for Mario to get to this point and how proud his parents would have been had they been alive to see the ceremony firsthand. I wondered if anyone sitting next to Mario on that stage knew of his early childhood struggles and his incredible perseverance. It was possible that some of the other graduates were also survivors of the internal armed conflict and genocide just like Mario. However, it was more likely that most of the graduates came from more privileged families from the capital, and, thus, emerged from the armed conflict and genocide relatively unscathed.

It was hard to contain my happiness for Mario as his name was finally called. I stood up and took as many photos as I could. After the ceremony, we hugged each other with tears in our eyes because we both knew very well how monumental this accomplishment really was for him. That little boy, who was nearly shot to death while on his sister's back and managed to survive after being lost for three days in the mountains unaccompanied and at the mercy of the nature that surrounded him, had achieved a goal that he could never have imagined when he was a child. I can only describe Mario's achievements as astounding, and yet he is always so grateful and gracious to everyone else for his success. He emphasized that not all orphaned child survivors have had the same luck and that he has been fortunate because of the opportunities he has been given in life. He has been steadfast in taking advantage of those opportunities and has been so grateful to everyone who contributed to his education along the way.

Following graduation, Mario continued to work as a music teacher at both private schools in Guatemala City. He found the work challenging and inspiring. He would soon rise up in the ranks and serve in an administrative position in addition to his teaching duties. He even developed a formal concert choir for one of the schools. In a conversation we had during a follow-up interview some years later, he excitedly revealed,

> I tell you that we are in exam week this week here in the school and two weeks ago, the new choir that I am directing had its debut and thank God, it was a total success!. . . . Everyone congratulated us: the parents, the teachers, the school director, and even the other students. Thank God! I was so nervous that day and the days leading up to it, but it went well!

Mario's life would continue moving forward, but his resilience and strength soon would be further tested. On January 1, 2009, Mario was in a near-fatal car accident on the dangerous winding Inter-American Highway at a point located on the western outskirts of the capital, which totaled the car that he had worked so hard to finance. Mario cannot recall all the details of the event, but he was profoundly moved by the experience: "I understand it as more than an accident. It was a miracle and God showed me that he loves me . . . " It took him a few weeks to recover from the accident. In the various conversations that we had following the event, he always foregrounded the conversation with his sincere gratitude for his life and consistently expressed that he does not take life for granted. When I asked him to summarize what he would like people to know about his life experiences as a person who grew up an orphaned child survivor in the highlands, Mario reflected,

> That one always has to be grateful and take advantage of the opportunities that present themselves, but especially not to give up and to fight for what one wants to be and do it with a lot of effort and goodwill. In conclusion, all of my achievements, besides any limitations that I have had, have been positive and you can never lose faith or hope. Do well unto others as you would do to yourself. Something important regarding the armed conflict is to not carry a grudge and

to not think of vengeance because that would not allow you to move forward . . . Thank God for those people [who have supported me] who I will never forget. My success is not mine alone.

In a more recent conversation that I had with Mario in 2019, he revealed that changes in school administration and funding brought his career as a music teacher to a close after twenty years as an educator. The unexpected change in his career gave him the freedom, however, to venture further into entrepreneurship. He had closed the Internet cafe a few years back as Internet services via cell phones and in residences had become more accessible, and competition among the few remaining Internet cafes had made profitability a challenge. Mario enjoyed his entrepreneurial venture with the Internet cafe and was eager to start a new business in one of the suburbs of the capital city. Partnering with a good friend, he opened a restaurant in 2019 that features what he describes as Tex-Mex food such as tacos, quesadillas, and nachos.

Today, Mario's restaurant continues to prosper. He lives with his wife of over ten years and their two children. Unfortunately, their third child died in 2013, and the loss has been difficult. He shared that losing a child was extremely challenging to overcome but that he and his family had to find the strength to keep moving forward (emblematic of the "*tiene que*" notion). Mario's life story is another example of the success and perseverance child survivors have exhibited in their lives while facing extreme adversity not only in childhood but also in adulthood. Despite having lost both of his parents and growing up in a permanent residential home for orphaned child survivors located some distance from his natal community, Mario developed into a resilient adult with strong self-confidence built on years of academic and other achievements. His adulthood has been a testament to both his strength and his ability to positively confront the hardships of being in a near-fatal accident and losing a child as well. Mario's positive attitude and generous heart continue to spread goodwill and inspiration to others.

Updates from Other Child Survivors

Through a recent short follow-up research stint in Guatemala and informally via social media, I was able to continue my conversations with many of the other twenty child survivors who participated in my research project. Most now are in their thirties and early forties and continue to move forward in life, pursuing their academic and career goals while raising families of their own. Nidia is a good example. She always enjoyed helping and nurturing children in the residential home ever since she was young. Fortunately, she began working in another home for children in a nearby city after she left the residential home in Santa Teresa at the age of eighteen. Within a few years, she married her boyfriend from a neighboring town of Santa Teresa, and they had their first child together, a daughter. Nidia's marriage was difficult at first because of her husband's violent temper, but over time, they were able to work through the challenges they faced and had two more daughters.

Nidia always wanted to attend college and initially sought a scholarship after leaving the residential home. I can confirm from my firsthand experience working with her during study halls in the residential home when I was a volunteer there that she is a brilliant and dedicated student with a deep penchant for learning. Unfortunately, her husband did not support her desire to attend college. With three small children, Nidia instead continued to dedicate herself to her family and to working with children in a private elementary school. The school is located in the same city where she worked in a residential home, which means an hour or more daily commute one way by bus. While balancing her job and family life is challenging, she loves her work and finds it a great blessing for her own intellectual growth and her personal life, as well as for her family. Nidia loves to teach, and when asked what her career goal is now, she responded, "I always try to maintain a permanent position at my job and to leave a positive impression." She also continues to challenge herself intellectually. Over the past decade, she has earned various certifications and participated in many trainings focused on special education for small children. Now in her early-40s, Nidia's academic goals have shifted from her own pursuits to those of her three daughters. She hopes that they achieve all they dream of academically and spiritually, as well as having families of their own. Her goal now is to fully support them along the way.

Much like his sister, Susana, Oscar followed in the footsteps of his older brothers and studied law as a young adult. When he left the residential home, he lived in his brother's home with his mom and sister in Santa Teresa. After a short while, he married and built his own home in Santa Teresa. Like his sister, he opened a store in the front of his home, which faced the main street running through Santa Teresa. In his store, he sold basic foodstuffs, but he especially focused on selling agricultural supplies such as seeds, fertilizers, herbicides, and tools. Profits from the store helped support his family and his academic pursuits. Oscar attended the University of San Carlos, working in his store in the mornings and attending classes in the afternoons and on the weekends. His wife tended the store in the afternoons while he was in school. He hoped to finish his degree and become a lawyer and notary, just like his brothers and sister. Part way through his studies, he began working in a legal organization in Antigua. The new job required him to make the forty-minute or more one-way commute there by bus in the early mornings. He then had to head to the capital in the afternoons to study, before making the two-hour or more commute back to Santa Teresa in the early evenings. The schedule was grueling, but Oscar was committed to getting his degree while providing for his growing family, which included two small children.

Unfortunately, as noted in Susana's update, Oscar was in a near-fatal car accident in 2010 and was left in a coma for a month. He lost much of his memory and has still not fully recovered. Because of his memory loss, he was forced to leave the university and did not graduate. He hopes that one day his memory will fully return so that he can resume studies to finish his degree, although he likely would have to entirely restart his degree program given the time that has passed since he was enrolled. Thankfully, Oscar was able to keep his job and continues to work there today. He also continues to operate his store with the help of his wife and children. Now a father of four, he has worked hard to make sure his children have a supportive home and ample access to education. His love for his children is palpable. Recently, I met Oscar outside of one of the local churches in Santa Teresa, and he was thrilled to show me how his kids have grown. Oscar is a wonderful father who continues to provide for his family despite unexpected setbacks in his adulthood. His memory may not be fully recovered, but his persistence and strength have not diminished.

With the financial support of the permanent residential home, Medelin attended a career-focused high school program in Antigua that specialized in tourism and hospitality. Once graduated from the program, she was on her own and set out to find work. She worked in various positions, eventually set-tling in a nearby city where she met her future partner. After dating for a time, they moved in together and had their first child, a son. She continued to work various jobs, while also caring for her infant. She hoped to one day attend college but made her son her priority at that point in her life. After several years together, her partner unexpectedly left her and moved to the capital. He returned on weekends to visit their son, and although Medelin was devastated by her now ex-partner's decision to leave the relationship, she was glad that he at least was still involved in their son's life.

One weekend, however, her ex-partner came to visit their son and said he was going to take him to the capital for the weekend as he normally did. Medelin kissed her son good-bye and told him to be a good boy. She told him she would see him when he returned Sunday evening. However, Medelin was terrified when Sunday evening came and went without her ex-partner return-ing her son. She panicked and called her ex-partner. There was no answer. She frantically called everyone she knew who might have seen her partner and son, but nobody had any idea where they were. Unable to sleep, Medelin kept trying to call her ex-partner. Her efforts were fruitless.

Her ex-partner essentially kidnapped her son, and she spent the next two years searching for him without any luck. She was absolutely devastated and desperately sought every possible solution to find her son. On her time off from work, she would drive her motorcycle into the capital and search for hours just hoping to spot her son somewhere. She even tried making the risky journey north to the US, thinking that if she could work for just a few years there, she could save enough money to hire a lawyer who would help find her son. She simply did not have enough money to hire a lawyer while living in Guatemala. Medelin made the grueling trek north and told me how the "coyotes" gave the women in her group who were heading north birth control pills as they likely would be sexually assaulted along the way. Despite the horrific conditions and warnings from others who had crossed, she was determined to make it. She had to find her son and she needed money to hire a lawyer. She felt she had only one option: risk everything and head north.

The journey north was as grueling as Medelin had anticipated despite her determination. At one point, she got separated from the group and wandered alone through the desert along the Mexico/US border. All her toenails had fallen off at that point and she quickly was becoming severely dehydrated. She eventually was found by an Arizona rancher who called the authorities to detain her. Medelin did not mind. She was so dehydrated and delusional at that point that she felt like she was on the verge of death. She was just happy to be found alive.

Medelin was deported back to Guatemala after a month in detention, and the money she managed to scrounge up to pay the "coyotes" was lost since she had to pay them up front and did not make it across successfully. There's no "return policy" with coyotes. You pay them and never see the money again regardless of how successful you are at crossing the border. Now she was back at square one with no savings, no job, and still emotionally devastated by the kidnapping of her son. She placed ads in the primary newspaper in the capital that asked for any information on his whereabouts, but to no avail. In addition, she sought help from a nonprofit organization that focused specifically on finding stolen children. Her case went nowhere, with no leads. It seemed her son had simply vanished, as if the earth swallowed him up. Putting one foot in front of the other each day seemed like an impossible feat. Medelin had become depressed and was losing hope. To make matters worse, her ex-partner had sent thugs to beat her up in her own apartment as a message to stop looking for her son. The beating was severe, and she feared that the next time might mean death. As a means of both distracting and protecting herself, she sought a university program in another Central American country where she studied for one year with the financial support of a benefactor who had a relationship with the residential home. She took her studies seriously and was able to advance her English language skills significantly. Once she completed the program, she spent a few months working in Mexico with friends of a former residential home volunteer and then returned to Guatemala in the hopes that the situation with her ex-partner had cooled off enough so that she could get on with her life and continue looking for her son.

Medelin found employment in the capital and worked in various jobs utilizing her now advanced English language skills. Eventually, she happened to meet up with a former junior high school classmate, and soon they began dating. The couple united, and Medelin moved to the town where her new partner grew up and where they had attended school together. A year later, they had their first child together, a daughter. She still has received no word on her son and can only hope that when he is old enough, he will search for her. She has been devastated by the loss of her son whom she loved and adored. She fears that he has been fed false information by her ex-partner and may never want to see her again as a result. She can only hope that her son will be able to figure things out on his own and give her the opportunity to explain what happened. She is still affected deeply, and some days are worse than others, but as Medelin shared, "I can't just stop. I have to keep living." Meanwhile, she is raising her daughter and working in a municipal position to help support her family. She is also working on her bachelor's degree in business administration and is nearly done with the program. Medelin is an incredibly strong woman who has had to overcome sometimes seemingly insurmountable obstacles. Yet she powers forward, and despite what happened with her son and her own experience growing up in the terrifying circumstances of the armed conflict and genocide, she maintains a positive spirit and attitude. She thanks God for the roof over her head, for never going without food, and for her family. Her daughter is growing every day, her mother-in-law is no longer ill, and her partner is doing well. In Medelin's words, "Life continues, and every day is another opportunity."

The life experiences presented in this chapter reveal both the achievements and struggles that child survivors have had in adulthood. Orphaned in childhood, they lost key family and natal community support systems that certainly could have made their transition into adulthood less arduous, stressful, and risky. Despite their limited resources and support, however, child survivors managed to enter adulthood with strong aspirations and the drive to make something of themselves and their lives. Their success and achievements are remarkable given the context in which they grew up and the multitude of obstacles that they have had to subsequently face. Their life stories are an inspiration and offer unique insights into their individual journeys into and through adulthood. Such insights are important for better understanding their experiences and for utilizing lessons learned to inform and develop more effective ways to support current and future orphaned children around the globe. These insights, which I now present as key themes, deserve further attention.

KEY THEMES ACROSS GUATEMALAN
CHILD SURVIVOR EXPERIENCES

Overall, child survivors in my research project have become positive, well-adapted adults despite having lived through dramatically disrupted and traumatic childhoods. That is not to say that all child survivors who grew up in the residential home in Santa Teresa have lived healthy, stable lives. A few died young as a result of alcoholism, other addictions, or gang violence. Others have struggled immensely with the long-term emotional, social, and economic consequences of having been orphaned when they were children. However, the vast majority, and particularly those who participated in my research project, have managed to build healthy, stable lives despite unwarranted circumstances in their childhoods. On their own in adulthood and without the financial support of the residential home, child survivors could easily have lost sight of their aspirations and lost their drive to make something of themselves and their lives as they struggled to just get by in the first few difficult years of transitioning into adulthood. Because they did not have family or natal community guidance or support, it would not have been surprising had they ended up living in poverty or been involved in risky behaviors as a means of coping, albeit in an unhealthy way, with their trauma and loss. However, as child survivors presented in this book clearly demonstrate, they did not fall victim to life obstacles or disadvantaged circumstances. Rather, they have achieved positive academic, career, and family goals in adulthood, all without safety nets derived from familial or natal community ties. In their view, they had no choice but to forge ahead, working hard to establish themselves and to create families of their own. Looking across their experiences reveals several commonalities, presented here as key themes, that help to elucidate their motivation for forging ahead and soundly establishing themselves in adulthood.

First, most child survivors have maintained the "*tiene que*" attitude that they had no choice but to keep moving forward and striving to make a better life in whatever way possible. This attitude is encapsulated in Juliana's comment, "But Shirley, you have to . . . you just have to continue moving forward and leave the past behind. What else is there?" For most, there simply was no other choice. Rather than centrally focusing on what they had lost in their childhoods and succumbing to their circumstances, child survivors set their sights on working hard and achieving what they could even though much of what they set out to do was in unfamiliar territory for them. As Susana pointed out, child survivors have had to depend on themselves in adulthood and make efforts on their own to get ahead in life because there was no one else to do it for them. Consequently, some had to learn how to navigate life in urban centers, while others became parents at a young age without the sage advice of their own parents to guide them. Navigating college was another challenge they had to figure out completely on their own but managed to do with great success.

Second, education has played a major role in child survivors' lives and has been key not only to their professional success but also to their intellectual development. Most child survivors have sought education beyond the high school level and at a much greater rate than their Santa Teresa peers who had the full and consistent support of their families growing up. Child survivors recognized early on in the residential home that education would become a central tool for helping them to establish themselves in life. With the help of the Catholic sisters in the residential home, child survivors were able to earn their career-specific high school diplomas as adolescents. Many of their peers at the time would not have been able to afford the high school programs, which are private and the most expensive programs in the country. With high school diplomas in hand, child survivors overcame a major hurdle (graduating from high school) and could then set their sights on college. Their hope was that a college degree would help them build a professional career, one that would increase their earning potential and better allow them to financially support themselves and their future families. Through much grit and determination, many child survivors not only earned a college degree but also attained or are now working toward advanced degrees. Examples include: Esteban, who earned a master's degree in human resources; Susana, who is working on completing her J.D. program; and Oscar, who was in the process of attaining his J.D. when he was involved in a near-fatal accident. While the path to higher education has not been an easy one, child survivors have taken on the challenge with unwavering determination and hard-earned success.

In addition to the professional and financial benefits of education, child survivors have also pursued education because they perceive it as contributing to their overall intellectual development. While many were not always keen on doing their homework when they were teenagers in the residential home—something I witnessed firsthand—most did develop an appreciation of and respect for education and the empowering knowledge that it can impart. For example, Esteban noted, "I am now very dedicated to education, and I really believe that, yes, I can do something for my community by providing others with an education." Mario not only appreciated the music and college education that he received but went on to teach for twenty years, imparting his profound love for music and education to many students over the years. Nidia and Debora were not able to attend college because their spouses did not support the idea. However, they both have continued to seek education in other forms because of their love for education. In Nidia's case, she has completed multiple certification programs and trainings, helping enrich her intellectual curiosity. She also teaches young children in elementary school, showing them how mind-opening and engaging education can be. As a stay-at-home mom, Debora has been considerably involved in her children's education, spending much time helping in their schools and encouraging them to do well so that they can go to college someday. The intellectual stimulation that education provides is clearly recognized by child survivors and continues to inspire them to seek education where they can, whether in law school, teaching others, or assisting in their children's own education.

Third, professional careers became commonplace for most child survivors in my research project. Because they were able to earn high school, college, and even advanced degrees, they became qualified for professional careers in areas such as education, business administration, legal services, and non-profit management. Without the education they attained, most of these professional careers would not have been accessible or achievable for them. Working hard to establish themselves as adults with stable incomes, child survivors made great efforts to earn their degrees so that they could access professional careers and, therefore, more readily support themselves and their own families financially. Many have worked countless hours, even adding part-time or second jobs and establishing their own businesses to their already busy schedules, all with the goal of becoming financially stable providers. For example, Oscar, Susana, and Mario attained professional careers and commensurate income that allowed them to expand their own businesses. Ultimately, having professional careers has meant that most child survivors could begin to overcome the economic consequences of having lost family, land, and assets because of the armed conflict and genocide. Their journey toward financial stability has not been an easy one, but many are now reaping the benefits of having studied and worked so hard in early adulthood. Several have built homes of their own and are able to send their children to private schools where they can get the best education possible. Their sacrifices have paid off, and their professional careers will likely continue to help them increase their earning potential as they move forward and more fully into middle adulthood.

Fourth, entrepreneurship has been a common experience for several child survivors in my research project. Mario owned an Internet cafe early on in his career and recently opened a restaurant in one of the most bustling neighborhoods of the capital. Susana opened a store in Santa Teresa while in college, and when she had her own home built, she relocated her store to the new home. Similarly, Oscar opened a store in his home that was also built in Santa Teresa and offers specialized products in agricultural supplies, demonstrating his keen recognition of the particular needs of local farmers. Esteban recently established his own real estate valuation business with the goal that its income will support his law school expenses. Lastly, Juliana established her own business of selling food to university students after carefully observing them for a while from her apartment rooftop when she would do laundry. While life circumstances prevented her from attaining a high school or college degree, the skills she learned from her elementary and junior high school experiences and from tutoring offered in the residential home have given her a solid foundational knowledge for entrepreneurship, and she is exceptional at it.

Successful entrepreneurship requires innovation and courage as it can be risky and may take a few years to turn a profit. Still, several child survivors, on their own and without parents or family members to model such endeavors, have boldly taken up the challenge of entrepreneurship. Fortunately, their efforts have been successful, and their creativity is inspiring. For example, Susana's ready-to-cook chicken idea and Mario's Tex-Mex restaurant serving food that is unique when compared to typical Guatemalan cuisine demonstrate their insightfulness and abilities to tailor products to their customers' changing needs and desires. Thus, child survivors' ventures into entrepreneurship further illustrates their resourcefulness and drive to establish themselves not only financially but also creatively as adults.

Fifth, successfully balancing school, work, and family while moving forward in adulthood is another key theme across child survivor experiences. Interestingly, even though several reported working multiple jobs while also going to college and raising children, they have never complained to me about their busy schedules or time demands placed on them. Instead, they have asserted that their busy schedules and efforts to balance all their responsibilities have been necessary to get ahead in life. Their ability to balance their responsibilities is remarkable given their incredibly busy schedules. For example, both Susana and Oscar worked full-time jobs, had their own stores, and attended college while raising small children and dealing with long commutes. Mario simultaneously worked two full-time jobs while operating his Internet cafe, attending college, and starting his own family. His Internet cafe was located thirty miles from the capital, requiring a daily commute until he could staff his business with a reliable manager. Fortunately, he hired as a manager a fellow alumnus from the residential home in Santa Teresa who was several years younger and had just turned eighteen. Mario was thrilled to give a fellow alumnus a job opportunity and to reduce the number of hours that he would have to spend at the cafe himself during his busy workweek. Balancing school, work, and family is not easy, but child survivors have managed to do it and without complaint. Certainly, there must have been times when they felt overwhelmed, exhausted, and overly stressed, but they have never expressed that in any interview or informal conversation that I have had with them over the past several decades. Instead, they focus on the possibilities and goals that their multiple efforts are helping them achieve. Their efforts to balance all that they are doing in adulthood is another testament to their resourcefulness, tenacity, and resilience.

Sixth, faith in God is another key theme that emerged in interviews and conversations not only with child survivors in my research project but also with most alumni of the residential home with whom I have maintained contact. When talking about her experiences, for example, Juliana noted that it has been with God's help that she has become a strong women who has a lot of love for her family. When speaking about his car accident, Mario asserted that his surviving the accident was a miracle and a sign that God loves him. He also thanked God for people who have supported him along the way. Medelin similarly thanked God for providing her with housing, food, and her family, while Debora credited God first with giving her a son who is so loving and is the strength in her life. Finally, Esteban stressed his gratitude toward God for his life after the hard time he had living in his natal village and for making him the man he is today. He believes that God has given him the best in life and feels so blessed as a result. He also believes God has a plan for his life, and he trusts that things happen because God wants them to occur. Child survivors' strong faith in God is evident in their interviews and the many conversations I have had with them over the years. They often gave thanks to God first and foremost when talking about their lives and what had transpired. Interestingly, many child survivor alumni of the residential home in Santa Teresa have converted from Catholicism (which they grew up initially within their families and then in the residential home) to evangelism. For many, the conversion occurred simply because they married into a family that is evangelical. Others converted on their own as increased efforts by evangelical churches to recruit new members have grown exponentially in Guatemala over the past several decades (Garrard-Burnett 2010; Samson 2007). Child survivors' conversion to evangelism would be an interesting topic of future research. Regardless, child survivors' central faith in God remains steadfast and offers them a sense of strength and stability to forge ahead in life. It has also given them gratitude and humility for all that they have achieved as adults.

The final key theme that emerged from child survivors' life experiences in adulthood involves creating families of their own. Having lost out on family life in their own childhoods, child survivors have placed great emphasis on creating their own healthy families and providing a loving home and bright future for their children. For example, Debora is grateful for her children and hopes to provide them with the loving home she did not have. Esteban's dedication to family is illustrated in the fact that he worked multiple jobs so that he and his two sisters could finally live together as a family. When his older sister's third child needed support, Esteban officially adopted her so that she would have the love and financial stability she needed. He then went on to have two children of his own and together with his wife, has established a nurturing home environment in which his children are cherished, protected, and empowered. Similarly, Nidia's primary focus in life now is on her daughters. While her marriage was rocky at first, she has dedicated herself to making a loving home for her daughters and works hard to provide them with the best education so that they can achieve their dreams and have loving families of their own.

While child survivors have created loving families of their own, they also have experienced devastating loss in their families. Juliana and Miguel lost their son when he was just two years old to an illness that remains undiagnosed. They shared that they are grateful for having their own angel in heaven now, but the loss was crushing. Mario and his partner also lost a child, which he had a hard time accepting at first. However, he believes God has a plan for him and is grateful for the short time he had with his third child. Medelin still struggles with the loss of her son, who was kidnapped by her ex-partner. She has good days and bad days but is hopeful that one day he will search for her and give her the opportunity to tell him the truth about what happened to separate them. She also focuses on her young daughter and is grateful that she was able to have another child. Losing a child has been excruciatingly difficult for some child survivors in my research project; at the same time, it has further deepened their gratitude for their surviving children. Having a loving, nurturing family is something that most child survivors could only have imagined when they were children and adolescents. Fortunately, they have been able to create the families they desired—families that offer them a source of love and support and that further strengthen their resilience.

Of their own accord, child survivors established life goals such as higher education, professional careers, entrepreneurship, and creating families of their own, and they achieved these life goals with little guidance or support from others. On their own, without family members to support and encourage them, most child survivors managed to figure out on their own how to access various resources, programs, and services in adulthood to help them on their journeys. It would be a great injustice to not recognize that child survivors, themselves, have been one of their own greatest assets in becoming positive, well-adapted adults. Although their abilities and skills were expanded and strengthened while living in the residential home in Santa Teresa, their drive and initiative in adulthood are purely their own and are truly extraordinary given the circumstances they were forced to face. Instead of succumbing to their challenging circumstances and multiple losses, child survivors have worked hard to move forward in life and to ultimately start overcoming the challenges forced upon them because of their orphan status. I believe it is imperative to further elucidate what they believe helped them in their journeys to become strong, resilient adults, given all that they have experienced and learned along the way. Knowledge gained from learning what aspects child survivors believe contributed to their resilience and adaptability could also help other orphaned children currently in the throes of surviving wars, armed conflicts, and genocide. With the aim of helping others in mind, I turn to child survivors' own explicit reflections on what they think helped them to develop resilience and positive adaptability while living in the residential home. I also include their advice for those working with orphaned child survivors in the world today.

REFLECTIONS AND ADVICE FOR HELPING OTHER ORPHANED CHILD SURVIVORS TODAY

During research and follow-up interviews, as well as in informal conversations, I often asked child survivors what they thought helped them become positive, well-adapted adults. In particular, I asked them what aspects of living in the permanent residential home that they thought contributed to their resilience and adaptability. The majority first responded by expressing gratitude for having had the opportunity to grow up in the residential home in Santa Teresa. Much like any typical family, however, each child survivor had unique experiences to share, and some had better experiences in the residential home than others. For example, Debora did not feel love in the residential home but at the same time was grateful for other opportunities and friendships with fellow child survivors that she developed while living there. Juliana and Esteban both were forced to leave the residential home before having had the opportunity to complete high school. Yet neither one of them was disgruntled. Instead, both appreciated their time in the residential home and recognized that their life choices caused them to miss out on additional opportunities afforded by the residential home. While each child survivor's experience in the residential home is as individual as they are, there are several commonly identified aspects that they concur were critical in helping to develop their resilience and adaptability. These aspects could help other orphaned child survivors, especially those now living in alternative care.

First is education. All child survivors in my research project and most of their fellow alumni from the residential home overwhelmingly agreed that having access to education was one of the most useful and practical assets the Catholic sisters bestowed upon them in the residential home. Time and again, child survivors have stressed the importance of having access to education. For example, Susana directly attributed much of her success to education. She asserted in a follow-up interview that the greatest advantage for the children living in the residential home, at the very least, was having access to an education that their families would not have been able to provide. Esteban also underscored the importance of having access to education and recognized that he would not have had the education he has today if he had not grown up for the majority of his childhood in the residential home: "I have an education, otherwise perhaps I would have been married at the age of fifteen and would not have even completed the sixth grade in elementary school perhaps." He and his fellow child survivors had the fortune of having the support of the residential home and of scholarships from organizations and benefactors that allowed them to go to school beyond sixth grade. Similarly, Nidia recognized that she and most of her fellow alumni of the residential home have made strides in overcoming the long-term economic consequences of the armed conflict and genocide precisely because of their access to education and the fact that many are now university graduates. Even Debora, who did not necessarily feel love from adult caregivers while living in the residential home, proclaimed, "A great advantage was that they gave us an education. If we wouldn't have been there in the home, we would not have been able to study."

Along with formal education, vocational training was another critical aspect that both engaged child survivors at the time of participation and contributed in important ways to their overall skill set. Having the option of training in carpentry, sewing/tailoring, or shoemaking, child survivors developed practical, hands-on skills that could contribute to their self-sufficiency in adulthood. They also were required to help with agriculture by tending to chickens and rabbits, harvesting corn, preparing the fields for planting, and weeding when needed, which advanced their practical life skills. The Catholic sisters purposely developed the vocational training program with skill development and self-sufficiency in mind. Many child survivors enjoyed their time in the workshops, which I observed when I was a volunteer. They also found the skills useful in adulthood. For example, Mario developed carpentry skills that he would later employ when establishing his own business locales. Debora and Nidia were in the sewing/tailoring workshop and still use those skills today, often sewing their own family household and clothing items. Interestingly, peers who grew up in Santa Teresa have also identified the vocational training that child survivors received as an important aspect of their living in the residential home. One peer, Dario, shared that he thinks that child survivors actually left the residential home with more advantages than he had living with his family. He noted that they came out with vocational skills and a strong work ethic, helping them secure gainful employment. Another peer, Andrea, likewise noted that child survivors were able to bring important vocational skills with them as they left the residential home; the vocational training they received taught them how to work and, thus, became an important asset for them. Dario, Andrea, and their peers from Santa Teresa simply did not have the same opportunities to gain vocational skills or to develop a similar strong work ethic by the time they reached early adulthood.

Economic stability in childhood and adolescence was another aspect that child survivors underscored as critical for helping them and other orphaned child survivors. Once enrolled in the residential home in Santa Teresa, they no longer had to fret over not having enough food to eat, finding safe housing, or being able to go to school. Clothing, housing, shelter, formal education, books, and other resources were made available immediately upon their arrival at the residential home. Working on a tight budget and the generosity of donations, the Catholic sisters managed to secure what the children needed as basic essentials even if, at the time, some of the items were unfamiliar or were quite basic. One example is some of the food received from foreign organizations. Once a year, the sisters would receive non-perishable food donations from an organization in Canada that often included expired food items discarded by companies such as crates full of heart-smart alfredo sauce and boxes of generic Cheerios. Children in the residential home loved the Cheerios, which was served in hot milk like a porridge, but had no idea what to do with the odd-tasting alfredo sauce. Another common complaint was that they had to eat lentils over and over again, not a favorite of most. While donated food, clothing, and other supplies were quite simple and sometimes even odd (some of the donated food, such as heart-smart alfredo sauce or blue corn tortilla chips, were not typical in Guatemala), child survivors still recognize how advantageous it was having access to those items. For example, when asked about the economic stability of living in the residential home, Juliana shared that she felt like they lived as wealthy people because they had all the basic items they needed and never went hungry or without decent clothing. Susana shared Juliana's sentiments: "Living conditions in the residential home were so good because they gave us everything."

Many child survivors went from living in abject poverty and dangerous conditions to having all their basic needs met when they enrolled in the residential home. They are fully aware of the benefits that having instant economic stability in the residential home afforded, and at the same time, they caution that such support can be detrimental to orphaned child survivors if they are not taught to appreciate it. For example, Juliana reflected that she had everything she could ever need in the form of food, shelter, and education in the residential home, but the experience also skewed her perceptions of reality: "They did not make us see the reality outside of the home. We had everything, but they did not teach us to appreciate it." Susana also acknowledged the economic benefits of living in the residential home, but similarly cautioned that after having grown accustomed to living in the residential home where everything was provided, child survivors had to confront the real world when on their own. According to her, she and her fellow child survivors did not have a good sense of the reality of living on their own; she noted that the provisions of the residential home failed to help child survivors envision a future in which they would have to financially struggle for what they wanted. Therefore, while child survivors identify economic stability in childhood and adolescence as imperative for potentially helping other orphaned child survivors, they also stress the importance of exposure to the economic realities of life so that the transition into adulthood is less economically shocking and strenuous.

Child survivors also stressed the importance of fostering greater community involvement as a way to help support orphaned child survivors. The Catholic sisters deliberately enrolled all children from the residential home in the local schools so that they would meet and mix with children from Santa Teresa and the local area. Many child survivors had friends from town as a result, and some residents of the town commonly attended events in the residential home to show their support for the Catholic sisters' work with orphaned children. However, child survivors did not always feel connected to the community. Even when I was a volunteer in the residential home, whenever vandalism took place in town, residents immediately blamed the children in the residential home because they were viewed as outsiders and inherently untrustworthy. Having been more involved in community activities and events, outside of the schools, could have helped smooth relationships in the town and modeled social networking for child survivors. Susana affirmed the importance of greater community involvement for orphaned children in one of our follow-up interviews. She perceived her peers from Santa Teresa as having been much more involved in community life, allowing them to form important relationships with individuals who are not relatives. Susana saw the residential home as more insular in that child survivors often formed bonds and relationships primarily with each other because they did not always have ample access to the greater community of Santa Teresa. Consequently, they did not get the opportunity to meet a lot of other people, other than their school classmates, until they left the residential home. For Susana, encouraging greater community involvement could have helped them build important social skills, nurture supportive community relationships, and provide important social networking to better support their transition into adulthood. Child survivors in the residential home did participate in some community involvement, but it certainly could have been expanded. Offering greater opportunities to participate in community life, if and when appropriate, is insightful advice that should not be overlooked when working with orphaned children today.

Another important aspect for helping contemporary orphaned children is formally fostering opportunities for them to share their experiences with each other. As I note in chapter four, self-disclosure and emotional expressiveness fostered in the residential home may have been a contributor to the significantly higher reported levels of post-traumatic growth among child survivors in my research project. Child survivors also acknowledge how useful it was to have other children to talk with whom shared similar experiences. For example, Debora related that her friends during her time in the residential home were mostly other orphaned child survivors. She found that they understood her struggles and loneliness better than anyone else because of their similar experiences. The Catholic sisters recognized that fact and informally supported child survivors sharing their experiences with each other. However, there was no official program or activity in the residential home designed to formally foster their willingness and engagement in sharing their stories and experiences. Sharing experiences can offer vital support and build strong peer attachments that contribute to healing and resilience (Calhoun, Cann, and Tedeschi 2010; Johnson, Thompson, and Downs; Mota and Matos 2013). In conversations I have had with various child survivors in more recent years, some revealed that they wish they would have had more opportunities to share their stories with others in the residential home in a more structured and guided way. Still they have been grateful for the friendships that they developed with each other. Giving orphaned children the guidance and structured context within which to safely share, listen, and dialogue about their struggles and experiences can provide them with the space they need to heal. It also can advance their interpersonal communication skills by helping them address what happened in their childhoods as a group and, therefore, encourage them to more readily enlist the help of others to confront and ultimately overcome whatever obstacles may lie ahead in their futures.

In a similar vein, fundamental nurturing and compassion are also imperative for effectively helping orphaned child survivors today. Nidia, who works with school-age children herself, advised that children must feel that they are loved and heard. For her, nurturing children and helping them overcome their problems can have the most lasting effect. Esteban, who has developed a profound desire to protect children so that they are not taken advantage of like he was by extended relatives, opined that orphaned child survivors especially need to feel understood. For him, recognizing that their attitudes and behaviors may be reflective of their troubled pasts is essential for developing genuine compassion for what they have been through. According to Esteban, protecting orphaned child survivors is also paramount to their healing and well-being as they are among the most vulnerable of children. He further suggested that by failing to recognize their struggles and failing to develop compassion for them, people working with orphaned children may unconsciously harm them in some psychological or emotional way.

While not all child survivors in my research project felt fully nurtured or treated with compassion in the residential home, they all recognized how important the elements they identified are for positive child development. At the same time, various child survivors continue to visit and maintain enduring relationships with certain caregivers who raised them in the residential home even though the caregivers no longer work for the Catholic sisters. I often hear from child survivors that they spent Christmas or other holidays with their former *tías* at their own homes. I also maintain friendships with several former *tías*, who likewise tell me about visits they receive regularly from grown child survivors whom they had cared for in the residential home. Nurturing and compassion are crucial for positive child development and vital to caring for orphaned child survivors. However, not all programs and services attending to the needs of orphaned child survivors place nurturing and compassion at the forefront of their activities or mission. Without these central elements, orphaned child survivors will continue to suffer despite having their other basic needs met, and such suffering can extend the long-term psychological consequences of their circumstances as survivors of war, armed conflict, and genocide.

Cultivating tenacity is an additional aspect that child survivors identified as key to helping them when they were children. Tenacity, for child survivors in my research project, involves an individual's own drive and efforts to make something of themselves and their lives regardless of their orphan status. In a poignant example, Mario asserted that orphan status simply no longer matters in adulthood because employers do not ask for that status. They are simply looking for someone who can do the job well. For Mario, what matters more is a person's ability to find an opportunity and work hard at taking advantage of it in a positive way. He explained that if a person gets a job in an office, for example, they have to start from the bottom and work their way up to a higher position. No one can force a person to make something of their life; they have to do it on their own, and that requires tenacity. He is adamant that it is tenacity and drive that help people get ahead in life and that orphaned child survivors, just like everyone else, have the capacity and the means to make something of themselves and their lives, so they should not waste the opportunity to use them.

Jacki likewise stressed that her own efforts to get ahead in life are far more important than her orphan status. She admitted that she does get frustrated at times because she was orphaned in childhood and sometimes says to herself, "I can't do it." However, she insisted that an attitude like that is problematic; she explained that she has a head, hands, feet, a heart, and a brain, so she is capable of anything that anyone else can do. She just needs to be persistent and stay focused on her goals. Child survivors commonly refer to tenacity as vital to their resilience and adaptability, explicitly identifying it as important for helping other orphaned child survivors. However, they did not offer concrete examples for how other organizations and individuals working with orphaned children today can cultivate that tenacity. Perhaps they recognized that cultivating tenacity depends on orphaned child survivors' particular contexts, or that they simply needed more time to think about concrete ways it can be developed. Regardless, for child survivors in my research project, cultivating tenacity is critical to the well-being of any child survivor and deserves further exploration.

Finally, structured support was deemed necessary to facilitate a smooth transition into adulthood economically, socially, and emotionally. Child survivors recognized that the Catholic sisters did their best to support them while they were minors and even as young adults if they had not yet finished high school. They also acknowledged that it is much more difficult to fundraise for projects that involve supporting older teens and young adults. However, their advice for nongovernmental organizations, governments, and individuals is to develop formal programming or practical structures that extend support of orphaned child survivors through the first few years of transitioning into adulthood. Extending such support could include financial assistance, helping expand their social networks to include individuals living in urban centers or locations where they plan to live, and offering extended psychological support services. Striking out on their own has been onerous and daunting for most child survivors. With just some basic transition support, they could have experienced less distress and anxiety in the process.

Intriguingly, several child survivors have since taken the lessons they learned from their own difficult transition into early adulthood and used them to help younger alumni from the residential home transition more smoothly into adulthood years later. For example, Mario hired a younger alumnus to help run his Internet cafe. I also have observed via social media that alumni continue to communicate and help younger alumni access resources, look for employment, and navigate life in urban centers. Thankfully, younger generations of alumni from the residential home now have the support of older alumni, especially in an era when support for the residential home and new regulations have shrunk the Catholic sisters' programming and funding significantly, such that they simply no longer have the resources to launch a supportive transition program. While alumni have taken it upon themselves to help younger alumni as best they can, they still assert that a more formal, structured transition support program must be considered when helping contemporary orphaned children and should be part of alternative care overall.

Despite limited funding offered by the Catholic sisters of the residential home in Santa Teresa, child survivors in my research project have expressed deep gratitude for the opportunities that living in the residential home afforded them. Interestingly, I have never heard a single survivor state that they wished they would have been adopted by a foreign family, or that they were ashamed that they grew up in the residential home. Instead, they have celebrated the fact that the residential home gave them unprecedented access to resources, stability, and enriching life experiences during their formative years in childhood. When asked about his experience in the residential home, for example, Esteban simply responded that the residential home was the best. He further explained that they had everything they needed even though they may not have taken advantage of it at the time. For Esteban, living in the residential home was nothing but advantageous because it gave him an education, taught him values, and formed his central principles. He viewed his time in the residential home as a time in which he could reshape his life through the help he received: "If I would have stayed in my village, I would be nobody. I would not have an education. I would barely have a wife and children. Now, even though I do not have many material things, I have the most important things in life which are an education, values, and well-formed principles." Susana is also grateful for all that the Catholic sisters and staff in the residential home provided and did for her. Having worked for them when she graduated from high school, she has known firsthand the extensive efforts required to support the residential home and children enrolled, and she has been especially thankful for all that she received and experienced when she was enrolled there.

Nidia also shared Esteban's and Susana's opinions: "For me, the residential home was something extraordinary in my life. I have no complaints. On the contrary, I am very appreciative of everything they did with and for me. I lacked nothing. I had much love, understanding, and all that a child yearns to have after living in the streets without anyone wanting to take care of you." She explained that in many cases, child survivors who grew up in the residential home in Santa Teresa were even better off than those who grew up with their parents because they had so many more opportunities provided by the residential home. Yohana recognized the many opportunities afforded by the residential home as well. She stressed that if she would not have taken advantage of the help or what they taught her in the residential home, she would have been a street kid: "I would have lived a very difficult life, but since I put in all my effort there to try to get ahead in life and to be someone in the future, to be someone in the sense of obtaining a profession, then I think I'm not doing so badly."

Child survivors' reflections on their own life experiences elucidate important insights from individuals who experienced alternative care firsthand. As orphaned child survivors of armed conflict and genocide, they are acutely aware of the trauma they were unjustly forced to endure. They also recognize the vital refuge that the residential home provided them—and the relief it gave to their few surviving family members who did not have the economic means to support them—amidst the brutality and chaos that enveloped the highlands region at the time of their enrollment in the residential home in the 1980s. Now as adults entering middle adulthood, child survivors have over thirty to forty years of life experiences on which to base their sound, practical advice for others currently working with orphaned children in alternative care. With families of their own, child survivors also have informed insight into the strength, nurturing, and positivity that family life can provide children. As parents, they are able to compare their childhood experiences in alternative care with those of their children living in loving, supportive families. Thus, they are not ignorant or dismissive of family living nor do they necessarily promote alternative care for other children when loving families are an option. However, they show no evidence of a bitter attitude about having lost out on living with their families when they were children. Instead, they are overwhelmingly grateful that they had the opportunity to be enrolled in the residential home and acknowledge the many benefits they received as a result. Accordingly, their reflections and advice are a testament to the positive outcomes and beneficial long-term consequences that alternative care can have for children, when living with loving, nurturing families simply is not an option and leaving the country to live with adoptive families would have cut any remaining ties they had with surviving family members and extended kin.

LOOKING TOWARD THE FUTURE

Despite having been orphaned and growing up in a permanent residential home for the majority of their childhoods, child survivors have made unprecedented strides and have achieved remarkable goals in adulthood. They have already achieved so much in their lives, and as they enter middle adulthood, they continue to work hard to advance themselves educationally and professionally, while supporting and empowering their own loving, nurturing families. The long-term consequences of having lost parents in the armed conflict and genocide, along with facing related sequential traumatization, will no doubt forever impact their lives. Still, they continue to work toward overcoming the obstacles they have been forced to face, and they do so with grace, humility, and generosity. Their futures remain bright, and whatever may unfold, child survivors' experiences to date boldly demonstrate their resilience and ability to handle whatever life may throw at them. While the future is unknown, what is certain is that child survivors in my research project will forge ahead, modeling for their own children and grandchildren the same tenacity and drive that have served them well. Their life journeys have been poignant, and I am confident they will inspire generations to come.

NOTE

1. The term "united" comes directly from the Spanish term "*unido*," which indicates that a couple has joined together in a *committed*/marriage-type relationship, but without legally marrying, which requires a separate civil and legal ceremony in Guatemala that is both costly and time-intensive.

Chapter Seven

Giving Away the Future

When I first arrived in Santa Teresa in 1994, I was first greeted by the Catholic sisters who founded and ran the permanent residential home. For my orientation as a newly-arrived volunteer, the Catholic sisters provided me with a brief history of their work there. Their mission in Santa Teresa was both to provide a loving, nurturing home for orphaned children, while also fostering their ethnic identities, Mayan languages, cultural practices, and sense of belonging, and maintaining children's family ties whenever possible. To the Catholic sisters, these children were Guatemala's future and a beacon of hope.

The Catholic sisters also shared their wariness of intercountry adoption processes in Guatemala and asked me to be vigilant of strangers. Intercountry adoption (ICA), or the adoption of children from one country by families from another country, had grown exponentially in Guatemala since the start of the internal armed conflict in 1960. For decades, no central Guatemalan authority existed to verify that these adoptions were actually legal and that the children were voluntarily and knowingly relinquished for adoption by their parents or surviving relatives. Such lack of regulation became evident even at the residential home in Santa Teresa. On various occasions, random individuals would show up with falsified documents in hand, ready to take one of the children away with them. Authorized by the state children and adolescents' court, the Catholic sisters, with permission of the children's surviving family members, held legal guardianship over all children enrolled in the residential home, and only a judge of the state court had the authority to change that legal guardianship status. Thus, the Catholic sisters stood their ground when strangers appeared, and they put the residential home complex in lockdown for the remainder of the day to keep children safe in case of a kidnapping attempt. The Catholic sisters would then report those instances to the court. During my time at the residential home, I witnessed firsthand that none of these strangers' assertions ever turned out to be legitimate or legal. The strangers would eventually leave but remained a constant threat. Because of these instances and their firsthand experiences with similar situations at other mission sites in the country, the Catholic sisters were rightfully skeptical of intercountry adoptions of Guatemalan children. Consequently, they insisted that orphaned child survivors enrolled in the residential home never be put up for adoption, nationally or internationally. The Catholic sisters, at that time, argued that Guatemalan children should not be placed in ICAs until there was a way to ensure that such an adoption was legitimate, in the best interests of the child and their families, and voluntarily agreed upon by the surviving parent or relatives.

The Catholic sisters saw ever-increasing numbers of other Guatemalan children being adopted out of the country over the years. They contended that sending away so many children meant those children would likely lose any remaining connections with surviving blood relatives. They also were concerned that by adopting so many children out of the country, Guatemala was essentially giving away its future. As one Catholic sister poignantly asked me, "If so many of our children leave Guatemala, how can we find hope for the future?" The Catholic sisters were adamant that caring for orphaned children within their own country could foster children's abilities to grow up resilient and lead the country's future. It also would maintain and strengthen the children's birth family, community, and cultural connections in ways that ICA simply could not.

Several years after returning from serving my volunteer term in the residential home in Guatemala, I began working for a Latino[1]-serving nonprofit organization in Minnesota and was surprised when a young college student came to volunteer with our organization. The student, Emily, had been adopted from Guatemala by a white, middle-class family from the US in 1981 at the height of *la violencia*. When Emily found out that I had lived in Guatemala and had worked as a volunteer with orphaned children at a residential home, she eagerly began to share with me her experiences as a Guatemalan adoptee growing up in a primarily white, rural, mid-size city in central Minnesota. She was the only student of color in her school and felt that she never really was accepted as part of her community. She noted that a cross once was burned in her adoptive family's yard because they had adopted her. Emily shared that in her support group of eleven Guatemalan adoptees, which was formed by the adoption agency that facilitated their adoptions, all but two had attempted suicide at least once during their adolescence. She reflected, "It's just that we're lost. We don't know who we are. I love my parents, but I wish they would've left me in Guatemala!" Emily knew very little about her ethnic or family background. She assumed that her biological parents must have been murdered in the internal armed conflict and genocide, but she did not know that for certain. Emily's lack of knowledge about her adoption case is emblematic of the often problematic and, at times, even illegitimate nature of Guatemala's adoption trade. With thousands of Guatemalan children having been adopted by families outside of the country for over five decades (Chenney and Rotabi 2014), there is no telling what long-term consequences their adoption experiences will have for them and for their own children.

INTERCOUNTRY ADOPTION AND GUATEMALA'S PROBLEMATIC ADOPTION TRADE

ICAs became increasingly popular after World War II. They were touted as a noble effort to "rescue" orphaned children, mostly from Germany, Greece, and Italy, through placement with adoptive families primarily in the US (Choy 2018). Having avoided the war-related destruction that occurred in Europe, US families were in better financial and living conditions to take in orphaned and impoverished European children. Even though numbers of European orphaned children began to dwindle by the early 1950s, ICAs with respect to other countries soon expanded. For example, the Korean War left many Korean children orphaned or abandoned, sometimes due to their mixed heritages (e.g., Korean mother and US military father) (Kim 2010, 127). By the end of the 1950s, an estimated 2,899 Korean children were adopted via ICA, with most sent to the US. During the 1960s as worsening economic conditions affected many families in South Korea, ICAs of Korean children grew to 6,166 and then rose sharply to 46,035 by the end of the 1970s. Again, the US remained the top receiving country by far. In addition, these adoptions contributed mightily to the massive global expansion of ICAs, with an estimated total of 103,000 Korean children having been adopted via ICAs from 1953 to 1986 and estimates of over 200,000 total from 1953 to the late 2000s, which is a sizable portion of the Korean population (ibid., 20–21).

New sources of adoptable Asian children after the Korean war also contributed to the rapidly growing number of ICAs in the last half of the twentieth century. Other Asian children placed in ICAs came from Chinese families who sought refuge in Hong Kong starting in the late 1950s through the early 1970s. Because they were relegated to living in extremely harsh conditions, many parents felt forced to give away their children, which fed into the ICA system (Choy 2018). The Vietnam War became another large source of children for ICAs. The US Agency for International Development (USAID) estimated that in 1975, over 900,000 children in South Vietnam had lost one or both parents because of the war (Forkert 2012, 428). In that same year, the US government announced an initiative to address the growing number of supposedly orphaned children. Known as "Operation Babylift," the initiative involved airlifting 2,500–2,700 Vietnamese children out of Saigon at the end of the war to send them to live with adoptive families, primarily in the US but also in Australia, France, West Germany, and Canada (Bergquist 2009, 622; Choy 2018, 153; Forkert 2012, 427). Advocates working with these children, however, often reported that the children spoke of their parents, suggesting that they were not actually orphaned (Forkert 2012, 439). Sadly, one of the flights crashed in 1975, killing an estimated 78 children and numerous adults (ibid., 436).

In the 1970s, the US was the largest recipient of children through ICAs worldwide, followed by Sweden, the Netherlands, and Norway (Selman 2012). The decade started with the US receiving 2,409 children via ICAs in just 1970 alone, double the number received by any other country at the time (Selman 2002, 211). Nearly a decade later when the number of ICAs would grow exponentially, the US continued as the largest recipient country (Choy 2018; Selman 2012). Even though some Asian nations began to restrict ICAs because of improved internal child welfare services, scores of other infants and children from Russia and Latin America began adding to the rapid growth of ICAs. With new sources of children, ICAs rose sharply in the last two decades of the twentieth century and kept rising as the new century unfolded, reaching its peak in 2004 with over 45,000 infants and children adopted worldwide in that single year alone (Gibbons and Rotabi 2016, 1; Selman 2016, 7). ICAs specifically to the US likewise peaked in 2004 at 22,728 for that year alone (Selman 2016, 7). From the period of 2000 to 2010, the US processed more than 230,000 foreign-born child adoption visas, representing 50 to 80 percent of all worldwide ICAs at that time (McBride 2017, 9). By the 2000s, top receiving countries after the US were Spain, France, Italy, Canada, and the Netherlands, with China, Russia, and Guatemala as the top sending countries (Selman 2016, 8). As a relatively small country in both population and area size relative to China and Russia, Guatemala's place as a top sending country of children for ICAs became both perplexing and concerning.

Guatemala's thirty-six-year internal armed conflict and genocide left an estimated 5,000,000 mainly Maya Indigenous children orphaned, abandoned, or displaced (Gresham, Nackerud, and Risler 2003, 5). As mentioned in chapter two, the REMHI (1999) truth report confirms that Maya Indigenous children during the armed conflict and genocide were commonly abducted by soldiers and covertly forced into domestic servitude to families in urban areas. Other children were kidnapped and placed in the homes of soldiers and military officers for either domestic servitude or to be raised as part of the family (ibid.). ICAs of Guatemalan children—most of whom came from Maya Indigenous families living in the most devastated areas of the highlands region—also began to increase during the armed conflict and genocide. Between 1979 and 1983, when the genocide was at its most heightened state, an estimated 438 Guatemalan children were placed in ICAs and adopted by US families (McConahay 2000). With the signing of the 1996 peace accords,

ICAs of Guatemalan children nearly doubled in a single year, from 731 in 1996 to 1,278 in 1997 (Dubinsky 2010, 108). Guatemala's close proximity to the US, lack of regulations, lower relative adoption costs compared to other countries, and availability of younger children (especially infants) contributed to making it one of the top three primary ICA sources of children who were adopted mostly by US families in the 1990s and 2000s (Gibbons, Wilson, and Schnell 2009; Rotabi, Morris, and Weil 2008; Selman 2009).

ICAs of Guatemalan children continued to increase rapidly from the late-1990s until 2008 (Choy 2018). With one of the highest birth rates in Latin America and increasing levels of extreme poverty in the wake of the armed conflict and genocide, Guatemala soon secured its position as the largest source of adopted children from the Americas, and the numbers are staggering (Gresham, Nackerud, and Risler 2003; McCreery Bunkers, Groza, and Lauer 2009; Selman 2009). Between 1996 and 2006, over 22,242 Guatemalan children were adopted by mainly US citizens (Rotabi, Morris, and Weil 2008, 3). ICAs of Guatemalan children then peaked in 2007 at 4,851 in a single year (Selman 2016, 11).

Child protection systems in Guatemala were plagued by weak implementation and regulation of protection policies, limited national budgets, and the centralization of service provision in urban centers quite distant from many regions in which children had been living in extreme poverty, or had been abandoned or orphaned (McCreery Bunkers, Groza, and Lauer 2009). Lacking Guatemalan government regulation of ICAs prior to 2008 meant that many of those ICAs were questionable at best and outright fraudulent at worst (Briscoe 2009). Private attorneys and notaries processing the ICAs of Guatemalan children became millionaires in the process (Chenney and Rotabi 2014). Charging increasingly exorbitant adoption fees upward of US$25,000-$40,000 or more per child, attorneys and notaries worked with judges to develop their own intricate, unregulated networks of international adoption agencies, intermediaries, and pre-adoption childcare providers to feed the burgeoning ICA market for Guatemalan babies adopted primarily by US families (Rotabi and Bloomfield 2012, 131). These networks also facilitated corrupt and fraudulent practices such as child kidnapping and trafficking, potentially creating an international black market for babies sold to the highest bidder (Briscoe 2009; Gibbons and Rotabi 2016; Gresham, Nackerud, and Risler 2003; San Román and Rotabi 2019).

Growing concerns regarding human rights, child protection, and child trafficking issues of Guatemalan children in ICAs surfaced for years both nationally and internationally (Blair 2005; Chenney and Rotabi 2014). With mounting international pressure and concerns, the UN sent a Special Rapporteur of the Commission on Human Rights on the Sale of Children, Child Prostitution, and Child Pornography to Guatemala in July 1999 to investigate ICAs and the potential sale and/or trafficking of children (Blair 2005; Campell 2000). In her published report, the Special Rapporteur, Ofelia Calcetas-Santos, revealed that attorneys were the most involved actors in the adoption process and, unsurprisingly, the ones who benefited the most. She further established that attorneys, who represented both the birth mother and the adopter and who issued the certificate of adoption, operated in collusion with other *"casas cunas"* (crib houses)—derisively referred to as "fattening houses"—where children who were stolen or purchased were cared for while awaiting final placement in an ICA (UN ECOSOC 2000).

The Special Rapporteur's report goes on to detail how, with minimal government supervision, attorneys paid rural midwives to register the birth of non-existent children and to use a false name for the birth mother. Another woman would act as the mother and was given an unrelated and often stolen baby to take to the capital to falsely "give up" for adoption. The baby was then placed in foster care in preparation for adoption proceedings. Many of the babies were bought from their mothers either through persuasion or deception while they were still in the womb. The Special Rapporteur also found that babies were procured by tricking or drugging illiterate birth mothers to place their thumbprint—in lieu of a signature—on a piece of legal paper that gave consent to adopt their babies even though the women had no idea what the documents were (ibid.). Overall, the Special Rapporteur concluded that the sale and/or trafficking of children out of Guatemala mainly occurred for the purpose of ICAs and on a large scale. According to the information she obtained, legal adoption of Guatemalan infants and children appeared "to be the exception rather than the rule" (ibid., 5).

The United Nations Children's Fund (UNICEF) followed by commissioning a study of ICAs originating in Guatemala with the Latin American Institute for Education and Communication (ILPEC). Their subsequent report likewise noted lack of government regulation of ICAs of Guatemalan infants and children, and also detailed the use of networks of *"jaladoras"* ("grabbers" who served as intermediaries affiliated with attorneys) that would locate children for adoption often through illicit means (Blair 2005, 368). Both the Special Rapporteur and ILPEC reports added to mounting pressure for an international response to the questionable practice of ICAs in Guatemala and to the call for regulations to safeguard Guatemalan children.

Regulating ICAs and Safeguarding Children in Guatemala

With both the special rapporteur and ILPEC substantiated reports at its disposal, the Special Commission on the Practical Operation of the Hague Intercountry Adoption Convention in 2000 focused attention on Guatemalan ICAs (Blair 2005). Delegates at the convention recommended that receiving countries, such as the US, should apply standards and safeguards of the Hague Convention to ICAs, even if sending countries, such as Guatemala, were not yet contracting states of the Hague Convention (ibid.). International pressure arose from entities such as UNICEF and the UN Office of the High Commissioner for Human Rights (OHCHR) to address the growing issue of child trafficking related to ICAs. In response to intensified pressure, the Guatemalan government ratified the Hague Convention on the Protection of Children and Co-operation in Respect of Intercountry Adoption agreement (or simply called the "Hague Convention") in 2002 and it officially came into full force in 2003, although it would be several years before ICAs would be directly affected (ibid.; Chenney and Rotabi 2014). The Hague Convention stems from the UN Convention on the Rights of the Child (CRC), which upholds the best interests of children worldwide and argues that ICAs should only be resorted to if suitable care cannot be provided in the country of origin (Briscoe 2009; UN OHCHR 2020e). Concluding in 1993, the Hague convention further advanced the goals of the CRC by establishing a framework of international standards of practices that promotes international cooperation and the development of laws and policies at the individual state level (Blair 2005; US Department of State 2020). By ratifying the Hague convention, countries agreed to develop systems to ensure the best interests of children, including taking active steps to prevent the sale, abduction, or trafficking of children for ICAs (Briscoe 2009; Rotabi and Bromfield 2012; Rotabi, Pennell, Roby, and Bunkers 2012).

The CRC was signed and ratified by Guatemala in 1990 (OHCHR 2020e), but to implement the standards of the Hague Convention and work toward meeting its ratification requirements, the Guatemalan government passed a new adoption law (Law 77/2007) in December 2007 (Rotabi, Pennell, Roby, and Bunkers 2012). The new adoption law eliminated the private adoption system and placed all adoption cases in the hands of the government (Rotabi and Bromfield 2012). The government subsequently funded the establishment of a central authority for adoption called the *Consejo Nacional de Adopciones* (National Council on Adoptions, or simply CNA) (Wilson and Gibbons 2005). The CNA was charged with scrutinizing and processing all adoption requests and immediately began reviewing all pending cases of ICAs in May 2008 (Posocco 2011). In reviewing just the first 150 of 3,000 pending cases, the CNA found 40 percent of birth mothers had not been asked whether they had voluntarily relinquished their child, and 10 percent of the cases had questionable records (McCreery Bunkers, Groza, and Lauer 2009, 653).

Along with establishing the CNA, the Guatemalan government no longer allowed any new adoptions to be registered until the CNA could fully implement the Hague Convention requirements, which essentially shut down new ICAs of children from Guatemala as of January 2008 (Chenney and Rotabi

2014; Gibbons, Wilson, and Schnell 2009). ICA cases already in process prior to December 31, 2007, however, were allowed to continue as long as the cases were registered with the CNA by spring 2008 (US Department of State 2020).

As Guatemala implemented its new adoption law, the US government imposed its own moratorium on new ICAs from Guatemala in January 2008, citing flaws in Guatemala's new system and concerns regarding vulnerabilities leading to widespread corruption (Selman 2016; US Department of State 2020). In November 2009, the CNA in Guatemala launched a pilot adoption program to permit limited adoptions but under greater restrictions with priority to adopt given to Guatemalan citizens over foreign families (Blair 2005; US Department of State 2020). New adoption stipulations required that a child could be considered for ICA only if they had been rejected by at least two Guatemalan families (Rotabi and Gibbons 2012). The new program was also designed to allow limited numbers of ICAs for children with special needs and sibling groups (Blair 2005; Rotabi 2010). The US was among the small group of countries invited to participate in the pilot program but withdrew from participation in the program on October 5, 2010, because of concerns that future adoptions still would not meet the requirements of the Hague Convention (US Department of State 2020). This all resulted in a drastic drop in ICA cases from Guatemala to only fifty cases in 2010 (Selman 2016, 11; US Department of State 2020). While cases already in process before December 31, 2007, were allowed to move forward, albeit slowly (some were not completed until as late as 2018), no new ICAs of Guatemalan children have occurred since 2008 (US Department of State 2020).

Pushback regarding the drastic decline in adoptions of Guatemalan children both from foreign adoptive families, especially from the US, and from proponents of ICA has been strong. Even prior to the moratorium on ICAs from Guatemala, increased attention to fortifying regulations in Guatemala and the US spurred adoptive parents, adoption agencies, and legislators to pressure the US government to ignore adoption laws and push hard for continued ICAs. Adoptive families and ICA proponents created embellished narratives of child desperation on social media, blogs, and websites to garner public support and justify the "rescue" of Guatemalan children via ICAs by US families (McCreery Bunkers, Groza, and Lauer 2009). Such child "rescue" narratives have proliferated and fuel what Cheney and Rotabi (2018) call the Orphan Industrial Complex (or OIC), which commodifies children without parental care and promotes ICAs as the optimal solution. The idea that ICAs are a form of child "rescue" and the optimal solution to the "orphan crisis" globally has colored proponents' views of the need to regulate ICAs in the best interests of children and their families. These proponents view ICAs as a noble and just cause regardless of the many flaws, fraud, and corruption involved in ICAs from countries such as Guatemala (Chenney and Rotabi 2014).

Harvard Law School professor and ICA proponent Elizabeth Bartholet (2007), for example, argues that there should be no in-country adoption preference so that children can be placed in adoptive homes as quickly as possible, regardless of where they are located. She also suggests that there is no evidence that in-country adoption works better for children (ibid.). What Bartholet lacks in her argument, however, is consideration of children's extended families and even their own parents, who may have felt forced to relinquish their child in the face of extreme poverty, threat, or coercion. Remaining in-country allows children to grow up in their own cultural contexts and to have access to their surviving family members who are not able to care for them often through no fault of their own. I believe that penalizing impoverished families by taking their children far away from them, their home countries, and natal communities is both cruel and inhumane. Furthermore, the voices that are missing from this debate are those of adoptees themselves. Much like Emily, who as a volunteer told me about her struggles, many adoptees are justifiably appreciative of their adoptive families. At the same time, however, many recognize that they have lost their fundamental sense of ethnic identity and belonging along the way. Fortunately, grown ICA adoptees are now beginning to publish works, post blogs, create support networks, and participate in documentary films that reveal their nuanced and complex experiences. Their own perceptions of their adoption experiences are vital for gaining valuable insight into ICA and for developing sound solutions to uphold and genuinely advance the best interests of orphaned and other disadvantaged children and their families globally. To better understand Guatemalan adoptee experiences in particular, the following examples of their works and stories best highlight their unique and vital perceptions.

GUATEMALAN ADOPTEE PERCEPTIONS
OF THEIR ADOPTION EXPERIENCES

Formal research designed to examine the experiences of individuals adopted from Guatemala through ICA and who are now adults is in shorty supply. However, publications, creative works, support networks, and social media posts by and about Guatemalan adoptees are beginning to gain momentum, shedding light on important issues and implications of ICA in a way that only adoptees can. For example, Maya Figueroa Ferreira (2020) published a reflection on her adoption experiences in the recently-established *Maya America: Journal of Essays, Commentary, and Analysis* , an interdisciplinary peer-reviewed, digital, bilingual, and open access publication hosted by the Maya Heritage Community Project (Maya America 2020). In her piece, Figueroa Ferreira explains that she was adopted by a white couple in the US before she had memory of it. Although her adoptive mother explicitly told her that her cultural heritage is "Maya," she was also told that she was white, leading her to question why she looked different from her white peers. After telling a classmate that she was Maya, the classmate responded, "All your people are dead, you do know that, right?" (ibid., 2).

Hurt by the comment, Figueroa Ferreira did not tell anyone else that she was Maya for another ten years. Meanwhile, she continued to struggle with the idea that she was white, which never felt authentic to her. When her thoughts went to Guatemalan and Maya history, she felt immense pain and heartache. Fortunately, after encountering the works of individuals she identifies as Black and brown writers, activists, bloggers, and online platforms creators, Figueroa Ferreira began to find her way through the mire of identity politics. She also sought more information about her birth family and notes that her adoption papers offered minimal information, which she identifies as a symptom of systematic oppression (ibid, 3). However, she eventually discovered that she has seven other siblings in the US who also had been adopted. They are now working together to build a family relationship and to search for their remaining relatives in Guatemala. Reflecting on her experiences, Figueroa Ferreira ponders, "Someone told me once that to claim to be Maya, I had to suffer Maya sufferings. I don't believe pain is a prerequisite to indigeneity, but if we are counting experiences, the adoption experience is a very Maya one" (ibid., 5). Clearly Figueroa Ferreira has had a complex ICA experience. Torn between two cultures and two countries, she has had to work hard to navigate the complexities and nuances of her adoption experience while trying to figure out who she is and where she belongs.

The complexities and nuances of ICA are also evident in the documentary film *Discovering Dominga* (Jaguar House Films 2002). In the film, director Patricia Flynn takes viewers on the journey of 29-year-old Iowa housewife Denese Becker. Denese, whose birth name is Dominga, was adopted by white US parents, an evangelical pastor and his wife, when she was eleven years old. Denese was just nine years old when her parents were murdered in the 1982 Rio Negro massacre in the Rabinal region, one of the hardest hit regions during the internal armed conflict and genocide. The film shows Denese returning to Guatemala years later to search for the truth and to try to find her father's remains so she can bury them with her mother's. Along the way, she rediscovers both happy and painful memories that she had long tucked away. In one scene, for example, she is in the local market and closes her eyes after picking up a bolt of cloth used for Maya women's *cortes*. She smells the cloth, which reminds her of her birth mother, and is instantly returned to her early childhood.

Describing her first trip back to Guatemala, Denese shares, "I could see the valleys and the mountains, and the hills and I could see the little children dressed in Maya clothing. All I could see is me as a little child with my mother and that was when I knew I was home" (Jaguar House Films 2002, 00:10:00). During her visit to Guatemala, Denese also discovers that her surviving family members searched fruitlessly for her in the chaos when she went missing. Responding to the plight of so many Guatemalan children who, like Denese, went missing and then were hurriedly placed in ICAs at the time, co-producer and journalist Mary Jo McConahay asks the question of whether the children from that period who were placed in ICAs were better off being raised elsewhere. She responds that there may never be an answer. She then asserts that as a journalist amid the brutal violence, "those of us who were meant to be watching events so closely did not track the region's youngest and most vulnerable inhabitants to the degree they deserved" (McConahay 2013, 74). What is certain from the film is that Denese was taken from her family, either through kidnapping or other means, and placed into ICA without her surviving relatives' knowledge. Her adoption clearly left a gaping hole in what remained of their family during a truly violent and traumatic time. It also affected Denese's sense of ethnic identity and belonging, contributing to lifelong struggles despite all the perceived advantages of living in the US.

When considering issues of ethnic identity and belonging in the film, Denese talks about how she never felt that she fit in as a child growing up in a small, nearly all white town in northern Iowa. Her journey back to Guatemala raised many questions regarding her ethnic identity. She admits that she has grown accustomed to cultural life in the US but also recalls the pain associated with never quite feeling like she belonged. She notes that she was often taunted at school in Iowa because kids thought she was Chinese and used a derogatory name for Chinese peoples when referring to her. However, she can remember her early life in Guatemala, and is nostalgic about the smells, sounds, and tastes that remain vivid in her memory. Toward the end of the film, Denese reveals that her fight for justice for her murdered parents, the emotional toll of dealing with resurfaced traumatic childhood memories, and her ongoing struggles with ethnic identity and belonging strained her marriage, resulting in a separation from her husband. She struggles to move forward with far more questions about her past than she has answers but remains steadfast in seeking justice for her parents. Denese's story is another vivid portrait of a Guatemalan adoptee's experiences, especially of those who survived the armed conflict and genocide. It also is a reminder of the complicated journeys they have endured not only in childhood but also in adulthood.

In his book, *Between Light and Shadow* (2011), journalist Jacob Wheeler explores Guatemalan adoptee experiences by centering on the particular life experiences of Ellie, a fourteen-year-old Guatemalan adoptee abandoned when she was seven and adopted via ICA by a middle-class white family living in Michigan. Ellie's birth mom, Antonia, had been abandoned by her husband, who decided to leave her for another woman and she and her children were forced to leave their humble home. Antonia tried to make ends meet, but they fell into extreme poverty and were forced to live in a small rustic shack. Not long after they moved in, a local woman began to show up, inquiring about the children, especially Ellie. The woman asked many questions and eventually brought a "friend" to visit who talked about better opportunities for Ellie, raising Antonia's suspicions. Antonia pondered the questions that the woman had been posing for months, and eventually gave in, telling Ellie, whose birth name is Bernice, that they would be traveling to the capital the next day. Ellie had no idea why they were going to travel to the capital, but she was excited, nonetheless. Antonia's decision to relinquish Ellie to ICA was forged in the hope that Ellie would have a better life and ample access to resources by escaping the crushing poverty that overshadowed her family. Antonia was also in desperate need of the money she had been promised for relinquishing her daughter, money which she never received.

From the age of seven onward, Ellie grew up in Traverse City, Michigan. When she was fourteen, Ellie and her adoptive parents decided to search for her birth mother in Guatemala. They enlisted the help of Wheeler to find her and after much effort, he obtained her information. Several months after her adoptive mom traveled to Guatemala first to meet Antonia and assess the situation, Ellie returned with her adoptive mother to Guatemala to finally reunite with her birth mother. The reunion between Ellie and Antonia was powerful and heart-wrenching. A little later in the day after the initial reunion, Antonia told Ellie, "I never thought I'd see this day. I thought I'd lost you forever" (Wheeler 2011, 165). Ellie was thrilled and relieved to finally know and be with her Guatemalan birth mother and brothers.

Overwhelmed by the situation, Ellie fled the hotel where they all were staying shortly after and set out with her brothers. Her brothers pleaded with her to stay in Guatemala and convinced her to head back to the region where their natal community is located. Ellie's adoptive mother was not going to permit her to visit her natal community on this first return trip because of safety concerns. After discovering that Ellie and her brothers left the hotel and following a painstaking search with the help of Antonia, Ellie's adoptive mom and Wheeler found Ellie safe and sound with her brothers near their natal community. Antonia instantly scolded her sons for running off with Ellie even though she must have understood their intentions. Fortunately, Ellie was safe but conflicted. While her brothers did not want her to leave, Ellie agreed to return to the US with her adoptive mom (Wheeler 2011).

Back at home, Ellie dealt with post-trip depression and a heavy, mixed-bag of emotions. She had reconnected with her birth family, but the conflicted feeling of being between two worlds, two families, and two cultures remained a constant in her life. At the start of her return trip to Guatemala and before reuniting with her birth family, Wheeler had asked Ellie what she thought of when she saw poor kids working on the side of the road. She answered, "When I see them it reminds me of when I was little and lived like them. I see how lucky I am to be with a good family, living the good life. . . . I feel really bad for them that they don't have much fun and they always have to work. I just feel really, really lucky" (Wheeler 2011, 158). The ambivalence of ICA seems to be a theme across adoptees' experiences. Like Ellie, many adoptees of ICAs are greatly appreciative of their adoptive families and lives. Yet they simultaneously experience ongoing feelings of loss regarding ethnic identity and birth family ties, and of guilt for living a "good life" economically when compared to those who remained behind in Guatemala, including their own siblings. Ellie's story is another poignant example of the complexities and nuances of ICA that surface with regularity in adoptees' stories.

The organization Next Generation Guatemala (or NGG), founded by Guatemalan adoptee Gemma Givens in 2007, has collected similar stories, experiences, and perceptions of Guatemalan adoptees who underwent ICA. NGG's aim is to provide a safe and supportive network of fellow adoptees who support each other in their journeys as adoptees living outside of Guatemala. Acknowledging the diverse experiences of Guatemalan adoptees, NGG designates itself as "an international community for this generation of adoptees wherever they find themselves along this incredible experience" (2020a) and proclaims that just as Guatemala never forgets its children, its children never forget Guatemala. With over 500 members from twenty countries around the world, NGG hosts a website that posts videos of adoptee experiences, maps the country location of participating members, advertises local and online events, and coordinates adoptee meet-up events in different cities throughout the US. The website offers links to a wide array of resources such as recommendations for literature on Guatemala, scholarships for adoptees searching for their birth families, guides for navigating the legal and medical systems, and adoptee creative works. Additionally, NGG provides access to post-reunion support networks of fellow adoptees who help others process their birth family reunion experiences or provide support when reunions are not possible.

By drawing together the varied and numerous stories of adoptees as a collective narrative, NGG aims to showcase the tremendous diversity that characterizes what it means to be adopted from Guatemala by families outside of the country. Brief stories of fellow adoptees posted to their website are both informative and poignant. Some stories are about the moment adoptees reunite with birth mothers and families. For example, in one reunion story that was video recorded and posted on NGG's website, twenty-three-year-old

Kayela meets her birth mom for the first time, and their teary embrace is moving to watch. Some of the statements adoptees share in online posts are also deeply meaningful. In one post, Maria, who was raised in Ireland, states, "Every emotion is valid when it comes to adoption. You can feel resentment, sadness, loss, happiness, you can be grateful, not feel anything at all . . . Your feelings can fluctuate and change as you evolve and change yourself" (NGG 2020b). For Maria, adoption is an adoptee's story, and she asserts that nobody—especially someone who is not adopted—has the right to tell any adoptee how to feel. In another poignant post, Val shares that she feels like her adoption was a contributing factor to her struggle with depression and that she has felt out of place most of her life. Growing up in a predominantly white community in the US, Val just wanted to be "normal" and accepted in her adoptive community. She reflects that there will always be a small empty place in her heart that her birth mother left, but she feels proud of who she is today and what she has become.

A final example of the illuminating posts on NGG's website is a link to an article in the University of California's (UC) *Berkeley News* on Gemma Givens, NGG's founder. Gemma shares her own adoption story, revealing that she was adopted from Guatemala when she was just four months old. Her adoptive mother in the US was a graduate student at UC Berkeley at the time. Gemma describes her childhood experience growing up in the US as feeling like a movie that skipped some parts. She remarks, "I felt like I was foundationless, or floating" (NGG 2020b). She had good days when she felt proud, but then bad days when she felt crippling depression. She did feel surrounded by love, family, and friends; however, she also felt completely alone in an existential way. As she grew older, Gemma was determined to find and meet her birth mother to help make sense of her world and of who she is.

Gemma first returned to Guatemala with a study abroad program and began to inquire about her birth mother. She was fortunate in that she knew her birth mother's full name. With some help, she was able to send word to her birth mother's community and a meeting was scheduled. Gemma went to the meeting with great anticipation and excitement. Unfortunately, she was greeted by relatives who told her that her birth mother had died. Deeply saddened, Gemma still was determined to understand who her birth mother was and why she gave her up for adoption. She continued to search for documents or anything that would provide clues. From what little she found, Gemma discovered that her birth mother, Esther, identified as Kaqchikel and worked as a live-in maid at her employer's home in the capital when she was pregnant with Gemma. While Gemma was unable to determine why her mother gave her up for adoption or if she had, indeed, voluntarily given her up at all, she did discover that she has a younger brother, and the two of them have since formed a special bond (ibid.).

Guatemalan adoptees' own voices are starting to be heard and deservedly so. Their insights are vital for understanding the full complexities and nuances of adoption experiences, especially for individuals who have been adopted through ICA. By learning directly from them, we can better assess and implement what is truly in the best interests of children who have been orphaned, abandoned, or neglected. We also gain a deeper sense of the long-term repercussions that kidnapping and child trafficking can have on children who often were placed in ICA under false and fraudulent pretenses. Furthermore, shedding light on and evaluating the experiences of adoptees of ICAs can contribute in important ways to research that involves comparisons of their experiences with those of their fellow orphaned, abandoned, or neglected peers who remained in-country.

Nothing can compare to a safe, loving, and nurturing family home. But when that home is located outside of the child's birth country and cultural community and away from extended family, it can make for challenging life experiences and cause children to feel conflicted and torn between two worlds. Based on a growing collection of creative works, published stories, support networks, and social media posts of Guatemalan adoptees, it is evident that many of them have sincere gratitude for their adoptive families. At the same time, however, themes of loneliness, sadness, standing out, and not feeling they belong permeate their stories.

For child survivors in my research project, themes of childhood distress and loss arise from their stories, but those themes are connected primarily to the trauma caused by the internal armed conflict and genocide and not with their experiences growing up in the residential home in Santa Teresa. In fact, the group of child survivors I interviewed generally do not characterize their experiences in the residential home overall as sad, lonely, or feeling like they did not belong. They recognize that the transition to and out of the residential home was difficult and even traumatic, but their time while living in the residential home generally was not one necessarily marred with negative emotion. Child survivors in my research project also do not report experiencing any sort of ethnic identity loss or "identity crisis" in the way that Guatemalan adoptees who were involved in ICAs do. That is not to say that all ICAs are necessarily bad for children. On the contrary, a series of meta-analyses of 270 studies suggests that children adopted via ICA may have better physical, cognitive, and emotional development than siblings left behind. However, the context in which siblings are left behind in such comparative analyses is imperative to explore because it may vary dramatically from one setting to the next and does not always include institutional care since many siblings remained with birth families or lived in some other form of alternative care (Juffer and IJzendoorn 2012). It is also important to point out that many adoptive families are loving parents doing their absolute best to provide the safe, loving, and nurturing home that their adopted children deserve. However, the many inconsistencies, lack of regulation, and often outright fraud found in the ICA system make many ICAs questionable. Furthermore, ICAs have come to overshadow healthy, supportive, and culturally-astute in-country alternative care options on a large scale, resulting in the frequent tendency to dismiss in-country solutions in favor of ICAs.

Given the relatively positive experiences that child survivors in my research project had in the residential home in Santa Teresa and the seemingly solid sense of ethnic identity and belonging they manifest, it is worth reconsidering the potential value that nurturing, family-style, in-country residential care, in particular, can have for children. Residential care can be a positive form of alternative care, especially when loving foster or adoptive families within the child's home country are not available or short-term care is needed until surviving family members are in a better economic position to care for the child in their homes or an in-country adoption can take place with the genuine voluntary consent of surviving family members. Such alternative care can be particularly vital in the throes of war, armed conflict, and genocide when families are turned upside down and surviving family members are often simultaneously suffering under the weight of crushing poverty by no fault of their own. In such cases, reconsidering residential care for children—even if as just a temporary solution only—is paramount.

RECONSIDERING RESIDENTIAL CARE FOR CHILDREN

There is long-standing stigma in the US and in many other countries around the world associated with permanent residential care for children, especially when the site of that care is explicitly called an "orphanage" (Braitstein 2015; Kendrick 2013). In the US, horrific conditions and treatment of Native American children in boarding schools at the turn of the last century, along with the abysmal portrayals of orphanages such as in *Little Orphan Annie* and *Oliver Twist*, have developed and promoted negative stereotypes for anything even slightly resembling an orphanage (e.g., Calheiros, Vaz Garrido, Lopes, and Patrício 2015; Child 2000). Some facets of these stereotypical views of permanent residential care are clearly founded, given the atrocities that took place at many Native American boarding schools and unregulated orphanages in the 19th and twentieth centuries (Braitstein 2015; Child 2000; Kendrick 2013; Søland 2015). However, the stigma and stereotypes do not apply to all permanent residential homes, such as the one in Santa Teresa.

Internationally, horrifying accounts of abuse and maltreatment in Russian and Romanian orphanages have also fed international contempt for any type of permanent residential care (e.g., Chisholm 1998; Fujimura, Stoecker, and

Sudakova 2005; Khlinovskaya Rockhill 2010; Philps and Lahutsky 2009).
While people across the globe, especially those in industrialized countries,
are quick to condemn programs they perceive as "orphanages," much less
attention has been paid to permanent residential homes that actually "work"
in the sense that they provide a loving, nurturing environment in which
orphaned children grow and develop into positive, resilient adults (Gray,
Ariely, Pence, and Whetten 2017; Huynh 2014; Kendrick 2013). Permanent
residential care "works" when it is truly a safe, loving, and nurturing home
and allows children to remain in their home countries, where their surviving
family members can maintain relationships with them whenever possible and
they can grow up in their own natal cultural, linguistic, and social contexts.
Such conditions are far more apt to foster a strong sense of ethnic identity and
belonging. Residential care can also provide children with access to important resources that otherwise would be unattainable for them.

A growing number of studies substantiate these claims (Huynh 2014;
Kendrick 2013). For example, economic professor Richard McKenzie
conducted one of the few longitudinal studies of its kind with "orphanage"
alumni in the US with the particular aim of examining the long-term effects
of permanent residential care on alumni later in adulthood (1999). Working
with alumni associations of nine homes for orphaned children in the South
and Midwest regions of the US, he recruited 1,589 participants who were
enrolled at homes during the 1960s. McKenzie, who also grew up at an
"orphanage" in North Carolina in the 1950s, found that alumni had outpaced
their counterparts in the general population on several emotional, economic,
and social indicators by statistically significant margins, especially in the
areas of education, income, and attitude toward life (ibid., 293). Based on
his personal experiences and on his formal research, McKenzie argues that
permanent residential care for orphaned children certainly can be a positive,
effective, and viable means of caring for orphaned and other disadvantaged
children, especially in light of the failing foster care system in the US—a
system that he deems little more than "permanent temporary care" for scores
of children (ibid.).

Brigitte Søland (2015) arrived at similar conclusions in her longitudinal
analyses of 140 oral history interviews conducted with individuals who spent
at least part of their childhoods in one or more orphanages mainly in the
Midwest region of the US between 1920 and 1970. Søland cautions that the
number of individuals whose interviews she analyzed is small relative to the
hundreds of thousands of people who were enrolled in orphanages during
that time period, and she notes that her findings cannot be construed as representing the experiences of all orphanage alumni. However, her findings do
elucidate several principal themes common across all the interviews.

For many alumni, living in residential care meant rescue, security, survival, and opportunities otherwise unattainable to them. In interviews, alumni tended to focus on these aspects instead of conveying any negative emotional repercussions from living in residential care. They contended that the residential care setting imbued them with personal strength and social awareness. Even across gender, racial, and generational contexts, alumni overwhelmingly agreed that residential care provided them with educational and vocational training, affording them critical skills and advantages that children living with families may not have had and the alumni certainly would not have had if they had not grown up in residential care. Several alumni also expressed gratitude for college funds provided by the orphanage where they grew up, as college would have been unattainable for other children from poor and working-class families. They likewise valued the stability and predictability that residential care offered, and those who grew up at larger orphanages were especially grateful for the ability to remain living with their siblings in residential care, something that may not have been possible had they been adopted or placed into foster care (Søland 2015).

Interviewees also felt that residential life fostered strong bonds with fellow children who were not related. Many referred to their fellow alumni as "sisters" and "brothers" in the orphanage and spoke of loyalty, mutuality, and protective sentiment when referencing other alumni. Coming from similar backgrounds and situations, they did not feel a stigma attached to their orphan status. Thus, besides meeting their basic needs of food, shelter, health, safety, and medical care, the orphanages helped them develop a sense of kinship and belonging. At the same time, many interviewees agreed that individual nurturing or affection by caregivers in the orphanages was sparse, if existent at all. Yet they were adamant that growing up in residential care provided them with positive life lessons and that they had grown into healthy, happy, wellfunctioning adults as a result. Their emotional survival and adult successes were not *in spite of* living in residential care, but *because* of it (ibid., 47). Søland's study offers critical evidence that residential care can be a positive form of alternative care that supports and advances child development instead of adversely affecting it.

Working with current orphaned children and children separated from their families, Whetten et al. (2014) also conducted a longitudinal study assessing the well-being of children who were living in either institutions or family dwellings in the five middle-income countries of Cambodia, Ethiopia, Kenya, India, and Tanzania. Whetton and her team randomly selected 1,357 institution-dwelling children ages six to twelve and 1,480 family-dwelling children of the same age and collected data biannually from both the children and their primary caregivers starting with a baseline and then completing data collection thirty-six months later (ibid., 1). Principal measures of child well-being centered on physical health and growth, emotional well-being, and learning ability and memory. Their findings revealed a few differences in that institution-dwelling children had significantly higher average height and better caregiver-reported physical health. Children living in family dwellings had fewer caregiver-reported emotional difficulties. Otherwise, no statistically significant differences on any of the other measures arose between the groups. Thus, these findings contradict the hypothesis that placement in any residential home inevitably affects child well-being in adverse ways. Whetton and her team further caution that, with an estimated 132 million single and double[2] orphaned children currently in low-and middle-income countries (with 95% over the age of five), removing residential care as a childcare option would not significantly improve child well-being (ibid., 1). In fact, it could actually worsen outcomes for children, especially if they are removed from a setting in which they are doing relatively well to one that is more deprived. The researchers conclude that the best way to improve the well-being of orphaned and separated children is to implement improvements in all care settings, including residential care and family dwellings (ibid.).

Utilizing a human rights framework, Embleton et al. (2014) similarly assessed the experiences of children currently in residential care. Their comparative study involved a total of 2,871 orphaned or separated children and adolescents aged eighteen or younger living either in residential care or in households in eight administrative locations within western Kenya (Embleton et al. 2014, 1). Sub-Saharan Africa is home to an estimated 55 million orphaned children, constituting an orphan crisis that is overwhelming many communities and weakening the abilities of extended relatives to provide childcare (ibid.). Embleton et al. sought to evaluate how children's basic human rights were being upheld in institutional versus community- or family-based care settings to help gauge the effectiveness of alternative care options, such as residential care, for the growing number of orphaned and separated children in this region of the world. Comparing the experiences of 1,390 children living in residential care with 1,481 living in community or family households, they found that community- or family-based care settings are significantly less likely to be able to provide a standard of living adequate for children's physical, mental, spiritual, moral, and social development (ibid.). Residential care, on the other hand, was better able to meet these adequate standards of living vital to child development. Residential care institutions also worked to facilitate family connections as a way of ensuring that children know and have contact with their kin. In addition, these care settings facilitated obtaining identity documents such as birth certificates, which very few children in other institutions or family-based care have obtained (ibid., 11–12). Without a birth certificate, children cannot access education and other important resources. Residential care settings were better equipped to register children and obtain their birth certificates. In terms of religion, most children in residential care settings were cared for by a faith-based organization and community. This meant that children did not necessarily have their right to freedom of religion upheld as the particular religion of the organization in charge of the institution was compulsory for children enrolled, much like the residential home in Santa Teresa. Most residential care settings also limit admission to children under the age of twelve, leaving many orphaned or separated teenagers with little or no care options when extended family are unable to care for them. Discrimination against orphaned or separated teenagers leaves them vulnerable to a whole host of risks (ibid.).

Based on their findings, Embleton et al. conclude that while adequate, supportive community- and family-based care is essential for child development and upholding children's rights, many households need significantly increased support (ibid., 16). Residential care is needed even if just as a last resort when community- and family-based care is not available or is inadequate. Therefore, residential care can act as an important safety net for vulnerable children. Given the increasing numbers of orphaned children in sub-Saharan Africa, automatically eliminating residential homes could be detrimental to child well-being and human rights. Embleton et al. recommend adopting a "both-and" rather than an "either-or" approach to childcare and support when considering residential care for children in relation to other forms of care (ibid., 18).

Kim, Hynes, and Lee (2017) examined the effects and efficacy of residential care with research specifically focused on children in Guatemala. Using an exploratory, grounded theory approach to assess two separate nonprofit family-style orphanages in two major cities (the residential home in Santa Teresa was not among them as it is in a rural area), they conducted and qualitatively analyzed semi-structured interviews with nine caregivers (also called "*tías*") who lived with the children; seven teachers who taught the children at schools associated with the orphanages; two directors (one at each orphanage); one psychologist; and one sponsor. Three major themes emerged across all content that interviewees associated with family-style residential care: sense of belonging, hope for the future, and the importance of structure (i.e., organization and schedule) (ibid., 1248–1250). Based on their findings, Kim et al. contend that family-style residential care can offer uniquely protective aspects that support children and can provide children with better quality relationships, greater resources, and more opportunities for the future (ibid.).

A final example of research underscoring the possible benefits of residential care is a recent study conducted by Mishra and Sondhi (2019). They examined the role of institutional care in promoting resilience among twenty orphaned adolescents (twelve females and eight males) residing in five orphanages in three states in India. Using small focus groups of no more than five youth that lasted one hour to ninety minutes in duration, Mishra and Sondhi analyzed data collected from the questions posed in the groups to determine emerging themes across all participants' perspectives. They found that adolescents viewed the institutions where they lived as a gateway to otherwise inconceivable, positive opportunities such as getting an education, perceiving a more positive view of their changed selves, fostering determination to stand on one's own feet, feeling encouraged, and cultivating pride in oneself. In addition, adolescents commonly spoke of residential care as instrumental in reducing their anxiety about the future, gaining them access to additional educational resources, enhancing their socialization skills necessary for the future, and providing them with active career guidance and institutional commitment for support in higher education once they moved out of residential care. Besides meeting their basic needs, residential care gave these individuals an opportunity to focus on higher order goals. Other important growth factors included: the opportunity to model positive behavior; motivation enhancing agents (e.g., receiving encouraging support from donors and volunteers); augmented exposure to books and film that widened children's worldviews and sense of future possibilities; and help navigating urban living that would be especially beneficial for adolescent participants later in adulthood. Overall, Mishra and Sondhi concluded that residential care in India does help children because it gives them a "good life" and helps encourage them to work for a desirable future. With over 44 million destitute children in India, of whom 12.44 million are orphaned children, Mishra and Sondhi contend that residential care can help promote resilience among children in culturally meaningful ways and as such, should be considered when other local alternative or family-based care options are unfeasible (ibid., 318, 335).

There is no substitute for a loving, nurturing family for children. However, the sampling of studies I present in this chapter, as well as my own research in Guatemala, offer telling counterpoints to the stigma and stereotypes associated with permanent residential homes for children. In our studies, orphaned children had positive experiences in residential care, gaining access to otherwise unattainable resources such as education, vocational training, and other skills training designed to help them become resilient, well-adapted adults. Furthermore, research, such as McKenzie's and my own, reveals that children raised in residential care have not only can grow up to be positive, resilient adults but have outpaced their peers on various emotional, economic, and social indicators. Based on our research, permanent residential care for orphaned children, in some instances, has proven to be a viable form of childcare, promoting resilience and supporting positive child development that translates into healthy, resilient adulthood. This does not mean that permanent residential care should replace all other alternative care options or local adoption by loving families. On the contrary, I believe that loving families should always—whenever possible—be the primary care option for orphaned and other disadvantaged children who deserve a permanent, nurturing, and loving home. However, in low- and middle-income countries where there may be little regulation of adoption and extreme poverty that prevents extended relatives or local peoples from having the economic resources to adopt or care for orphaned children, I argue that other locally-developed alternatives for caring for children, such as family-style permanent residential care, should be considered. This is especially pertinent when combined with family group conferencing (FGC), which involves kinship networks in carefully assessing and determining the best possible domestic solution for children and their birth families (Roby et al. 2014; Rotabi, Pennell, Roby, and McCreery Bunkers 2012). In some cases, families participating in FGC may deem residential care the best possible solution for their children. Therefore, reconsidering residential care rather than automatically dismissing it because of global stigma or stereotypes is vital because it gives children in low-and middle-income countries the possibility of remaining in their homelands where they are better able to maintain vital familial, cultural, linguistic, and social ties. These essential ties can help strengthen children's resilience and foster a strong sense of belonging. Moreover, residential care, as well as other forms of local alternative care, can empower and safeguard children's futures as well as the futures of their families and home countries—something rarely mentioned in debates regarding alternative care and especially ICA.

SAFEGUARDING THE FUTURE RATHER THAN GIVING IT AWAY

In late January of 2010, ten US citizens were arrested for illegally taking thirty-three children, ages two months to twelve years, out of Haiti in the aftermath of the January 12th earthquake that devastated most of the country (Guyler Delva 2010). These US citizens, who claimed membership in the Idaho-based charity called "New Life Children's Refuge," had no documents to prove that the children actually were orphaned, or that they had the legal authority to place the children in ICA. Lacking any legal authority whatsoever, they were suspected of being involved in an illicit adoption scheme and were detained in Haiti. This incident raised immediate fears that traffickers would further exploit the chaos and turmoil following the earthquake by taking more children out of the country to feed the seemingly insatiable hunger for children in ICAs, particularly ICAs involving potential adoptive parents in the US (ibid.). With declining numbers of ICAs worldwide due to increased regulation of adoptions under the Hague Convention, sources of relinquished or orphaned children available for ICAs had diminished significantly (Rotabi and Bromfield 2012). With narrowing sources from which to attain children to feed into the ICA system, child traffickers and others involved in ICA began taking advantage of natural disasters, such as in Haiti, to quickly source more infants and children before government authorities were aware of what is happening and called law enforcement to protect vulnerable children and their families (Guyler Delva 2010; Monico, Rotabi, and Lee 2019).

The more recent immigration crisis at the Mexico/US border is another example of egregious child-grabbing. In spring 2018, the Donald Trump administration adopted a "zero-tolerance" policy that criminalized illegal entry of child migrants and their families into the US (Monico, Rotabi, and Lee 2019). This policy led to hundreds of migrant children being forcibly separated from their parents and resulted in many children being placed in foster care with unrelated, unfamiliar adults in the US. The children and their families were mostly from Guatemala, El Salvador, and Honduras where political and economic living conditions have drastically deteriorated, especially in the past several years leading up to 2018 (ibid.). Cheney and Rotabi (2018) argue that the forced separation of so many migrant children, while egregious, was predictable by those who have studied ICAs and global child issues and human rights. They assert that Trump's "zero-tolerance" policy was only the latest effort to feed the powerful Orphan Industrial Complex, or OIC, which is propelled by the orphan "rescue" narratives that so often spur child exploitation and trafficking. Cheney and Rotabi (ibid.) note that the OIC is driven by North American and European desires for children but with the recent immigration crisis, the source of children is now on our own soil. With migrant birth parents unable to pay the high costs of foster care and/or reunification—especially if they are still in detention on the border while their children are in another state far away—their children are declared "abandoned." The children are then made available for adoption, which is fully legal in US courts, especially when parents are detained so far away as to be unable to appear before the court where their child is located (ibid.). The result: children are taken from their parents and thrust into adoption without any regard for their human rights or the rights of their parents. At the time of publication of their article in 2018, Cheney and Rotabi noted that an adoption agency in Michigan with ties to the billionaire US Department of Education Secretary Betsy de Vos placed eighty such migrant children in foster care hundreds of—and in some cases well over a thousand—miles away from the southern Mexico/US border where their parents were being detained, ensuring that their parents would not be able to appear in court. The actions of the Trump administration are egregious and inhumane, yet they highlight just how pervasive and powerful the OIC remains today.

A newer trend on the horizon for children in ICAs is global surrogacy, which primarily involves women in low- and middle-income countries who are enticed or coerced to become pregnant and deliver a baby for another individual or couple from an upper-middle- or high-income country who would have paid considerably more for a surrogate in their home country (Rotabi and Bromfield 2012). The problem with such arrangements is that they involve vulnerable women in low- and middle-income countries, who, as among the poorest and most oppressed women in the world, may feel economically forced into the surrogacy arrangement (ibid., 137). With few protective regulations to support them, women in low- and middle-income countries likely sell their eggs and their bodies without the true option of voluntary consent or free will. Much like ICAs, global surrogacy takes advantage of the power imbalance between impoverished surrogate mothers in low- and middle-income countries and wealthier "consumer parents" in wealthier countries, especially the US (ibid.). The global surrogacy industry is growing rapidly and must be addressed both locally and globally so that appropriate regulations can be implemented to protect vulnerable women and their children worldwide before the industry gets out of hand and further hinders the future of so many children, women, and countries around the world.

These examples demonstrate just how prevalent and serious child-grabbing has become on a global scale. Children deserve to grow up in safe, loving, and nurturing environments. They also have the right to grow up in their homelands where they can maintain and strengthen natal familial, cultural, linguistic, and social bonds. For orphaned and other disadvantaged children, living with their families may not be feasible, but that does not mean that they should be stripped of their basic human rights and taken far away from their home countries simply to satisfy the desires of privileged families in the US and other upper middle- and high-income countries. Their surviving family members also have basic human rights that include the right to maintain healthy relationships with their child relatives even if they are not able to care for them because of extreme poverty that has been forced upon them. Likewise, women in low- and middle-income countries also have basic human rights that should be upheld so that they do not feel forced into surrogacy arrangements because of their vulnerable status. The imbalance of power between children, families, and women in low- and middle-income countries relative to individuals, couples, and families in wealthier countries has stripped so many vulnerable peoples of their rights and of their own children. Furthermore, if children are our future—and they are—then we all have a responsibility to protect them and to uphold their human rights no matter where they live. Residential care, while never capable of fully replacing a loving, nurturing family, can help protect children's rights and the rights of their families, especially in low- and middle-income countries. By dismissing residential care as a viable form of alternative care and supporting its full and automatic elimination worldwide without considering the specific cultural, economic, social, and political contexts in which children are living, we undercut our ability to support children and their surviving family members. We also fail to safeguard their futures and the futures of so many low- and middle-income countries around the world. Instead of giving away their futures, we must help safeguard them and residential care can be one viable and proven way to do that.

NOTES

1. The organization continues to use the term "Latino" to describe the population that it serves in the Minneapolis/St. Paul area of Minnesota, so I have used the term here. See https://oportunidad.org/about/ for more information.

2. Single orphans are defined as children who have lost one parent who had died, while the designation of double orphans indicates that a child has lost both parents due to death (Whetten et al. 2014).

Conclusion

The Guatemalan government deliberately sought to destroy Maya Indigenous children either through murder or by making living conditions so unbearable—including murdering parents so children would endure extreme poverty—that children had to struggle through some of the harshest living conditions just to survive. Guatemalan orphaned child survivors who participated in my research project were among those who struggled. They experienced some of the most tragic events and abrupt disruptions imaginable in childhood. Having lost one or both parents either directly (e.g., via murder or kidnapping) or indirectly (e.g., as a consequence of related illness or suicide), they have lived through more hardships, distress, and struggles in their early childhoods than most individuals do in an entire lifetime. Making matters worse, child survivors have continued to face challenges caused by the long-term consequences of the internal armed conflict and genocide precisely because of their orphan status.

Instead of confronting these challenges in negative or maladaptive ways, child survivors featured in this book have actively engaged in creative and constructive practices to develop resilience, to establish themselves economically, and to develop a strong sense of ethnic identity and belonging as adults in the Guatemalan nation-state today. I draw *Child Survivors of Genocide* to a close in this chapter by underscoring several primary conclusions drawn from my research project and by highlighting central sources of influence that I believe have helped child survivors adapt positively and confront some of the long-term consequences of the armed conflict and genocide. I also discuss implications of my research and propose future research based on my findings. I close with some final remarks regarding child survivors' experiences and finding hope in the aftermath of Guatemala's tragic history.

PRIMARY CONCLUSIONS DRAWN FROM RESEARCH

The first of three central questions I posed in my research was: *What long-term consequences of the internal armed conflict and genocide have affected and continue to affect grown orphaned child survivors today in adulthood?* Child survivors who participated in my research project have, indeed, faced long-term consequences and are still affected by them even today in adulthood. As I have demonstrated throughout this book, the long-term consequences that they most commonly identified and discussed are sequential traumatization, economic loss, severed familial and natal community ties, and lost aspects they associate with ethnic identity.

Overall, child survivors reported suffering more genocide-related childhood trauma than their peers. Child survivors recognize that the armed conflict and genocide have left indelible lifelong emotional and psychological scars. They also described facing greater economic challenges because of sustained economic loss. Their orphan status left them without any kind of economic, familial, or emotional safety net to help them transition into and sustain themselves in adulthood, making their early adult years, in particular, much more economically challenging. Without the support of family or natal communities, child survivors have had to confront long-term economic consequences in adulthood solely on their own. In addition, severed familial and natal community ties that resulted from the military's deliberate efforts to wipe out Maya Indigenous peoples and their identities caused some of the most abrupt and long-term consequences for child survivors. By destroying familial and natal community ties, the military commonly severed child survivors' connections with their primary centers of socialization and enculturation during the most formative years of childhood. These centers typically play a principal role in influencing how individuals perceive and express ethnic identity. Dramatically uprooted from their families and natal communities, child survivors found themselves in an entirely novel social context disruptive to identity formation, and subsequently, lost some aspects they associate with ethnic identity as a result (e.g., language, traditions, customs, etc.).

Long-term consequences of the armed conflict and genocide certainly could have resulted in child survivors being much more disadvantaged emotionally, economically, and socially throughout adulthood. However, that is simply not the case with those survivors who participated in my research project. This leads to another primary conclusion that I draw from my research project, one that answers my second research question: *How have grown orphaned child survivors responded in their life experiences to the challenges of these long-term consequences?* Instead of succumbing to emotional, economic, and social disadvantages, child survivors have responded to these challenges in creative and constructive ways. In particular, they have responded to the challenge of childhood trauma by engaging in positive, thriving behaviors. They have become resilient, well-adapted adults who even report having grown in positive ways from their childhood trauma and hardships. They have responded to the challenge of sustained economic loss by building their own financially viable lives through various creative and constructive practices such as pursuing higher education at a much greater rate than their peers from Santa Teresa, securing professional work positions, and becoming entrepreneurs. Lastly, they have responded to the challenge of severed familial and natal community ties and lost aspects of ethnic identity by maintaining a strong internalized sense of ethnic identity that is deeply located within their being where others cannot harm, erase, or destroy it. They have also employed creative and transformative practices regarding ethnic identity, adapting in positive, constructive ways to their circumstances as orphaned child survivors. This leads to the final conclusion drawn from my research project.

The third and final research question that I posed was: *How have the long-term consequences and grown orphaned child survivors' responses to them influenced child survivors' own senses of ethnic identity and belonging in the Guatemalan nation-state today?* Despite severed ties with families and natal communities, child survivors both reported and demonstrated that they have not lost their overall sense of ethnic identity or their sense of belonging as primarily Maya Indigenous citizens in the Guatemalan nation-state today. On the contrary, they perceive and express a strong sense of ethnic identity that includes a dynamic conceptualization of both continuity and active participation in creative practices. The dynamic manner in which child survivors perceive and express their identities allows them to maintain a sense of profound rootedness impervious to external forces, while fostering their active and creative adaptation to novel and varied situations and circumstance. Participating in such active and creative processes does not denote merely "passing" (or becoming *ladino*) or being molded into the "ideal *ladino* citizen" according to the Guatemalan state. Rather, child survivors have and continue to engage in creative and transformative practices regarding ethnic identity in their own right and for their own reasons, which has expanded what it means for them to be Maya Indigenous Guatemalans today. Child survivors' abilities to form such a strong sense of ethnic identity and belonging in creative and constructive ways—all while facing difficult challenges brought about by the long-term consequences of the armed conflict and genocide—are remarkable and leave one to wonder what ultimately helped them develop such positive, well-adapted abilities and resilience. Many factors have likely contributed, but I believe two sources of influence are central.

CENTRAL SOURCES OF INFLUENCE
FOR CHILD SURVIVORS

Based on both my research and my observations of the life experiences of child survivors over the past few decades, I identify the permanent residential home's programming as a central source of influence for fostering child survivors' coping skills, resilience, and adaptability. Residential home programming was designed to meet more than just the basic needs of orphaned children. While food, housing, and safety were the most immediate concerns for child survivors upon their initial enrollment, provision of formal education and educational support, along with vocational training, allowed them access to essential skill-building resources that they most likely would never have been able to access had they remained living with surviving family members due to economic constraints. The majority of child survivors had little or no access to formal education prior to arriving at the residential home, and vocational training was not common in the rural highlands at the time. At the residential home, the Catholic sisters, staff, and volunteers worked with child survivors to develop their educational and vocational skills with a constant eye toward the future. The aim was to help them develop lifelong skills that would strengthen their abilities to respond to adversity and challenges in positive, well-adapted ways not only at the time of childhood and adolescence but also in adulthood after they no longer had the financial support of the residential home. As the various participant quotes presented throughout this book demonstrate, child survivors have been grateful for the educational and vocational training and support they received. They also clearly have recognized just how influential that training and support have been in helping to develop their abilities to support themselves and achieve their desired goals in adulthood.

The fact that child survivors were living together as children who shared similar childhood experiences with trauma and loss also likely helped mitigate some of the pain and struggles they suffered, as discussed in chapter four. By living together and sharing experiences with each other, they built peer attachments, which has been shown in trauma literature to strengthen child survivors' critical emotional and social support systems (Heying et al. 2016). Just how much growing up with other children who had experienced similar trauma and loss has helped child survivors positively adjust to their circumstances is difficult to gauge. However, there is no doubt that it played a major role in their childhood experiences given the detailed information that child survivors could readily provide about each other's stories in interviews and informal conversations I have had with them over the years.

Furthermore, relationships that child survivors established with the adults at the residential home, with the Catholic sisters, *tías*, staff, and volunteers, also likely facilitated their development of strong relational skills, which helped them become resilient, well-adapted adults today. The *tías*, staff, and vocational training instructors, especially, developed nurturing relationships with most child survivors during their enrollment in the residential home. In fact, many child survivors still return to the residential home or to the homes of their former *tías* or instructors on a regular basis today to visit because they recognize them as having been important role models in their childhood and adolescence. Fortunately, child survivors were able to establish strong attachments with positive, supportive adults in the absence of their surviving family members. These positive relationships certainly have contributed to their social skills in establishing and maintaining healthy relationships, carrying forward to their positive, well-adapted abilities in adulthood.

The Catholic sisters' intentional efforts to support, encourage, and celebrate child survivors' ethnic identities and cultural heritage were another important factor in the residential home programming. The Catholic sisters went to great lengths to hire *tías* from diverse ethnic backgrounds who could help child survivors maintain their cultural traditions and languages. The sisters also traveled to other regions to purchase the specific community *traje* of the girls enrolled in the residential home to help foster their Maya cultural heritage and some sense of connection with their natal communities. Furthermore, cultural activities, a positive multicultural environment, religious formation, and agricultural training were part of daily life in the residential home, further helping to facilitate child survivors' pride in their ethnic identities and cultural heritage. Finally, relatives were encouraged to visit child survivors in the residential home to help maintain their connections with their families whenever possible. Maintaining connections with family members encouraged continuity in child survivors' experiences with relationships and identity, which likely helped cultivate their cultural pride. All of these deliberate efforts within the residential home programming were aimed at strengthening child survivors' ethnic identity and sense of rootedness in their cultural heritage that, in turn, helped reinforce their positive sense of self, which is vital for developing positive coping skills, resilience, and adaptability.

A final influential factor of the residential home programming was the integration of child survivors into the local community of Santa Teresa. Integrating child survivors helped them develop their social skills, contributing to their abilities in adulthood to adapt to new communities and social circumstances in positive ways. The residential home was intentionally designed to be part of the community instead of serving as an inward-facing, self-contained institution. To integrate child survivors from the residential home into the local community, the Catholic sisters enrolled the children in the local schools with other children from the community, required them to attend Sunday mass at the Catholic Church in town, and encouraged them to participate in community activities such as the annual town patron saint feast day celebration. Child survivors also were involved with local sports teams, often joining their friends from town in area soccer or basketball tournaments and commonly going to the homes of friends from town to work on projects for school or community events. Consequently, friendships were common between child survivors and children from town. Many survivors also had supportive godparents and sponsors from town for the Catholic rites of baptism, first communion, and confirmation. While some of the orphaned survivors indicated a desire for even greater community life involvement (discussed in chapter six), the deliberate efforts that were carried out to include them in the daily life of the community helped them to establish important friendships with other children their age and positive relationships with other adult mentors. I believe these relationships further contributed to their social skills and, thus, added to their resilient, well-adapted abilities.

The second central source of influence that I believe has helped child survivors become resilient, well-adapted adults, despite having lived through dramatically disrupted and traumatic childhoods, is their own ambition and drive to make something positive of themselves and their lives. While enrolled in the residential home, child survivors enjoyed a consistent and wide range of emotional, educational, spiritual, cultural, and social support from adults who focused on serving their best interests. In adulthood, on their own and without the primary financial support of the residential home, they could easily have lost sight of their future aspirations to make something of themselves and their lives. It would not have been surprising or inconceivable had they succumbed to their circumstances because they did not have family or natal community guidance or support. Yet my research clearly demonstrates that this was not the case.

Child survivors, of their own accord and with the moral support of the Catholic sisters, *tías*, staff, and volunteers, established life goals, such as higher education and entrepreneurship, and actively engaged in creative and constructive practices to achieve those goals in adulthood. On their own and often without one or both parents to support and encourage them, they figured out how to access the higher education system, worked hard in their professional fields, and established businesses of their own. It would be a great injustice to not recognize that child survivors, themselves, have been one of their own greatest resources for becoming resilient, well-adapted adults. Although their abilities and skills were indeed expanded and strengthened while living at the residential home in Santa Teresa, their initiative in adulthood is their own and is truly remarkable given the circumstances they were unjustly forced to face. This is especially notable as the long-term consequences of the armed conflict and genocide resurfaced in adulthood because of their orphan status and often did so in the most challenging ways. Given child survivors' experiences and their noteworthy abilities to confront and ultimately work to overcome these challenges as revealed in this book, my research yields several important implications.

IMPLICATIONS OF RESEARCH

The first implication of my research is that research focused exclusively on the experiences of orphaned child survivors who are now adults is both necessary for validating their particular experiences and challenges and essential for contributing to the construction of an accurate historical account of the thirty-six-year Guatemalan internal armed conflict and genocide. Child survivors' experiences demonstrate that children who lost one or both parents have faced their own distinct set of challenges and circumstances not only in childhood or in the immediate aftermath of the *la violencia* but also well into adulthood. Elements of trauma and loss, as well as economic loss, severed familial and natal community ties, and lost aspects they associate with Maya Indigenous identities, remain and likely will persist in some form throughout their lifetimes. Even though child survivors are working to confront and overcome those long-term consequences, persistent elements of those consequences must be recognized as part of their experiences to validate the hardships, distress, and struggles they have endured as a distinct group of survivors. This is not to say that other Guatemalan genocide survivor groups have not experienced similar and sometimes even graver suffering. Rather, I contend that orphaned children's particular experiences warrant further attention in their own right, especially given that this group of individuals constitutes such a relatively large segment of Guatemalan survivors.

Collecting, recording, and analyzing grown child survivors' experiences is also vital for the construction of an accurate historical account of the armed conflict and genocide that has been underway in various forms, especially after the signing of the 1996 peace accords in Guatemala. The REMHI (1998) and CEH (1999) truth reports have been instrumental in collecting, recording, and analyzing survivor testimonies. Some of the testimonies have even come from individuals who were orphaned as children during the armed conflict and genocide, and both reports dedicate a section specifically to child survivors' experiences generally. Post-conflict anthropological scholarship has similarly examined the particular experiences of women who were widowed during the genocide in Guatemala (Green 1999; Zur 1998). The accounts collected in those studies with widows have elucidated the distinct hardships, distress, and struggles widowed women have had to endure. Work with refugees, both resettled in-country and outside of the country, has also contributed to the construction of an accurate historical account of the genocide (e.g., Falla 1994; Manz 1988; Montejo 1999; Stolen 2007; Taylor 1998). Furthermore, research detailing the general events, historical forces, and perpetrators of the genocide in Guatemala has been prolific in the past four decades (e.g., Handy 1984; Grandin 2011; May 2001; Nelson 1999; Sanford 2003; Schirmer 1998).

Nevertheless, research carried out solely with survivors who were orphaned in childhood remains limited. With estimates of the number of children orphaned during the thirty-six-year armed conflict and genocide as high as 200,000 (CITGUA 1989, 18; WOLA 1989, 1) and likely more, it is evident that this group constitutes a large segment of the survivor population. Yet relatively few publications exist that focus specifically on this segment of survivors. My research clearly demonstrates the importance of recognizing and examining orphaned child survivors' experiences to comprehend the full lengths to which the Guatemalan state went to eradicate Maya Indigenous peoples and to "destroy the seed" (their children). Therefore, greater efforts must be made to include grown child survivors' particular experiences in the construction of a historical account of the armed conflict and genocide if the accuracy necessary and desired by survivors and their communities is to be fully achieved.

A second implication of my research involves the ways in which contemporary ethnic identity in Guatemala is conceptualized and examined. Research must continue expanding to include analyses of the internalized sense of continuity exemplified by participants in my research project. The simultaneous creative and transformative practices surrounding ethnic identity should also continue to be further explored. Contemporary scholars have moved well past the analytical confines of a dichotomous identity construct when examining identity in Guatemala. They also recognize the complexity of both Indigenous and *ladino* identities. However, many scholars working in Guatemala continue to examine Maya Indigenous identities, in particular, as inextricably linked with familial and natal community ties, which is appropriate in some contexts. These ties have been especially associated with Maya Indigenous identities even when individuals actually reside in locations other than their natal communities, as illustrated in research conducted by Walter Little (2004), for example. For many survivors of the armed conflict and genocide, however, these connections may no longer remain or have been impaired, yet any lost connections do not inextricably equate with a lost sense of ethnic identity or any sort of ethnic "identity crisis." Child survivors in my research project clearly show that they did not lose their sense of Maya Indigenous identity simply because their familial and natal community ties were severed. Instead, they speak of ethnic identity as being deeply located within them where it cannot be destroyed and tied to their Maya cultural heritage that has millennia-old roots. Their rootedness and pride in their heritage certainly were fostered in the residential home by the Catholic sisters who deliberately celebrated child survivors' cultural heritages, but they also continue well into adulthood. Therefore, it is imperative that scholars continue to consider the internalized sense of ethnic identity and rootedness, particularly in the absence of familial and natal community ties, when analyzing Maya Indigenous identities today. This is becoming even more imperative as increasingly large numbers of Maya Indigenous Guatemalans are now relocating to urban centers and to other countries where ties with natal communities and, in some cases, with family members are becoming more difficult to maintain. Given the strong sense of ethnic identity child survivors in my research project perceive and express, one cannot assume that compromised familial and natal community ties unavoidably result in a lost sense of ethnic identity or "identity crises." This is particularly important to keep in mind when working with Maya Indigenous peoples living in contexts either permanently or temporarily separate from families and natal communities in Guatemala.

Along with continuity, it is also important to recognize the creative practices that Guatemalan Indigenous peoples, in general, engage in regarding ethnic identity, especially as they become increasingly involved in larger, dynamic relations and systems. I argue that one of the most powerful forms of resistance that Indigenous peoples of Guatemala have had over the past five centuries is their use of creative practices to adapt to their often horrendous, changing circumstances and contexts brought about by external forces and the state. In the past, non-Maya peoples and even some late scholars may have equated Indigenous peoples' participation in creative practices, such as formal education or second language acquisition, as simply "passing" in that an Indigenous individual was unavoidably giving in and becoming a *ladino* simply because they now included what were viewed as "non-Indigenous" practices in their life experiences. This oversimplified assumption of "passing" is not only inherently mistaken but also is demeaning and dismissive as Indigenous peoples have a long history of engaging in complex, dynamic conceptualizations and practices regarding ethnic identity.

Dismantling the erroneous assumption that creative practices do not contribute to sustaining and promoting Indigenous identities—and thus, connote a "de-Indigenizing" process—is especially important when examining Indigenous peoples' pursuit of higher education in contemporary Guatemala. Following previous presentations or discussions that I have given on my research, several scholars suggested to me that child survivors' pursuit of higher education simply meant that "they're just becoming the *ladinos* the state wants them to be." On the contrary, child survivors in my research project argue that they are attending college because they perceive higher education as an asset that can help them achieve the economic and career goals that they have set for themselves and their families. While they fully recognize the need to decolonize educational institutions, they also do not view higher education as eroding their Maya Indigenous identities. In fact, several have used their college degrees to give back to support their communities, implement policy changes, and preserve their Mayan languages and heritages for future generations. Therefore, accessing higher education is but another example of their agentive use of creative and constructive practices in perceiving and expressing their Maya Indigenous identities. Pursuit of higher education in Guatemala was not as financially feasible or socially acceptable for most Indigenous young adults in the past. With the dramatic increase in Indigenous peoples accessing higher education in the past two decades, higher education and Indigenous identities should not and cannot be considered mutually exclusive. Therefore, we contemporary scholars should continue to challenge any underlying assumptions that higher education is principally the realm of non-Indigenous peoples and that entering that realm necessarily negates Indigenous identities or worldviews. This is an elitist assumption that not only fails to recognize the perceptions and lived experiences of Indigenous peoples but also turns a blind eye to the ways in which Indigenous peoples are actively transforming higher education in new, constructive, and decolonizing ways through their participation and leadership in it.

The third and final implication stemming from my research, as discussed in chapter seven, is that scholars and practitioners should reconsider the potential of in-country permanent residential care as a viable option for nurturing and caring for children who have been orphaned, even if that care is short-term until in-country adoption or other alternative care can take place. While there is no substitute for a loving, nurturing family for children, studies have substantiated cases of children reared in permanent residential care who grew up to be resilient, well-adapted adults and even outpaced their nonresidential care peers on various emotional, economic, and social indicators in adulthood (e.g., Embleton et al. 2014; McKenzie 1999; Mishra and Sondhi 2019; Whetten et al. 2011). Various studies, including my own, illustrate that permanent residential care for orphaned children can be a viable form of nurturing and caring for children, especially during human-made and natural disasters when children can get caught up in the chaos, lose track of their families, and end up being placed in ICAs, all without the knowledge or genuine, uncoerced voluntary consent of their family members. Residential care can also help families maintain connections with their child relatives for whom they may not be able to care because of extreme poverty. This is especially important in the face of worldwide child-grabbing that has often fed into unregulated ICAs. The drive for ICAs commonly fails to address the imbalance of power between poor families living in low- and middle-income countries and those in wealthier countries who ignore the value of family, community, and cultural connections within the children's own birth country. Residential care can help protect children's rights and the rights of their families in such cases. Finally, the global trend to eliminate all residential care around the world is dismissive and fails to consider the specific cultural, linguistic, economic, social, and political contexts in which children are actually living. As my research and that of scholars working in other countries have substantiated, nurturing, family-style residential care can be a viable option for certain contexts and should be considered along with other solutions if we truly are to meet the best interests of children and their surviving family members. That is not to say that all permanent residential homes are good for children. Certainly, there have been various cases, including in Guatemala itself, where permanent residential care has been harmful to children (e.g., Plasencia 2018; Wilson 2003). Yet quality care offered via a nurturing, family-style residential home can provide families with much needed in-country care options. Rather than focusing solely on foreign solutions to local problems regarding orphaned and disadvantaged children, we must reconsider the most appropriate and effective in-country, local solutions (see also Leinaweaver 2008) and residential care might be one of them.

FUTURE RESEARCH

My research with child survivors has illustrated the importance of working with the individuals who were orphaned in childhood during the armed conflict and genocide. I believe that future research must expand to focus not only on the experiences of child survivors raised in the residential home in Santa Teresa but also on the experiences of many other individuals who are among the estimated 200,000 or more children orphaned during that period. As stated earlier, inclusion of orphaned child survivors' experiences in the construction of an accurate historical account of the armed conflict and genocide is not only vital for the accuracy of the historical account but also for validating the particular experiences of such a large segment of survivors who form a distinct group deserving of attention in its own right. I believe that without concentrated and expanded efforts to work with orphaned child survivors to examine their experiences, the full scope and long-term consequences of Guatemala's armed conflict and genocide will never be entirely exposed.

282 _Conclusion_

Therefore, they cannot be fully understood, making the road to justice and reconciliation even longer and more elusive.

Continued scholarship on ethnic identity and the dynamic conceptualization of Indigenous identities is critical for better understanding and validating the experiences of all Guatemala's Indigenous citizens, not only today but also in the past. Further analyses of the internalized sense of continuity despite severed familial and natal community ties is especially important because it is an aspect of Indigenous identities that has not yet been fully explored. At the same time, I believe that the most effective way to examine the internalized sense of continuity and the dynamic conceptualization of Indigenous identities at the local level in Guatemala is by supporting Indigenous peoples' pursuit of higher and advanced education and their own scholarship so that they can undertake these analyses from a truly emic point of view. Important work by Indigenous Guatemalan scholars, such as Jakaltek Maya anthropologist Victor Montejo, has been imperative. Continued support of current and future Indigenous scholars is also essential, especially because they can write "as" and "with" their own peoples, offering greater insight.

A final area of future research that would contribute considerably to both anthropological and other literature, as well as to the work of practitioners, is a comparative analysis of the experiences of child survivors who remained in Guatemala in permanent residential care following the aftermath of _la violencia_ with the experiences of individuals of corresponding ages and circumstances who were adopted outside of the country by foreign families during that same period. Such a comparative analysis would not only advance the knowledge of what happened to children who were orphaned or abandoned as a result of armed conflict and genocide but also would provide further poignant insight into what types of care are genuinely in the best interests of orphaned and other disadvantaged children, especially in the wake of state-perpetrated violence. A comparative analysis would also illuminate pertinent and informative issues surrounding ethnic identity and continuity. Such a project can greatly fortify anthropological and other literature, as well as advance pivotal childcare policies and practices in meaningful and lasting ways.

FINDING HOPE

In early December of 2010, I returned to Guatemala to participate in the twenty-fifth anniversary celebration of the permanent residential home in Santa Teresa. Alumni, past volunteers, townspeople, other supporters, Catholic sisters, and former _tías_ and staff all joined the current sisters, _tías_, staff, volunteers, and children living in the residential home in a nine-day, event-filled celebration that ended with a Catholic Mass and a festive lunch on the feast day of the patron saint of the residential home. Picture-taking abounded among the alumni, and alumnus Mario, featured in this book, composed a song for the residential home, which he performed after the lunchtime meal. It was a festive day with a lot of heart-filled emotions and reminiscing. I was grateful that I could participate in such a moving event celebrating not only the work of the residential home and of all the adults, past and present, who had been involved in meeting the needs of child survivors but also the tremendous growth and achievements of the orphaned child survivor alumni. While the anniversary celebration was deeply meaningful for me, there was something that I felt was still missing from my return trip to Guatemala that year.

The next day, I hopped into my little rental car and stopped by child survivor Sofia's house a few blocks away from the residential home. I had spoken with Sofia at the celebration just the day before, and she had agreed to call her mother, Lucia, who had worked at the residential home for many years as a *tía* and who had shared her story as a widowed survivor of the *la violencia* with me when I was first a volunteer. *Tía* Lucia could not make the long trip in from her home to Santa Teresa to attend the anniversary event that year because of her worsening arthritis. Sofia told her mother during a brief phone call that we would be arriving the next day for a visit, and *tía* Lucia was elated, as was I. The next day I arrived at Sofia's house as she was gathering up her three children (all under the age of twelve at the time) and some fresh produce to deliver to her mother. Loading everyone and everything into the car, we embarked on a two-hour drive through the lush green mountainous backcountry of the municipalities of Santa Teresa and San Juan.[1]

After bumping over the back dirt roads and strategically navigating several minor landslides and huge dips and ruts in the road, all in a small car with low clearance, we eventually arrived in Sofia's natal community. I parked the car at the bottom of the hill where the path to *tía* Lucia's house begins. Because of recent rapid expansion of cellular phone towers constructed throughout the highlands, Sofia actually called her mother just moments before we arrived at the bottom of the hill, allowing *tía* Lucia to come and meet us the moment we arrived. When we all got out of the car, *tía* Lucia's grandchildren ran to her and smothered her in hugs and kisses. I also gave *tía* Lucia a huge bear hug and told her how wonderful it was to see her again. She was excited that we were all visiting, and as her grandchildren ran ahead of us, we discussed the latest happenings in our lives, strolling along the 50-yard length of path leading to her home.

I only had been to *tía* Lucia's home one other time. When I was a volunteer at the residential home, the internal armed conflict was still being waged and travel in the backcountry, where *tía* Lucia's tiny hamlet is located, was still considered too dangerous. On subsequent return trips to Guatemala, I simply did not have sufficient time or the means to travel the distance to *tía* Lucia's home as there is only one local bus that travels between her hamlet and Santa Teresa, and it does not have a set daily route. As such, it was not until I was conducting fieldwork and I had my own vehicle that I finally had the time and the means to visit *tía* Lucia's home for the first time. It was during that first trip that I was profoundly moved by a tree that *tía* Lucia had pointed out in the small dirt courtyard in front of her home. *Tía* Lucia explained to me that she had planted that tree in the spot where her husband was brutally shot point-blank in the back of the head by military soldiers in 1980, which Sofia discussed in chapter four. She had planted the tree there shortly after her husband's murder as a way of honoring him and of replacing the horror that occurred in that spot with something positive and hopeful like a tiny seedling.

On this second trip to *tía* Lucia's home, I was taken aback the moment we turned the corner and finally reached her house. The tree in the center of the patio had grown dramatically since my last visit just two years earlier. Around the base of the tree, *tía* Lucia had planted annual flowers in various plastic receptacles, making the center patio look so colorful and vibrant. After finishing a delicious lunch of chicken stew and freshly made thick corn tortillas, *tía* Lucia and I sat outside on the perimeter of the patio under the shade provided by the tin awning of her simple cement block house. We chatted and laughed for several hours and in the course of the conversation, I told her all about my research project and what I had been discovering in the process. I also shared how her story had influenced my own life trajectory, including my decision to attend graduate school and conduct research in Guatemala. After some tears and some laughter, *tía* Lucia took a deep breath, motioned toward the tree planted in the middle of the patio, and said to me, "Ah, Shirley, it's just that you have to look for hope even in the most horrible situations."

When I set out to begin my research project, I was not focused on looking for hope. Based on what I had witnessed first-hand as a volunteer at the residential home during child survivors' adolescence, I was certain that I would find debilitating trauma, despair, and devastation persisting among them well into adulthood. Consequently, I set out to gather information that would substantiate why this group of child survivors likely "fell through the cracks" or why they "never had a chance" at life. However, my research results clearly contradict what I had expected to find. In place of their succumbing to prolonged trauma, despair, and devastation, I found grown child survivors demonstrating resilience, strength, and pride in who they are. In her work in Guatemala, Sanford notes that survivors are those who taught her of *la violencia,* and that they taught her of their human agency (2003, 22). I found a similar experience with child survivors. There is absolutely no doubt that child survivors have suffered immensely because of the armed conflict and genocide. But in the same place of devastation and destitution, they have grown positively and adaptively into remarkable adults today, who are profoundly rooted in their own families and an unwavering sense of ethnic identity and belonging. Much like *tía* Lucia's flourishing tree, child survivors have worked to positively confront the horrors that they have had to endure in childhood with tremendous growth and tenacity in adulthood. Child survivors' experiences boldly illustrate that, as *tía* Lucia suggests, even in the long-term aftermath of the most brutal, inhumane treatment of humankind that is genocide, one must look for, and indeed can find, hope.

NOTE

1. As with Santa Teresa, I am using a fictitious name for this town to protect my research participants as using its real name could reveal the location of the residential home.

Bibliography

Adalian, Rouben Paul. 2009. "The Armenian Genocide." In *Century of Genocide: Critical Essays and Eyewitness Accounts*, edited by Samuel Totten and William S. Parsons, 55–92. New York: Routledge.

Adams, Richard Newbold. 2001. "Strategies of Ethnic Survival in Central America." In *Nation-States and Indians in Latin America*, edited by Greg Urban and Joel Sherzer, 181–206. Tucson: Hats Off Books.

Adams, Walter Randolph, and John P. Hawkins. 2007. "Introduction: The Continuing Disjunction between Traditional and Western Medical Beliefs and Practices in Guatemala." In *Healthcare in Maya Guatemala: Confronting Medical Pluralism in a Developing Country*, edited by Walter Randolph Adams and John P. Hawkins, 3–26. Norman: University of Oklahoma Press.

Afflitto, Frank M., and Paul Jesilow. 2007. *The Quiet Revolutionaries: Seeking Justice in Guatemala*. Austin: University of Texas Press.

Aguilera Peralta, Gabriel, and John Beverly. 1980. "Terror and Violence as Weapons of Counterinsurgency in Guatemala." *Latin American Perspectives* 7 (2–3): 91–113.

American Psychiatric Association (APA). 1994. *Diagnostic and Statistical Manual of Mental Disorders* (4th Edition). Washington: American Psychiatric Association.

American Psychiatric Association (APA). 1980. *Diagnostic and Statistical Manual of Mental Disorders* (3rd Edition). Washington: American Psychiatric Association.

Amir, Marianne, and Rachel Lev-Wiesel. 2003."Time Does Not Heal all Wounds: Quality of Life and Psychological Distress of People who Survived the Holocaust as Children 55 Years Later." *Journal of Traumatic Stress: Official Publication of the International Society for Traumatic Stress Studies* 16 (3): 295–299.

Amnesty International. 1998. *Guatemala: All the Truth, Justice for All*. New York: Amnesty International Publications.

Amnesty International. 1976. *Amnesty International Briefing: Guatemala*. London: Amnesty International Publications.

Anderson, E. N., and Barbara Anderson. 2013. *Warning Signs of Genocide: An Anthropological Perspective*. New York: Lexington Books.

Andradé, Dale. 1990. *Ashes to Ashes: The Phoenix Program and the Vietnam War.* New York: Lexington Books.

Arias, Arturo. 1990. "Changing Indian Identity: Guatemala's Violent Transition to Modernity." In *Guatemalan Indians and the State: 1540–1988*, edited by Carol Ann Smith and Marilyn M. Moors, 230–257. Austin: University of Texas Press.

Armenian Genocide Museum-Institute Foundation (AGMI). 2020. "Armenian Children Victims of Genocide." Genocide-Museum.am. http://www.genocide-museum.am/eng/online_exhibition_3.php

Armenian National Institute (ANI). 2020. "Frequently Asked Questions about the Armenian Genocide." Armenian-Genocide.org. https://www.armenian-genocide.org/genocidefaq.html

Arsanjani, Mahnoush H. 1999. "The Rome Statute of the International Criminal Court." *The American Journal of International Law* 93 (1): 22–43.

Asselbergs, Florine. 2004. *Conquered Conquistadors: The Lienzo de Quauhquechollan, A Nahua Vision of the Conquest of Guatemala.* Boulder, CO: University Press of Colorado.

Atkinson, P. A., C. R. Martin, and J. Rankin. 2009. "Resilience Revisited." *Journal of Psychiatric and Mental Health Nursing* 16: 137–145.

Avakian, Paul N. 2018. "Denial in Other Forms." *Genocide Studies and Prevention: An International Journal* 12 (1): 3–23.

Ball, Patrick, and Megan Price. 2018. "The Statistics of Genocide." *CHANCE* 31 (1): 38–45.

Barel, Efrat, Marinus H. van IJzendoorn, Abraham Sagi-Schwartz, and Marian J. Bakermans-Kranenburg. 2010. "Surviving the Holocaust: a Meta-analysis of the Long-term Sequelae of a Genocide." *Psychological Bulletin* 136 (5): 677.

Bartholet, Elizabeth. 2007. "International Adoption: Thoughts on the Human Rights Issues." *Buffalo Human Rights Law Review* 13: 151–203.

Becker Richards, Julia, and Michael Richards. 1996. "Maya Education: A Historical and Contemporary Analysis of Mayan Language Education Policy." In *Maya Cultural Activism in Guatemala*, edited by Edward F. Fischer and R. McKenna Brown, 208–221. Austin: University of Texas Press.

Beltrán Adriana. 2016. "A New Era of Accountability in Guatemala?" *Current History* February: 63–67.

Benson, Peter, and Edward F. Fischer. 2009. "Neoliberal Violence: Social Suffering in Guatemala's Postwar Era." In *Mayas in Postwar Guatemala: Harvest of Violence Revisited*, edited by Walter E. Little and Timothy J. Smith, 151–166. Tuscaloosa: The University of Alabama Press.

Bergquist, Kathleen Ja Sook. 2009. "Operation Babylift or Babyabduction?: Implications of the Hague Convention on the Humanitarian Evacuation and 'Rescue' of Children." *International Social Work* 52 (5): 621–633.

Bermejo-Toro, Laura, and María Prieto-Ursúa. 2006. "Teachers' Irrational Beliefs and Their Relationship to Distress in the Profession." *Psychology in Spain* 10 (1): 88–96.

Betancourt, Theresa Stichick, and Kashif Tanveer Khan. 2008. "The Mental Health of Children Affected by Armed Conflict: Protective Processes and Pathways to Resilience." *International Review of Psychiatry* 20 (3): 317–328.

Betancourt, Theresa S., Stephen E. Gilman, Robert Thomas Brennan, Ista Zahn, and Tyler J. VanderWeele. 2015. "Identifying Priorities for Mental Health Interventions in War-Affected Youth: A Longitudinal Study." *Pediatrics* 136 (2): e344–e350.

Blair, Marianne. 2005. "Safeguarding the Interests of Children in Intercountry Adoption: Assessing the Gatekeepers." *Capital University Law Review* 34: 349–403.

Bloxham, Donald. 2003. "The Armenian Genocide of 1915–1916: Cumulative Radicalization and the Development of a Destruction Policy." *Past & Present* 181: 141–191.

Bolstad, Bret R., and Richard E. Zinbarg. 1997. "Sexual Victimization, Generalized Perception of Control, and Post-traumatic Stress Disorder Symptom Severity." *Journal of Anxiety Disorder* 11: 523–540.

Bonanno, George A. 2004. "Loss, Trauma, and Human Resilience: Have We Underestimated the Human Capacity to Thrive after Extremely Aversive Events?" *American Psychologist* 59 (1): 20–28.

Booth, John A., Christine J. Wade, and Thomas W. Walker. 2010. *Understanding Central America: Global Forces, Rebellion, and Change*. Boulder: Westview Press.

Bowen, Rachel E. 2019. "The Weight of the Continuous Past: Transitional (In)Justice and Impunity States in Central America." *Latin American Politics and Society* 61 (1): 127–147.

Bracken, Peter J. 2001. "Post-Modernity and Post-Traumatic Stress Disorder." *Social Science & Medicine* 53 (6): 733–743.

Bragin, M. 2007. "The Psychological Effects of War on Children: A Psychosocial Approach." *Trauma Psychology: Issues in Violence, Disaster, Health, and Illness* 1: 195–229.

Braitstein, Paula. 2015. "Institutional Care of Children in Low- and Middle-Income Settings: Challenging the Conventional Wisdom of Oliver Twist." *Global Health: Science and Practice* 3 (3): 330–332.

Breslau, Naomi, Howard D. Chilcoat, Ronald C. Kessler, and Glenn C. Davis. 1999. "Previous Exposure to Trauma and PTSD Effects of Subsequent Trauma: Results from the Detroit Area Survey of Trauma." *American Journal of Psychiatry* 156: 902–907.

Brett, Roddy. 2016. "Peace Without Social Reconciliation? Understanding the Trial of Generals Rios Montt and Rodriguez Sanchez in the Wake of Guatemala's Genocide." *Journal of Genocide Research* 18 (2–3): 285–303.

Briscoe, Erica. 2009. "Hague Convention on Protection of Children and Co-Operation in Respect of Intercountry Adoption: Are its Benefits Overshadowed by its Shortcomings?" *Journal of American Academy of Matrimonial Law* 22 (2): 437–460.

Broder, John M. 1999. "Clinton Offers his Apologies to Guatemala." NewYorkTimes.com. https://www.nytimes.com/1999/03/11/world/clinton-offers-his-apologies-to-guatemala.html

Brown, R. McKenna. 1996. "The Maya Language Loyalty Movement in Guatemala." In *Maya Cultural Activism in Guatemala*, edited by Edward F. Fischer and R. McKenna Brown, 165–177. Austin: University of Texas Press.

Brown, R. McKenna, Edward Fischer, and Raxché (Demetrio Rodríquez Gauján). 1998. "Mayan Visions for a Multilingual Society: The Guatemalan Peace Accords on Indigenous Identity and Languages." *Fourth World Bulletin* 6: 28–33.

Burrell, Jennifer L. 2013. *Maya After War: Conflict, Power, and Politics in Guatemala*. Austin: University of Texas Press.

Burt, Jo-Marie. 2016. "From Heaven to Hell in Ten Days: The Genocide Trial in Guatemala." *Journal of Genocide Research* 18 (2–3): 143–169.

Burt, Jo-Marie, and Paulo Estrada. 2018. "Court Finds Guatemalan Army Committed Genocide, but Acquits Military Intelligence Chief." IJMonitor.org. https://www .ijmonitor.org/2018/09/court-finds-guatemalan-army-committed-genocide-but -acquits-military-intelligence-chief/

Burt, Martha R., and Bonnie L. Katz. 1987. "Dimensions of Recovery from Rape: Focus on Growth Outcomes." *Journal of Interpersonal Violence* 2: 57–81.

Calheiros, Maria Manuela, Margarida Vaz Garrido, Diniz Lopes, and Joana Nunes Patrício. 2015. "Social Images of Residential Care: How Children, Youth and Residential Care Institutions are Portrayed?" *Children and Youth Services Review* 55: 159–169.

Calhoun, Lawrence G., Arnie Cann, and Richard G. Tedeschi. 2010. "The Post-traumatic Growth Model: Sociocultural Considerations." In *Post-traumatic Growth and Culturally Competent Practice: Lessons Learned from Around the Globe*, edited by Tzipi Weiss and Roni Berger, 1–14. Hoboken: John Wiley & Sons, Inc.

Calhoun, Lawrence G., Richard G. Tedeschi, Arnie Cann, and Emily A. Hanks. 2010. "Positive Outcomes Following Bereavement: Paths to Post-traumatic Growth." *Psychologica Belgica* 50 (1–2): 1–2.

Calvert, Peter. 1985. *Guatemala: A Nation in Turmoil.* Boulder: Westview Press, Inc.

Campaign for Peace and Life in Guatemala. 1999. *Refusing to Forget: Joining with Guatemalans to Recover Our Historical Memory; A Study Guide on Guatemala: Never Again.* Washington: Campaign for Peace and Life in Guatemala.

Campbell, Christopher D., and Tessa Evans-Campbell. 2011. "Historical Trauma and Native American Child Development and Mental Health: An Overview." In *American Indian and Alaska Native Children and Mental Health: Development, Context, Prevention, and Treatment,* edited by Paul Spicer, Michelle C. Sarche, Patricia Farrell, and Hiram E. Fitzgerald, 1–26. Santa Barbara: Praeger.

Campbell, Duncan. 2000. "Guatemalan Babies 'Sold to Highest Bidders': A UN Report Says that the Trafficking of Children for Adoption is Widespread but Many Reject its Claims." TheGuardian.com. https://www.theguardian.com/world/2000/jun/13/internationalcrime

Carey Jr., David. 2001. *Our Elders Teach Us: Maya-Kaqchikel Historical Perspectives*. Tuscaloosa: The University of Alabama Press.

Carlsen, Robert S. 2011. *The War for the Heart & Soul of a Highland Maya Town*. Austin: University of Texas Press.

Carmack, Robert. 2012. *The Quiché Mayas of Utatlán: The Evolution of a Highland Guatemala Kingdom*. Norman: University of Oklahoma Press.

Casaús Arzú, Marta Elena. 2008. *Genocidio: ¿La Máxima Expresión del Racismo en Guatemala?* Guatemala: F&G Editores.

Castillo Méndez, Iván. 2008. *Descolonización Territorial, Del Sujeto y La Gobernabilidad: Examen Crítico del Discurso Restringido de la Inclusión (Individual) del Indígena Maya en el Sistema de Partidos Políticos*. Guatemala: Universidad Rafael Landívar.

Chalk, Frank, and Kurt Jonassohn. 1990. *The History and Sociology of Genocide*. New Haven: Yale University Press.

Cheney, Kristen E., and Karen Smith Rotabi. 2018. "The Orphan Industrial Complex Comes to Roost in America." ISSBlog.nl. https://issblog.nl/2018/07/12/the-orphan -industrial-complex-comes-home-to-roost-in-america-by-kristen-cheney-and -karen-smith-rotabi/

Cheney, Kristen E., and Karen Smith Rotabi. 2014. "Addicted to Orphans: How the Global Orphan Industrial Complex Jeopardizes Local Child Protection Systems." In *Conflict, Violence and Peace, Volume 11*, edited by Christopher Harker, Kathrin Hörschelman, and Tracey Skelton, 89–107. Singapore: Springer.

Child, Brenda J. 2012. *Holding our World Together: Ojibwe Women and the Survival of Community*. New York: Penguin Books.

Child, Brenda J. 2000. *Boarding Schools Seasons: American Indian Families, 1900–1940*. Lincoln: University of Nebraska Press.

Chisholm, K. 1998. "A Three-year Follow-Up of Attachment and Indiscriminate Friendliness in Children Adopted from Romanian Orphanages." *Child Development* 69 (4): 1092–1106.

Choy, Catherine Ceniza. 2018. "International Adoption and Cultural Insecurity." In *Handbook of Cultural Security*, edited by Watanabe Yasushi, 146–166. Cheltenham: Edward Elgar Publishing.

Cicchetti, Dante. 2010. "Developmental Psychopathology." In *The Handbook of Life-Span Development: Social and Emotional Development, Volume 2*, edited by Michael E. Lamb and Alexandra M. Freund, 511–589. Hoboken: John Wiley & Sons, Inc.

Ciencia y Tecnología para Guatemala (CITGUA). 1989. *Situación de la Mujer en Guatemala IV*. México: CITGUA.

Clark, Janine Natalya. 2011. "Peace, Justice and the International Court: Limitations and Possibilities." *Journal of International Criminal Justice* 9: 521–545.

Cojtí Cuxil, Demetrio. 1997. *El Movimiento Maya (en Guatemala)/ Ri Maya' moloj pa Iximulew*. Guatemala: Editorial Cholsamaj.

Cole, Wade M. 2015. "Mind the gap: State Capacity and the Implementation of Human Rights Treaties." *International Organization (2015)*: 405–441.

Comisión de Derechos Humanos de Guatemala (CDHG). 1991. *1981–1991: 10 Años de Impunidad, Ejecuciones Extrajudiciales en Guatemala*. Guatemala: Comisión de Derechos Humanos de Guatemala.

Comisión de Derechos Humanos de Guatemala (CDHG). 2004. *Conclusiones y Recomendaciones: Guatemala, Memoria del Silencio*. Guatemala: F&G Editores.

Comisión de Derechos Humanos de Guatemala (CDHG). 1999. *Guatemala: Memoria del Silencio, vols. 1–12.* Guatemala: Comisión para el Esclarecimiento Histórico.

Comisión de Derechos Humanos de Guatemala (CDHG). 1999a. *Guatemala: Memoria del Silencio, vol. 1: Causas y Orígenes del Enfrentamiento Armado Interno.* Guatemala: Comisión para el Esclarecimiento Histórico.

Comisión de Derechos Humanos de Guatemala (CDHG). 1999b. *Guatemala: Memoria del Silencio, vol. 2: Las Violaciones de los Derechos Humanos y los Hechos de Violencia.* Guatemala: Comisión para el Esclarecimiento Histórico.

Comisión de Derechos Humanos de Guatemala (CDHG). 1999c. *Guatemala: Memoria del Silencio, vol. 3: Las Violaciones de los Derechos Humanos y los Hechos de Violencia.* Guatemala: Comisión para el Esclarecimiento Histórico.

Comisión de Derechos Humanos de Guatemala (CDHG). 1999d. *Guatemala: Memoria del Silencio, vol. 5: Conclusiones y Recomendaciones.* Guatemala: Comisión para el Esclarecimiento Histórico.

Consorcio Actoras de Cambio. 2006. *Rompiendo el Silencio: Justicia para las Mujeres Víctimas de Violencia Sexual durante el Conflicto Armado en Guatemala.* Guatemala: Consorcio Actoras de Cambio, La Lucha de las Mujeres por la Justicia, Instituto de Estudios Comparados en Ciencias Penales de Guatemala.

Cook, John L. 1997. *The Advisor: The Phoenix Program in Vietnam.* Atglen: Schiffer Publishing.

Dadrian, Vahakn N. 2003. "Children as Victims of Genocide: The Armenian Case." *Journal of Genocide Research* 5 (3): 421–437.

Davis, Shelton H. 1988. "Introduction: Sowing the Seeds of Violence." In *Harvest of Violence: The Maya Indians and the Guatemalan Crisis*, edited by Robert M. Carmack, 3–36. Norman: University of Oklahoma Press.

Davis, Shelton H., and Julie Hodson. 1983. *Witnesses to Political Violence in Guatemala: The Suppression of a Rural Development Movement.* Boston: Oxfam America.

DeForest, Orrin, and David Chanoff. 1990. *Slow Burn: The Rise and Bitter Fall of American Intelligence in Vietnam.* New York: Simon and Schuster.

Derogatis, Leonard R. 1983. *SCL-90-R: Administration, Scoring & Procedures Manual-II for the R(evised) Version and Other Instruments of the Psychopathology Rating Scale Series.* Townson: Clinical Psychometric Research.

Derogatis, Leonard R. 1977. *The SCL-90 Manual I: Scoring, Administration and Procedures for the SCL-90-R.* Baltimore: Clinical Psychometrics Research.

Desjarlais, Robert, and Arthur Kleinman. 1994. "Violence and Demoralization in the New World Disorder." *Anthropology Today* 10 (5): 9–12.

Dill, Kathleen. 2009. "Reparations and the Illusive Meaning of Justice in Guatemala." In *Waging War, Making Peace: Reparations and Human Rights*, edited by Barbara Rose Johnston and Susan Slyomovics, 183–206. Walnut Creek: Left Coast Press, Inc.

Doyle, Kate. 2012. "Justice in Guatemala." *NACLA Report on the Americas* 45 (1): 37–42.

Dubinsky, Karen. 2010. *Babies without Borders: Adoption and Migration across the Americas.* New York: New York University Press.

Durst, Nathan. 2003. "Child-Survivors of the Holocaust: Age-Specific Traumatization and the Consequences for Therapy." *American Journal of Psychotherapy* 57 (4): 499–518.

Dyregrov, Atle, Rolf Gjestad, and Magne Raundalen. 2002. "Children Exposed to Warfare: A Longitudinal Study." *Journal of Traumatic Stress* 15 (1): 59–68.

Dyregrov, Atle, Leila Gupta, Rolf Gjestad, and Eugenie Mukanoheli. 2000. "Trauma Exposure and Psychological Reactions to Genocide among Rwandan Children." *Journal of Traumatic Stress* 13 (1): 3–21.

Eber, Christine. 2000. *Women and Alcohol in a Highland Maya Town: Water of Hope, Water of Sorrow.* Austin: University of Texas Press.

Ejército de Guatemala. 1983. *Plan de Campaña "Firmeza 83."* Guatemala: Ejército de Guatemala.

Ekmekcioglu, Lerna. 2013. "A Climate for Abduction, a Climate for Redemption: The Politics of Inclusion During and After the Armenian Genocide." *Comparative Studies in Society and History* 55 (3): 522–553.

Eliach, Yaffa. 1991. Keynote Address. *The First Annual Gathering of Children Hidden during World War II*, May 26–27. Marriott Marquis Hotel, New York City.

Embleton, Lonnie, David Ayuku, Allan Kamanda, Lukoye Atwoli, Samuel Ayaya, Rachel Vreeman, Winstone Nyandiko, Peter Gisore, Julius Koech, and Paula Braitstein. 2014. "Models of Care for Orphaned and Separated Children and Upholding Children's Rights: Cross-Sectional Evidence from Western Kenya." *BMC International Health and Human Rights* 14 (1): 1–18.

Falla, Ricardo. 1994. *Massacres in the Jungle: Ixcán, Guatemala, 1975–1982.* Boulder: Westview Press.

Falla, Ricardo. 1988. "Struggle for Survival in the Mountains: Hunger and Other Privations Inflicted on Internal Refugees from the Central Highlands." In *Harvest of Violence: The Maya Indians and the Guatemalan Crisis*, edited by Robert M. Carmack, 235–255. Norman: University of Oklahoma Press.

Fassin, Didier, and Richard Recthman. 2009. *The Empire of Trauma: An Inquiry into the Condition of Victimhood.* Princeton: Princeton University Press.

Fear-Segal, Jacqueline. 2010. "Institutional Death and Ceremonial Healing: The Carlisle Indian School Cemetery." *Museum Anthropology* 33 (2): 157–171.

Fernando, Chandi, and Michel Ferrari. 2013. "Resilience in Children of War." In *Handbook of Resilience in Children of War*, edited by Chandi Fernando and Michel Ferrari, 287–301. New York: Springer.

Figueroa Ferreira, Maya. 2020. "Who Am I? A Reflection of the In-Between." *Maya America: Journal of Essays, Commentary, and Analysis* 2 (1): 3–5.

Figueroa Ibarra, Carlos. 1991. *El Recurso del Miedo: Ensayo Sobre el Estado y el Terror en Guatemala.* Costa Rica: Editorial Universitaria Centroamericana.

Fischer, Edward F. 2006. *Broccoli and Desire: Global Connections and Maya Struggles in Postwar Guatemala.* Stanford: Stanford University Press.

Fischer, Edward F. 2004a. "The Janus Face of Globalization: Economic Production and Cultural Reproduction in Highland Guatemala." In *Pluralizing Ethnography: Comparison and Representation in Maya Cultures, Histories, and Identities,* edited by John M. Watanabe and Edward F. Fischer, 257–290. Santa Fe: School of American Research Press.

Fischer, Edward F. 2004b. "Beyond Victimization: Maya Movements in Post-War Guatemala." In *The Struggle for Indigenous Rights in Latin America,* edited by Nancy Grey Postero and Leon Zamosc, 81–104. Brighton: Sussex Academic Press.

Fischer, Edward F., and R. McKenna Brown. 1996. "Introduction: Maya Cultural Activism in Guatemala." In *Maya Cultural Activism in Guatemala,* edited by Edward F. Fischer and R. McKenna Brown, 1–18. Austin: University of Texas Press.

Fischer, Edward F., and Carol Hendrickson. 2003. *Tecpán Guatemala: A Modern Maya Town in Global and Local Context.* Boulder: Westview Press.

Fischer, Edward F., and Judith M. Maxwell. 1999. "Political Linguistics and Maya Worldview: The Creation of Neologisms in Kaqchikel Mayan." *Texas Linguistic Forum* 42: 64–73.

Forkert, Joshua. 2012. "Refugees, Orphans and a Basket of Cats: The Politics of Operation Babylift." *Journal of Australian Studies* 36 (4): 427–444.

Foxen, Patricia. 2007. *In Search of Providence: Transnational Mayan Identities.* Nashville: Vanderbilt University Press.

Frank, Luisa, and Philip Wheaton. 1984. *Indian Guatemala: Path to Liberation; the Role of Christians in the Indian Process.* Washington: EPICA Task Force.

Fujimura, Clementine K., Sally W. Stoecker, and Tatyana Sudakova. *Russia's Abandoned Children: An Intimate Understanding.* Westport: Praeger Publishers.

Gálvez Borrell, Víctor. 2008. *Política y Conflicto Armado: Cambios y Crisis del Régimen Político en Guatemala (1954–1982).* Guatemala: Editorial de Ciencias Sociales.

García Ferreira, Roberto. 2013. *Operaciones en Contra: La CIA y el Exilio de Jacobo Arbenz.* Guatemala: FLASCO.

Garrard-Burnett, Virginia. 2010. *Terror in the Land of the Holy Spirit: Guatemala under General Efraín Ríos Montt, 1982–1983.* New York: Oxford University Press.

Gegout, Catherine. 2013. "The International Criminal Court: Limits, Potential and Conditions for the Promotion of Justice and Peace." *Third World Quarterly* 34 (5): 800–818.

Geltman, Paul L., Wanda Grant-Knight, Supriya D. Mehta, Christine Lloyd-Travaglini, Stuart Lustig, Jeanne M. Landgraf, and Paul H. Wise. 2005. "The 'Lost Boys of Sudan': Functional and Behavioral Health of Unaccompanied Refugee Minors Resettled in the United States." *Archives of Pediatrics & Adolescent Medicine* 159 (6): 585–591.

Gibbons, Judith L, and Karen Smith Rotabi. 2016. "Introduction." *Intercountry Adoption: Policies, Practices, and Outcomes*, edited by Judith L. Gibbons and Karen Smith Rotabi, 1–4. New York: Routledge.

Gibbons, Judith L., Samantha L. Wilson, and Alicia M. Schnell. 2009. "Foster Parents as a Critical Link and Resource in International Adoptions from Guatemala." *Adoption Quarterly* 12 (2): 59–77.

Gibney, Mark, and David Warner. 1999. "What Does It Mean to Say I'm Sorry-President Clinton's Apology to Guatemala and Its Significance for International and Domestic Law." *Denver Journal of International Law & Policy* 28: 223–233.

Goldín, Liliana, and Brenda Rosenbaum. 2009. "Everyday Violence of Exclusion: Women in Precarious Neighborhoods of Guatemala City." In *Mayas in Postwar Guatemala: Harvest of Violence Revisited,* edited by Walter E. Little and Timothy J. Smith, 67–83. Tuscaloosa: University of Alabama Press.

Gong, Jie, Xiaoming Li, Xiaoyi Fang, G. Zhao, Y Lv, Jianglin Zhao, Xiuyun Lin, L Zhang, Xinguang Chen, and Bonita Stanton. 2009. "Sibling Separation and Psychological Problems of Double AIDS Orphans in Rural China–A Comparison Analysis." *Child: Care, Health and Development* 35 (4): 534–541.

González de Rivera, J.L., L.R. Derogatis, C. De las Cuevas, R. Gracia Marco, F. Rodríguez-Pulido, M. Henry-Benítez, and A.L. Monterrey. 1989. *The Spanish Version of the SCL-90-R. Normative Data in the General Population.* Towson: Clinical Psychometric Research.

Gramsci, Antonio. 1957. *The Modern Prince & Other Writings.* New York: International Publishers.

Grandin, Greg. 2011. *The Last Colonial Massacre: Latin America in the Cold War.* Chicago: University of Chicago Press.

Grandin, Greg. 2004. *The Last Colonial Massacre: Latin American in the Cold War.* Chicago: University of Chicago Press.

Grandin, Greg. 2000. *The Blood of Guatemala: A History of Race and Nation* (Revised Edition). Durham: Duke University Press.

Gray, Christine L., Sumedha Ariely, Brian W. Pence, and Kathryn Whetten. 2017. "Why Institutions Matter: Empirical Data from Five Low-and Middle-Income Countries Indicate the Critical Role of Institutions for Orphans." In *Child Maltreatment in Residential Care,* edited by Adrian V. Rus, Sheri R. Parris, and Ecaterina Stativa, *379–400.* Switzerland: Springer International Publishing.

Green, Emily. 2019. "Guatemala Shut Down Its Anti-Corruption Commission. Now Its People Worry about Impunity." Pri.org. https://www.pri.org/stories/2019-10-14/guatemala-shut-down-its-anti-corruption-commission-now-its-people-worry-about

Green, Linda. 1999. *Fear as a Way of Life: Mayan Widows in Rural Guatemala.* New York: Columbia University Press.

Greene, Jerome A., and Douglas D. Scott. 2004. *Finding Sand Creek: History, Archeology, and the 1864 Massacre Site.* Norman: University of Oklahoma Press.

Gresham, Katie, Larry Nackerud, and Ed Risler. 2003. "Intercountry Adoption from Guatemala and the United States: A Comparative Policy Analysis." *Journal of Immigrant & Refugee Services* 1 (3–4): 1–20.

Grey Postero, Nancy, and Leon Zamosc. 2004. "Indigenous Movements and the Indian Question in Latin America." In *The Struggle for Indigenous Rights in Latin America,* edited by Nancy Grey Postero and Leon Zamosc, 1–31. Brighton: Sussex Academic Press.

Groark, Kevin P. 1997. "To Warm the Blood, to Warm the Flesh: The Role of the Steambath in Highland Maya (Tzeltal-Tzotzil) Ethnomedicine." *Journal of Latin American Lore* 20 (1): 3–96.

Guarnaccia, Peter J., and Pablo Farias. 1988. "The Social Meanings of Nervios: A Case Study of a Central American Woman." *Social Science and Medicine* 26: 1223–1231.

Guatemalan Human Rights Commission (GHRC). 2019. "Assassination of Bishop Gerardi." GHRC-USA.org. http://www.ghrc-usa.org/our-work/important-cases/assassination-of-bishop-gerardi/.

Güell, Rosa, Vanesa Resqueti, Mercedes Sangenis, Fatima Morante, Bernardi Martorell, Pere Casan, and Gordon H. Guyatt. 2006. "Impact of Pulmonary Rehabilitation on Psychosocial Morbidity in Patients with Severe COPD." *Chest* 129: 899–904.

Gugelberger, Georg M. 1999. "Stollwerk or Bulwark?: David Meets Goliath and the Continuation of the Testimonio Debate." In *Latin American Perspectives* 26 (6): 47–52.

Guillén, José. 2007. *Historia Analítica de Guatemala del Popul Wuj al TLC.* Guatemala: Alvagrafic.

Gunson, Phil. 2018. "Gen Efraín Ríos Montt Obituary: Guatemalan Military Dictator Charged with Genocide and Crimes Against Humanity." TheGuardian.com. https://www.theguardian.com/world/2018/apr/02/gen-efrain-rios-montt-obituary

Gutierrez, Gustavo. 1988. *A Theology of Liberation.* London: SCM Press.

Guyler Delva, Joseph. 2010. "Americans Arrested Taking Children Out of Haiti." Reuters.com. https://www.reuters.com/article/us-quake-haiti-arrests-idUSTRE60T23I20100130

Hale, Charles R. 2006. *Más que un Indio (More than an Indian): Racial Ambivalence and Neoliberal Multiculturalism in Guatemala.* Santa Fe: School of American Research Press.

Hale, Charles R. 1999. "Travel Warning: Elite Appropriations of Hybridity, Mestizaje, Antiracism, Equality, and Other Progressive-Sounding Discourses in Highland Guatemala." *Journal of American Folklore* 112 (445): 297–315.

Handy, Jim. 1984. *Gift of the Devil: A History of Guatemala.* Boston: South End Press.

Hazard, Carol. 2017. "John Dau, One of the Lost Boys of Sudan: A Story about Courage, Suffering and Redemption." Richmond.com. https://www.richmond.com/news/local/john-dau-one-of-the-lost-boys-of-sudan-a/article_65e72860-dfb5-58dd-9661-5acf63d3fad8.html

Heberer, Patricia. 2011. *Children During the Holocaust.* Lanham: AltaMira Press.

Hendrickson, Carol. 1995. *Weaving Identities: Construction of Dress and Self in a Highland Guatemalan Town.* Austin: University of Texas Press.

Heying, Shirley, David C. Witherington, Jane E. Smith, and Judith L. Gibbons. 2016. "Post-traumatic Distress and Growth Among Guatemalan War Orphans in Adulthood." *International Perspectives in Psychology: Research, Practice, Consultation* 5 (1): 18–33.

Holiday, David. 2001. "Guatemala's Precarious Peace." *Current History* 99 (634): 78–84.

Holland, Dorothy, William Lachicotte Jr., Debra Skinner, and Carole Cain. 1998. *Identity and Agency in Cultural Worlds.* Cambridge: Harvard University Press.

Huynh, Hy V. 2014. "Vulnerable Children Policy and Research: A Focus on Supporting 'Suitable' Institutions When Placement is 'Necessary' for a Child." *American Journal of Orthopsychiatry* 84 (4): 1–8.

Jack, Fiona, Shelley Macdonald, Elaine Reese, and Harlene Hayne. 2009. "Maternal Reminiscing Style During Early Childhood Predicts the Age of Adolescents' Earliest Memories." *Child Development* 80 (2): 496–505.

Jaguar House Films. 2002. *Discovering Dominga*. Patricia Flynn, Director and Co-producer. Mary Jo McConahay, co-producer. Berkeley: Berkeley Media.

Johnson, Howard, Andrew Thompson, and Maria Downs. 2009. "Non-Western Interpreters' Experiences of Trauma: The Protective Role of Culture Following Exposure to Oppression." *Ethnicity & Health* 14 (4): 407–418.

Jonas, Susanne. 2009. "Guatemala: Acts of Genocide and Scorched-Earth Counterinsurgency War." In *Century of Genocide: Critical Essays and Eyewitness Accounts* (3rd Edition), edited by Samuel Totten and William S. Parsons, 377–411. New York: Routledge.

Jonas, Susanne. 2000. *Of Centaurs and Doves: Guatemala's Peace Process*. Boulder: Westview Press.

Jonas, Susanne. 1991. *The Battle for Guatemala: Rebels, Death Squads, and U.S. Power.* Boulder: Westview Press.

Jones, Adam. 2016. *Genocide: A Comprehensive Introduction* (3rd Edition). New York: Routledge.

Jones, Frank L. 2005. "Blowtorch: Robert Komer and the Making of Vietnam Pacification Policy." *Parameters* 35 (3): 103–118.

Jones, Laura K., and Jenny L. Cureton. 2014. "Trauma Redefined in the DSM-5: Rationale and Implications for Counseling Practice." *The Professional Counselor* 4 (3): 257–271.

Juffer, Femmie, and Marinus H. van IJzendoorn. 2012. "Review of Meta-Analytical Studies on the Physical, Emotional, and Cognitive Outcomes of Intercountry Adoptees." In *Intercountry Adoption: Policies, Practices, and Outcomes*, edited by Judith L. Gibbons and Karen Smith Rotabi, 175–186. Surrey: Ashgate Publishing Limited.

Julian, Megan M. 2013. "Age at Adoption from Institutional Care as a Window into the Lasting Effects of Early Experiences." *Clinical Child and Family Psychology Review* 16 (2): 101–145.

Kahn, Hilary E. 2006. *Seeing and Being Seen: The Q'eqchi' Maya of Livingston, Guatemala, and Beyond.* Austin: University of Texas Press.

Keilson, Hans. 1979. *Sequentielle Traumatisierung bei Kindern: Deskriptiv-Klinische und Quantifizierend-Statistische Follow-Up Untersuchung zum Schicksal der Jüdischen Kriegswaisen in den Niederlanden.* Stuttgart: Enke.

Kendrick, Andrew. 2013. "Relations, Relationships and Relatedness: Residential Child Care and the Family Metaphor." *Child & Family Social Work* 18 (1): 77–86

Kepner, Timothy J. 2000. "Torture 101: The Case Against the United States for Atrocities Committed by School of the Americas Alumni." *Dickinson Journal of International Law* 19 (2000): 475.

Khlinovskaya Rockhill, Elena. 2010. *Lost to the State: Family Discontinuity, Social Orphanhood, and Residential Care in the Russian Far East.* New York: Berghahn Books.

Kiernan, Ben. 2007a. *Blood and Soil: A World History of Genocide and Extermination from Sparta to Darfur.* New Haven: Yale University Press.

Kiernan, Ben. 2007b. "Introduction: A World Turned Upside Down." In *Children of Cambodia's Killing Fields*, edited by Kim DePaul, xi–xvii. New Haven: Yale University Press.

Kim, Eleana J. 2010. *Adopted Territory: Transnational Korean Adoptees and the Politics of Belonging.* Durham: Duke University Press.

Kim, Oh Myo, Kevin C. Hynes, and Richard M. Lee. 2017. "Guatemalan Family-Style Orphanages: A Grounded Theory Examination of Caregiver Perspectives." *International Social Work* 60 (5): 1244–1254.

Kinsbruner, Jay. 2000. *Independence in Spanish America: Civil Wars, Revolutions, and Underdevelopment.* Albuquerque: University of New Mexico Press.

Kinzer, Stephen. 2018. "Efraín Ríos Montt, Guatemalan Dictator Convicted of Genocide, Dies at 91." NewYorkTimes.com. https://www.nytimes.com/2018/04/01/obituaries/efrain-rios-montt-guatemala-dead.html

Konefal, Betsy. 2010. *For Every Indio who Falls: A History of Maya Activism in Guatemala, 1960–1990.* Albuquerque: University of New Mexico Press.

Kramer, Wendy. 1994. *Encomienda Politics in Early Colonial Guatemala, 1524–1544: Dividing the Spoils.* Boulder: Westview Press.

Kravić, Nermina, Izet Pajević, and Mevludin Hasanović. 2013. "Surviving Genocide in Srebrenica During the Early Childhood and Adolescent Personality." *Croatian Medical Journal* 54 (1): 55–64.

Krell, Robert. 1985. "Therapeutic Value of Documenting Child Survivors." *Journal of the American Academy of Child Psychiatry* 24 (4): 397–400.

Kulkarni, Madhur, Nnamdi Pole, and Christine Timko. 2013. "Childhood Victimization, Negative Mood Regulation, and Adult PTSD Severity." *Psychological Trauma: Theory, Research, Practice, and Policy* 5 (4): 359–365.

Leinaweaver, Jessica. 2008. *The Circulation of Children: Kinship, Adoption, and Morality in Andean Peru.* Durham: Duke University Press.

Lepore, Stephen, and Tracey Revenson. 2006. "Resilience and Post-traumatic Growth: Recovery, Resistance, and Reconfiguration." In *Handbook of Post-traumatic Growth: Research and Practice*, edited by Lawrence G. Calhoun and Richard G. Tedeschi, 24–46. Mahwah: Lawrence Erlbaum Associates.

Lev-Wiesel, Rachel, and Marianne Amir. 2000. "Post-traumatic Stress Disorder Symptoms, Psychological Distress, Personal Resources, and Quality of Life in Four Groups of Holocaust Child Survivors." *Family Process* 39 (4): 445–459.

Levenson, Deborah T. 2013. *Adiós Niño: The Gangs of Guatemala City and the Politics of Death.* Durham: Duke University Press.

Levenson, Deborah T. 2002. "Reactions to Trauma: The 1976 Earthquake in Guatemala." *International Labor and Working-Class History* 62: 60–68.

Levinger, Laurie. 2009. *What War? Testimonies of Maya Survivors.* West Hartford: Full Circle Press.

Liefaard, Ton, and Julia Sloth-Nielsen. 2017. "25 Years CRC: Reflecting on Successes, Failures and the Future." In *The United Nations Convention on the Rights of the Child: Taking Stock after 25 years and Looking Ahead*, edited by Ton Liefaard and Julia Sloth-Nielsen, 1–13. Leiden: Brill Nijhoff.

Little, Walter E. 2008. "A Visual Political Economy of Maya Representations in Guatemala, 1931–1944." *Ethnohistory* 55 (4): 633–663.

Little, Walter E. 2004. *Mayas in the Marketplace: Tourism, Globalization, and Cultural Identity.* Austin: University of Texas Press.

López Raquec, Margarita. 1989. *Acerca de los Alfabetos para Escribir los Idiomas Mayas de Guatemala.* Guatemala: Proyecto Lingüístico Franciso Marroquín.

López, Steven R., and Peter J. Guarnaccia. 2000. "Cultural Psychopathology: Uncovering the Social World of Mental Illness." *Annual Review of Psychology* 51: 571–598.

Lovell, William George. 2015. *Conquest and Survival in Colonial Guatemala: A Historical Geography of the Cuchumatán Highlands, 1500–1821* (4th Edition). Montreal: McGill-Queen's University Press.

Lovell, William George. 2000 [1995]. *A Beauty that Hurts: Life and Death in Guatemala* (Revised Edition). Austin: University of Texas Press.

Luján Muñoz, Jorge. 2018. *Breve Historia Contemporánea de Guatemala. México* (4th Edition: 3rd Reprint). Mexico: Fondo de Cultura Económica.

Luthar, Suniya S., Elizabeth J. Crossman, and Phillip J. Small. 2015. "Resilience and Adversity." In *Handbook of Child Psychology and Developmental Science, Volume 3*, edited by Michael E. Lamb, 247–286. Hoboken: John Wiley & Sons, Inc.

Lutz, Christopher H., and W. George Lovell. 1990. "Core and Periphery in Colonial Guatemala." In *Guatemalan Indians and the State: 1540–1988*, edited by Carol A. Smith, 35–51. Austin: University of Texas Press.

Madley, Benjamin. 2015. *An American Genocide: The United States and the California Indian Catastrophe.* New Haven: Yale University Press.

Mam, Kaylanee. 2006. "The Endurance of the Cambodian Family Under the Khmer Rouge Regime: An Oral History." In *Genocide in Cambodia and Rwanda: New Perspectives*, edited by Susan E. Cook, 119–162. New Brunswick: Transaction Publishers.

Manyena, Siambabala Bernard. 2006. "The Concept of Resilience Revisted." *Disasters* 30 (4): 433–450.

Manz, Beatriz. 2008. "The Continuum of Violence in Post-War Guatemala." *Social Analysis* 52 (2): 151–164.

Manz, Beatriz. 2004. *Paradise in Ashes: A Guatemalan Journey of Courage, Terror, and Hope.* Berkeley: University of California Press.

Manz, Beatriz. 1988. *Refugees of a Hidden War: The Aftermath of Counterinsurgency in Guatemala.* New York: State University of New York.

Martínez Peláez, Severo. 2009. *La Patria del Criollo: An Interpretation of Colonial Guatemala,* translated by Susan M. Neve and W. George Lovell, and edited by W. George Lovell and Christopher H. Lutz. Durham: Duke University Press.

Masten, Ann S., Karin Best, and Norman Garmezy. 1990. "Resilience and Development: Contributions from the Study of Children who Overcome Adversity." *Development and Psychopathology* 2: 425–444.

Masten, Ann S., Angela J. Narayan, Wendy K. Silverman, and Joy D. Osofsky. 2015. "Children in War and Disaster." In *Handbook of Child Psychology and Developmental Science, Volume 4,* edited by Marc H. Bornstein and Tama Leventhal, 704–745. Hoboken: John Wiley & Sons, Inc.

Mato Nunpa, Chris. 2014. "Historical Amnesia: The 'Hidden Genocide' and Destruction of the Indigenous Peoples of the United States." In *Hidden Genocides: Power, Knowledge, Memory,* edited by Alexander Laban Hinton, Thomas La Pointe, and Douglas Irvin-Erickson, 96–108. New Brunswick: Rutgers University Press.

May, Rachel. 2001. *Terror in the Countryside: Campesinos Responses to Political Violence in Guatemala, 1954–1985.* Athens: Ohio University Press.

Maya America. 2020. "Journal of Essays, Commentary, and Analysis." DigitalComm ons.Kennesaw.edu. https://digitalcommons.kennesaw.edu/mayaamerica/.

McAllister, Carlota, and Diane M. Nelson, eds. 2013. *War by Other means: Aftermath in Post-genocide Guatemala.* Durham: Duke University Press.

McBride, Becca. 2017. *The Globalization of Adoption: Individuals, States, and Agencies across Borders.* Cambridge: Cambridge University Press.

McCall, Robert B. 2011. "IX. Research, Practice, and Policy Perspectives on Issues of Children Without Permanent Parental Care." *Monographs of the Society for Research in Child Development* 76 (4) (2011): 223–272.

McConahay, Mary Jo. 2013. "Discovering Dominga: Adoptions and Tangled Truths." *ReVista: Harvard Review of Latin America* XIII (1): 74–75.

McConahay, Mary Jo. 2000. "New Hope for Missing Kids: Victims of Guatemala's Civil War Are Likely to Be Alive, Report Says." SFGate.com. https://www.sfgate .com/news/article/New-Hope-for-Missing-Kids-Victims-of-3303502.php

McCreery, David. 1994. *Rural Guatemala: 1760–1940.* Stanford: Stanford University Press.

McCreery Bunkers, Kelley, Victor Groza, and Daniel P. Lauer. 2009. "International Adoption and Child Protection in Guatemala: A Case of the Tail Wagging the Dog." *International Social Work* 52 (5): 649–660.

McKenzie, Richard B. 1999. *Rethinking Orphanages for the 21st Century.* California: Sage Publications.

McPherson, Alan. 2006. *Intimate Ties, Bitter Struggles: The United States and Latin America Since 1945.* Washington: Potomac Books

McSherry, J. Patrice. 2002. "Tracking the Origins of a State Terror Network: Operation Condor." *Latin American Perspectives* (29) 1: 38–60.

Menéndez, Luis Antonio. 2002. *La Educación en Guatemala: Enfoque Histórico-Estadístico.* Guatemala: C.J.C. Computación.

Miller, Edward. 2017. "Behind the Phoenix Program." NYTimes.com. https://www .nytimes.com/2017/12/29/opinion/behind-the-phoenix-program.html

Ministerio de Trabajo y Previsión Social. 2010. "Salario Mínimo Guatemala." MinTrabajo.gob.gt. https://www.mintrabajo.gob.gt/

Minow, Martha. 2010. "XII. The Hope for Healing: What Can Truth Commissions Do?" *Truth v. Justice: The Morality of Truth Commissions*, edited by Robert I. Rotberg and Dennis Thompson, 235–260. Princeton, NJ: Princeton University Press.

Mishra, Rachna, and Vanita Sondhi. 2019. "Fostering Resilience among Orphaned Adolescents through Institutional Care in India." *Residential Treatment for Children & Youth* 36 (40): 314–337.

Molina Mejía, Raúl, and Patrice McSherry. 2001. "Justice in the Gerardi Case but Terror Continues." *NACLA Report on the Americas* 35 (1): 8–11.

Monbiot, George. 2001. "Backyard Terrorism." TheGuardian.com. https://www.theguardian.com/world/2001/oct/30/afghanistan.terrorism19

Monico, Carmen, Karen S. Rotabi, and Justin Lee. 2019. "Forced Child-Family Separations in the Southwestern U.S. Border Under the 'Zero-Tolerance' Policy: Preventing Human Rights Violations and Child Abduction into Adoption (Part 1)." *Journal of Human Rights and Social Work* 4 (3): 164–179.

Montejo, Victor. 2005. *Maya Intellectual Renaissance: Identity, Representation and Leadership.* Austin: University of Texas Press.

Montejo, Victor. 2004. "Angering the Ancestors: Transnationalism and Economic Transformation of Maya Communities in Western Guatemala." In *Pluralizing Ethnography: Comparison and Representation in Maya Cultures, Histories and Identities*, edited by John M. Watanabe and Edward F. Fischer, 231–255. Santa Fe: School of American Research Press.

Montejo, Victor. 1999. *Voices from Exile: Violence and Survival in Modern Maya History*. Norma: University of Oklahoma Press.

Moser, Caroline, and Cathy McIlwaine. 2001. *Violence in a Post-Conflict Context: Urban Poor Perceptions from Guatemala*. Washington: The World Bank.

Moskovitz, Sarah. 1985. "Longitudinal Follow-up of Child Survivors of the Holocaust." *Journal of the American Academy of Child Psychiatry* 24 (4): 401–407.

Mota, Catarina Pinheiro, and Paula Mena Matos. 2013. "Peer Attachment, Coping, and Self-Esteem in Institutionalized Adolescents: The Mediating Role of Social Skills." *European Journal of Psychology of Education* 28 (1): 87–100.

Munyandamutsa, Naasson, Paul Mahoro Nkubamugisha, Marianne Gex-Fabry, and Ariel Eytan. 2012. "Mental and Physical Health in Rwanda 14 Years After the Genocide." *Social Psychiatry and Psychiatric Epidemiology* 47 (11): 1753–1761.

Museo Comunitario Rabinal Achi. 2003. *Oj K'aslik: Estamos Vivos. Recuperación de la Memoria Histórica de Rabinal (1944–1996)*. Rabinal: Museo Comunitario Rabinal Achi.

Nash, June. 2004. "Beyond Resistance and Protest: The Maya Quest for Autonomy." In *Pluralizing Ethnography: Comparison and Representation in Maya Cultures, Histories, and Identities*, edited by John M. Watanabe and Edward F. Fischer, 163–198. Santa Fe: School of American Research Press.

Nelson, Diane M. 1999. *A Finger in the Wound: Body Politics in Quincentennial Guatemala*. Berkeley: University of California Press.

Next Generation Guatemala (NGG). 2020a. "Next Generation Guatemala." NextGenGuate.wixsite.com. https://nextgenguate.wixsite.com/home

Next Generation Guatemala (NGG). 2020b. "Next Generation Guatemala Facebook Page." Facebook.com. https://www.facebook.com/NextGenGuate/

Ng, Lauren C., Naphtal Ahishakiye, Donald E. Miller, and Beth E. Meyerowitz. 2015. "Narrative Characteristics of Genocide Testimonies Predict Post-traumatic Stress Disorder Symptoms Years Later." *Psychological Trauma: Theory, Research, Practice, and Policy* 7 (3): 303.

Nguyen-Gillham, Viet, Rita Giacaman, Ghada Naser, and Will Boyce. 2008. "Normalising the Abnormal: Palestinian Youth and the Contradictions of Resilience in Protracted Conflict." *Health and Social Care in the Community* 16 (3): 291–298.

Norris, Fran H., and Julia L. Perilla. 1996. "The Revised Civilian Mississippi Scale for PTSD: Reliability, Validity, and Cross-Language Stability." *Journal of Traumatic Stress* 9 (2): 285–298.

Oglesby, Elizabeth, and Diane M. Nelson. 2016. "Guatemala's Genocide Trial and the Nexus of Racism and Counterinsurgency." *Journal of Genocide Research* 18 (2–3): 133–142.

Oglesby, Elizabeth, and Amy Ross. 2009. "Guatemala's Genocide Determination and the Spatial Politics of Justice." *Space and Polity* 13 (1): 21–39.

Organization of American States (OAS). 2020. "Department of International Law." http://www.oas.org/en/sla/dil/international_law.asp.

Otzoy, Irma. 2017. *Ru'x.* Guatemala: F&G Editores.

Otzoy, Irma. 1996. "Maya Clothing and Identity." In *Maya Cultural Activism in Guatemala,* edited by Edward F. Fischer and R. McKenna Brown, 141–155. Austin: University of Texas Press.

Papageorgiou, V., Frangou-Garunovic, A., Iordanidou, R., Yule, W., Smith, P., and Vostanis, P. 2000. "War Trauma and Psychopathology in Bosnian Refugee Children." *European Child and Adolescent Psychiatry* 9 (2): 84–90.

Parkhurst Moss, Beverly. 2008. *Dark Exodus: The Lost Girls of Sudan.* Dallas: The P3 Press.

Pedersen, Geir, and Sigmund Karterud. 2004. "Is the SCL-90R Helpful for the Clinician in Assessing DSM-IV Symptom Disorders?" *Acta Psychiatrica Scandinavica* 110 (3): 215–224.

Perera, Victor. 1993. *Unfinished Conquest: The Guatemalan Tragedy.* Berkeley: University of California Press.

Philippe, Frederick L., Samuel Laventure, Genevieve Beaulieu-Pelletier, Serge Lecours, and Natasha Lekes. 2011. "Ego-Resiliency as a Mediator between Childhood Trauma and Psychological Symptoms." *Journal of Social and Clinical Psychology* 30 (6): 583–598.

Philps, Alan, and John Lahutsky. 2009. *The Boy from Baby House 10: From the Nightmare of a Russian Orphanage to a New Life in America.* New York: St. Martin's Press.

Plasencia, Madeleine M. 2018. "The Torture of Children and Adolescents Living and Dying in Guatemala's Institutions." *Journal of International Law & Policy* 25 (1): 37–68.

Poitevin, René. 2001. *Nadie Quiere Soñar Despierto: Ensayos sobre Juventud y Política en Guatemala.* Guatemala: Magna Terra Editores, S.A.

Posocco, Silvia. 2011. *"Expedientes*: Fissured Legality and Affective States in the Transnational Adoption Archives in Guatemala." *Law, Culture and the Humanities* 7 (3): 434–456.

Pran, Dith. 1999. *Children of Cambodia's Killing Fields: Memoirs by Survivors*. New Haven: Yale University Press.

Pratt, Richard H. 1973 [1892]. "The Advantages of Mingling Indians with Whites." In *Americanizing the American Indians: Writings by the 'Friends of the Indian,' 1880–1900*, edited by Francis Paul Prucha, 260–271. Cambridge: Harvard University Press.

Rabe, Stephen G. 2016. *The Killing Zone: The United States Wages Cold War in Latin America* (2nd Edition). New York: Oxford University Press.

Recovery of Historical Memory Project (REMHI). 1999. *Guatemala: Never Again!* New York: Orbis Books.

Recuperación de la Memoria Histórica (REMHI). 1998. *Guatemala: Nunca Más, vol. 1: Impactos de La Violencia*. Guatemala: Oficina de Derechos Humanos del Arzopbispado de Guatemala.

Reddy, Suma Narayan. 2003. "The Agonising Plight of Orphans of War: A National Survey." *Indian Journal of Social Work* 64 (3): 307–332.

Rensink, Brenden. 2009. "The Sand Creek Phenomenon: The Complexity and Difficulty of Undertaking a Comparative Study of Genocide vis-à-vis the Northern American West." *Genocide Studies and Prevention* 4 (1): 9–27.

Restall, Matthew, and Florine Asselbergs. 2007. *Invading Guatemala: Spanish, Nahua, and Maya Accounts of the Conquest Wars*. University Park: The Pennsylvania State University Press.

Reynolds, Louisa. 2017. "Death of 41 Girls after Fire in Guatemala Shelter Leads to Charges of Abuse and Neglect." *Latin America Digital Beat* 80284: 1–3.

Robinson, S., M. Rapaport-Bar-Sever, M., and J. Rapaport. 1994. "The Present State of People who Survived the Holocaust as Children." *Acta Psychiatrica Scandinavica* 89 (4): 242–245.

Roby, Jini L., Joan Pennell, Karen Rotabi, Kelley McCreery Bunkers, and Sully de Ucles. 2014. "Contextual Adaptation of Family Group Conferencing Model: Early Evidence from Guatemala." *The British Journal of Social Work* 45 (8): 2281–2297.

Roht-Arriaza, Naomi, and Almudena Bernabeu. 2008. "The Guatemalan Genocide Case in Spain." *Berkeley Review of Latin American Studies* Fall 2008: 1–4.

Rosenau, William, and Austin Long. 2009. *The Phoenix Program and Contemporary Counterinsurgency.* Santa Monica: RAND Corporation.

Ross, Amy. 2016. "The Rios Montt Case and Universal Jurisdiction." *Journal of Genocide Research* 18 (2–3): 361–376.

Rotabi, Karen Smith. 2010. "From Guatemala to Ethiopia: Shifts in Intercountry Adoption Leaves Ethiopia Vulnerable for Child Sales and Other Unethical Practices." *Social Work and Society Online News Magazine* June 2010. file :///C:/Users/DRSHIR~1/AppData/Local/Temp/June2010-Rotabi__Kara_Smith-_From_Guatemala_to_Ethiopia__Shifts_in_intercountry_adoption_leaves_ethopia_vunerable_for_child_sales_and_other_unethical_practies-1.pdf

Rotabi, Karen Smith, and Nicole Bromfield. 2012. "The Decline in Intercountry Adoptions and New Practices of Global Surrogacy: Global Exploitation and Human Rights Concerns." *Affilia* 27 (2): 129–41.

Rotabi, Karen Smith, and Judith L. Gibbons. 2012. "Does The Hague Convention on Intercountry Adoption Adequately Protect Orphaned and Vulnerable Children and Their Families?" *Journal of Child and Family Studies* 21 (1): 106–119.

Rotabi, Karen Smith, Alexandra W. Morris, and Marie O. Weil. 2008. "International Child Adoption in a Post-Conflict Society: A Multi-Systemic Assessment of Guatemala." *Journal of Intergroup Relations* XXXIV (2): 9–41.

Rotabi, Karen Smith, Joan Pennell, Jini L. Roby, and Kelley McCreery Bunkers. 2012. "Family Group Conferencing as a Culturally Adaptable Intervention: Reforming Intercountry Adoption in Guatemala." *International Social Work* 55 (3): 402–416.

Saavedra, Alfredo. 2001. *El Color de la Sangre: Cuarenta Años de Represión y de Resistencia en Guatemala.* Guatemala: Grupo de Apoyo Mutuo.

Sabino, Carlos. 2013. *Tiempos de Jorge Ubico en Guatemala y el Mundo.* Guatemala: Fondo de Cultura Económica de Guatemala, S.A.

Sabino, Carlos. 2007. *Guatemala, La Historia Silenciada (1944–1989). Tomo I: Revolución y Liberación.* Guatemala: Fondo de Cultura Económica de Guatemala, S.A.

Sack, William H., John R. Seeley, and Gregory N. Clarke. 1997. "Does PTSD Transcend Cultural Barriers? A Study from the Khmer Adolescent Refugee Project." *Journal of the American Academy of Child and Adolescent Psychiatry* 36: 49–54.

Saigh, Philip A., and J. Douglas Bremner. 1999. "The History of Post-traumatic Stress Disorder." In *Post-traumatic Stress Disorder: A Comprehensive Text*, edited by Philip A. Saigh and J. Douglas Bremner, 1–17. Needham Heights: Allyn & Bacon.

Samson, C. Mathews. 2007. *Re-enchanting the World: Maya Protestantism in the Guatemalan Highlands.* Tuscaloosa: The University of Alabama Press.

San Román, Beatriz, and Karen Smith Rotabi. 2019. "Rescue, Red Tape, Child Abduction, Illicit Adoptions, and Discourse: Intercountry Adoption Attitudes in Spain." *International Social Work* 62 (1): 198–211.

Sanford, Victoria. 2008. "Breaking the Reign of Silence: Ethnography of a Clandestine Cemetery." In *Human Rights in the Maya Region: Global Politics, Cultural Contentions, and Moral Engagements*, edited by Pedro Pitarch, Sahnnon Speed and Xochitl Leyva Solando, 233–255. Durham: Duke University Press.

Sanford, Victoria. 2003. *Buried Secrets: Truth and Human Rights in Guatemala.* New York: Palgrave Macmillan.

Schaal, Susanne, and Thomas Elbert. 2006. "Ten Years After the Genocide: Trauma Confrontation and Post-traumatic Stress in Rwandan Adolescents." *Journal of Traumatic Stress* 19 (1): 95–105.

Schirmer, Jennifer. 1998. *The Guatemalan Military Project: A Violence Called Democracy.* Philadelphia: University of Pennsylvania Press.

Schlenger, W. E., J. A. Fairbank, B. K. Jordan, and J. M. Caddell. 1999. "Combat-Related Post-traumatic Stress Disorder: Prevalence, Risk Factors, and

Comorbidity." In *Post-traumatic Stress Disorder: A Comprehensive Text*, edited by Philip A. Saigh and J. Douglas Bremner, 69–91. Needham Heights: Allyn & Bacon.

Schlesinger, Stephen, and Stephen Kinzer. 2005. *Bitter Fruit: The Untold Story of the American Coup in Guatemala.* Cambridge, MA: Harvard University Press.

Schwartz, Rachel A. 2019. "Guatemala's Anti-Corruption Struggle Teeters on the Edge." *NACLA-Report on the Americas* 51 (2): 200–205.

Selman, Peter. 2016. "The Rise and Fall of Intercountry Adoption in the 21st Century: Global Trends from 2001 to 2010." In *Intercountry Adoption: Policies, Practices, and Outcomes*, edited by Judith L. Gibbons and Karen Smith Rotabi, 7–27. New York: Routledge.

Selman, Peter. 2012. "The Rise and Fall of Intercountry Adoption in the 21st Century." *International Social Work* 52 (5): 575–594.

Selman, Peter. 2009. "The Rise and Fall of Intercountry Adoption in the 21st Century." *International Social Work* 52 (5): 575–594.

Selman, Peter. 2002. "Intercountry Adoption in the New Millennium: The 'Quiet Migration' Revisited." *Population Research and Policy Review* 21 (3): 205–225.

Shapiro-Phim, Toni. 2002. "Dance, Music, and the Nature of Terror in Democratic Kampuchea." In *Annihilating Difference: The Anthropology of Genocide*, edited by Alexander Laban Hinton, 179–193. Berkeley: University of California Press.

Sharer, Robert J. 2005. *The Ancient Maya* (6th Edition). Stanford: Stanford University Press.

Simon, Jean-Marie. 1987. *Guatemala: Eternal Spring-Eternal Tyranny.* New York: W.W. Norton & Company.

Smith, Carol A. 1990a. "Preface." In *Guatemalan Indians and the State: 1540–1988*, edited by Carol Ann Smith and Marilyn M. Moors, vii–ix. Austin: University of Texas Press.

Smith, Carol A. 1990b. "Introduction: Social Relations in Guatemala over Time and Space." In *Guatemalan Indians and the State: 1540–1988,* edited by Carol Ann Smith and Marilyn M. Moors, 1–30. Austin: University of Texas Press.

Smith, Carol A. 1990c. "Origins of the National Question in Guatemala: A Hypothesis." In *Guatemalan Indians and the State: 1540–1988*, edited by Carol Ann Smith and Marilyn M. Moors, 72–95. Austin: University of Texas Press.

Smith, Carol A. 1990d. "Class Position and Class Consciousness in an Indian Community: Totonicapán in the late 1970s." In *Guatemalan Indians and the State: 1540–1988*, edited by Carol Ann Smith and Marilyn M. Moors, 205–229. Austin: University of Texas Press.

Smith, Carol A. 1988. "Destruction of the Material Bases for Indian Culture: Economic Changes in Totonicapán." In *Harvest of Violence: The Maya Indians and the Guatemalan Crisis*, edited by Robert M. Carmack, 206–231. Norman: University of Oklahoma Press.

Søland, Birgitte. 2015. "'Never a Better Home': Growing Up in American Orphanages, 1920–1970." *The Journal of the History of Childhood and Youth* 8 (1): 34–54.

Spinden, Herbert J. 1999. *Ancient Civilizations of Mexico and Central America.* Mineola: Dover Publications, Inc.

Stavenhagen, Rodolfo. 1998. "Challenging the Nation-State in Latin America." In *Crossing Currents: Continuity and Change in Latin America*, edited by M. B. Whiteford and S. Whiteford, 13–23. Upper Saddle River: Prentice-Hall, Inc.

Stern, Marie. 2005. *Naming Security-Constructing Identity: 'Mayan Women' in Guatemala on the Eve of 'Peace.'* New York: Manchester University Press.

Stolen, Kristi A. 2007. *Guatemalans in the Aftermath of Violence: The Refugees' Return.* Philadelphia: University of Pennsylvania Press.

Stout, Mary A. 2012. *Native American Boarding Schools.* Santa Barbara: Greenwood.

Summerfield, Derek. 2000. "Childhood, War, Refugeedom and 'Trauma': Three Core Questions for Mental Health Professionals." *Transcultural Psychiatry* 37 (3): 417–433.

Taylor, Clark. 1998. *Return of Guatemala's Refugees: Reweaving the Torn.* Philadelphia: Temple University Press.

Tedeschi, Richard G., and Lawrence G. Calhoun. 2004. "Post-traumatic Growth: Conceptual Foundations and Empirical Evidence." *Psychological Inquiry* 15 (1): 1–18.

Tedeschi, Richard G., and Lawrence G. Calhoun. 1996. "The Post-traumatic Growth Inventory: Measuring the Positive Legacy of Trauma." *Journal of Traumatic Stress* 9 (3): 455–472.

Tedeschi, Richard G., and Lawrence G. Calhoun. 1995. *Trauma and Transformation: Growing in the Aftermath of Suffering.* Thousand Oaks: Sage.

Thabet, Abdel A., and Panos Vostanis. 2000. "Post Traumatic Stress Disorder Reactions in Children of War: A Longitudinal Study." *Child Abuse & Neglect* 24 (2): 291–298.

Thompson Jr., Charles D. 2001. *Maya Identities and the Violence of Place: Borders Bleed.* Aldershot: Ashgate.

Tierney, Nancy Leigh. 1997. *Robbed of Humanity: Lives of Guatemalan Street Children.* St. Paul: Pangaea.

Tischler Visquerra, Sergio. 1998. *Guatemala 1944: Crisis Y Revolución, Ocaso y Quiebre de una Forma Estatal.* Guatemala: Cuadal S.A.

Turse, Nick. 2013. *Kill Anything that Moves: The Real American War in Vietnam.* New York: Metropolitan Books.

Ungar, Michael, Marion Brown, Linda Liebenberg, Rasha Othman, Wai Man Kwong, Mary Armstrong, and Jane Gilgun. 2007. "Unique Pathways to Resilience Across Cultures." *Adolescence* 42 (166): 287–310.

United Nations (UN). 2020a. "About the UN." UN.org. https://www.un.org/en/about-un/index.html

United Nations (UN). 2020b. "Universal Declaration of Human Rights." UN.org. https://www.un.org/en/universal-declaration-human-rights/index.html

United Nations (UN). 2022. "The Genocide Convention." UN.org. https://www.un.org/en/genocideprevention/genocide-convention.shtml.

United Nations Economic and Social Council (UN ECOSOC). 2000. *Commission on Human Rights, Report of the Special Rapporteur on the Sale of Children, Child Prostitution and Child Pornography, January 14, 2000.* Geneva: United Nations.

United Nations Office of the High Commissioner for Human Rights (UN OHCHR). 2020a. "Convention on the Prevention and Punishment of the Crime of Genocide." OHCHR.org. https://www.ohchr.org/EN/ProfessionalInterest/Pages/CrimeOfGenocide.aspx

United Nations Office of the High Commissioner for Human Rights (UN OHCHR). 2020b. "International Covenant on Economic, Social and Cultural Rights." OHCHR.org. https://www.ohchr.org/EN/ProfessionalInterest/Pages/CESCR.aspx

United Nations Office of the High Commissioner for Human Rights (UN OHCHR). 2020c. "International Covenant on Civil and Political Rights." OHCHR.org. https://www.ohchr.org/EN/ProfessionalInterest/Pages/CCPR.aspx

United Nations Office of the High Commissioner for Human Rights (UN OHCHR). 2020d. "Convention on the Rights of the Child." OHCHR.org. https://www.ohchr.org/EN/ProfessionalInterest/Pages/CRC.aspx

United Nations Office of the High Commissioner for Human Rights (UN OHCHR). 2020e. "Status of Ratification Interactive Dashboard." OHCHR.org. https://indicators.ohchr.org/

United Nations Office of the High Commissioner for Human Rights (OHCHR). 2020f. "Protocol Additional of the Geneva Conventions of 12 August 1949, and Relating to the Protection of Victims of Non-International Armed Conflicts (Protocol II)." OHCHR.org. https://www.ohchr.org/EN/ProfessionalInterest/Pages/ProtocolI.aspx.

United Nations Office of the High Commissioner for Human Rights (OHCHR). 2020g. "International Human Rights Law." OHCHR.org. https://www.ohchr.org/EN/ProfessionalInterest/Pages/InternationalLaw.aspx

US Bureau of the Census. 1937. *Fifteenth Census of the United States, 1930: The Indian Population of the United States and Alaska.* Washington, DC: US Government Printing Office.

US Department of State. 2020. "Intercountry Adoption." Travel.state.gov. https://travel.state.gov/content/travel/en/Intercountry-Adoption.html

US Holocaust Memorial Museum. 2020. "Introduction to the Holocaust." Ushmm.org. https://encyclopedia.ushmm.org/content/en/article/introduction-to-the-holocaust\

US Office of Refugee Resettlement. 2014. "The Lost Boys of Sudan. Annual ORR Reports to Congress." https://www.acf.hhs.gov/orr/resource/annual-orr-reports-to-congress-2005-iii-the-lost-boys-of-sudan

Valentine, Douglas. 1990. *The Phoenix Program.* New York: Morrow.

van der Hal-van Raalte, Elisheva, Marinus H. van IJzendoorn, and Marian J. Bakermans–Kranenburg. 2007. "Quality of Care after Early Childhood Trauma and Well-Being in Later Life: Child Holocaust Survivors reaching Old Age." *American Journal of Orthopsychiatry* 77 (4): 514–522.

van der Kolk, Bessel A. 2014. *The Body Keeps the Score: Brain, Mind, and Body in the Healing of Trauma.* New York: Penguin Books.

van der Kolk, Bessel A., Lars Weisaeth, and Onno van der Hart. 1996. "History of Trauma in Psychiatry." In *Traumatic Stress: The Effects of Overwhelming Experience on Mind, Body, and Society*, edited by Bessel van der Kolk, Alexander McFarlane, and Lars Weisaeth, 47–76. New York: The Guilford Press.

Van Schaack, Beth. 1999. "The Civil Enforcement of Human Rights Norms in Domestic Courts." *ILSA Journal of International and Comparative Law* 6: 295–303.

Veronen, Lois J., and Dean G. Kilpatrick. 1983. "Rape: A Precursor of Change." In *Life-Span Developmental Psychology: Nonnormative Life Events*, edited by Edward J. Callahan and Kathleen A. McCluskey, 167–191. New York: Academic Press.

Warren, Kay B. 1998. *Indigenous Movements and Their Critics: Pan-Maya Activism in Guatemala*. Princeton: Princeton University Press.

Warren, Kay B. 1993. "Interpreting *La Violencia* in Guatemala: Shapes of Mayan Silence & Resistance." In *The Violence Within: Cultural & Political Opposition in Divided Nations*, edited by Kay B. Warren, 25–56. Boulder: Westview Press.

Washington, Karla. 2007. "Research Review: Sibling Placement in Foster Care: A Review of the Evidence." *Child & Family Social Work* 12 (4): 426–433.

Washington Office on Latin America (WOLA). 1989. *The Administration of Injustice: Military Accountability in Guatemala*. Washington: WOLA.

Watanabe, John M. 1992. *Maya Saints and Souls in a Changing World*. Austin: University of Texas Press.

Watanabe, John M., and Edward F. Fischer. 2004. "Introduction: Emergent Anthropologies and Pluricultural Ethnography in Two Postcolonial Nations." In *Pluralizing Ethnography: Comparison and Representation in Maya Cultures, Histories, and Identities*, edited by John M. Watanabe and Edward F. Fischer, 3–33. Santa Fe: School of American Research.

Weaver, Frederick Stirton. 1999. "Reform and (Counter)Revolution in Post-Independence Guatemala: Liberalism, Conservatism, and Postmodern Controversies." *Latin American Perspectives* 26 (2): 129–158.

Weisbart, Caren. 2018. "Diplomacy at a Canadian Mine Site in Guatemala." *Critical Criminology* 26 (4): 473–489.

Weiss, Tzipi, and Roni Berger. 2006. "Reliability and Validity of a Spanish Version of the Post-traumatic Growth Inventory." *Research on Social Work Practice* 16 (2): 191–199.

Wheeler, Jacob. 2011. *Between Light and Shadow: A Guatemalan Girl's Journey through Adoption*. Lincoln: University of Nebraska Press.

Whetten, Kathryn, Jan Ostermann, Brian W. Pence, Rachel A. Whetten, Lynne C. Messer, Sumedha Ariely, Karen O'Donnell, Augustine I. Wasonga, Vanroth Van, Dafrosa Itemba, Misganaw Eticha, Ira Madan, Nathan M. Thielman, and The Positive Outcomes for Orphans (POFO) Research Team. 2014. "Three-Year Change in the Wellbeing of Orphaned and Separated Children in Institutional and Family-Based Care Settings in Five Low-and Middle-Income Countries." *PLoS One* 9 (8): e104872.

Whetten, Kathryn, Jan Ostermann, Rachel Whetten, Karen O'donnell, Nathan Thielman, and Positive Outcomes for Orphans (POFO) Research Team. 2011. "More than the Loss of a Parent: Potentially Traumatic Events Among Orphaned and Abandoned Children." *Journal of Traumatic stress* 24 (2): 174–182.

Whetten, Kathryn, Jan Ostermann, Rachel A. Whetten, Brian W. Pence, Karen O'donnell, Lynne C. Messer, and Nathan M. Thielman. 2009. "A Comparison of the Wellbeing of Orphans and Abandoned Children Ages 6–12 in Institutional and Community-Based Care Settings in 5 Less Wealthy Nations." *PLoS One* 4 (12): e8169.

Wilson, Samantha L. 2003. "Post-Institutionalization: The Effects of Early Deprivation on Development of Romanian Adoptees." *Child and Adolescent Social Work Journal* 20 (6): 473–483.

Wilson, Samantha L., and Judith L. Gibbons. 2005. "Guatemalan Perceptions of Adoption." *International Social Work* 48 (6): 742–752.

Woodward Jr., Ralph L. 2008 [2005]. *A Short History of Guatemala.* Guatemala: Editorial Laura Lee.

World Bank. 1978. *Guatemala: Economic and Social Positions and Prospects.* Washington: World Bank.

Zur, Judith N. 1998. *Violent Memories: Mayan War Widows in Guatemala.* Boulder: Westview Press.

Index

About the Author

Shirley A. Heying earned an MA and a PhD in anthropology from the University of New Mexico. She currently serves as an applied anthropologist working primarily in the government sector in the United States. She taught anthropology courses at the University of New Mexico Albuquerque and Gallup campuses, as well as at Western Oregon University. She remains an affiliated faculty member and adjunct instructor for the University of New Mexico. As a sociocultural anthropologist and genocide scholar, Dr. Heying continues to examine the intersections of mental health (particularly genocide-related trauma, resilience, and post-traumatic growth), indigenous identity, race relations, human agency, and state power in Guatemala. She has a deep passion for educating others about genocides. As board member of New Mexico Human Rights Projects in Albuquerque, she has helped select and lead groups of New Mexico high schools students to participate in the Kreisau-Initiative's Model International Criminal Court program in Poland.

www.ingramcontent.com/pod-product-compliance
Lightning Source LLC
Chambersburg PA
CBHW022300280326
41932CB00010B/931